AF609347

The Art of Status

The Art of Status

Looted Treasures and the Global Politics of Restitution

Jelena Subotić

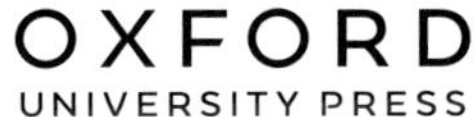

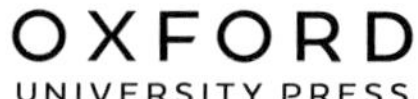

Great Clarendon Street, Oxford, OX2 6DP,
United Kingdom

Oxford University Press is a department of the University of Oxford.
It furthers the University's objective of excellence in research, scholarship,
and education by publishing worldwide. Oxford is a registered trade mark of
Oxford University Press in the UK and in certain other countries

© Jelena Subotić 2025

The moral rights of the author have been asserted

All rights reserved. No part of this publication may be reproduced, stored in a retrieval system, transmitted, used for text and data mining, or used for training artificial intelligence, in any form or by any means, without the prior permission in writing of Oxford University Press, or as expressly permitted by law, by licence or under terms agreed with the appropriate reprographics rights organization. Enquiries concerning reproduction outside the scope of the above should be sent to the Rights Department, Oxford University Press, at the address above.

You must not circulate this work in any other form
and you must impose this same condition on any acquirer.

Published in the United States of America by Oxford University Press
198 Madison Avenue, New York, NY 10016, United States of America

British Library Cataloguing in Publication Data

Data available

Library of Congress Control Number: 2025933796

ISBN 9780198909750

DOI: 10.1093/oso/9780198909750.001.0001

Printed in the UK by
Bell & Bain Ltd., Glasgow

The manufacturer's authorised representative in the EU for product safety is Oxford University Press España S.A. of El Parque Empresarial San Fernando de Henares, Avenida de Castilla, 2 – 28830 Madrid (www.oup.es/en or product.safety@oup.com). OUP España S.A. also acts as importer into Spain of products made by the manufacturer.

Links to third party websites are provided by Oxford in good faith and
for information only. Oxford disclaims any responsibility for the materials
contained in any third party website referenced in this work.

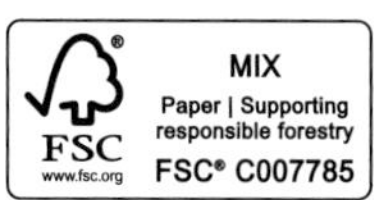

For my parents

Preface and Acknowledgments

Sometime in 1935, Erich Šlomović, a 20-year-old Yugoslav Jew from a small town of Đakovo in today's Croatia, arrived in Paris, in search of art greatness.[1] Since a very young age, Šlomović was obsessed with modern art. His dream was to become an art collector and open his own gallery. Once in Paris, he struck incredible luck by becoming an apprentice of the legendary French art dealer Ambroise Vollard. Widely regarded as perhaps the most important French art dealer of the period, Vollard introduced Šlomović to the art business but also to the bustling Parisian art scene of the 1930s. Through Vollard, Šlomović befriended Pablo Picasso, Henri Matisse, Marc Chagall, Jean Cocteau, Georges Rouault, and many other art giants of the era. These artists would on occasion sketch a little drawing and give it to Erich as a present, or make a doodle in his scrapbook, which he called *Kolektanea* and carried everywhere with him.

By 1939, Erich Šlomović had a sizeable collection of his own—some 600 art pieces, mostly prints and drawings but also a number of important and valuable oil paintings by Picasso, Bonnard, Renoir, Derain, and others. As the war broke out in Europe, Ambroise Vollard prepared to move from his estate in the French countryside to Paris, where he had already stored as many as 10,000 artworks. The famed art dealer, however, never made it to Paris. His car skidded off the wet road and he died in the crash.

With no Vollard to provide employment and connections and with the Nazi occupation of France looming, Erich Šlomović decided to flee. He hurriedly rented a vault in the Société General bank in Paris and deposited some 150 artworks there. Šlomović rented the Paris bank vault in his own, visibly Jewish name, presumably not worried about potential Nazi seizures. One of the many mysteries regarding his biography is the fact that the artwork remained in the vault throughout the Nazi occupation of France and was not Aryanized like much of French Jewish property.

[1] Not much is known or confirmed about the biography of Erich Šlomović. Even his name is spelled in many different ways in various accounts (Slomovic, Chlomovitch). This account of his life is based on D'Arcy, "Mysterious Mr. Slomovic"; Perry, *Stolen Art*; Coblence and Laufer, "Memorandum"; Rabinow, Druick, Dumas, Groom, Roquebert, and Tinterow, *Cezanne to Picasso*, as well as the documentary film *The Mysterious Mr. Slomovic* (2017, dir. by Miodrag Ćertić), which includes oral testimony by some of Šlomović's surviving relatives.

In March 1940, he returned to Belgrade, Yugoslavia with the remaining bulk of his collection—some 450 pieces. His grand idea was to open a Museum of Modern Art in Belgrade where he would display his French art treasures. A friend he met in Paris—the legendary architect Le Corbusier—accompanied him to Belgrade where he was to make sketches of the future museum. He also arranged to display his collection at a special exhibition in Zagreb in November 1940, to great local reception. The exhibition was open for two months and drew huge crowds.

Erich Šlomović and Yugoslavia were, however, all living on borrowed time. Just five months after the opening of the Zagreb exhibition, Nazi Germany occupied Yugoslavia in April 1941. From Belgrade, Erich and his family—parents Bernard and Roza and brother Egon—fled to the Serbian countryside and the village of Baćina. They hid in a country house, where Erich built a double wall with the help of a local farmer and deposited his artwork inside. Sometime in 1942, a local German patrol—by some eyewitness accounts helped by the collaborationist village mayor—discovered the Šlomović family hideout. They spared Roza, but picked up Erich, Egon, and Bernard. They were most likely immediately shot in a series of retribution killings Nazi German occupation authorities instituted in retaliation for the increasingly heavy toll Yugoslav communist partisan resistance was inflicting on German forces. The exact date and location of the Šlomović murders remains unknown.[2]

Erich's mother Roza and the hidden art collection survived, but only for a while. A few months after the liberation of Yugoslavia in October 1944, Roza Šlomović was able to get in touch with Yugoslav communist leadership and negotiate the gift of Erich's collection to the Yugoslav state—she asked that the collection bear Erich's name—in exchange for "just compensation." On December 31, 1944, she boarded a special train to Belgrade, arranged by the Yugoslav government. She was accompanied by her cousin Mara Hertzler, Mara's two small children, and Erich's vast art collection. In a final cruel twist, the train collided head-on with a Bulgarian train that was transporting retreating soldiers. Roza Šlomović and Mara's children were killed on the spot. The art was strewn around the vast area of the train crash, intermingling with human remains, belongings, and the country dirt and mud. Mara, the

[2] Since the Šlomović family did not have close direct survivors, their murder in the Holocaust has remained unmemorialized. In 2016 as part of my research on Erich Šlomović, I prepared individual pages of testimony for Erich, Egon, and Bernard Šlomović with as much information about their lives as I could find and submitted them to the Yad Vashem Shoah Names database (https://yvng.yadvashem.org), in which they are now included.

only survivor, salvaged some art and eventually handed it over to communist authorities. Some art pieces were destroyed, some looted from the scene, some forever disappeared.

It took about three years for the Yugoslav government to decide what to do with the collection. It was eventually turned over to the National Museum in Belgrade (then called the Art Museum), where it had remained ever since. The new inventory listed around 350 artworks, including pieces by Cézanne, Degas, Gauguin, Renoir, Matisse, Bonnard, Derain, and other masters. The Yugoslav government reneged on its promise of compensation to Roza or any of her descendants. Since she was now dead, the government declared the Šlomović collection heirless, and the property of the state. A few distant surviving relatives in Israel and the United States filed a series of unsuccessful lawsuits against the Yugoslav government, but were rebuffed by Yugoslav courts.

Since 1949, the National Museum of Serbia owns the Šlomović collection, which represents the bulk of its European holdings, and is one of the Museum's most visible attractions. The collection has, however, been under a legal cloud since 1979, when the Société General bank in Paris finally opened the Šlomović vault and put up the rest of his collection for auction. This piqued the interest of Ambroise Vollard's heirs, who claimed that these pieces were, in fact, the property of Vollard and not Šlomović who, they claimed, was a nobody, "a small Yugoslav Jew," as one of the claimants complained, an art hustler, who was not sophisticated enough nor famous enough to amass such a precious collection. The French courts sided with Vollard's descendants, who after obtaining rights to the Paris part of the collection in 2012 sued the National Museum of Serbia for the remaining, much larger and more valuable collection. The Museum refused to cooperate—the Šlomović paintings were removed from the public exhibition and stored in a vault during the Museum's renovation (2003–2018), where they remained for almost fifteen years, hidden from view. At one point, they became entangled in the process of Holocaust restitution payments in Serbia, where for a while the Jewish community advocated for their sale and for proceeds to be distributed to the small remaining Jewish community. Nothing came of this.

Instead, after the Museum reopened in 2018, the "Erich Šlomović collection" was displayed again as the major part of the museum's modern European holdings. Not a single caption anywhere in the museum indicates that this vast and invaluable collection—the jewel of the National Museum's treasures—is art that belonged to the victim of the Holocaust, art seized by the state, and incorporated into, first, Yugoslav, and after the federation's breakup,

Serbian national heritage without any attempt at restitution or acknowledgment of provenance. There is not even a basic panel with Erich's biography or the history of the collection, as is common museum practice. Erich Šlomović did, finally, get his paintings displayed in a Belgrade museum, as was his dream. But the Serbian state made these paintings its own, and in the process removed Erich Šlomović from history, erased his and the biography of his art objects, and completely ignored the historical context in which he collected, preserved, and ultimately lost his precious art. His beautiful paintings still hang on the walls of the Museum, but the violent path they took to get there does not seem to be on the minds of either the Museum or its visitors.

This is a book about the violence states perpetrated in pursuit of their public collections of art. It is also a story about how this violently extracted art became absorbed into the national cultural heritage of states that acquired it, a process of appropriation that erased the histories of the people these objects were taken from. But it is also a book about the changing moral framework of art ownership, and the long path it took to get to this current moment when returning looted art has become, at the very least, part of the international conversation.

What I hoped to accomplish in writing this book is to reconsider art in the context of international politics, and reconsider international politics in the context of art. We go to museums to admire famous pieces of art, but so much of the art we enjoy was extracted through systematic political violence, or through theft, looting, sales under duress, deception, bribery, or greed. The objects of art we come to see carry stories of their own—and some are stories of occupation, imperialism, colonial brutality, oppression, and genocide. How an art object was acquired, under what political conditions, through what means of extraction, whose hands did it pass through, where was it displayed, who owned it, who relinquished it, and why—should also be an integral part of how we observe, evaluate, and process art collections. The violent biographies of these objects are imprinted on them and part of fully appreciating the art in front of us is knowing how it got here in the first place. I hope I did these stories justice.

This book was shaped by many conversations with friends and colleagues, who all helped with various parts of the project over many years: Yoni Abramson, Rebecca Adler-Nissen, Michael Barnett, Martin Bayly, Gemma Bird, Franziska Boehme, Saša Brajović, Adrian Calmettes, Mia Ćertić, Miodrag Ćertić, Emile Chabal, Mark Copelovitch, Haris Dajč, Chris Deacon, Lauren Eastwood, Jakub Eberle, Kristin Eggeling, Filip Ejdus, David Feldman, Wesley Fisher, Lene Hansen, Laura Hastings, Evanthis Hatzivassiliou, Naomi Head, Aida Hozić, Alastair Iain Johnston, Eirini Karamouzi, Emil Kerenji,

Catarina Kinnvall, Višnja Kisić, Jeff Kopstein, Ron Krebs, David Laufer, Philipp Lepenies, Aliza Luft, Staffan Lundén, Amir Lupovici, Maria Mälksoo, Jennifer Mitzen, Katarina Melić, Mary-Ann Middelkoop, Iver Neumann, Josh and Diana Oboler, Meg O'Mahoney, Vincent Pouliot, Galia Press-Barnathan, Cresa Pugh, Sigrid Quack, Ciraj Rassool, Brent Steele, Rouven Symank, Jelena Todorović, Ann Towns, Ruth Weinberger, Lerna Yanık, and Ayşe Zarakol.

I am very grateful to Jean-Marc Dreyfus who explained the methodology behind the invaluable *Göring Catalogue* he put together in 2015 and to Wesley Fisher for spending the time to outline in detail the work of the Looted Art and Cultural Property Initiative of the Conference on Jewish Material Claims Against Germany and World Jewish Restitution Organization. Marina Duque, Elif Kalaycioglu, and Jason Sharman took the time to read many chapters of the book and provide detailed and nuanced feedback. The book is immeasurably better because of their engagement. My friends at the Norwegian Institute for International Affairs in Oslo (NUPI) hosted a book workshop in May 2024 to help me put the book together. I am grateful for the comments of everyone at the workshop, but especially to Paul Beaumont, Benjamin de Carvalho, Halvard Leira, Ole Jacob Sending, and Pål Røren, who spent so much of their time and effort in improving the manuscript. Truly, I owe you.

The early versions of this project were presented at various venues, and I always benefited from informed and enthusiastic exchanges. Thank you to participants in the panels where I presented this work at the International Studies Association-Midwest Annual Conference in St. Louis in 2021, the Western Political Science Association Annual Meeting in Portland, OR in 2022, the Social Science History Association Annual Conference in Chicago in 2022, the International Studies Association Annual Convention in Montreal in 2023, and the American Political Science Association Annual Conference in Philadelphia in 2024. I also benefited enormously from the feedback I received at a number of workshops I participated in with this project: on ontological security at Hebrew University in Jerusalem in 2022, on the role of the European historian today at the American College of Greece in Athens in 2022, on diplomacy at the Royal Danish Society of Sciences and Letters in Copenhagen in 2022, on exceptionalism at NUPI in Oslo in 2023, and on "objects from afar" at Free University in Berlin in 2024. I also introduced this project to extremely knowledgeable audiences at the Institute of International Relations in Prague, the University of Gothenburg, and the University of Duisburg, all in 2023. I particularly enjoyed talking through this book with my students at Georgia State University, and the students in my masterclass on historical memory at Hebrew University in Jerusalem in 2023. I am also very thankful to Georgia State University for a number of awards that made this research possible and to Anaya Wilson for excellent research assistance.

Dominic Byatt at Oxford University Press was an enthusiastic supporter of this book when it was still only an idea. My deepest gratitude to Dominic for the excellent stewardship of this project, as well as to everyone at OUP for making it happen so smoothly. I also thank Cambridge University Press for granting permission to republish material from my article "Nineteenth Century 'Antiquities Rush' and the International Competition for Cultural Status," *Review of International Studies* 51 (2025).

And to my family. They are, simply, the best. My husband Doug Rose is my biggest cheerleader and has helped in every aspect of this project, from discovering the latest news about some hot restitution case, down to the technical details of photography, images, and layout. He also patiently went along my multiple museum visits in many countries and pointed out things he thought I may have missed. He is also just incredibly fun to be around. Our son Leo—a book author in his own right!—is the coolest kid that ever was. As he prepares to leave home for college and embark on his own writer's journey (no, I won't be OK, thanks for asking), I keep being amazed at his talent, joy, and kindness. How lucky am I. My family also knows that my life revolves around two things—writing books and playing tennis (what I lack in skill I compensate for in competitiveness). My Atlanta tennis friends, especially Jen Denbo and Dak Perry, deserve their own round of thanks, as they make every day I spend on the court a joy.

I am very grateful to my sister Ivana Subotić for helping me track down and translate Italian sources for this book, as well as to my cousin Irina Ljubić and her amazing daughters Lara and Hana Stojanovski for, well, just being awesome. Thank you also to my generous in-laws Karol and Doug Ross. Finally, my parents Irina and Gojko Subotić, both art historians, made the world of art a constant background to my childhood as early as I can remember. I resisted it for years, rolling my teenage eyes at having to visit yet another museum, church, or archeological site. And how glad I am that they persisted. My mother also read this entire manuscript with a keen interest and decades of firsthand experience as a former curator at the National Museum of Serbia and a prominent art critic and cultural policy commentator. I hope my parents realize their hard work at making me fall in love with art, eventually, paid off. This book is dedicated to them.

Contents

List of Figures

List of Abbreviations

BCE	before common era
CCP	Central Collecting Point
CDMP	Documentation Centre for Property Transfers of the Cultural Assets of WWII Victims
CGJA	Commissariat-General for Jewish Affairs
EMKP	Endangered Material Knowledge Programme
ERR	*Einsatzstab Reichsleiter Rosenberg* (Reichsleiter Rosenberg or "Special" Taskforce)
FESTAC	Festival of International Black Art
FMAS	Front Multiculturel Anti-Spoliation (Multicultural Anti-Spoliation Front)
FRG	Federal Republic of Germany
GDR	German Democratic Republic
ICOM	International Council of Museums
JCR	Jewish Cultural Reconstruction
MCP	Munich Collection Point
MFA&A	Monuments, Fine Arts, and Archives program
MNR	Musées Nationaux Récupération (National Museum Recuperation)
MOMA	Museum of Modern Art
MOWAA	Museum of West African Art
MP	Member of Parliament
NAGPRA	Native American Graves Protection and Repatriation Act
NARA	National Archives and Records Administration
OMGUS	Office of Military Government of the United States
PM	Prime Minister
RSG	Restitution Study Group
SHAEF	Supreme Headquarters Allied Expeditionary Force
SS	Schutzstaffel (Protection Squadron)
UNESCO	United Nations Educational, Scientific and Cultural Organization
USGCC	United States Group Control Council for Germany
USSR	Union of Soviet Socialist Republics
V&A	Victoria & Albert Museum
WJRO	World Jewish Restitution Organization

1

The International Problem of Looted Art

A few months after Nazi Germany occupied the Netherlands in May 1940, Irma Klein, a divorced actress living with her mother in Amsterdam, became financially destitute. As a Jew, she could not work, and the divorce alimony payments from her former husband Robert Lewenstein stopped coming after his sewing factory was Aryanized. Irma had no money, but she had the paintings Robert left behind. One of these was *Painting with Houses* by the now famed abstract artist Wassily Kandinsky. The painting went up for sale at the auction held on October 8–9, 1940 in Amsterdam. The buyer was the Amsterdam city Stedelijk Museum. Whether Irma actively put up the painting for a duress sale, or whether it was taken from her and sold by third parties, is a matter still under dispute.[1]

What is clear from the records is that the October 1940 auction included individual collectors' paintings, as well as parts of the collection of Jacques Goudstikker, the most prominent art dealer in the Netherlands at the time.[2] Goudstikker was Jewish and fled the Netherlands as soon as Germany invaded in May 1940. He managed to get on a ship to England but fell into the boat's hold by accident and died on the spot. He left behind a vast collection of mostly Old Masters—some 1,400 paintings in total—all of which the Nazis consequently looted on direct orders by Hermann Göring, Hitler's de facto second in command, who kept most of the valuable art pieces for himself.[3]

The auction of October 1940, therefore, was already understood by all parties as an under-sale auction where parts of the Goudstikker estate and other paintings by smaller collectors would be "officially sold" but for absurdly low prices. Irma Klein's Kandinsky was thus sold for only 160 Dutch guilders, the today's equivalent of $1,600 for a painting whose value was many times higher already at the time, and by now is estimated at more than 20 million dollars. It is unclear if she ever actually received the proceeds from the sale. Throughout the German occupation, Irma was arrested and detained by the

[1] Restitution Committee Report.

[2] Ibid.

[3] Genocchio, "Seized, Reclaimed." For background on the Goudstikker collection and continuing search for his looted paintings, see the Goudstikker Art Research Project, https://goudstikker.com.

Gestapo many times. In 1942, she tried to escape detention by jumping out of the window, but instead she suffered a concussion and memory loss. By sheer luck and some bureaucratic confusion regarding her designation as a Jew (she claimed she was "half-Aryan"), Irma survived the war in Amsterdam and lived there until her death in 1983.[4] Her Kandinsky has been on display at the Stedelijk Museum for more than eighty years. It represented one of the jewels of the museum's modern art collection and the question of its provenance was not a matter of much interest.

The slow wheels of restitution began to turn in 1998, when a major international conference on Nazi-looted art was held in Washington, DC. The conference produced a guiding document, the *Washington Principles on Nazi-Confiscated Art*, agreed to by forty-four states, which urged countries to develop their own mechanisms for identifying and restituting art looted during the Holocaust.[5] In 1999, in display of its commitment to the Washington Principles, the Netherlands initiated an audit of its art collections acquired during and immediately following the Nazi occupation. This project, *Museum Acquisitions 1940–1948*, immediately identified the questionable provenance of Irma Klein's Kandinsky. The project report stated, "the purchase of a painting by Kandinsky at a sale at the firm of Frederik Muller & Co. in October 1940 is an area of attention. Before the war this painting was probably part of the collection of a Jewish collector. It is not known who gave instructions for the painting to be sold."[6]

However, no action was taken to restitute it. A few years later, in 2001, the Dutch government issued another report on looted art by the so-called Ekkart Committee. One of the Committee's explicit recommendations was that all sales by Jews in the Netherlands from the first day of occupation, May 10, 1940, until the very end of the war, should be considered "involuntary sales," unless there was clear evidence to the contrary.[7] Still, there was no action by the Stedelijk Museum.

In 2002, the Netherlands established the Advisory Committee on the Assessment of Restitution Applications for Items of Cultural Value and the Second World War (the Restitution Committee), a state agency tasked with adjudicating restitution claims for Nazi-looted art. It is to this Committee that Irma Klein and Robert Lewenstein's descendants submitted their application for restitution of *Painting with Houses* in 2013. After five years of

[4] Restitution Committee Report.
[5] US Department of State, "The Washington Principles."
[6] Restitution Committee Report.
[7] Restitution Committee Report.

research and deliberations, the Restitution Committee issued a binding opinion in 2018. The Committee agreed with the family claimants that the art was most likely sold under duress and that, in any case, and following the Dutch government's own principles, all art sales by Jews during the occupation were in some form or another made under duress. The Committee also recognized that the family claimants were legitimate heirs of Klein and Lewenstein.

And yet, the Committee's Binding Opinion determined that the Kandinsky should remain at the Stedelijk Museum and not returned to the family due to "public interest."[8] Specifically, the Committee declared, "the work has a significant place in the Stedelijk Museum's collection."[9] The Committee ended the report without any recommendation for a settlement with the family, or a suggestion for financial compensation in exchange for the painting remaining in the Amsterdam museum. The painting, in other words, was too important to be returned, and the interest of the state in maintaining its public art stock outweighed the Netherlands' commitment to restitution.[10] The 2018 decision came on the heels of a massive restitution claim by the family of the art collector Jacques Goudstikker, some of whose paintings ended up in the same 1940 auction as Irma Klein's Kandinsky. The Goudstikker descendants in 2006 successfully reclaimed 202 paintings from the Dutch museums.[11] After this major restitution, the Dutch museums, it seemed, were done pulling paintings off their walls.

The Restitution Committee's decision not to restitute Klein's Kandinsky, however, led to swift international backlash and questions regarding Dutch moral standing in the international society. "These developments risk turning the Netherlands from a leader in art restitution to a pariah," international restitution experts warned.[12] Ronald Lauder, then president of the Jewish World Congress, argued that "Dutch moral leadership on the issue had been dented."[13]

Other Jewish families claiming art from Dutch museums joined the chorus of criticism and disappointment. The family of Johanna Margarethe Stern-Lippmann, whose large art collection was seized by the Nazis after she was deported from Amsterdam to Auschwitz and murdered there in 1944, filed a claim against the city museum of Eindhoven, which owned and displayed their own family's Kandinsky painting, *View of Murnau with Church*. They,

[8] Liphshiz, "Jewish Family."
[9] Restitution Committee Report.
[10] Boffey, "Dutch Art Panel's Ruling."
[11] Genocchio, "Seized, Reclaimed."
[12] Liphshiz, "Jewish Family."
[13] Boffey, "Dutch Art Panel's Ruling."

too, were rebuffed by the Dutch state. The Stern family accused the Dutch restitution officials of "careless mistakes and a lack of empathy."[14]

This international criticism stung as the Netherlands considered itself a pioneer in restitution efforts.[15] It was one of the only five state signatories of the Washington Principles that actually complied with the document's recommendations and set up restitution committees. It also took pride in how it dealt with return of looted art to its former colony Indonesia and considered itself a leader in international restitution efforts.[16] All of these international commitments grew out of and were domestically justified by the Dutch self-understanding of *gidsland* (good country), which is a guiding principle of the state and has shaped its foreign policy for decades.[17]

The Netherlands needed to respond to these criticisms of its moral convictions, and so in 2020, it set up an official review of its restitution practices, focusing on both its "legal and moral aspects."[18] The review, named *Striving for Justice*, determined that the interests of the museums and concerns about the public art stock should no longer be relevant in adjudicating restitution claims and that the state needed to conduct more comprehensive research into art looted from the Jews in the Netherlands during the Holocaust.[19] Critically, the report said, "the Dutch reputation as a role model for other countries 'has been undermined by a limited number of requests . . . that have been rejected in recent years.'"[20]

In August 2021, the Amsterdam City Council in charge of the Stedelijk Museum announced that Kandinsky's *Painting with Houses* would be restituted to the family of Irma Klein and Robert Lewenstein. The city officials said in a statement that Amsterdam had a "moral obligation" to return the painting: "The city stands for a fair and clear restitution policy, returning as much looted art as possible to the rightful owners or the heirs of the owners."[21] In September 2022, Kandinsky's *View of Murnau with Church* was also restituted from the city museum of Eindhoven to the family of Johanna Margarethe Stern-Lippmann. "We are thrilled that the Kandinsky has been returned to us," descendants of Stern-Lippmann wrote in a statement.

[14] Boztas, "Jewish Family."
[15] Oost, "From 'Leader to Pariah'"?
[16] Scott, *Cultural Diplomacy*.
[17] Herman, "Dutch Drive for Humanitarianism."
[18] The statement establishing the Evaluation Review is available at https://www.raadvoorcultuur.nl/documenten/adviezen/2020/03/17/committee-appointed-to-evaluate-dutch-restitution-policy-on-nazi-looted-art.
[19] DutchNewsl.nl, "Interest of Museums Irrelevant."
[20] Boztas, "Jewish Descendants Welcome Report."
[21] Villa, "Amsterdam to Restitute Kandinsky Painting."

> The painting used to have a prominent position hanging in our [great] grandparents' house and represents much of our family's story . . . Its coming back to us now marks an important moment. It won't bring back the nine immediate family members who were so tragically murdered, but it's an acknowledgment of the injustice that we, and so many like us, have endured.[22]

Understanding the international restitution race

The demands for art restitution today, however, are much broader in scope than the cases of Nazi-looted art. In the past decade, building in part on the perceived success of Nazi-era art restitution but also on the increased visibility and impact of national and global social movements demanding racial justice and institutional decolonization, major world museums have come under ever stronger pressure to return other categories of looted art—art plundered as part of European imperialism and colonial occupations in Africa, Asia, Latin America, and Oceania.

Perhaps the most organized of the current campaigns is the effort to return the so-called "Benin Bronzes"—a vast collection of various artifacts looted from the Kingdom of Benin (in today's Nigeria) and dispersed across major international museums, most prominently the British Museum in London and the Humboldt Forum in Berlin, but also in the Field Museum in Chicago, the Museum of Archaeology and Anthropology in Cambridge, the Dresden State Art Collection, the Weltmuseum in Vienna, the Penn Museum in Philadelphia, the Metropolitan Museum of Art in New York City, among others. Since 2020, several museums have pledged to return their holdings of Benin Bronzes and restitute them to Nigeria, where there are plans for a major new museum to be built to display them in Benin City.[23]

The major announcement by French president Emmanuel Macron in 2017 that France should return its looted African art produced a comprehensive report outlining the process for repatriation and opening up the gates for other museums to follow.[24] The return of part of the Benin Bronzes collection from Cambridge to Nigeria in 2021, a major announcement from the Smithsonian Museum about doing the same, and the restitution of most of

[22] Liphshiz, "Reversing Earlier Stance."

[23] Brown, "New Museum in Nigeria." Some examples of pledges to restitute Benin Bronzes are described in Stevens, "Smithsonian Moves"; Nayeri and Onishi, "Looted Treasures"; BBC, "Cambridge University."

[24] Sarr and Savoy, *Restitution of African Cultural Heritage.*

the Bronzes from Germany back to Nigeria in 2022 are indications of this trend.[25]

The question of international art restitution is politically urgent as we are witnessing a dramatic change in how states evaluate the contents of their national museums. Just as the Netherlands seriously engaged in restitution efforts after its reputation as a "good country" was internationally challenged, many other states have directly tied their restitution policies to their international standing and status ambition. Sweden, for example, has passed a policy on restitution of looted art in 2016 that states that "the Swedish practice shall be *exemplary* with regards to 'identifying and repatriating or restituting objects in museum collections where there may be special ethical considerations for return.'"[26]

And yet, many states resist restitution of their valuable art collections, despite the increasing calls for their return. This is the situation with perhaps the most famous case for restitution—the movement to return the Parthenon "Elgin" marbles from the British Museum to the Acropolis in Athens.[27] The British Museum, of course, is not the only national museum that snubs restitution demands. The Thyssen-Bornemisza Museum, one of the three major national art museums in Madrid, has persistently refused to return the painting by Camille Pissarro which the Nazis seized from a Jewish family in Germany in 1939. The Spanish museum, against much international legal consensus, claims that it is the painting's rightful owner.[28] And the National Museum of Serbia in Belgrade owns and displays an entire collection of valuable European art that was looted by the Nazis in Italy, France, Austria, and elsewhere and then through fraud brought to communist Yugoslavia in the chaotic aftermath of World War II.[29] The National Museum has steadfastly refused not only to restitute the paintings but even to acknowledge that their provenance is an issue of concern.

This dramatic change and variation in restitution practices is puzzling. How did the international race to acquire these objects of art transform into a race for their return? What accounts for this change in international practices

[25] CNN, "Cambridge University"; Stevens, "Smithsonian Moves."

[26] Museum of World Cultures, Gothenburg, Sweden, "Policy for return of objects," https://www.varldskulturmuseerna.se/siteassets/pdf/aterlamnande/final-policy-for-return-of-objects_eng.pdf, emphasis mine.

[27] Marshall, "As Europe Returns Artifacts."

[28] Kuo, "Setback for Heirs." The museum displays the painting with no visible description of its provenance, other than a small QR code placed on the wall that interested visitors can open on their phones and read the Thyssen-Bornemisza Museum's legal brief justifying the continuing ownership of the painting. Author's visit to the Museum, Madrid, February 2023.

[29] Akinsha, "Ante Topic Mimara."

and the normative expectations surrounding them? And how do we explain restitution resisters?

The argument I advance in this book is that acquisition and restitution of looted art should be understood in the context of state concerns for international status, reputation, and prestige. Most existing explanations of restitution politics focus on development, diffusion, and institutionalization of international norms, expectations of proper behavior that states are increasingly finding difficult to resist. These normative changes are usually explained by the emergence and institutionalization of the politics of decolonization and transitional justice or global human rights more broadly.[30]

While taking the normative change as a given, I instead focus on the objects themselves and their changing status value for states, over time. I begin with the assumption that states construct their identities in part through interaction with material objects, including artifacts, which they imbue with value—economic, discursive, emotional, and status-affirming. States compete with other states for status, prestige, and cultural worth in an explicitly hierarchical international society. The content of national art collections, their quantity and expert-assessed quality, are markers of cultured status in international society, measured by a shared international understanding of what constitutes "high culture."[31] However, the same art objects that granted states desirable cultural attributes and, hence, high international cultural status when they were first acquired, have over time come to represent international status liabilities. The status value of the objects themselves has changed because the standards of status recognition have changed. My focus on art restitution, then, introduces an important dynamic element into our understanding of how states seek, maintain, and manage international status and provides a different explanation for how states address demands for art restitution.

This choice of focus, however, inevitably favors a more macro, structural explanation for changes in norms and practices of restitution and pays less attention to the micro explanations that would center on norm entrepreneurs—restitution activists and social movements. While my main argument focuses on states, I engage in a more extensive discussion about restitution movements and agents of normative change in the book's Conclusion.

[30] A comprehensive and pioneering norms-based study of art restitution in IR is Sandholtz, *Prohibiting Plunder*. Also see Boehme, "Normative Expectations"; McAuliffe, "Complicity or Decolonization?"

[31] Van Laar and Diepeveen, *Artworld Prestige*.

Art and international status

Art has always been inextricably linked to status. Owning, displaying, and consuming art brings joy and pleasure, but it also communicates taste and social and cultural capital.[32] In sociology, the connection between art and status has been understood in different ways. For Thorstein Veblen, the link between the two is an issue of conspicuous consumption, as art is acquired to display wealth and social class.[33] For Bourdieu, it is instead a matter of taste and distinction, as high art can only be properly understood and appreciated by small groups who have acquired that ability through elite education or upbringing.[34] This acquired and cultivated taste to make distinctions (between beautiful and ugly, good and bad art, and even between what *is* and *isn't* art) is a marker of the group's status, which then becomes socially reproduced.[35] For those on the lower rungs of the cultural hierarchy, there is always a problem of catching up with the cultural tastes of the elite. By the time status-seekers have caught up with elite cultural consumption patterns, the elite taste has moved on to a different cultural product or practice.[36]

As this book demonstrates, however, acquisition of art has historically been an important practice not just for individuals, but also for states in their pursuit and maintenance of international status. States that were former great imperial powers with recognized high international status had first-mover advantage in establishing museums and setting up norms and standards of civilization which those lower on the hierarchy then followed, trying to catch up. Discussing another international cultural status symbol, the opera house, Leira and de Carvalho identify the same dynamic: "For the first movers, the status was sought through signaling grandeur, for all latecomers, the point has been to demonstrate civilizational belonging."[37]

In the field of International Relations, there has been a renewed interest in the relationship between art and state international status-seeking.[38] This scholarship builds on a recent surge in attention to the questions of international status more broadly.[39] Regardless of what precise mechanism

[32] Ostrower, "Arts as Cultural Capital."
[33] Veblen, *Theory of the Leisure Class*. Also see Chan, *Social Status*.
[34] Bourdieu, *Distinction*.
[35] DiMaggio, "Classification in Art."
[36] In a Bordieuan context, by the time the aspiring members of a country club have learned to play tennis, the old-money club members have already moved on to golf.
[37] Leira and De Carvalho, "Importance of Being Civilized."
[38] E.g. MacKay, "Art World Fields"; Yanık and Subotić, "Cultural Heritage"; Hansen and Spanner, "National and Post-National Performances."
[39] MacDonald and Parent, "The Status of Status."

is at work, it has become quite clear that a great deal of world politics is difficult to explain absent some notion of status. Historically, status was understood as mostly a reflection of "prized attributes" such as "military power, economic development, cultural achievements, diplomatic skill, and technological innovation."[40] Status, however, is also social and relational. It sets expectations of behavior within a particular club of peers.[41]

If they cannot compete for status on the basis of material capabilities, some states can seek their higher status position on the basis of their normative or moral authority, or their exemplary action, as has been demonstrated in the case of Norway, for instance.[42] Without explicitly linking it to international status, scholars of cultural heritage have attempted to define these attributes with the concept of "cultural wealth," which would "include the number and the significance of [the state's] cultural and natural heritage sites, its stock of art and artifacts exhibited in the top international museums of art, and the number of widely recognized international prizes earned by its citizens."[43] For example, it is out of this desire for international cultural recognition that the National Museum of Norway proudly boasts that it is the first museum in the world to acquire one of Claude Monet's works, already in 1890.[44] But cultural status is also an important political asset for states that can claim status because they have more art or cultural sites than other states at the same level of economic wealth or with other similar material attributes.[45] It is art and culture that confers high international status on, for example, Italy, Greece, or Mexico that their level of economic development otherwise would not grant.

States do not only seek higher status because of whatever material or instrumental benefits it provides them, but also because higher status creates a sense of self-esteem.[46] In fact, this intrinsic, psychological drive for status is the core underpinning of Social Identity Theory, the primary foundation for nonmaterial explanations of status-seeking.[47] But there may be other reasons why states seek status. Some of them are rooted firmly in domestic politics. States may seek international status because of domestic political pressures brought on by electoral competition, or at particular moments of domestic crisis when international status-seeking can bring about domestic political

[40] Larson and Shevchenko, *Quest for Status.*
[41] Renshon, *Fighting for Status;* Duque, "Recognizing International Status."
[42] Wohlforth, De Carvalho, Leira, and Neumann, "Moral Authority and Status."
[43] Bandelj and Wherry, "Introduction."
[44] The Monet painting is *Rain, Étretat* (1886). Author's visit to the National Museum, Oslo, September 2022.
[45] Askew, "Magic List."
[46] Clunan, "Why Status Matters."
[47] For application of SIT to IR, see Larson, "Social Identity Theory."

legitimacy.[48] Status-seeking can also go on domestically even in the absence of international recognition. States can construct and seek status markers themselves, even if no international actor grants this process much attention.[49] As the case of art restitution demonstrates, there can be a significant gap in what domestic elites may assume grants them status, versus what other international actors consider worthy of recognition.

Status-seeking can also be quite local, as states compete for status in local rivalries.[50] As the next chapter's discussion of the "antiquities rush" in the nineteenth century demonstrates, much of art looting as a status-seeking practice in the nineteenth century was the result of rivalries between Great Britain and France, later joined by Germany.[51] The colonial "scramble for Africa" has already been successfully retold from the perspective of international status competition in Joslyn Barnhart's influential account.[52] But while noting in passing that the symbolic value of empires is socially constructed and changeable, Barnhart's explanation is silent on the processes of how that value is constituted, maintained, contested, and understood by elites and citizens.

My focus on art objects extracted from imperial expansions and colonial occupations shows that cultural artifacts were important status symbols for empires. It also demonstrates the amount of narrative work needed to give artifacts this symbolic value. As the cases of the Parthenon Marbles and the Benin Bronzes will show, once these objects were brought to European imperial capitals, the state put in a lot of effort, beyond just displaying them in museums, but through popular culture, media, even national currency, to give them the symbolic value they continue to hold. This indicates that artifacts only become status symbols if social actors confer on them symbolic value and discursively link their possession with desirable high status in, to them, meaningful social hierarchy.[53]

An important practice by which states may seek status is by investing in functionally unnecessary status symbols (aircraft carriers or other expensive projects such as space programs), which nevertheless inscribe on them the trappings of a modern, advanced developed state. In the realm of culture, status symbols may be opera houses or national museums, which claim a

[48] Ward, *Status*; Lin and Katada, "Striving for Greatness."

[49] Beaumont, *Grammar of Status Competition*.

[50] Renshon, *Fighting for Status*.

[51] As the remainder of the book shows, these rivalries continue today as France and Germany have raced to be the first to restitute looted art, firmly leaving Britain in the dust.

[52] Barnhart, "Status Competition."

[53] Beaumont and Røren, "Status Symbols."

certain standard of civilization.[54] This state search for symbolic capital can then explain seemingly irrational, costly, or nonbeneficial investments and priorities.[55] It is this performance of conspicuous consumption that then grants states higher status in a desired group.[56]

This is important because status symbols are well-defined boundary markers.[57] They pull together those that possess them within the same status rank (e.g. the nuclear powers), while clearly keeping those that do not outside of that status rank. Acquisition and display of art has historically been a prime example of such state practice. This was exactly the logic behind aggressive efforts by the United Arab Emirates to rebrand itself as a cultural hub by opening grand museums in Dubai and a Louvre extension in Abu Dhabi. Collecting and displaying art, here, was supposed to quite literally buy UAE higher international status and place it in the status group of high culture states.[58]

Looted art as international stigmata

The symbolic value of these objects of status, however, does not remain stable. In fact, it may increase if they are coveted by others. As this book demonstrates, the contested ownership of specific collections of art—both the competition for their acquisition and for their restitution—keeps these status symbols internationally visible, and it is this very process of contested ownership that further reproduces their symbolic value. However, even successful acquisitions of status symbols can generate domestic contestation and ultimately backfire on states that put too much effort into obtaining them in the first place.[59] Acquiring status symbols can then lead not only to status gain, but to status loss as well.

Possession of looted art turned out to be a practice that could lead to status loss. As a new international legal and normative architecture that governs art provenance developed after World War II and became institutionalized in the 1990s and 2000s, it has established not only that looting is wrong but, more important, that restitution is morally right.[60] Holding on to a looted object has come to be understood as holding on to a part of someone else's identity.

[54] Leira and De Carvalho, "Importance of Being Civilized."
[55] Musgrave and Nexon, "Defending Hierarchy"; Barnhart, "Status Competition."
[56] Gilady, *Price of Prestige*, building on Veblen, *Theory of the Leisure Class.*
[57] Goffman, "Symbols of Class Status."
[58] Ajana, "Branding, Legitimation." For a similar dynamic, also see Eggeling, "Cultural Diplomacy in Qatar."
[59] Beaumont, Paes, and Maglia, "Prestige and Punishment."
[60] Joy, *Heritage Justice*; Sandholtz, *Prohibiting Plunder.*

This is "the harm of retention."[61] As a result of this reframing of what it means to "own" art, an artifact's historical provenance is now considered to be a core element of its value.[62] What makes art collections highly valuable markers of cultured status has changed.

This becomes a problem for museum collections that include looted art and for states that rely on their national museums to claim international cultural status. Not only do looted art objects now possess a different kind of value, but, more important, they can also be material evidence to a mass crime (colonial subjugation or genocide) and as such the search for their provenance is a path toward confronting historical accountability for crimes of the past.[63] As Geoffrey Robertson powerfully argues, these objects are "freighted with the meaning of their removal."[64] The provenance of these objects and the violence inscribed on them are, therefore, not just irritants and inconveniences to state museums. The search for their provenance and demands for restitution are a direct threat to state status.

As the case studies that follow demonstrate in detail, some states and their national museums may fear that the continuing possession of looted art might lead to reputational stigma, which, if upheld, would lead to status loss. Here, state concern is not about status-seeking, but about stigma and status management.[65] The art objects themselves still have immense value for states, but the value is now in their return and, specifically, the *narratives* about their return. Of course, states can only restitute art objects once, but they can remind the world of their moral action and build status in the international moral hierarchy that far outlasts the point at which these objects are removed from the halls of national museums.

Not all states, however, react the same to the threat of status loss brought on by changing valuation of looted art. For some states, having been exposed as possessing and flaunting looted art raises questions about a state's biography, its sense of being a "good country," a "cultured country."[66] Instead, a state is exposed as an ordinary thief. And the way out of this shame and embarrassment is for national museums—as agents of the state—to reconceptualize what makes objects valuable to them. No longer is art valuable only because of its market price or artist prestige; it is valuable because of its clean provenance. Restitution of looted art, then, recaptures lost status and helps reposition the state back as a moral leader in international society. In contrast to much existing work on status symbols that assumes that their value to

[61] Joy, *Heritage Justice*, p. 19.
[62] Feigenbaum and Reist, *Provenance*.
[63] Boehme, "Normative Expectations."
[64] Robertson, *Who Owns History?*, p. 12.
[65] Adler-Nissen, "Stigma Management."
[66] For a discussion of state moral authority and international status, see Wohlforth et al., "Moral Authority and Status."

states is in their acquisition (specifically, according to Gilady, their visibility, costliness, and exclusivity), this book demonstrates that some status symbols may remain valuable also through the process of deaccession—restitution or return.

But other states may have alternative available narratives that resonate more deeply and enable an alternative response to demands for restitution. These narratives may have built up national resentment because, while major European imperial powers collected and looted "the best art" over centuries, some smaller, or more peripheral states had to be satisfied with cultural leftovers. For those states (as the case of Serbia will demonstrate later in the book), possessing precious art—of questionable provenance or not—is still a ticket to high cultural status, and such states often plan to resist calls for restitution as long as they can. For other states instead, as I describe in the case of Great Britain, through various cultural practices and narrativizing through museums and other cultural institutions, these collections of art have become deeply embedded in national stories of greatness. Even when the international normative environment has changed and their ownership has begun to be regarded as stigmatizing, some states and their museums have found the prospect of these objects' restitution too painful a narrative rupture to withstand.

And yet for other states, as I show in the case of France, restitution can serve seemingly unrelated status-affirming purposes. It can help project the state's soft power onto particular regions of the world (such as Africa) and compete with other states (such as China) for regional influence.[67] Restitution claims can also help to forge international alliances, as states (for example, Greece) may lobby other states for support in their repatriation campaigns in exchange for agreements regarding other, distinct diplomatic issues. The process of restitution—both offers to return and demands to reclaim—can, therefore, help states assert their political clout in different international arenas. Negotiations over restitution, here, are no longer an item of diplomacy; restitution *is* diplomacy.[68]

Museums as state actors

The problem of art restitution is often discussed as an issue of primarily museum choices and decisions—it is museums that acquire, display, and sometimes return artifacts. Art restitution, however, as I present it in this book, is fundamentally a political question and one inextricably linked to

[67] For speculation along these lines, see Herman, "Restitution—What's Really Going On?"
[68] Winter, "Heritage Diplomacy."

state competition over international status and prestige. As the case studies demonstrate, the process of looted art extraction as well as its restitution involve both states and museums, but also additional substate actors (such as culture ministries or professional associations). In fact, as we shall see, states and museums have often been at odds regarding restitution claims and have pursued their own, distinct, status games (museums competing for status with other museums, states with other states).

All of which is to reiterate that museums are, at their core, political institutions; they are "public enterprises with public motives."[69] As Alice Procter convincingly argues, museums are hardly neutral spaces; everything they own, curate, and display is political, and "shaped by the politics of the world that made it."[70] But museum collections and decisions regarding what to do with them are shaped not only by the historical moment in which they were created and acquired but also by the historical and political moment of the present. As this book demonstrates, museums play a pivotal role in politics of their nations as agents of nation-building and identity construction. They produce and represent the nation.[71] This also means that politics plays a major role in how museums operate, how they see their national responsibilities, and to what extent they represent their state in international society.

The international history of art restitution is, therefore, a story of many actors and complex relationships between them. Although there is certainly significant overlap, cases of looted art I describe in the book deal mostly with looting as a political act—artifacts taken from their original owners on orders from and through action by the state for the purposes of broader social, cultural, or political change, which distinguishes them from primarily commercial motives of individual grave robbers, looters, and traffickers.[72] The artifacts I focus on were taken by the state and then often housed in large state, national museums that are, albeit to a different degree, themselves acting as direct agents of the state. Sometimes, they have very little autonomy in restitution decisions as they are, quite literally, governed by state ministries of culture or the policies about restitution are encoded in national law, which leaves little to no room for autonomous action. And yet, some museum directors and curators disagree with their government positions and find ways to resist state mandates. Other times, however, locations of restitution

[69] McAuley, *House of Fragile Things*, p. 188.
[70] Procter, *Whole Picture*, p. 16.
[71] Levitt, *Artifacts and Allegiances*, p. 2.
[72] Gaudenzi and Swenson, "Looted Art and Restitution," pp. 495–96.

controversies are city, local, or regional museums that respond to different kinds of local or community pressures.

Cases of restitution also play out within the walls of private, not public museums, and the relationship between the museum and the state may appear less direct. To complicate the cast of characters further, private dealers and auction houses (such as the giants Christie's or Sotheby's) are also part of the larger political economy of art collection, authentication, appraisal, sale and return. Part of the challenge my book takes on is mapping out this complex political terrain of the international art world. As will become clear in the remainder of the book, what unifies the restitution cases I discuss is that they are all considered part of the larger cultural heritage of the state which took possession of them, and it is that claim to heritage that is being disputed as restitution demands grow.

Marbles, bronzes, and pictures

Theoretically, the objective of this book is to historicize rules of status competition and recognition and demonstrate their change over time. To carry this out, the book explores the international politics of restitution of three major categories of looted art: (1) art looted during European imperial expansions; (2) art looted during colonial occupations in the aftermath of the Berlin conference (1884–1885); and (3) art looted by Nazi Germany during World War II. Even though the three categories of looted art are quite different in terms of the historical context of looting as well as ownership claims (by individual owners vs. modern independent states), the movements for their restitution and the resistance to it are all part of larger questions of how national cultural heritage is internationally constructed, and how it serves states' desire for international status and prestige—questions that form the core research interest of my book. By taking a broader view and analyzing imperial, colonial, and Nazi-era looting and restitution, my book also joins recent calls for a global and transnational perspective on this topic.[73]

The book is organized around three groups of artifacts: the Parthenon Marbles, the Benin Bronzes, and Nazi-looted art. I made this choice for three principal reasons.

First, the looting of art during the imperial and colonial periods, as well as during the Nazi occupation of Europe, was an international endeavor. Imperial powers looted art in large part to compete with their rivals who were

[73] Gaudenzi and Swenson, "Looted Art and Restitution."

doing the same. These looted artifacts were then bought and sold through various intermediaries and ended up dispersed all over the world. While we most associate the Parthenon Marbles with the British Museum and the Acropolis Museum in Athens, pieces of the Parthenon are still on display at the National Museum in Copenhagen, at the Louvre in Paris, as well as in museums in Munich, Vienna, and Würzburg and, until very recently, at the Vatican and in Palermo.[74] The restitution of the Parthenon Marbles, therefore, is not simply a dispute between the United Kingdom and Greece.

The Benin Bronzes are equally dispersed. While the bulk of the collection was in London and Berlin, there were pieces displayed in several museums in Nigeria, but also in Aberdeen and Cambridge, in Philadelphia, Chicago, and New York City, as well as in Vienna, Stuttgart, Cologne, and Hamburg. As I recount in Chapter 4, the UK, Germany, and France all had very different responses to Benin Bronzes restitution claims. Looking at the same group of artifacts but tracing very different state responses to campaigns for their restitution illuminates the role that collecting and repatriating art plays in how different states understand and go about seeking and maintaining international status and prestige.

Similarly, like colonial looted art, Nazi-looted art was also internationally dispersed. As I recount in detail later in the book, Holocaust victims' property, including thousands of paintings declared "heirless" after the war as no owner survived to claim them, were handed out to various European museums. Often, they were simply distributed in bulk to countries they were looted from but not to individuals from whom they were taken. These valuable art pieces then remained in these countries' national museums and became part of their national cultural heritage. The international circulation and dislocation of these artifacts, then, also offers insights into how cultural heritage is internationally constructed, how it affects state cultural status, and how restitution claims are perceived as status threats.

The second dimension along which I selected the three groups of artifacts is time. While both the Marbles and the Bronzes were looted as part of the British imperial enterprise, the looting took place almost a hundred years apart. Lord Elgin removed parts of the Parthenon sculptures between 1801 and 1812, while most of the Benin Bronzes were looted during the British

[74] In January 2022, the Antonino Salinas Regional Archaeological Museum in Palermo sent on an extensive loan to Acropolis the so-called "Fagan fragment" of the Parthenon sculptures. *Greek City Times*, "Sicily returns a fragment." In December 2022, Pope Francis returned to Greece the three Parthenon stones held in the Vatican for over two hundred years. The gift was framed as a donation of the Pope to the Orthodox Christian archbishop of Athens in a sign of ecumenical reconciliation. Winfield, "Pope Returns Greece's Parthenon Sculptures." In May 2023, the Kunsthistorisches Museum in Vienna announced talks to return on loan its pieces of the Parthenon to the Acropolis Museum. Reuters, "Austria Says Talks Underway."

"punitive expedition" of 1897. This time gap then allows for the analysis of how these different objects were incorporated into European museums at different times, how different constellations of European powers at the time shaped the "antiquities rush" and competition among European museums for the best and most valuable art.

Nazi looting took place between 1933 and 1945, at the time when norms about the criminality of looting have already begun to take shape. Yet, it was not only Nazi Germany that engaged in an unprecedented scale of plunder; it was followed by the Soviet Union as its troops advanced across Eastern Europe in their defeat of the Nazis. Further, it took many decades after the war for the museums to begin to engage with restitution claims filed by Jewish families. While we often assume that Holocaust-looted art claims have mostly been resolved while the restitution campaigns for colonial looted art have just recently gained momentum, there are around 35,000 artworks looted in the Holocaust still hanging on the walls of state museums, and it is important that we understand why.[75]

Finally, in choosing to compare the outstanding restitution claims for Nazi-looted art with repatriation claims for imperial- and colonial-looted art, my goal is to connect the much more well-known cases of the Parthenon Marbles and the Benin Bronzes with often very obscure national collections of Nazi-looted art kept and displayed in much less visible, smaller museums that have for decades managed to escape global scrutiny. Some of the art collections I discuss contain very valuable artworks by major artists such as Tintoretto, Robert, Cézanne, Renoir, and Picasso, but the search for their restitution has received almost no international attention, only because the museums that hold them are on the international cultural periphery. To put it bluntly, the British Museum and the Louvre can't hide; the National Museum of Serbia can.

This imbalance in the global attention paid to different looted artifacts, then, also allows us to explore how different states understand the relationship between their art collections and their international status. Importantly, however, some states on the international cultural periphery (as I discuss regarding the Congo and Nigeria) have been at the forefront of restitution claims. It has been through the activism of those states that the criteria by which imperial- and colonial-looted art is to be understood have profoundly changed. Where a state is located in the international cultural hierarchy can influence state responses to restitution claims in quite different ways.

[75] The German government's Lost Art Database regularly updates the number of Nazi-era looted artworks in public museums. Database is available at https://www.lostart.de/en/start.

The book is based on extensive fieldwork which included visits to various museums and locations that are sites of disputes about restitution claims in Amsterdam, Athens, Belgrade, Berlin, Bogota, Cambridge, Copenhagen, Gothenburg, Istanbul, Jerusalem, London, Madrid, New York City, Oslo, Philadelphia, Prague, Tel Aviv, and Washington, DC. I analyzed primary archival and secondary literature sources on looted art and restitution, newspaper articles, museum exhibitions and catalogs, auction house records, feature and documentary films, memoirs, and novels. Over the course of three years (2022–2024), I conducted dozens of interviews with museum workers and local art historians and experts to ascertain their perspective on why certain artworks should or should not be restituted. How these local art experts conceptualize the role of these disputed artifacts in their own national cultural heritage that they—as museum workers—directly construct, is a key element of this story.

Plan of the book

This book has two main goals. The first is to demonstrate the political importance of art objects for states and the enduring power they have for state identity and the fight for international status, recognition, and prestige. The second is to introduce a new dynamic to our understanding of international status-seeking and status management. By showing how the status value of certain objects can change over time (from desirable status symbols to international stigmata), the book demonstrates that the standards of status recognition also change over time.

Chapter 2 provides the historical background to modern state-sponsored campaigns of art looting and reframes them as international status-seeking competitions. I begin with Napoleon and take us through the colonial era "antiquities rush" and all the way to the Nazi plunder during World War II. I sketch out how the systematic looting of cultural artifacts shaped the construction of national cultural heritage of European states that collected mass quantities of these items and the role that national museums played in this form of international cultural competition. The chapter then describes the slow road to normative change after World War II, when the ideas about stigmatizing possession of looted art and mandating restitution began to take shape and became institutionalized in a number of international resolutions. I document the path toward the current international cultural environment which places restitution within the larger context of decolonization and search for global cultural justice.

Chapters 3 and 4 deal with imperial- and colonial-looted art. Chapter 3 focuses on perhaps the most well-known case of international art restitution—the campaign to return pieces of the Parthenon taken by the British ambassador to Ottoman Turkey Lord Elgin in the early nineteenth century and housed in the British Museum. The chapter outlines the historical context of Elgin's removal of the Parthenon sculptures from the Acropolis in Athens and the very lively debates about the morality of his actions that existed at the time. I place Elgin's actions within the context of British status-seeking and especially its status competition with France. I then analyze the role of the British Museum as the home of this treasure and the meaning the "Elgin Marbles" have for British claims to world cultural superiority, both at the time and today. The chapter documents the sustained campaign by Greece to return the Marbles to the Acropolis and discusses the identity politics behind both the Greek restitution campaigns and British continuing resistance to them.

Chapter 4 moves a hundred years forward to the very end of the nineteenth century and the British "expedition" to the Kingdom of Benin in today's Nigeria. As an illustration of a widespread colonial practice, the chapter presents a brief historical account of the Benin expedition which removed art objects from the Royal Palace of Benin through tremendous physical violence, and then populated British museums with artifacts for which other European powers then competed. I document the long path of the Benin Bronzes restitution campaign, including a failed effort of repatriation in the 1960s, in the immediate aftermath of decolonization. The chapter takes us until today, when the restitution campaign has regained momentum and has already managed to secure pledges of return from a number of states. Both chapters discuss in detail the practical, legal, and ethical problems of repatriation, the cultural nationalism embedded in repatriation claims, and the question of who is the rightful country-heir of artifacts created in an era before these states were constituted.

Chapter 5 discusses Nazi-looted art. The chapter begins with the historical context of Nazi looting, explains its unprecedented scope, and the monumental obstacles facing survivors in getting their property, including artifacts, back. I describe the efforts—both by Jewish organizations and by the Allied forces—to document Holocaust "heirless" property and often contentious debates within these efforts regarding what to do with it. The chapter then outlines the massive art transfer throughout Europe of some of the "heirless" looted art and the way in which this art seamlessly became incorporated into the national cultural heritage of various European states.

The chapter anchors the discussion of Nazi-looted art on the case of the National Museum of Serbia, which houses a valuable collection of paintings that it received as a "restitution package" from the Allies after World War II. This collection, however, was in fact erroneously designated as having been looted in occupied Yugoslavia and its origins are instead in looted collections in France, the Netherlands, Austria, and elsewhere, many from Jewish owners. Through multisite primary archival research, the chapter reconstructs for the first time the international journey of these artworks, the manner in which they were incorporated into first Yugoslav and then Serbian cultural heritage, and explains Serbia's continuing refusal to not only restitute the art but even publicly acknowledge its problematic origins. I contrast this case with other recent cases of Nazi-looted art controversies, such as those involving Hungarian, Russian, Czech, and Polish museums, to demonstrate very different approaches to restitution claims in the context of international status management.

In the book's Conclusion, I take stock of the state of international politics of restitution to note the global political moment in which it appears that floodgates for restitution have, indeed, opened. This change was, in part, spurred by broader calls for social and racial justice, and reckoning with the way in which cultural institutions have supported and benefited from imperial and colonial projects. The Conclusion discusses whether the value of material objects has, indeed, permanently changed to include provenance as their core value, or if instead we are living through a fleeting moment of reckoning with the legacy of past crimes that will not make a permanent change. The final concluding thoughts revolve around some newer, creative models to deal with disputed restitution claims such as, for example, the idea to repatriate the Parthenon Marbles from the British Museum to Athens and replace them with a computer-generated 3D model in London.[76] Or to follow the example of the Museum of Rescued Art in Rome, which is a form of a holding museum for artifacts with disputed provenance, where they are displayed until successful repatriation.[77] These creative ideas then open up the space for rethinking the value of artifacts and even reimagine concepts such as authenticity, originality, and provenance.

The global cultural understanding of art ownership, appropriation, provenance, and display is changing.[78] This transformation raises important questions for international politics and practice. As my book demonstrates, the debates about art restitution reflect concerns about international status and

[76] Lidz, "Robot Guerrilla Campaign."
[77] Povoledo, "In Rome, a New Museum."
[78] Arvanitis and Tythacott, *Museums and Restitution.*

are much more directly rooted in global politics than a conventional understanding of the role of art in the world would suggest. Restitution claims go to the core questions regarding our understanding of the roles and responsibilities of contemporary statehood—a central concern of International Relations. What does a state have the right to own, when does this ownership begin, who inherits ownership from states and polities that no longer exist, but also who inherits responsibilities of care over material objects and cultural heritage in a globalized, multicultural world—these are all questions of international politics, as much as cultural practice.

The international history of art restitution I tell in this book is also a history of competing nationalisms, imperial pursuits, and construction of national heritage—powerful forces and movements with long historical legacies. Art restitution, then, should be understood not only as a difficult process of states relinquishing problematic ownership of valuable material objects, but also as a much more difficult process of recasting fantasies of cultural greatness.

2
Museums, Restitution, and International Status

Looting of various material objects, including artifacts, was common and largely unremarkable feature of warfare throughout history. Several passages in the Bible's Old Testament refer to the looting of art objects from Jerusalem by the Egyptian pharaoh Shoshenq I in 926 BCE.[1] In ancient Rome, it was routine practice to show the public looted artifacts from various Roman conquests. In a series of processions through the city, citizens of Rome could look at the objects that were individually carried by soldiers or piled up together in carriages.[2] The Christian Crusaders did the same upon their return to Venice after the pillaging and looting of artifacts from Constantinople during the Fourth Crusade in 1204.[3] So did Cortés's conquistadors after returning from Mexico to Spain with looted Aztec treasures.[4] Sweden looted art throughout Northern Europe during the Thirty Years' War (1618–1648), and under orders from Queen Christina, Swedish troops stole more than 1,000 paintings and other art objects from Prague and transported them to Stockholm in 1649, where the Queen, an avid art collector, amassed a huge personal art treasure.[5]

What we today refer to as art looting was understood for most of history as acquisition of "spoils of war." This practice was an obvious means of material enrichment for soldiers or higher up officers, but it also had a broader strategic purpose. It demonstrated military supremacy of the victorious party and the humiliating loss of the defeated.[6] It was also a way of showing cultural domination over the conquered and vanquished opponents.

As the historical account presented in this chapter demonstrates, however, it was also a form of international competition over cultural status. States, and especially empires with means of cultural extraction at their disposal,

[1] Lemaire, "Tribute or Looting."
[2] Sandholtz, *Prohibiting Plunder*, p. 33.
[3] Sandholtz, *Prohibiting Plunder*, p. 33.
[4] Thomas, *Conquest*.
[5] Lindsay, *History of Loot*.
[6] Evans, "Art in the Time of War."

competed to accumulate material artifacts as a sign of prestige and cultural wealth. And while looting was a long-standing practice throughout history, what changed in the modern era—and specifically with Napoleon—was the manner in which the mass accumulation of looted artifacts began to shape the construction of national cultural heritage. Napoleon's ransacking of Europe and the broader Mediterranean was so extensive and systematic that it also ushered in a shift from understanding plunder as "spoils of war" to treating it as "looted art."

It is at this time—broadly, the turn of the nineteenth century—that national museums that now housed and displayed this art came to play a critical role in the construction of national cultural heritage. Where states competed for accumulation of art, they now also competed for the largest and richest museum collections. This international competition for cultural status was, therefore, historically situated. As I recount in detail below, norms about looting and owning looted art also underwent a profound transformation in the twentieth century. Contemporary status competition has increasingly become competition about restitution.

But before we get to restitution, we need to start with Napoleon.

For the glory of France

Everybody looted, but nobody looted like Napoleon Bonaparte. It was not just the scale and reach of Napoleon's French army looting that was astonishing; it was also the systematic and deliberate way in which it was executed and then institutionalized as state practice for the explicit purpose of constructing French cultural heritage and superiority over its international rivals. The French state created a series of institutions in 1794 with the specific goal of organizing and streamlining the plunder of art from various territories France was conquering. The institutions included the Commission of Trade and Supply with the mandate to "extract" the artifacts from Belgium and take them to France; another Commission of Public Instruction which proposed "sending secretly after our armies educated citizens who will be commissioned to identify and to have removed with care the masterpieces that are found in the countries entered by our armies;" as well as the Temporary Art Commission which was to "compile lists of artistic and scientific objects in countries where the French armies were expected to enter."[7] As they progressed through Europe from Belgium toward Rhineland, French troops

[7] Sandholtz, *Prohibiting Plunder*, p. 49.

seized paintings and sculptures, manuscripts, precious gems, and coins. They looted churches and cathedrals, monasteries, city halls, and private homes from Bruges to Cologne to Bonn.[8]

When in 1796 Napoleon took full command of the French Army, he almost immediately went on the offensive against Italy. Looting of art was on the top of Napoleon's military agenda; it was not just an afterthought. On May 1, 1796, in a letter to the French emissary in Genoa, Napoleon ordered, "send me a list of the pictures, statues, cabinets and curiosities at Milan, Parma, Piacenza, Modena and Bologna."[9] Here is where looting kicked into high gear. The system of plunder became systematized and institutionalized through a series of treaties France imposed on various Italian states, making art requisition seem formalized and legalized—a mechanism of formalized looting Nazi Germany would perfect during World War II. As part of these "peace treaties," cities of Parma, Modena, Venice, Milan, Bologna, Perugia, and numerous others, including the Vatican, were emptied of their precious paintings, sculptures, and other art collections. Of course, plunder also went on outside the confines of the treaties. For example, Napoleon's army simply removed the massive statues of the four horses of the apocalypse from St. Mark's Square in Venice and took them home to Paris.[10]

It is during the looting of Venice in 1797 that Napoleon's army engaged in perhaps the most daring art looting scheme yet—the theft of Veronese's *Wedding Feast at Cana*, a massive painting weighing one-and-a-half tons that was, already at the time, considered a masterpiece of High Renaissance. Napoleon ordered the painting simply cut in half and then put together upon its arrival in Paris, where it was ceremoniously displayed at the Louvre in 1801.[11] The *Wedding Feast at Cana* was never returned to Italy. It still hangs at the Louvre today, on the wall across from the *Mona Lisa*.

Public display of looted art was a central feature of Napoleonic plunder.[12] Following the triumph of the conquest of Italy, a celebration was organized in July 1798 in Paris, one of the central features of which was the art treasures parade. A total of twenty-nine carts of stolen art, including masterpieces by Raphael, Titian, and Veronese, were marched through Paris. The parade was headed by a banner that read, "Greece gave them up; Rome lost them; Their fate changed twice; It won't change again."[13] At the end of the parade, the art was transported directly to the Louvre, as Napoleon's mission was to make

[8] Sandholtz, *Prohibiting Plunder*, p. 50.

[9] Saltzman, *Plunder*, p. 11.

[10] Sandholtz, *Prohibiting Plunder*, p. 50.

[11] Lindsay, *History of Loot*, p. 266. For a detailed account of the theft of the *Wedding Feast*, see Saltzman, *Plunder*.

[12] Sandholtz, *Prohibiting Plunder*, p. 47.

[13] Cited in Sandholtz, *Prohibiting Plunder*, p. 51.

Paris the new capital of European culture. Paris was to be "the asylum of all human knowledge . . . the capital of the arts, the school of the universe," wrote the French politician Boissy d'Anglas in 1794.[14] Paris, in other words, was to be the new Rome, and France was the only civilized country worthy of appreciating and displaying such artistic masterpieces (as the next chapter recounts, however, Great Britain begged to differ).[15]

Art looting, therefore, was directly linked to expressions of military supremacy—the most commonly recognized attribute of state status. The acquisition of art for the Louvre was understood to be a question of paramount military significance for France. As Webb argues, "Art and arms were not opposed; rather, the possession of masterpieces was a proof and an indication of superior military prowess."[16] Norms of warfare historically sanctioned art looting as a practice, and states engaged in it because it offered them the opportunities to acquire objects of art as status symbols. As I show later in this chapter, this alignment between art possession and military superiority began to break down when the possession of looted art became no longer valued, but instead stigmatized. The historically established practice of art looting that used to elevate state status, over time came to present a potential for status loss.

It was out of this notion of French cultural, political, and military supremacy that it conferred upon itself the responsibility to "protect civilization," understood, of course, very narrowly as Western European civilization. This protection was to be achieved through capturing Europe's finest art and denying the enemies of France, "the enemies of humanity," from possessing and enjoying it.[17] The widespread looting of European art, then, allowed France to position itself at the very top of the hierarchy of international cultural status. It was not just the victories in war that propelled France to this position; it was also the symbols France acquired in those war campaigns that provided it with crucial status markers and emblems, a collection of physical and beautiful reminders of French military feats and thus its superior status. To mark this status achievement, a song chanted during the parade of Italian looted art through Paris in 1798 ended its last verse with, "Rome is no more in Rome. It is all in Paris."[18]

And indeed, the extraordinary volume of Napoleon's looted treasure displayed at the Louvre made Paris an instant international tourist attraction at the turn of the nineteenth century, and visitors from all over Europe

[14] Quoted in McClellan, *Art Museum*, p. 236.
[15] Evans, "Art in the Time of War."
[16] Webb, "Appropriating the Stones," p. 75.
[17] Gilks, "Attitudes to the Displacement of Cultural Property," p. 122.
[18] McClellan, *Art Museum*, p. 237.

flocked to see the art and hail the Louvre as the best museum in the world.[19] But the French also justified the plunder and the parade of these foreign art objects as an opportunity for public education, accumulation of encyclopedic knowledge, and furthering of Enlightenment ideas of scientific and cultural progress. Napoleon claimed he acquired this art for the French nation and, true to his republican commitments, wanted it displayed not in the private palaces of French royalty but in a public museum he named after himself.[20]

The collecting of high art was not, however, understood only as an issue of war booty or in simply monetary terms. For Napoleonic France, acquiring and displaying the best art of Europe was a direct measurement of France's cultural greatness—its cultured status, which the French understood in part to be that of "liberty" as opposed to feudal "tyranny." Not only did the best art belong to France, but the best artists were to be considered *French*: "every man of genius . . . whatever country he may have been born, is a French citizen," claimed Napoleon.[21] French officials were quite explicit in this regard. The French Directorate instructed Napoleon in 1796, "The Executive Directory is convinced, Citizen General, that you see the glory of the Fine Arts as attached to that of the army you command. Italy owes to them [the Fine Arts] a great part of its riches and its fame; but the time has come when their reign must pass to France to solidify and embellish that of liberty."[22] What we today understand as state looting on a massive scale, Napoleonic France understood as a form of restitution—return of the arts to the civilized and the free.[23] In positioning themselves as the curators of the world, the French also put themselves in the position of determining what kind of culture matters, and what counts and does not count as culture in the first place.

Construction of national cultural heritage

Napoleon's massive looting of art, however, is also directly related to the creation and development of the Louvre, still considered the world's premier art museum.[24] The officials of the French Directorate instructed Napoleon in no uncertain terms that the purpose of his acquisition of Italian art was to enrich the collections at the Louvre: "The National Museum should hold the most

[19] Saltzman, *Plunder*.
[20] Saltzman, *Plunder*.
[21] Quoted in Gilks, "Attitudes to the Displacement of Cultural Property," p. 120. This vision of France did not die with Napoleon. Charles de Gaulle famously wrote in 1954, "France cannot be France without greatness." Gildea, "Myth, Memory and Policy," p. 60.
[22] Saltzman, *Plunder*, pp. 15–16.
[23] Gaudenzi and Swenson, "Looted Art and Restitution," p. 499.
[24] For a comprehensive account of the history of the Louvre, see McClellan, *Inventing the Louvre*.

famous monuments of all the arts, and you will not neglect enriching it with those pieces for which it waits from the present conquests of the Army of Italy and those that are still to come."[25] The roots of the Louvre's extensive collection of world art are, therefore, to a significant extent found in Napoleonic theft and plunder.[26]

The major world museums that developed and expanded on the Louvre's model—the British Museum, first among many—then also copied the French state model of filling their museums with objects of art procured as spoils of war. For example, the Rijksmuseum in Amsterdam built its large collection in large part on the objects looted and brought back as trophies from Dutch colonies. When the King of Holland Louis Napoleon (Napoleon's younger brother) returned to the Netherlands with crates of loot in 1806, at the head of his convoy was a banner which read, "Louis Napoleon, King of Holland, presents to his capital Amsterdam these trophies seized by brave Netherlanders from their enemies."[27] For Louis Napoleon, whose rule over the Netherlands was never considered quite legitimate by the Dutch, looted objects, included looted art, were to serve as legitimating tools of governance.

Napoleon's expeditions of plunder continued after the Italian triumph—his armies ransacked art collections throughout German lands, Austria, and Spain, and plundered huge number of antiquities during the expedition to Egypt in 1798. The French army was accompanied by 167 scholars and artists (the *savants*), whose role was to find, evaluate, and extract Egyptian treasures.[28] Much of this looted art also ended up at the Louvre. However, perhaps the most precious piece Napoleon took from Egypt, the famous Rosetta Stone, was seized by the British expeditionary force in 1801 and taken to the British Museum, where it remains.

But after Napoleon's first defeat and abdication in 1814, some of the countries his army plundered (such as Prussia and Austria) began to ask for their art to be returned. Great Britain and Russia, however, advocated against restitution out of fear that this fraught process would destabilize the new French state.[29] Charles-Maurice de Talleyrand-Périgord, French leading

[25] Saltzman, *Plunder*, p. 16.

[26] Bergvelt, Meijers, Tibbe, and van Wezel, *Napoleon's Legacy*.

[27] Author's visit to Rijksmuseum, Amsterdam, October 2023. For background, see Van Beurden, *Inconvenient Heritage*.

[28] Evans, "Art in the Time of War." Bringing artists on missions was a common European colonial practice. A hundred years earlier, Johan Maurits van Nassau-Siegen, the governor general of Dutch Brazil brought to Brazil in the 1640s a group of scholars and artists, who were to research and document the local landscape. Some of the paintings from this mission are today displayed at the Rijksmuseum in Amsterdam. Author's visit to Rijksmuseum, October 2023.

[29] For a detailed account of the debates about restitution following Napoleonic wars, see Sandholtz, *Prohibiting Plunder*, chs. 2 and 3. Also, see Sandholtz, "Plunder, Restitution, and International Law," p. 150 and Vrdoljak, *International Law*.

diplomat at the time, considered the failure of restitution to be a huge triumph for otherwise defeated France. In his memoirs, he wrote, "we have retained all of the admirable pieces of art conquered by our arms in nearly all the museums of Europe."[30]

After the French defeat at Waterloo in 1815, there were renewed calls for restitution of looted art. This time Britain, led by the Duke of Wellington, spearheaded the campaign for restitution and amassed a coalition of like-minded countries (Austria, Spain, the Low Countries, the German states, the Italian states, and the Vatican) to negotiate the return of plundered art at the Congress of Vienna.[31] The Duke of Wellington argued for restitution on the grounds of both morality as well as national cultural heritage claims: "The same feelings which induce the people of France to wish to retain the pictures and statues of other nations . . . would naturally induce other nations to wish, now that success is on their side, that the property should be returned to their rightful owners."[32] There were also cartoons in the British media mocking Napoleon's plundering frenzy (see Figure 2.1).

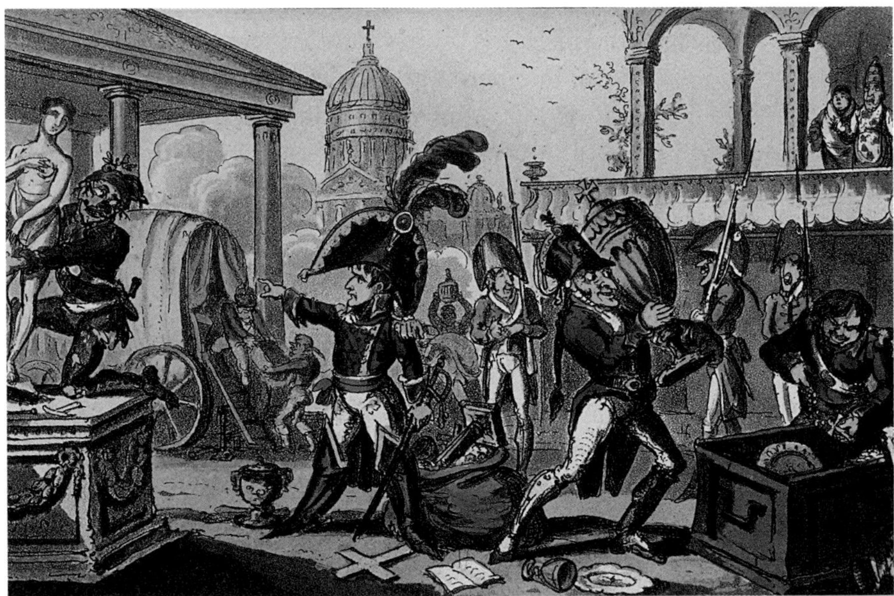

Figure 2.1 George Cruikshank, *Seizing the Italian Relics*, cartoon, 1815 (Wikimedia Commons)

[30] Cited in Sandholtz, "Plunder, Restitution, and International Law," p. 150.
[31] Sandholtz, "Plunder, Restitution, and International Law," p. 151.
[32] Quoted in Evans, "Art in the Time of War," p. 18.

France was compelled to return some 5,000 pieces of art, but refused to restitute a few hundred artifacts, including the expansive collection of Egyptian art. Much of the looted art was transported from the Louvre to smaller French provincial museums in an attempt to avoid repatriation.[33] Some of the art was repatriated from the Louvre by force—the Belgian delegates, for example, grew so impatient with French resistance to return that they simply took the art from the museum themselves and carried it back home.[34]

These early calls for restitution indicate the historically contingent understanding of looted art as a status symbol. The international criticism of France was that it was in possession of objects that should go back to origin countries and give those countries a status lift. The process of repatriation itself began to construct the concept of national cultural heritage in European public consciousness.[35] The French public, for instance, was aghast at the process of repatriating Napoleon's loot, which it had come to consider as part of *French* cultural heritage.[36] There are reports of women gathering outside the Louvre and weeping as crates of art were spirited away.[37] The return of plundered art to Belgium, on the other hand, was met with cheers from the assembled crowd in Brussels.[38] The vigorous debates about whether or not to repatriate stolen art then created a sense that various countries had claims to their own artworks, and that these artworks were important for their sense of identity and international cultural status. Napoleon's pillaging and subsequent calls for repatriation and restitution, therefore, gave birth, in significant part, to the idea that cultural objects represented the identity of the nation, and were important for the processes of nation-building.

In the aftermath of Napoleon's ravaging through Europe's art collections, European states started to catalog, classify, and protect their art holdings and conceptualize of them as not just individual objects of art but integral and inalienable part of national cultural patrimony.[39] As European nations began to consolidate as states and invent their traditions, artifacts in museums were material evidence of these states' "new past."[40] And as nation-building progressed, so did the idea that a nation should be distinguished by a particular and unique aesthetic that would be expressed through material objects.[41]

[33] Miles, *Art as Plunder*, p. 341.
[34] Quynn, "Art Confiscations of the Napoleonic Wars."
[35] Marchand, "Dialectics of the Antiquities Rush," p. 191.
[36] For a complex range of responses to both plunder and restitution in Napoleonic France, see Gilks, "Attitudes to the Displacement of Cultural Property."
[37] Miles, *Art as Plunder*, p. 334.
[38] Sandholtz, *Prohibiting Plunder*, p. 67.
[39] Evans, "Art in the Time of War," p. 18.
[40] Barkan, "Amending Historical Injustices," p. 18.
[41] Rose-Greenland, "Parthenon Marbles," p. 660.

The mid-eighteenth to early nineteenth century was also the time when, across Europe, the fine arts came to be valued as an essential expression of "national character" that attached people to their emerging nation-states.[42] Art objects became "imbued with national significance" and a particular attachment developed between material culture and national identity.[43]

This growing public interest in national cultural heritage also spurred the development of national museums as well as museum-led archaeological expeditions to find, excavate, and extract antiquities and bring them back to imperial capitals. These newly acquired collections served as material examples of the success of European imperial pursuits, the extent of their imperial reach, and the cultural diversity under their control. In the competition of national museums for quantities and qualities of these objects, a new sense of national heritage was created, and with it, a particular international cultural order.[44]

The international status competition of the "antiquities rush"

Massive art looting, of course, did not stop with Napoleon. If anything, it "normalized and legitimized" the colonial looting that came after.[45] The European imperial "scramble for Africa" in the nineteenth century was accompanied by what Suzanne Marchand memorably termed "the antiquities rush," or the simultaneous attempt by multiple actors to "take advantage of an opportune moment to extract antiquities for export."[46] What distinguishes this era of art looting from previous bouts of plunder is the involvement of the full state apparatus—primarily the public national museums, but also art commissions, ministries, and professional organizations.[47]

After Napoleon's retreat from Egypt, Egyptian antiquities became a veritable art playground for amateur archaeologists, tomb raiders, shady art dealers, but also scholars sent on missions by major European museums, which acted as arms of their states and their imperial projects. Between Great Britain, France, Bavaria, and Prussia, thousands of Egyptian stone statues, papyri, mummies, and many other objects were brought to museums

[42] Hoock, *Empires of the Imagination*, p. 14.
[43] McAuley, *House of Fragile Things*, p. 51.
[44] Gaudenzi and Swenson, "Looted Art and Restitution."
[45] Effros, "Berber Genealogy," p. 63.
[46] Marchand, "Dialectics of the Antiquities Rush," p. 192.
[47] Marchand, "Dialectics of the Antiquities Rush," p. 195.

in London, Paris, Berlin, or Munich.[48] The discovery and transport of the Rosetta Stone from Egypt to London was an international phenomenon and created an entire scholarly field of Egyptology. This antiquities rush was often chaotic, violent, and completely unregulated. Sounding much like Indiana Jones, British archaeologist Howard Carter, famous for discovering the tomb of Tutankhamun in 1922, lamented the passing of the glory days of nineteenth-century plundering of Egypt, "Those were the great days of collecting. Anything, for which a fancy was taken, from a scarab to an obelisk, was just appropriated and if there was a difference of opinion with a brother excavator one laid for him with a gun."[49]

This period also marks archaeology as a field of status competition between rival European powers that raced to dig up Greco-Roman ruins in the broader Mediterranean. Archaeology was also in direct service of colonial projects. French and Italian troops in North Africa, for example, were used to excavate Roman ruins "to establish a visual and ideological link between past and present colonialism."[50] In a broader sense, however, the antiquities rush also represented the international competition for the accumulation of mass quantities of art objects from newly acquired colonies—an international race for symbols of status.

Colonial powers have, obviously, gained economic assets through sale or repossession of stolen objects. But the antiquities rush of the nineteenth century (or in Marchand's more precise timeframe, the period 1800–1930) was also a way to enrich national museums and build the cultural repertoire of imperial seats of power. For example, the British Undersecretary of State for Foreign Affairs instructed the incoming British consul to Egypt Henry Salt in 1815 to acquire as many Egyptian antiques as possible, as a way of competing with rival nations: "Whatever the expense of the undertaking, it would be most cheerfully supported by an enlightened nation, eager to anticipate its rivals in the prosecution of the best interests of science and literature."[51] Salt did as he was told, procuring a tremendous number of antiques for the British Crown—and the British Museum—but also kept or sold numerous pieces for himself.[52]

Often, colonial administrators agonized over artifacts "left to rot" in their locations of origin, while they should have been sent to Europe instead. For example, in his description of the looting of Ottoman lands, Michael

[48] Lindsay, *History of Loot*, p. 322.
[49] Quoted in Lindsay, *History of Loot*, p. 324.
[50] Dyson, *In Pursuit of Ancient Pasts*, xiv.
[51] Lindsay, *History of Loot*, pp. 325–26.
[52] Lindsay, *History of Loot*, p. 333.

Greenhalgh quotes a British colonial chaplain E.J. Davis who wrote in 1879, despairing about an abandoned sarcophagus he found near the site of ancient Derbe (in today's Turkey), "it is a pity some European museum does not possess it, rather than it should be lying in the moist earth of Lycaonia."[53] This argument—that artifacts, even if looted, should remain in major Western museums because they will be better preserved there than if they were sent back to inferior conditions in countries of origin—is a common argument opponents of restitution continue to make.[54]

That the scramble for artifacts, and the international competition to collect more and more of them, culturally impoverished colonized and occupied nations is too obvious of a point. Art objects were acquired through a variety of means—aboveboard purchasing, but also bribery or outright looting, and often some murky mix of all. But the scramble of the antiquities rush also destroyed the integrity of cultural sites in many different ways—aesthetically, structurally, environmentally, and even semiotically. Objects were excavated, extracted, broken up into smaller pieces, and moved to various destinations for sale or depository into national museums. Stone statues were sawed off from their pedestals for ease of transport and would then appear in European museums without their feet that remain attached to the now discarded slab of stone at their original location.[55] These extractive practices then also changed the meaning of the artifact once it arrived at and was displayed in a European museum. An object that could have had spiritual, religious, or ritual purpose and meaning in its own habitat now became interpreted as an object of "art," valued and measured by the European standards of art appraisal at the time. As the discussion of the Benin Bronzes in Chapter 4 demonstrates in detail, at different historical moments, the same objects may have had quite different meaning and their value may have been determined by who owns them, and not by who created them. They served as material evidence of cultural status and acted as claims for status recognition.

The birth of the national museum

The development of national museums as agents of international status-seeking, therefore, is historically constituted. There were always collectors of artifacts, but for most of human history only the nobility or the political elite were able to enjoy precious objects of culture in their private homes. This began to change after the Renaissance. The origin of the modern museum

[53] Quoted in Greenhalgh, *Plundered Empire*, p. 523.
[54] See Van Beurden, "Loot," for an overview of some of these arguments.
[55] Thompson, *Possession*, p. 58.

is often traced to the sixteenth century, when the idea of a *wunderkammer* became popular among European nobility.[56] These "cabinets of curiosities" typically contained some specimens from the natural world, as well as objects of science, art, and curiosities brought from afar.[57] These were private collections, and the concept of the modern public museum did not really exist as such until the seventeenth century, when the Ashmolean Museum opened in 1683 to house the cabinet of curiosities donated by antiquary Elias Ashmole to the University of Oxford.[58]

With the rise of democratic pressures in the late eighteenth and early nineteenth centuries, various European states began to establish national museums to display art and material objects to the popular masses.[59] It is in this era that the British Museum (the first public institution to be named "British")[60] was founded in 1753, the Louvre in Paris in 1793, the Rijksmuseum in 1798 in the Hague, the Prado in Madrid in 1819, followed by the National Gallery in London in 1824, the Altes Museum in Berlin in 1830, the State Hermitage Museum in St. Petersburg in 1852, the Bavarian National Museum in Munich in 1855, and the Ethnological Museum in Berlin in 1873, among others.[61]

The political purpose of establishing national museums was both domestic and international. Domestically, national museums provided a physical location of national fantasies and desires expressed through material culture. They constructed national and cultural identities through emotional attachments to familiar material objects that represented a connection between national identity and the state.[62] Historically, they also served as critical institutions of nation-building by classifying and narrating various material objects as expressions of a particular national ("our") art and culture, therefore solidifying a sense of we-ness.[63] By turning nation-states and their publics into collectors of art, national museums served to further shore up national identity and shared cultural belonging.[64]

[56] Geczy, "Curating Curiosity."
[57] Impey and MacGregor, *Origins of Museums*.
[58] Impey and MacGregor, *Origins of Museums*.
[59] Brusius and Singh, "Introduction," p. 3.
[60] This is according to its former director, Neil MacGregor, "Britain Is at the Centre."
[61] The Louvre was opened in 1793 as Muséum central des arts de la République. In 1803, it was renamed Musée Napoléon. It came to be referred to more broadly as Le Louvre since 1815. While the British Museum was established in 1753, it initially was selective about who could visit and opened to select audiences in 1759. It only fully opened to the public in 1837. The Rijksmuseum was founded in 1798 in the Hague and moved to Amsterdam in 1808. The Hermitage Museum was founded in 1764, but only opened to the public in 1852. Madrid's Prado was founded in 1785 and opened to the public in 1819.
[62] Auslander and Zahra, "Things They Carried."
[63] Sylvester, *Art/Museums*, p. 29. This is a process well established since Anderson, *Imagined Communities*.
[64] Macdonald, "Collecting Practices," p. 85.

They also solidified the relationship between the citizen and the state by presenting the museum's valuable collections as belonging to the public, to the people themselves, and no longer just to the prince or the king. They were the property of the nation.[65] The national museum, then, was critical for the public to experience and practice their own citizenship.[66] Museums organized their collections in a way that not only allowed the public to experience art at the popular level, but also through a set of often ritualistic performances and routines organized the relationship between the visiting public and their cultural heritage and defined the public's own place in the national cultural system.[67] Possessing artifacts from other cultures and from far away colonized lands was also integral to the process of nation-building because these collections of "other people's things" demonstrated to the public that their state was an important actor on the international stage.[68]

Internationally, national museums represented the state in the international competition for cultured status. That states compete in the world of art and culture has already been well established.[69] Like with other examples of conspicuous consumption in world politics, states used their art collections in national museums to compete because other states competed.[70] They established national museums and raced to populate them with prestigious objects because their neighbors, peers, and aspirational states did so and so they needed to keep up. The institutional form of the museums also diffused.[71] While these major museums were established to be encyclopedic, grandiose, and "universal" in scale, they also clearly represented and often celebrated the nations that built them.[72] They were their nations' flattering "self-portraits."[73]

But this rush to populate museums with art treasures was also a form of global cultural entanglement—as objects were moved from one location to another, they obtained new cultural meaning. This massive cultural extraction and transfer also produced an encounter with non-European art, and an opportunity for European artists and art professionals to engage with this, for them, novel art in meaningful ways. For some scholars, this educational consequence of colonial art presentation in European museums is too often lost in the debates about restitution. It is certainly true that these

[65] Duncan and Aln Wallach, "Universal Survey Museum," p. 52, p. 55. Also Macdonald, "Museums."
[66] Duncan and Wallach, "Universal Survey Museum," p. 52.
[67] Bennett, *Birth of the Museum*.
[68] Macdonald, "Museums."
[69] MacKay, "Art World Fields."
[70] Gilady, *Price of Prestige*.
[71] Meyer, Boli, Thomas, and Ramirez, "World Society"; DiMaggio and Powell, "Iron Cage Revisited."
[72] McAuley, *House of Fragile Things*, p. 185.
[73] McAuley, *House of Fragile Things*, p. 187.

colonial entanglements enriched European art and made it less Eurocentric and parochial, extending the boundaries of what is considered "beauty" or even "art." From this perspective, art repatriation campaigns are often small-minded expressions of cultural nationalism and will lead to further cultural isolationism, as art will come to be seen as "national" property and not a universal cultural value.[74] I return to these arguments later.

National museums and international cultural power

Not only was there international competition to acquire art, but there was competition to establish national museums. The establishment of the magnificent Louvre was inspiring but also threatening to France's European rivals. For example, in 1807, Prussian education minister Karl vom Stein zum Altenstein advised King Friedrich Wilhelm III to make the fine arts accessible to everyone in a national museum, as art is "the expression of the highest condition of mankind."[75] It should not be only France, but also Prussia that had made its art collections the principal claim to international cultural status. This equation of national museums with high international status has remained present through time. When Pakistan emerged as an independent state in 1947, one of its first goals was to establish several national museums as its leaders believed, "the number of museums in a country is taken as indication of the cultural level that country has reached."[76] National museums held "discursive power" for European imperial states in the eighteenth century, but also for postcolonial states in the mid-twentieth.[77]

From their very emergence, therefore, national museums were profoundly political; they were state actors that pursued state interests through the collection, management, and display of artifacts.[78] They quite explicitly embodied the state through architecture and monumentality. Both from the outside and from within the exhibit halls, these museums conveyed a sense of national stability and progress.[79] Almost always built in grandiose, classical style, and located in prominent and highly visible locations in city centers, often in close proximity to other government buildings, these museums were purposefully designed to resemble ancient temples or palaces. As Timothy Mitchell has argued, the boundaries between state and society are often drawn internally

[74] For a forceful recent statement of this argument, see Kuper, *Museum of Other People*.
[75] Quoted in Duncan and Wallach, "Universal Survey Museum," p. 52.
[76] Quoted in McClellan, *Art Museum*, p. 5.
[77] Bellisari, "Art of Decolonization," p. 641.
[78] McClellan, *Art and Its Publics*; Carrier, *Museum Skepticism*; Gray, *Politics of Museums*.
[79] Macdonald, "Museums," p. 277.

through specific practices, such as proximity and distance to government buildings.[80] Grand national museums were, similarly, built to be a symbol of the state, one that "equates state authority with the idea of civilization."[81]

Culturally, through their collections and curation of those collections in grand national museums, European imperial powers claimed the classical heritage of ancient civilizations as their own ancestral culture, and then positioned themselves as bearers of that standard of civilization.[82] They were able to do this because being recognized as a state with high status involves the ability to speak on behalf of the international community, for example by determining what has universal cultural value. As Duque argues, "great powers arrogate to themselves the ability to act in the name of the international community as a whole."[83] By narrating their own history of Western civilization through appropriation of numerous antiquities from ancient Egypt, Greece, and Rome, these European states through their museums created a particular "universal survey" of art history which begins in antiquity and culminates in contemporary European political and aesthetic dominance.[84]

In the eighteenth and nineteenth centuries, while bowing to democratic movements domestically, the newly established national museums were also critically embedded in various European powers' imperial projects and pursuits.[85] Museums worked closely and shared expertise with colonial administrations.[86] They encouraged colonial staff, missionaries, or individual explorers to bring back material objects from colonial expeditions. For example, the Royal Museum for Central Africa in Tervuren, Belgium was established in 1897 with a specific mandate by King Leopold II to present Belgium's acquisition of the Congo as its new colony. Significantly from the perspective of international competition for status, the museum was opened as part of the 1897 World Fair in Brussels, as a showcase of Belgium's advances in Africa.[87] In fact, using colonial museums to claim international status was quite routine, as the world's first anthropological museum, Musée

[80] Mitchell, "Limits of the State."

[81] Duncan and Wallach, "Universal Survey Museum," p. 47.

[82] On the concept of "standard of civilization" in international politics, see Bowden, "In the Name of Progress"; Gong, *Standard of "Civilization."*

[83] Duque, "Concept of Status."

[84] Singh, "Museum Is National." On the concept of "universal survey museum," see Duncan and Wallach, "Universal Survey Museum."

[85] For broader context, see Stahn, *Confronting Colonial Objects.*

[86] Longair and McAleer, *Curating Empire.*

[87] Silverman, "Diasporas of Art."

d'Ethnographie du Trocadéro in Paris, was also established specifically to be shown at the Paris World Fair in 1878.[88]

These museums were also active participants in colonial art collecting, which of course included art looting. The British Museum, for example, directly participated in British colonial expeditions as part of the British administration abroad, which I describe in detail in Chapter 4. Using the full powers of the British military, navy, and the diplomatic service, as well as the government-facilitated and logistically complex transports of acquired antiquities from abroad, the British Museum amassed large quantities of art objects in this period.[89] Its collections could now stand up to the Louvre. The Museum's experts and curators worked next to other British colonial staff, as they collected valuable artifacts and brought them back for study and display in London.[90] While they also showcased local, national art and buttressed the local sense of cultural identity, these museums also displayed artifacts acquired through imperial expansions and incorporated this art into their own national cultural heritage. The art brought back from the colonies, then, became part of British, French, or Dutch cultural heritage, but it served a different purpose than the incorporation of Greco-Roman antiquity. It did not represent civilizational continuity, but instead civilizational difference.

That the role of colonial museums in the imperial project was central should by now be clear. Even more direct was the role of the anthropological or ethnological museums, museums that collected "curiosities" about various exotic peoples, and displayed their material objects, artifacts, objects of daily life and cultural customs, but also often their skulls and other human remains. These museums should then be understood as weapons of colonialism themselves, not only complicit in but also actively producing and disseminating racial hierarchies.[91] The objects they displayed that were extracted, often forcibly, from their locales of creation, were then used by the museums to not only construct the knowledge of the colonized others, but to legitimate their control and subjugation.[92]

These museums were now projections of international cultural and political power. Their collections represented their nation-states' political ambition and claims to international cultural status by demonstrating their "possession and mastery of the world."[93] By doing so they also justified their states'

[88] DeGroff, "Ethnographic Display." For a broader look at the role of world fairs in imperial projects, see Rydell, *All the World's a Fair.*

[89] Hoock, "British State."

[90] Sylvester, *Art/Museums*, p. 32. Also see Hicks, *Brutish Museums*; Phillips, *Loot.*

[91] Hicks, *Brutish Museums.*

[92] Donington, "Relics of Empire?"

[93] Macdonald, "Collecting Practices," p. 85.

imperial projects.[94] As Simon Njami writes, these grand national museums "represented a showcase through which colonial countries displayed their grandeur to their peers, an immense cabinet of curiosities that was meant to provoke envy and respect."[95] European imperial museums also directly competed with one another.[96] They raced to acquire and display more and more valuable objects in an "international chase for objects around the globe to fill the new treasure houses."[97] The wealth of state collections and their constant appetite for more also reflected in the most direct terms the colonial race between various European powers.[98]

It is important to emphasize, yet again, just how essential the imperial state, with its military and diplomatic arms, was in the process of antiquities acquisition in the nineteenth century. This was not just the hobby of rich explorers or adventurers trying to collect—often through simple plunder—antiquities and sell them to the highest bidder. European states—foremost France, Britain, and Prussia—coordinated and financed many expeditions to the Mediterranean, Middle East, and later Africa and Asia, and organized the transport of collectables back to their big national museums using naval vessels and providing logistical support and administration.

We have direct contemporary evidence of this competition. For example, in the aftermath of Napoleon's defeat in 1815, as various countries sent delegates to Paris to collect their looted art from the Louvre, French officials rebuffed these claims arguing that the British push for restitution is a thinly veiled attempt by Britain to amass its collections by taking artifacts away from the Louvre:

> If we yield to the claims of Holland and Belgium, we deprive the [Louvre] Museum of one of its greatest assets, that of having a series of excellent colorists . . . Russia is not hostile, Austria has had everything returned, Prussia has a restoration more complete . . . there remains only England, who has in truth nothing to claim but who, since she has just bought the bas-reliefs of which Lord Elgin plundered the Temple at Athens, now thinks she can become a rival of the Museum, and wants to deplete this Museum in order to collect the remains [for herself].[99]

This passage is important not only because it demonstrates that both art collection and restitution were direct forms of international status

[94] Levitt, *Artifacts and Allegiances*, p. 7.
[95] Jules-Rosette and Osborn, *African Art Reframed*, xiv.
[96] Hoock, "British State."
[97] Gaudenzi and Swenson, "Looted Art and Restitution," p. 503.
[98] Greenhalgh, *Plundered Empire*, ch. 16.
[99] Quoted in Quynn, "Art Confiscations," p. 451.

competition, but also because it is evidence that Elgin's plundering of the Acropolis was considered immoral at the time not only by some British intellectuals—the poet Lord Byron perhaps most prominently—but also by Britain's principal international rivals, a topic explored in depth in the next chapter. Amusingly, Elgin himself justified his looting of the Acropolis by one-upping Napoleon. Bragging about his Parthenon Marbles, Elgin wrote, "Bonaparte has not got such a thing from all his thefts in Italy."[100]

The calls for restitution

While some of the arguments against art restitution today claim that art looting was legal and morally unquestioned at the time, there were strong contemporary voices, as well as institutional efforts to limit plunder.[101] If we understand international norms as always productive of hierarchy, these early arguments against looting indicate that there did exist a rival normative order, even if less salient.[102] At the peak of Napoleon's plunder of Italy, the French archaeologist Quatremère de Quincy complained in his *Letters to Miranda on the Displacement of Monuments of Art from Italy* (1796) that looting of art was in contradiction to the goals and values of the French Republic, as "the arts and sciences belong to all of Europe, and are no longer the exclusive property of one nation."[103] After Napoleon's defeat in 1815, in addition to the Duke of Wellington's efforts to restitute Napoleon's loot to various European nations, likely the first formal recognition that art and other cultural property should not be at the mercy of invading armies was actually made during the American Civil War by the Union Army in 1863. The document that became known as Lieber's *Instructions* (or the Lieber Code after its author, the Prussian-American jurist Francis Lieber) states, "Classical works of art, libraries, scientific collections, or precious instruments, such as astronomical telescopes, as well as hospitals, must be secured against all avoidable injury, even when they are contained in fortified places whilst besieged or bombarded."[104]

Over the next few decades, there were numerous diplomatic conferences where the issue of protection of cultural property during wartime was

[100] Cited in St Clair, *Lord Elgin*, p. 100.

[101] Sandholtz, *Prohibiting Plunder*.

[102] Towns, *Women and States*.

[103] Quoted in McClellan, *Art Museum*, pp. 243–44.

[104] Instructions for the Government of Armies of the United States in the Field, prepared by Francis Lieber, promulgated as General Order No. 100 by President Abraham Lincoln, Washington, D.C., 24 April 1863, Article 35. Available at https://ihl-databases.icrc.org/en/customary-ihl/v2/rule38. For an extensive discussion of Lieber's activism and jurisprudence, see Sandholtz, *Prohibiting Plunder*, ch. 4.

discussed. At the initiative of Russian tzar Alexander II, representatives of major European powers met in Brussels in 1874 to further specify emergent international law on the conduct of war, including treatment of art by the invading armies. The Brussels Declaration made explicit note of art looting during warfare, and its Article 39 states, "Pillage is formally forbidden."[105] In 1880, international lawyers and diplomats met again, this time in Oxford, and expanded upon these various existing documents to create what became known as the *Oxford Manual.* These principles were then further internationally institutionalized at the Hague conference in 1899, later enshrined in the Hague convention in 1907, which again explicitly prohibited "pillage." The Hague convention also demanded that an occupying country protect, not destroy the property of the defeated state and its people.[106]

As Sandholtz documents in detail, the norms against looting and destruction of art were already so strong in the early twentieth century that they constrained Germany's wartime behavior during World War I. When a suggestion was made in the German media that the German army, as it advanced through Belgium, should capture the country's best art, this idea was rejected with horror by German scholars, artists, and museum workers, who considered it uncivilized and reminiscent of the savagery of Napoleonic plundering pursuits.[107]

Of course, these norms against destruction and plunder of cultural property were conceived exceedingly narrowly, to constrain behavior within Europe and the West. They did not apply to behavior of occupying forces in Eastern Europe and certainly not outside of Europe in colonized lands.[108] During World War I, the armies of the Central Powers did steal and destroy cultural property, including burning to the ground the buildings that during the Austro-Hungarian occupation (1916–1918) housed the Serbian National Museum in Belgrade. This destruction has become an important historical marker for the assertion of Serbian ownership over various artifacts collected since World War I and, as I discuss extensively in Chapter 5, to a large degree explain the Museum's resistance today to even discuss possible restitution of looted art it continues to display. Germany, however, was punished for the destruction of cultural property in World War I. For its destruction of art in Belgium, most notoriously the burning of the Library of Louvain, Germany was required by Article 247 of the Versailles Treaty to restitute a number of

[105] Sandholtz, *Prohibiting Plunder*, pp. 88–89.
[106] Evans, "Art in the Time of War," p. 19.
[107] Sandholtz, *Prohibiting Plunder*, pp. 106–07.
[108] Barkan, "Amending Historical Injustices," p. 19.

Belgian artworks that were taken to museums in Berlin and Munich and give them back to Belgium.[109]

In the aftermath of World War I, the international norms against wartime looting further developed through various agencies and committees of the League of Nations, most directly the International Museums Office established in 1926. This work culminated in the 1938 Preliminary Draft International Convention for the Protection of Historic Buildings and Works of Art in Time of War which read, in part, "destruction of a masterpiece, whatever nation may have produced it, is a spiritual impoverishment for the entire international community."[110] It is of utmost historical irony that this document was created right on the eve of World War II, the war that unleashed an unprecedented scale of destruction of humanity and its art and culture.

Restitution architecture after World War II

While massive art looting since Napoleon and throughout the era of European colonial expansion in the eighteenth and nineteenth centuries populated European museums with innumerable works of art, the systematic looting of art by Nazi Germany during World War II was an effort on an altogether different scale. As I detail in Chapter 5, Nazi looting of art was so extensive—estimates are that several million unique pieces of art were stolen—that it almost defies imagination.[111] Nazi plunder was followed by massive looting by the Soviet Army. The magnitude of the looted art problem, the geographic dispersal of art pieces, the different and often contradictory national policies and legislation regarding reparations, initially made the question of restitution seem overwhelming and often futile. But the devastation of World War II and the difficult process of postwar restitution also helped forge a global sentiment that cultural property is a matter of international concern, and that culture is the shared heritage of humanity.[112]

In the aftermath of the war, there was renewed effort at the international level to further institutionalize rules against wartime destruction of cultural property. In 1954, thirty-seven countries signed the Hague Convention for the Protection of Cultural Property in the Event of Armed Conflict. The

[109] Treaty of Versailles, p. 158. For more details on the Belgian claim, see Sandholtz, *Prohibiting Plunder*, pp. 114–15.

[110] Sandholtz, *Prohibiting Plunder*, p. 124.

[111] Nicholas, *Rape of Europa*. By other estimates, the Nazis looted 20 percent of European artworks. Lindsay, *History of Loot*, p. 6.

[112] Greenfield, "Return of Cultural Property," p. 29. For a broader look at the politics of claiming world cultural heritage, see Kalaycioglu, *Politics of World Heritage*.

Hague conference proceedings also included a separate Protocol, which obligated signatory states (twenty-two states signed this separate document) to return any cultural property illegally taken from an occupied territory—a move clearly aimed at preventing the mass removal of property from European countries occupied by Nazi Germany.[113]

Throughout the 1960s and 1970s, UNESCO (the United Nations Educational, Scientific and Cultural Organization) was active in creating additional international documents aimed at protecting cultural property. UNESCO activities in this period, however, pivoted from issues of restitution to preventing illicit trafficking of art, mostly antiquities. This is indicative of a larger problem with UNESCO's lack of clear focus and internal agreement on what its mission, really, was.[114] In 1970, UNESCO adopted the Convention on the Means of Prohibiting and Preventing the Illicit Import, Export and Transfer of Ownership of Cultural Property. The 1970 convention established the norm that states had a natural right to their cultural heritage, but it made these norms non-retroactive, specifically to make claims for restitution during colonialism difficult to pursue.[115] The convention urged the governments "to become increasingly alive to the moral obligations to respect [their] own cultural heritage[s] and that of all nations."[116]

Only a few years later in 1972, UNESCO adopted the Convention for the Protection of the World Cultural and Natural Heritage, which focused on physical cultural sites (such as monuments, buildings, and archaeological sites), but did not deal with issues of art restitution.[117] The Convention's narrow mandate to deal only with immovable heritage technically limited its remit to cultural heritage that, other than the contested case of the Parthenon Marbles, had historically not been the subject of restitution demands.[118] The 1972 Convention, however, did deal, quite explicitly, with questions of international status, as it established the coveted UNESCO List of World

[113] Sandholtz, *Prohibiting Plunder*, p. 184. By 2023, 133 states have ratified the 1954 Hague Convention. UNESCO, Report on the status of ratification of the 1954 Hague Convention for the Protection of Cultural Property in the Event of Armed Conflict and its two Protocols (1954 and 1999), available at https://unesdoc.unesco.org/ark:/48223/pf0000379633.

[114] Haas, *When Knowledge Is Power* and, more recently, Kalaycioglu, *Politics of World Heritage*.

[115] Van Beurden, "Art of (Re)Possession," p. 156.

[116] UNESCO, Convention on the Means of Prohibiting and Preventing the Illicit Import, Export and Transfer of Ownership of Cultural Property, Paris, November 14, 1970, available at https://en.unesco.org/about-us/legal-affairs/convention-means-prohibiting-and-preventing-illicit-import-export-and.

[117] Sandholtz, *Prohibiting Plunder*, p. 187.

[118] In 1995, another international convention, UNIDROIT Convention on Stolen or Illegally Exported Cultural Objects was signed in Rome, which set out conditions ("minimum legal rules") for claims of restitution or return of stolen or illegally exported cultural objects. But like the 1970 UNESCO convention, UNIDROIT was not retroactive, and was limited to cases after the convention went into force. UNIDROIT, available at https://www.unidroit.org/instruments/cultural-property/1995-convention.

Heritage Sites. The List created an often acrimonious international competition among states as they began to regularly run campaigns to have their cultural site included. The UNESCO Heritage List itself came to represent a shorthand for international cultural status.[119] At its inception, the List had a "high-civilizational emphasis," by which universal cultural value was ascribed to monumental architectural styles that elevated European cathedrals or Roman amphitheaters at the expense of other, non-European cultural sites. In other words, it was certain kind of art, and from certain countries, that was ascribed universal cultural value.[120]

Decolonization and the push for repatriation

On the heels of the African decolonization wave that began in the late 1950s, the issue of international art restitution and, especially, repatriation to countries of origin, began to gain momentum. For some newly independent countries, art restitution was an integral part of decolonization. The Republic of Congo in Kinshasa demanded restitution of Congolese art from the Royal Museum for Central Africa (formerly the Royal Museum of the Belgian Congo in Tervuren) as part of the independence negotiations with Belgium.[121] More broadly, restitution of looted art became a symbol of a new imagined international cultural order where a new relationship of cultural justice would be constructed between the former colonizers and the formerly colonized.

In 1969, a group of African cultural heritage activists published the *Pan-African Cultural Manifesto*, which situated the restitution of cultural heritage as an integral part of the decolonization struggle:

> The preservation of culture prevented the African peoples from becoming peoples without a soul and without a history. Culture protected them. It therefore makes sense that they now desire for culture to assist them in finding a way towards progress and development; since culture, as permanent and continuous creation, not only determines personalities and connects people, but also supports progress. For this reason, Africa takes such care, and attaches such value to the recovery of its cultural heritage, to the defence of its personality, and to the flourishing of new branches of its culture.[122]

[119] Askew, "Magic List."
[120] Kalaycioglu, *Politics of World Heritage*.
[121] Van Beurden, "Art of (Re)Possession."
[122] Quoted in Savoy, *Africa's Struggle*, p. 10.

The issue of art restitution, in other words, now became political and was leveled at states, not only individual museums and collections. This put European states and their national museums immediately on the defensive.[123]

In this period, much of the action related to restitution efforts was taking place at the United Nations within the broader discussion about decolonization and what former colonial powers owed the colonized. But the discussion about national cultural heritage and art restitution was also part of an effort by the decolonized nations to seek international recognition. It is no coincidence that establishing national museums was one of the first acts of newly decolonized states. For example, both the National Museum of Ghana in Accra (1957) and the Botswana National Museum and Art Gallery in Gaborone (1967) were opened as part of the statewide celebrations of newly acquired independence.[124]

Diplomatic activity on the specific question of restitution was sparked in 1973 at the UN General Assembly by Mobutu Sese Seko, president of the Democratic Republic of Congo (Zaire), who gave a fiery speech against apartheid and continued economic colonization of Africa. Toward the end of the speech, Mobutu turned to the question of looted art and restitution owed to countries that had been "victims of expropriation" and have thus been relegated to the lower rungs of the international cultural hierarchy through violence and theft:

> During the colonial period we suffered not only from colonialism, slavery, economic exploitation, but also and above all from the barbarous, systematic pillaging of all our works of art. In this way the rich countries appropriated our best, our unique works of art, and we are therefore poor not only economically but also culturally. Those works of art, which are to be found in museums of the rich countries are not our primary commodities but the finished products of our ancestors . . . This is why I would also ask this General Assembly to adopt a resolution requesting the rich Powers which possess works of art of the poor countries to restore some of them so that we can teach our children and our grandchildren the history of their countries.[125]

The context of Mobutu's call for restitution, however, is also important. It came as part of his broader domestic campaign for "national authenticity," the aim of which was to return Zaire to its precolonial, African roots. Restitution of art to Zaire, then, would confer on the state guardianship of its cultural

[123] Scott, *Cultural Diplomacy*, pp. 1–2.
[124] Bekenova, "African Museums," p. 144.
[125] United Nations General Assembly, Address by General Mobutu Sese Seko.

heritage, and that guardianship was necessary for the state to obtain, and then sustain its cultural and political legitimacy.[126] The campaign for repatriation of looted art should then be understood not only as a question of international justice but also of domestic nation-building.[127]

Mobutu's speech sparked quite a burst of activity. The following year, Ghana's kingdom of Asante (Ashanti) officially requested from the British Museum the return of royal gold regalia the British troops looted during the Third Anglo-Ashanti war when the British raided the Ashanti Royal Palace in Kumasi in 1874.[128] The British Parliament denied the request. Addressing the assembly, Baroness Jennie Lee of Asheridge and a former Minister of Arts warned, "When it comes to returning booty from this country, we should tread warily; it may turn into a striptease."[129]

But there was some success, as well. Between 1976 and 1981, Belgium did return 114 artifacts to Zaire but under the condition that this not be considered restitution but a "gift."[130] A few months after Mobutu's speech, in December 1973, the UN General Assembly adopted Resolution 3187 on the Restitution of Works of Art to Countries Victims of Expropriation. The Resolution called for restitution on two principal grounds—international cooperation and postcolonial justice, as "the prompt restitution to a country of its *objets d'art*, monuments, museum pieces, manuscripts and documents by another country, without charge, is calculated to strengthen international cooperation insomuch as it constitutes just reparation for damage done."[131] In 1976, UNESCO committee of experts met in Venice and reiterated the main principles of the 1973 Resolution, concluding, "the restitution or return of these objects . . . is a principle which should govern the action of Member states and to which they should give concrete form in a spirit of international solidarity and good faith."[132] Following the Venice meeting experts' recommendation, as well as the 1977 International Council of Museums (ICOM) comprehensive report on restitution, in 1978 UNESCO established the Intergovernmental Committee for Promoting the Return of Cultural Property to its Countries of Origin or its Restitution in Case of Illicit Appropriation.[133]

[126] Van Beurden, "Art of (Re)Possession," p. 145.

[127] Dunn, *Imagining the Congo*.

[128] In 2024, the British Museum and the Victoria & Albert Museum that also holds some of Ashanti artifacts agreed to loan the objects to Ghana for the first time. The artifacts will stay in Ghana until 2027 after which they will be returned to the UK. Folk, "British Museum."

[129] Quoted in Lucas, "Forgotten Movement."

[130] Van Beurden, *Authentically African*.

[131] UN General Assembly, Resolution 3187.

[132] UNESCO, Report of the Committee of Experts.

[133] ICOM, *Study on the Principles*.

This standing committee was supposed to adjudicate disputes between states and work on a case-by-case restitution of looted art.

By this time, the issue of restitution of colonial looted art had become a major topic of international cultural diplomacy. Museum officials at the time were becoming acutely aware that colonial restitution claims were going to diffuse and implicate them as well. For example, in 1974, then director of the National Museum of Ethnology in Leiden, Netherlands, which was in possession of Indonesian artifacts acquired by the Dutch during its colonial rule, warned the Dutch government not to unilaterally return objects to Indonesia without discussing this problem with other countries, as restitution of colonial art had become "a sharp matter with international aspects."[134]

That the question of restitution had already led to emotionally charged political debates is documented in the 1979 special issue of UNESCO's journal *Museum*, dedicated to cases of art restitution.[135] The special issue *Return and Restitution of Cultural Property* begins with the Editorial, which claims right from the start, "The activities undertaken by UNESCO to promote the return of cultural property to the countries having lost it as a result of colonial or foreign occupation have aroused here and there strong reactions and misunderstandings. Pathetic requests have sometimes been met with timid hesitations, certain accusations with irritability."[136]

The special issue of *Museum* included a number of articles that detailed bilateral agreements on restitution signed between France and Algeria, the Netherlands and Indonesia, Italy and Ethiopia, Australia and Papua New Guinea, and others. These cases were meant to exemplify successes in art restitution, and in a way balance the more well-known, negative cases of failed restitution, such as the Parthenon Marbles and the Benin Bronzes.[137] The issue also included an emotional "Plea for the return of an irreplaceable cultural heritage to those who created it" by the Secretary-General of UNESCO, the prominent Senegalese scholar Amadou Mahtar M'Bow, who on June 8, 1978 addressed the Paris headquarters of UNESCO with these words, "These men and women who have been deprived of their cultural heritage therefore ask for the return of at least the art treasures which best represent their culture, which they feel are the most vital and whose absence causes them the greatest anguish. This is a legitimate claim."[138] M'Bow's speech stirred up a lot of discussion about restitution, especially in France,

[134] Quoted in Scott, *Cultural Diplomacy*, p. 152.

[135] *Museum*, vol. 31, no. 1 (1979). Special issue "Return and restitution of cultural property."

[136] Fradier, "Editorial," p. 2.

[137] Scott, *Cultural Diplomacy*, pp. 1–2.

[138] M'Bow, "A Plea for the Return," p. 58.

where the UNESCO event took place. There was immediate backlash in the conservative newspapers, but there were also pro-restitution articles and TV shows.[139] The issue of restitution became topical, and globalized. This was no longer a fight Nigeria, Algeria, or Ghana were fighting on their own.

The new moral order of restitution

A further push to deal with restitution of art looted during the colonial era came from the UNESCO representatives from the Global South and it took central stage at the Second World Conference on Cultural Policies held in Mexico City in 1982. Couched in the language of international cultural cooperation, representatives from the Global South made impassioned pleas for the looted artifacts to be returned to their countries, noting that many of these objects were not only of artistic but also of spiritual or religious importance.[140] The Mexico City Conference Final Report also included specific recommendations regarding restitution, such as an ambitious demand that UNESCO creates a comprehensive list of looted art objects.[141] What is notable about these efforts is that the demands for restitution were already being made in the context of international cultural status. Colonial looting was understood to have reduced cultural standing of colonized states, at the expense of European colonial powers who have created international cultural hierarchies and placed themselves at the top.[142]

And yet, even with all this international diplomatic activism, very few, if any artifacts were actually restituted. As Bénédicte Savoy documents, however, the decolonial push for restitution did not just fizzle out. It was resoundingly defeated by a concerted effort of Western states and their museums who invoked the frightening future of grand museums' emptied displays to effectively block efforts at restitution. Museum leaders and government officials ignored and undermined international restitution commissions, they played up issues of poor upkeep and maintenance of African (and other Global South) museums but, most effectively, they simply refused to cooperate by not providing inventories and provenance details.[143]

Changes in the understanding of provenance and moral obligation to return, however, did begin to further develop during the 1980s. By the end of this decade, new laws were passed in the United States dealing with the

[139] Savoy, *Africa's Struggle*, pp. 72–75.
[140] UNESCO, Second World Conference on Cultural Policies, p. 13.
[141] UNESCO, Second World Conference on Cultural Policies, p. 31.
[142] Kalaycioglu, *Politics of World Heritage*, ch. 2.
[143] Savoy, *Africa's Struggle*.

protection of Native American heritage.[144] They established new procedures on how Native American artifacts, but also human remains, were to be presented and narrated in US museums. Of course, these laws elided the core paradox of returning cultural property without returning, in any meaningful sense, the land it is located on. I return briefly to this problem in the book's Conclusion. However incomplete, these laws certainly influenced how museums began to contextualize the history, provenance, and original functions or meanings of other types of artifacts in their possession.[145] And then, a decade later, a new set of international negotiations began to take place about a very different category of looted art—art looted by the Nazis during World War II. Developed somewhat in isolation from one another, these restitution campaigns converged on a stronger set of principles about how to determine the provenance, the biography, of a looted artifact, and what to do with it once the provenance became known.

In November 1998, the US State Department convened an international conference on Holocaust-era assets in Washington, D.C. Forty-four countries sent their delegates. The Washington Conference recommendations, which became known as the Washington Principles, demanded the full cataloging of all Holocaust-era art looted by the Nazis, but also the restitution of that art to its original owners. Most important, however, the Principles recognized that restitution was a moral act, an ethical imperative, even in cases of ambiguity of provenance. Article 4 of the Principles states, "In establishing that a work of art had been confiscated by the Nazis and not subsequently restituted, consideration should be given to unavoidable gaps or ambiguities in the provenance in light of the passage of time and the circumstances of the Holocaust era."[146] Similarly, the Native American Graves Protection and Repatriation Act (NAGPRA) passed a few years prior applies not only to clearly looted objects or remains, but even to those that were obtained through what was at the time authorized sale or excavation and which museums may hold a legal title to.[147] In other words, the normative commitment to return, which understands restitution as justice, takes precedent over claims to legal acquisition of art at the time. This very tension—between morality of return and legal ambiguity of ownership—lies at the core of continuing debates about art restitution. I return to this question throughout the book.

[144] The National Museum of the American Indian Act (1989) and the Native American Graves Protection and Repatriation Act (1990) were especially significant.

[145] La Follette, "Looted Antiquities," p. 669.

[146] US Department of State, "Washington Principles."

[147] La Follette, "Looted Antiquities," p. 676.

The Washington Conference represented an accelerated path toward the new moral order of restitution, and it introduced a set of formal rules and best practices regarding determining the provenance and possible restitution of looted art. The relative success of these international regimes and the gradual, if slow, return of Holocaust-looted art in many ways opened the normative and legal pathways for more recent debates and calls for return of colonial-plundered art—still displayed en masse across European museums. The restitution of Holocaust-looted art put the broader issue of art restitution firmly at the center of the international cultural agenda.[148]

The grand national museums, however, were not going to go down without a fight.

The universal museum

The end of the imperial epoch and the diffusion of decolonization in the 1950s and 1960s reshaped international hierarchies and constellations between states. It also changed the meaning, purpose, and justification for former imperial grand national museums.[149] Exhibiting artifacts to project imperial desires and domains was no longer an explicitly stated purpose of major national museums. Instead, these museums reframed their mission as being not only national, but also global depositories of world culture. They redefined their vision as being one of universalism, preserving and showcasing the best art of all humankind.[150]

These museums took pride in being the children of the Enlightenment, but their problem was that they were also children of colonialism.[151] And what followed political decolonization was cultural decolonization, in the form of demands for restitution or repatriation. The claim that material objects taken from their location of production during colonial occupations and now displayed in grand Western museums needed to "come home" put these museums immediately on the defensive, challenging not only their inventory, but also the way in which they narrated and presented to the public their vast collections.

In response to mounting campaigns for cultural decolonization and, specifically, restitution of artifacts, in 2002, eighteen major European and North American museums jointly published a *Declaration on the Importance*

[148] Herman, *Restitution*.
[149] Chambers, De Angelis, Ianniciello, and Orabona, *Postcolonial Museum*.
[150] McClellan, *Art Museum*.
[151] Chaniotis, "Divided Monument."

and Value of Universal Museums.[152] The Declaration reads as a manifesto of museum universalism—"Museums serve not just the citizens of one nation but the people of every nation." But it was also a clear warning against restitution and repatriation—"we should not lose sight of the fact that museums too provide a valid and valuable context for objects that were long ago displaced from their original source."[153] The Declaration nowhere mentions that passive "displacement" was, quite often, very active theft, looting, and plunder.[154] Nor does it mention how these "displaced" objects found their way to the grand museums, or, even, why historical provenance of these objects matters.

At its most ambitious and abstract, the universalist vision is one of global cosmopolitanism: "an attempt to create a new kind of citizen, a citizen who would be a citizen of the whole world and able to compare what happens in one part of the world to what happens in another, and above all to see how connected the world is."[155] James Cuno, former director of the Art Institute of Chicago and one of the initiators of the Declaration wrote extensively and eloquently about universal museums "as liberal, cosmopolitan institutions, [that] encourage identification with others in the world, a shared sense of being human, of having in every meaningful way a common history, with a common future."[156]

For the proponents of the universal museum idea, universalism is a contemporary standard of civilization. Max Hollein, the director of the Metropolitan Museum of Art in New York, the signatory institution to the Declaration, wrote in a letter to the Met's staff in 2023,

> We live in a time when the idea of a cosmopolitan, global society is being challenged, and some more nationalist voices embrace cultural artifacts less as ambassadors of a people but more as evidence of national identity . . . It's not that we are taking objects and closing them away just because we want to own them. We collect objects because we want to share them, we want to contextualize them, we want people to understand more about them.[157]

[152] The initial signatories of the Declaration were the Louvre in Paris, the Hermitage in St. Petersburg, the Metropolitan Museum in New York, the Berlin State Museum, Prado Museum in Madrid, Rijksmuseum in Amsterdam, as well as a number of other major museums in Europe and the United States. The British Museum immediately published the Declaration on its website.

[153] Declaration on the Importance and Value of Universal Museums, full text available in Bailey, "We Serve All Cultures."

[154] For further critique of the Declaration, see Curtis, "Universal Museums."

[155] Neil MacGregor, former director of the British Museum, quoted in Levitt, *Artifacts and Allegiances*, p. 2.

[156] Cuno, *Who Owns Antiquity?*, xxvii. Also see Cuno, "View from the Universal Museum."

[157] Quoted in Pogrebin and Bowley, "After Seizures."

And in his 2023 book, anthropologist Adam Kuper presented a vision of universal museums as places where visitors can appreciate art that was previously unknown to them, by, for example, making connections between non-Western and Western art and understanding how non-Western art influenced art schools in the West. This is an educational vision that incorporates non-Western art into the universal art canon and does not conceive of it as separate, localized, nationalized, and particularized.[158]

The cosmopolitan vision of the universal museum certainly purports to overcome the small-mindedness of nationalist claims to exclusive ownership and primordial belonging.[159] The problem, however, is that it is completely depoliticized and devoid of any recognition of international hierarchies. It perpetuates international status stratification by rewarding former imperial powers for their cultural conquests and asks no acknowledgment of harm or reparations in return. As David Lowenthal so aptly remarked, "Universalism endows the haves at others' expense."[160] It does not understand or care that its center of gravity is in a particular part of the world (the West, Europe, Britain, London, Bloomsbury) that many citizens of the world cannot access and cannot participate in. The vision for the universal museum would be more palatable if it called for establishment of universal museums in Mumbai and Dakar and Johannesburg and Bangkok. But it did not. None of the major museums outside of Europe and North America were invited to, or even considered worthy of invitation in the preparation of the Declaration.[161] This makes it difficult to evaluate the idea of a universal museum outside of its geographic and postimperial positioning.

Outside of the signatories of the Declaration, the broader international museum community, including its main professional organization ICOM, was critical of its main goals, and quickly surmised that the Declaration's purpose was not so much the establishment of some cosmopolitan cultural utopia, but a narrow self-interest of museums fighting restitution claims.[162] And this is exactly what museum experts outside of Europe and North America expressed. For example, George Abungu, former director of the National Museum of Kenya, stated simply that the Declaration "is a way of refusing to engage in dialogue around the issue of repatriation."[163]

[158] Kuper, *Museum of Other People*.

[159] For a similar forceful statement of cultural cosmopolitanism and the universalist vision, see Appiah, "Whose Culture Is It?"

[160] Lowenthal, *Heritage Crusade*, p. 242.

[161] Fiskesjö, "Commentary."

[162] O'Neill, "Enlightenment Museums," p. 191.

[163] Abungu, "Declaration on Universal Museums."

Worse, this perception of extreme Eurocentrism of the universalism project was not helped by some of its most outspoken promoters' narrow ideological positions in favor of protecting Western art markets, thus further perpetuating cultural and economic status of a select group of high-status states. Arguing against UNESCO declarations in favor of restitution policies, John Henry Merryman, the Stanford law professor and a leading voice of universalism, presented the issue of restitution in the stark language of "socialist source countries" (countries that are pursuing restitution claims) and "market nations" (countries that are the targets of restitution claims) and worried that restitution legislation might hurt the art markets in the West.[164] Locations of art production are, therefore, reduced to being simply sources for Western markets, with no agency of their own to pursue claims of art reunification or return.

The universal museums put up a good fight, but their arguments sounded increasingly stale and outdated. The new winds of change, ironically, blew in from France.

Global justice—the new status marker

A major international breakthrough on questions of restitution of colonial looted art came in 2017, when in a speech delivered in Burkina Faso, French president Emmanuel Macron made a surprising announcement that France would return its looted African art to countries of origin:

> African heritage cannot be only in private collections and European museums. It must be showcased in Paris, but also in Dakar, Lagos, Cotonou. This will be one of my priorities . . . In the next five years, I want the conditions to be met for the temporary or permanent restitution of African heritage to Africa . . . African heritage cannot be a prisoner of European museums.[165]

Macron then commissioned a special report that would identify African art objects taken through illicit means to France and recommend a procedure for their restitution. While Macron's announcement was met with skepticism and his true motives questioned (much more on this in Chapter 4), it set in motion a series of responses by other states, which did not want to appear as being behind the times. Status competition, as discussed in the previous chapter, is particularly important among peers, and the French claim to moral

[164] Merryman, "Licit International Trade."
[165] Codrea-Rado, "Emmanuel Macron Says."

authority on issue of restitution spurred its own race among European states and their national museums.[166]

In quick succession, Germany signed an agreement in 2019 pledging the return of looted artifacts to countries of origin, with a special focus on restitution to former German colonies.[167] The Preamble to the document, the *Framework Principles for Dealing with Collections from Colonial Contexts*, states, "The injustices committed during the colonial era and their repercussions, some of which pertain still today, must not be forgotten."[168] The French Parliament passed a law in 2020 ordering the return of twenty-seven items, looted during French colonial missions to Africa in the nineteenth century, to Benin and Senegal.[169] In 2021, the Netherlands pledged to return all of the country's colonial-era looted art. "There is no place in the Dutch state collection for cultural heritage objects that were acquired through theft. If a country wants them back, we will give them back," said the Dutch culture minister.[170] A year later, Belgium followed suit by creating a partnership with the Democratic Republic of Congo to return looted art to its former colony.[171] Decisions regarding restitution, however, have also frequently depended on quite local political circumstances, such as, for example, in Sweden, where specific restitution claims moved forward or backward depending on whether the left- or the right-leaning coalition was in government.[172]

In 2022, the Smithsonian Institution, the premier US federal network of museums and education centers, announced its own new comprehensive policy of restitution that formally authorized all Smithsonian organizations to return items that were looted, stolen, or otherwise unethically acquired. The Smithsonian presented this decision as an issue of cultural leadership and institutional status: "Smithsonian will be the place people point to, to say, 'This is how we should share our collections and think about ethical returns,'" the Smithsonian Secretary said.[173] And the Metropolitan Museum of Art in New York City perhaps went the furthest in its commitment to provenance research by announcing in May 2023 the establishment of a four-person provenance research team, dedicated exclusively to research on origins of various artifacts among its 1.5 million objects collection.

[166] On status as peer competition, see Renshon, "Status Deficits"; Røren, "Status Seeking."
[167] Boehme, "Normative Expectations."
[168] German Federal Government, "Framework Principles."
[169] Rea, "France Has Approved."
[170] Cascone, "Dutch Government Just Promised"; Corder, "Dutch Museums Will Return."
[171] Chow, "Inching Toward Restitution."
[172] Author interview with Adriana Muñoz, Curator, Museum of World Cultures, Gothenburg, October 17, 2023.
[173] Stevens, "In a Nod."

"Whatever unlawfully entered our collection should not be in our collection," Met director proclaimed.[174]

There was international movement in this regard as well. In 2021, the UN General Assembly adopted the Resolution on the Return or Restitution of Cultural Property to the Countries of Origin.[175] In its continuing campaign to repatriate the Parthenon Marbles, it was purposefully Greece that introduced the Resolution. In 2019, the European Parliament passed a sweeping Resolution that called for a pan-European database of looted art, additional funding for provenance research, and changes in laws that would eliminate statute of limitations.[176] The 2019 Resolution, importantly, does not explicitly mention European colonialism or colonial crimes but does refer throughout to illegally acquired and excavated antiquities, which would certainly include colonial looting. The reluctance to use the language of colonialism demonstrates the lack of broadly shared consensus among European political leaders that colonialism, at its very nature, was a criminal enterprise and not just a historical period that also brought European colonial states high and sustained international status. This normative conflict between acknowledging that looting is unjust but not accepting that the colonial project, itself, was fundamentally unjust and that high cultural status former colonial powers continue to enjoy is rooted in an international crime, as we shall see lies at the core of the still marked difference between how debates about restituting Nazi-looted art vs. colonial looted art are playing out in European capitals and their museums.[177]

But, as more and more museums made announcements about the return of their looted artifacts, the more the idea of restitution became normalized and legitimized.[178] These developments, however, need to be placed within a particular global political context of the time. The already existing debates about global racism and legacies of colonialism were accelerated in 2020 during the summer of Black Lives Matter protests. From the initial protests in the United States over police racism and brutality, the Black Lives Matter movement diffused globally and became nationalized and particularized. Protesters in each country and, indeed, each location, added local context to the larger grievance about global racial injustice. Many protests also included demands for removal of statues of problematic historical figures, especially those with links to global slavery. These demands led to a wave of removal

[174] Pogrebin and Bowley, "After Seizures."
[175] UN General Assembly, Resolution on the Return.
[176] European Parliament, Cross-border Restitution.
[177] Stahn, "Confronting Colonial Amnesia."
[178] Joy, *Heritage Justice*, p. 10.

of Confederate monuments in the United States, as well as removal of highly visible statues elsewhere, such as the statue of slave trader Edward Colston in Bristol in the UK.[179]

The mass participation in these protests and the quick mobilization around removal of monuments was unprecedented, but so was the backlash against them.[180] The debates also quickly included discussion about restitution of colonial-era looted art to countries of origin, and these discussions were couched within the language of global racial justice.[181] Art restitution came to be seen as a form of reparations and this gave campaigns for restitution new life.[182] These debates became not only discussions about the past and how to make amends, but also about present, ongoing global cultural and racial inequality, and how to chart a more equal path forward.[183]

The floodgates have now opened for restitution claims, and it is becoming increasingly difficult for states and national museums to ignore them. The terms of the debate have also shifted where restitution is now broadly understood to be a moral imperative. What enabled this shift was a shift in the meaning of artifacts as symbols of status. While they represented symbols of civilization and high cultural status on their acquisition, these same objects today are symbols of theft and international shame. In the subsequent chapters, I document the acquisition and then calls for restitution of three groups of artifacts—the Parthenon Marbles, the Benin Bronzes, and Nazi-looted art, to explain how the meaning and value of these objects to states that acquired them changed over time, and how state responses to restitution demands reflect their own understanding of their international status but also its external recognition.

179 Green, "Shifting Landscapes."
180 Mohdin and Storer, "Tributes to Slave Traders."
181 Hickley, "How Recent Anti-Racism Protests."
182 Boehme, "Normative Expectations."
183 Joy, *Heritage Justice*, p. 2.

3
The Marbles

Perched on a hill overlooking Athens, the Parthenon is one of the most recognizable cultural monuments in the world. It orients the visitors to the city. It attracts millions of tourists each year who climb up the winding stone path up to the top of the Acropolis in the heat of Greek summer. Its image is reprinted on millions of shirts, mugs, posters, tote bags, postcards, refrigerator magnets, and is the background of innumerable Instagram profiles. It is the visual symbol of UNESCO, the organization that protects cultural heritage of the world. The Parthenon is so familiar and its image so ubiquitous that it has transcended its meaning as an ancient Greek temple and has become an enduring symbol of Western culture and civilization, and even a visual representation of democracy (Figure 3.1).[1]

While the Parthenon has over time come to represent many European and, broadly, Western aesthetic and political ideals, its meaning has changed

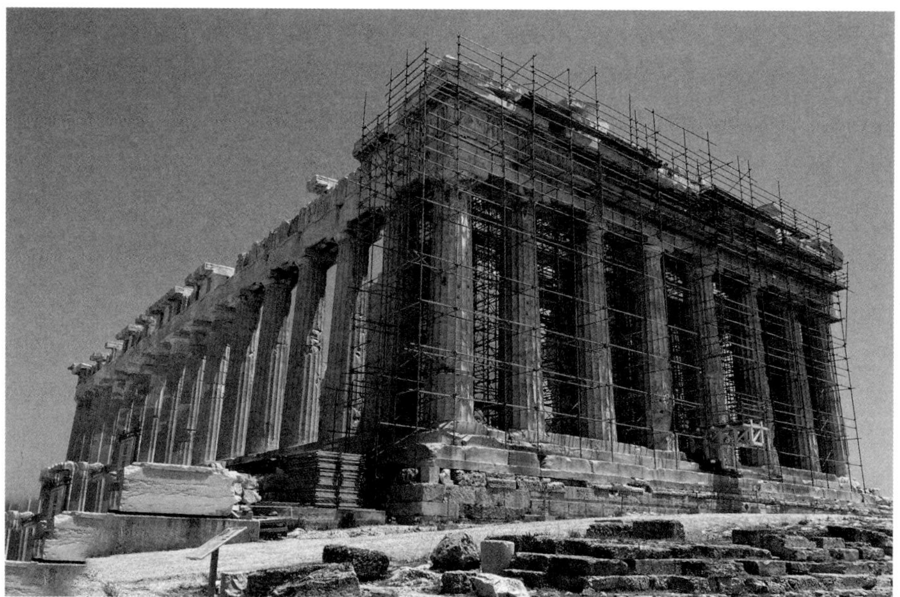

Figure 3.1 Parthenon on the Acropolis, Athens (photograph by author)

[1] St Clair, "Looking at the Acropolis."

dramatically over its long history for the inhabitants of Athens where it stands, for Greece, for Europe, for the West and for the world at large.[2] The Parthenon has also always been modern, in the sense that it has always served as a projection of contemporary cultural and political values. While today it is often used as a visual symbol of democracy, it almost certainly did not invoke democracy for the citizens of Pericles' Athens in 5th century BCE. In fact, the Parthenon often symbolized democracy's absence. For example, during the Roman times, the Parthenon was used for the unveiling of honorary monuments for various political leaders and thus for the legitimation of authority and control.[3]

In the course of its long life, the Parthenon was appropriated for many other, distinctly nondemocratic projects. Cecil Rhodes viewed the Parthenon (favorably, of course), as a manifestation of imperialism: "Through art, Pericles taught the lazy Athenians to believe in Empire."[4] For Nazi Germany, the Parthenon was the pinnacle of Aryan civilization and cultural accomplishment. During the German occupation of Greece, the Nazis planted a flag on the Acropolis and a number of high-profile Nazi officials were photographed with the Parthenon and the swastika in the background. This is why the actions of two Greek students on May 30, 1941 in taking the Nazi flag down became one of the most famous acts of Greek resistance during the occupation.[5]

The Parthenon is important to Greece, of course, and it sits at the foundation of contemporary Greek national identity, but it is also important to the broader Western cultural world that continues to trace its origin story to antiquity and, especially, to ancient Greece. The Parthenon is so old that its biography predates what we today culturally understand as Europe or even the West. Its weathered stones embody the memories of rising and waning empires, violence, destruction, occupation, and liberation. And like Athens, over which it majestically presides, the Parthenon had many owners and many occupants.

The many lives of the Parthenon

Dedicated to Athena, the goddess of wisdom, the Parthenon was built in many phases, but most of it was finished in the 5th century BCE during what is

[2] St Clair, *Who Saved the Parthenon?*

[3] Hamilakis, *Nation and Its Ruins*, p. 249.

[4] Quoted in Connelly, *Parthenon Enigma*, xiii.

[5] Beard, "Latest Scheme"; Stockings and Hancock, *Swastika over the Acropolis*; Yalouri, *Acropolis*.

considered the golden age of Athens under Pericles.[6] This was the time when Athens was the center of art and culture in the entire Greek world. Pericles ordered a construction project of unprecedented architectural sophistication and ambition for the time, to be carried out under the supervision of the great sculptor and architect Phidias. The complex at the Acropolis, of which the Parthenon and the surrounding structures are a part, was meant to project the glory and power of Athens, but also its commitment to humanism and its cultural and artistic richness. Pericles made it one of his missions to invest in the arts, culture, philosophy, and architecture, and the Parthenon on the Acropolis was to place Athens at the center of culture for all the ancient world, its beauty and greatness unmatched. It was also a clear case of conspicuous consumption, an over-the-top expensive and extravagant project meant to embody Athens' unrivaled cultural status and reputation and demonstrate its cultural superiority over other ancient Greek city states, as well as its preeminence over the recently defeated Persia.[7]

Integral to the Parthenon building, on the outermost columns, were large carved plaques (metopes), each representing different moments in Greek history—the destruction of Troy, battles between Olympian gods and the Giants, between Athenians and the Amazons, as well as weddings, feasts, and processions. Inside the Parthenon was a 38-feet-high statue of Athena Parthenos, carved in ivory and gold by Phidias, and now forever lost. Additional sculptures were on the pediments (gable triangles of the roof at each short end of the temple). The Eastern side represented Athena's birth from the head of her father Zeus, the Western the struggle between Athena and Poseidon over control of Attica. Decorating the Parthenon above the inner columns was a 524-feet-long frieze which displayed a procession of citizens of Athens, offering various gifts to Athena.[8] The frieze was in color-painted high-relief marble and depicted 378 individual human figures and 245 animals.[9] Between the Parthenon and Propylaea, the giant entry gateway to the Acropolis, stood another huge bronze statue of Athena Promachos, also by Phidias, and also lost to time. The entire complex on the Acropolis was vibrant with color, with diverse and unusual sculptures interspersed between the Parthenon, Erechtheion, the Temple of Athena Nike, and many smaller temples and structures. The Acropolis was a wonder of its time and at its heart stood the Parthenon.

[6] There exist innumerable studies and histories of the Parthenon. This brief historical overview is based mostly on Beard, *Parthenon*; Connelly, *Parthenon Enigma*; St Clair, *Lord Elgin*.

[7] Hamilakis, *Nation and Its Ruins*, p. 248.

[8] Connelly offers a revisionist account of the Parthenon frieze, interpreting the procession as a mythological succession of events in Athens' past, including the controversial claim of human sacrifice. Connelly, *Parthenon Enigma*.

[9] Neils, "'With Noblest Images.'"

As the supremacy of Athens and the broader ancient Greek world declined in the centuries that followed, the Parthenon came to represent the values and symbols of the new rulers of Athens. The Parthenon lived on as a temple dedicated to the goddess Athena for almost 1,000 years until Roman emperor Theodosius II declared in 435 CE that all pagan temples in the Eastern Roman Empire were to be shattered. A hundred years later, the Parthenon was converted into a Christian church, dedicated to Virgin Mary, and it became an important destination of Christian pilgrimage during the Middle Ages.

The Ottoman Empire conquered Athens in 1456, and in the coming decades the Parthenon was turned into a mosque. The tower built during the Latin Empire's control of the temple was now replaced with a minaret. During the Morean War between Venice and the Ottomans, the Ottoman army used the Parthenon as an ammunition depot during the siege of the Acropolis in 1687. By some accounts, the Ottomans specifically chose the Parthenon for this purpose as they thought Venice would not fire at a structure of such cultural and religious significance. But the Venetians did fire directly at the Parthenon, which erupted in an explosion that killed 300 people and severely and irreparably damaged the structure. Three of the four walls, the roof, the columns, as well as the sculptures from the temple's frieze collapsed. The Venetians then went on to loot the ruins, further destroying the structure by removing by force the marble decorations. Much of the Parthenon was reduced to rubble, and for the next hundred years, it was consistently looted for building scraps and valuable ornaments. Two heads from pediment figures were looted by Venetians and are today at the Louvre. Two other heads from a fallen metope were looted and sold on the streets of Athens to the Danish naval officer Moritz Hartmann who was employed by the Venetian fleet. Today, they are displayed at the National Museum in Copenhagen.[10]

During the eighteenth century, the Parthenon began to capture the imagination of cultured Europeans, who now flocked to see and admire the ruins, sometimes as part of the rite-of-passage Grand Tour, the tourist itinerary across Europe often taken by British and other northern European men of prestige and wealth.[11] It was this same desire for a cultural education that made Paris the preferred destination for Europe's nobility and the Louvre a major tourist attraction—developments I described in the previous chapter.

But Greece, Athens, and the Parthenon specifically, also became of special interest to educated Europeans in the eighteenth and especially the nineteenth century in the context of philhellenism. This intellectual movement

[10] Author's visit to the National Museum of Denmark, Copenhagen, August 2022.

[11] For more on the Grand Tour, see Chaney, *Evolution of the Grand Tour.*

that elevated all things Greek attracted writers, poets, and artists across Europe and included such diverse figures as Lord Byron, Victor Hugo, Johann Wolfgang von Goethe, and, later, Friedrich Nietzsche. It introduced the field of Classics as a requirement for proper education, especially in Great Britain and Germany.[12] Philhellenism was also an ideological movement that reduced Greekness to an "essence," and rejected the possibility of cultural hybridity that has entangled Greek culture over the past thousand years with its newer cultural influences of Christianity or Islam. It was during this period and through the lens of philhellenism that the classic Greek art and culture became newly appraised and appreciated as the origin but also the pinnacle of European civilization, the zenith of European aesthetic and cultural accomplishment. Philhellenism was also political. While it culturally elevated the significance of classical Greece to European culture, it also politically organized Western European support for Greek independence from the Ottoman Empire.

For the history of the Parthenon itself, no philhellene was more consequential that Lord Elgin.

Elgin at Acropolis

Thomas Bruce, the 7th Earl of Elgin, was a Scottish nobleman who served in the British Army and then in the diplomatic service of the British Crown.[13] After serving a few short-term diplomatic posts in Austria, Belgium, and Prussia, Elgin was appointed ambassador to the Ottoman Empire in 1798. As a philhellene, and a noble one at that, Elgin fully embraced the cultural spirit of his time, which held that "educated Englishmen were the true heirs of classical civilization."[14] Elgin was enchanted with Greek art and architecture, and in 1800, at his own expense, he dispatched a team of artists and architects to make sketches and drawings of major classical Greek sites, premier of which was, of course, the Acropolis. While Elgin's motives may have been driven in part by his philhellenism, he also had a careerist motive, as he wished to make his post at the embassy "beneficial to the progress of the Fine Arts in Great Britain," which would presumably have helped him in his pursuit of English peerage.[15] Other accounts suggest he mostly wanted to make the casts

[12] Stray, "Culture and Discipline"; Marchand, *Down from Olympus*.

[13] Geoffrey Robertson describes him unkindly but amusingly as "under-bright but overambitious Tory." Robertson, *Who Owns History?*, p. 59. A comprehensive account of Elgin's adventures at the Acropolis that I draw from here is in St Clair, *Lord Elgin*. A more accessible popular account is in Hitchens, *Elgin Marbles* and the second edition with a notable title change, Hitchens, *Parthenon Marbles*.

[14] Evans, "Art in the Time of War," p. 17.

[15] St Clair, *Lord Elgin*, p. 7; Robertson, *Who Owns History?*, p. 60.

of Parthenon Marbles to decorate his estate at Broomhall in Scotland.[16] What happened next is at the root of the continuing international dispute about the ownership of the Parthenon Marbles.

In the summer of 1800, Elgin hired Giovanni Battista Lusieri, an Italian landscape painter, as well as a team of modelers and sketchers and sent them all to Athens, where they were tasked with making drawings of various antique monuments on the Acropolis. Elgin claimed that in 1801 he had procured a *firman* (decree) from the Ottoman administrators of Athens allowing his team to not only make copies and casts of the Parthenon sculptures that were dispersed on the ground around the temple, but also "to take away any pieces of stone with old inscriptions or figures thereon" to preserve them from further looting and damage.[17] The document, however, does not explicitly indicate any permission to "take away" the sculptures from the Parthenon temple itself. Elgin's chaplain Phillip Hunt who was on the ground in Athens self-servingly interpreted the *firman* to allow just that; many opponents of Elgin's actions—at the time and since—interpreted the document to allow the "taking away" of only materials scattered on the ground.[18] The original Turkish *firman* did not survive, which of course fueled endless and mostly unresolved speculation about its narrow or expansive license given to Elgin by Ottoman officials.[19] While interpretations of what the *firman* actually allowed for continue to be hotly debated, the British Museum's position that Elgin "acted with the full knowledge and permission of the legal authorities of the day in both Athens and London" is, therefore, overreaching at best.[20]

Even if Elgin initially did not plan on taking the sculptures back to England, his chaplain Hunt made the decision for him. The Elgin team went on to remove fifty-six of the surviving ninety-seven panels of the Parthenon frieze (75 meters in length), fifteen metopes and seventeen sculpture fragments, as well as one of the caryatids (female statues that supported the structure), and a column, both from the Erechtheion temple. Fragments of sculptures were also removed from Propylaia (the gate to the Acropolis), as well as the Temple

[16] Greenhalgh, *Plundered Empire*, p. 513.

[17] Quoted in Greenhalgh, *Plundered Empire*, p. 513.

[18] Robertson claims that not only did the *firman* not authorize removal from the Parthenon structure, but that the document itself was not even an official *firman* at all, but an unofficial letter from local authorities who Elgin had bribed. Robertson, *Who Owns History?*, p. 63. Rudenstine argues that *firman* was unsigned and therefore invalid. Rudenstine, "Trophies for the Empire."

[19] The British Museum today owns the Italian translation of the *firman* prepared by the British embassy in Constantinople. For deep dives into this document and its meaning, see Williams, "Lord Elgin's Firman"; Robertson, *Who Owns History*; St Clair, *Lord Elgin*; Beard, *Parthenon*; Greenhalgh, *Plundered Empire*; Rudenstine, "Trophies for the Empire." For a more recent anti-restitution account arguing that Elgin's actions were legal and defensible, see Malcolm, "Elgin Marbles."

[20] The British Museum, The Parthenon Sculptures: The Trustees' statement, https://www.britishmuseum.org/about-us/british-museum-story/contested-objects-collection/parthenon-sculptures/parthenon.

of Athena Nike. The removals were done through brute force that included chiseling or sawing off pieces and sculptures from the temple, damaging both the Parthenon and the backs of the sculptures themselves. One metope was broken during removal, and one part of the frieze during the transport to the port of Piraeus.[21] The east pediment of the Parthenon was permanently destroyed during wrenching and lifting the sculptures from the structure.[22] Removal of the caryatid and the column from Erechtheion also caused a serious structural risk to that temple.[23] And when Elgin himself first arrived in Athens in 1802, he carved his name into a Parthenon column, a small act of vandalism at the time quite common for English travelers visiting ancient sites.[24]

Once removed, the first part of Elgin's loot was shipped to Britain in 1803. However, this voyage was its own tale of misfortune, as the ship *Mentor* which Elgin procured for this transport sank near the Kythera island, southeast of the Peloponnese. It took three years and most of the remaining Elgin fortune for the divers to recover the Marbles.[25] Elgin's contractor Lusieri remained in Athens, where he supervised continuing removals. In 1812, additional crates of antiquities from Greece arrived in London.[26]

Elgin's exploits on the Acropolis bankrupted him. To recover his huge debt, he sold the sculptures to the British government in 1816, after the House of Commons voted eighty-two for and thirty against the purchase.[27] The Marbles were then vested in trusteeship to the British Museum, where they have been displayed ever since. It is therefore the British government, and not the British Museum, that purchased the Marbles. This will become important in the discussion of restitution later in the chapter.

To his dismay, Elgin only received £35,000 for the Marbles, half of his asking price. It hardly seemed that the adventure was worth it.

Elgin's homecoming

The official British position today—of both the government and the governing trustees of the British Museum—claims that the British ownership of the

[21] Robertson, *Who Owns History?*, p. 69.

[22] Greenfield, *Return of Cultural Treasures*, p. 63.

[23] Hamilakis, *Nation and Its Ruins*, p. 251. The Acropolis Museum in Athens has a very vivid visual presentation of the chiseling and hacking off of pieces by Elgin's team. Author's visit to the Acropolis Museum, May 2022.

[24] Robertson, *Who Owns History?*, ch. 3.

[25] Diving expeditions to explore the remains of the *Mentor* continue to yield new insights into Elgin's ill-fated transport. Vardas, "From the Depths of Despair."

[26] St Clair, *Lord Elgin*, p. 214.

[27] The fact that the British government purchased the Marbles is also important in the context of international law, as it is the British government that incurs responsibility for the legality of the circumstances surrounding its acquisition. Robertson, *Who Owns History?*

Marbles is lawful (pointing to the infamous *firman*), as well as morally justified (as the British Museum is the home of the "heritage of humanity").[28] This position often presents British ownership as uncontroversial and settled at the time. But this was hardly the case. Upon finally getting the Marbles to Britain, Lord Elgin was grilled at the 1816 House of Commons Select Committee hearing where both his motives, legality, and methods were scrutinized.[29] In fact, it is partly because of the dubiousness of Elgin's claims, his lack of proper documentation, and the tawdry methods he used to both bribe the Ottoman officials and also primitively hack off slabs of marble from the temple, that the British government was willing to pay him only half of his asking price.

But in addition to the brusque questioning at the British Parliament, many of Elgin's contemporaries—in the UK as well as abroad—vehemently protested his actions, finding them crude and illegal. Member of the British Parliament John Morritt testified to the Select Committee that on his own visit to Athens in 1795 he was denied license to take as "a souvenir" a part of the Parthenon metope that was partially detached from the building. The Marbles, Morritt claimed, "were looked on as the property of the state" and the Ottoman administrators stopped anyone from whisking them away.[30] Another MP, Hugh Hammersley, argued that Britain should not accept the Marbles "on the grounds of the dishonesty of the transaction by which the collection was obtained." Hammersley memorably added he was "not so enamored of those headless ladies as to forget another lady, which was justice."[31] Sir Francis Ronalds, the English inventor of the electric telegraph, wrote dismissively of Elgin in his travelogue through Athens, "If Lord Elgin had possessed real taste in lieu of a covetous spirit he would have done just the reverse of what he has, he would have removed the rubbish and left the antiquities."[32]

But the most piercing of Elgin's contemporary British critics was Lord Byron. Himself a passionate philhellene, Byron famously wrote of Elgin's despoliation of the Parthenon in *Childe Harold's Pilgrimage* in 1812,

> Dull is the eye that will not weep to see
> Thy walls defaced, thy mouldering shrines removed
> By British hands, which it had best behoved
> To guard those relics never to be restored.
> Curst be the hour when from their isle they roved,

[28] For a recent elaboration of this position, see Malcolm, "Elgin Marbles."
[29] Select Committee of the House of Commons, "Report."
[30] Select Committee of the House of Commons, "Report," p. 130.
[31] House of Commons Parliamentary Debate (June 7, 1816), volume 34, col. 1031.
[32] Sir Francis Ronalds' Travel Journal: Athens, June 21, 1820, https://www.sirfrancisronalds.co.uk/athens.html.

And once again thy hapless bosom gored,
And snatched thy shrinking gods to northern climes abhorred!

Byron was even more incensed in *The Curse of Minerva* (1811), where line after line of the poem harshly accuses Elgin of plunder: "That all may learn from whence the plunderer came; The insulted wall sustains his hated name." Even through his anger, Byron was clear to point out that although the shame of this act should fall on Britain, it should not fall on England:

Daughter of Jove! in Britain's injured name,
A true-born Briton may the deed disclaim.
Frown not on England; England owns him not:
Athena, no! thy plunderer was a Scot.

It is worth noting that there was also considerable hypocrisy in the contemporary outrage at Elgin, considering that the practice of taking "mementos" from ancient cites was routine at the time. Well-known figures such as the writer François-René de Chateaubriand, painter and archaeologist Edward Dodwell, or Edward Daniel Clarke, the traveler and later professor at Cambridge University, all admitted to taking pieces of antiques, including from the Acropolis. And it was Byron himself who etched his initials into the ancient Greek temples throughout his various travels and also had no qualms about hitching a ride out of Greece on *Hydra*, one of the British warships carrying the Marbles.[33] Elgin's loot, however, was so massive and so high profile that he made himself an easy mark.

"No Elgin, no marbles"

While Byron was disgusted with the despoliation of the Acropolis, other intellectuals of the time warmly welcomed the Marbles to Britain. JW Goethe, for example, rejoiced at the prospect of the Marbles heralding "a new age of great art," while John Keats wrote a sonnet, *On Seeing the Elgin Marbles*, after visiting them at the British Museum in 1817, in which he extolled the beauty and wonder of the antique sculptures.[34]

While for many other contemporary writers, it was clear that Elgin acted in bad faith, their low opinion of the Turks and a view of British cultural superiority inclined them to argue that the Marbles should stay in London.

[33] Webb, "Appropriating the Stones," pp. 86–88; Beard, "Latest Scheme."
[34] Beard, *Parthenon*, p. 16.

For example, the French classicist Peter Edmund Laurent wrote in 1821 that the Parthenon sculptures should remain in Britain, "under the safe-guard of a nation fond of art, rather than be left exposed to the senseless fury of the Turks, the depredations of private collectors, and the insults of ignorant travellers."[35] That Britain was "a nation fond of art" implied its high international cultural status, that was to be compared to that of France, which also, as we saw earlier, justified populating the Louvre with looted art on account of its national fine taste and artistic sophistication.

There were also productive suggestions for how to salvage the situation. Indeed, some of these suggestions are the same options proposed today. For example, the French archeologist Quatremère de Quincy who, as described in the previous chapter, complained about Napoleon's looting of Italy, suggested in 1818 that instead of originals, casts of the sculptures Elgin took should be made and displayed at the British Museum.[36] MP Hammersley suggested the Marbles be held "only in trust till they are demanded by the present, or any future, possessors of the city of Athens."[37]

Edward Dodwell suggested in 1819 that the looted Erechtheion temple sculptures be restored on the Acropolis, while the Elgin sculptures in the British Museum replaced with casts. He specifically argued, with a heavy touch of Orientalism thrown in for good measure, that this goodwill gesture would impress British's rivals: "We should be esteemed for such an action by all nations, and particularly by the Greeks and Turks; who, from such an example, would learn to respect the ancient monuments of their country."[38] John Cam Hobhouse, English politician, fellow philhellene, and Byron's close friend, similarly was clear on the British cultural superiority being the logical reason for housing the Marbles in London:

> It is pretty evident, that an infinitely greater number of rising architects and sculptors must derive benefit from these studies, if they can be pursued in a museum at London or Paris, than if they were to be sought in the Turkish territories; and surely, we can hardly complain, if they are to be found in our capital.[39]

The argument here, again mirroring French arguments about how Napoleon's thefts are in fact acts of restitution, is that Elgin acted as a savior of the Parthenon, rescuing the Marbles from their certain destruction, neglect, and looting under "the Turks." This same position was pursued for decades

[35] Quoted in Greenhalgh, *Plundered Empire*, p. 408.
[36] Greenhalgh, *Plundered Empire*, p. 515.
[37] Parliamentary debate, June 7, 1816.
[38] Quoted in Greenhalgh, *Plundered Empire*, p. 515.
[39] Hobhouse, "Note on Lord Elgin's Pursuits," pp. 345–49.

by the British Museum itself, under the slogan "No Elgin, no marbles."[40] The world, according to this position, should be thankful for, not critical of Elgin, as it is due to his actions that the world gets to see, enjoy, and appreciate the wonders of the Parthenon sculptures.[41] An act of looting is repackaged as a commendable act of restitution. This narrative lives on the walls of the British Museum today. One of the captions in the Greek rooms at the Museum reads,

> The elements of the Erechtheum and Athena Nike temple now displayed in this room came to the British Museum in 1816 as part of Lord Elgin's collection. They were *rescued* from the ruins of the Acropolis, and have since been preserved from weathering and modern atmospheric pollution.[42]

And while there certainly is strong evidence that the Parthenon was dilapidating with time from exposure to the elements and pollution, and that the Ottoman administrators treated it with neglect and turned a blind eye to (and profited from) persistent looting for scrap or sale, these arguments are strong arguments in favor of conservation and preservation of the Parthenon.[43] However, they do not logically, and certainly not ethically, justify conservation and preservation of the Parthenon *in London.*

This position has become especially absurd since 2009, when a state-of-the-art museum opened at the foothills of the Acropolis in Athens, ready to accept removed Marbles and preserve and store them on the location and within the cultural, historical, and geographic context of their creation. But the British opposition persists, even if the arguments are increasingly trivial. The 2023 report on the future of the Marbles written by the well-known historian Noel Malcolm includes this gem, which seems to argue for keeping the Marbles in London for the benefit of the resource-strapped international tourist:

> And which museum-goers matter here? In the 'return' scenario, only the ones who go to Athens. But if we are to consider benefits to future people in relation to the Marbles, we should also think about the much larger number of museum-goers who see them in London (and, incidentally, do so for free; the entrance charge

[40] The slogan was first used by Sir David Price, a Conservative Party MP, during the parliamentary debate on the Marbles in the House of Commons on November 21, 1983. Transcript of the debate is available at https://hansard.parliament.uk/Commons/1983-11-21/debates/cd01da84-47bc-4256-bbbc-ea3dcb8c700a/ElginMarbles. The slogan was then often used in defense of keeping the Marbles in the British Museum by Museum curators and experts, such as Ian Jenkins, the senior curator in charge of the Parthenon Marbles. "Ian Jenkins Obituary," *The Times*, December 15, 2020. For Jenkins' scholarly elaboration of this position, see Jenkins, *Parthenon Sculptures*, p. 9, p. 16.

[41] This argument is also defended in Malcolm, "Elgin Marbles."

[42] Author's visit to the British Museum, February 2024, emphasis added.

[43] On evidence of degradation and looting of the Acropolis before Elgin's arrival, see Beard, *Parthenon*; Greenhalgh, *Plundered Empire*.

to the Acropolis Museum in the tourist season is 15 Euros), and about the severe disbenefit of taking away that experience.[44]

The arguments for keeping the Marbles at the British Museum, therefore, are not about conservation; as the next section of this chapter shows, they are about the international competition for cultural status. And it is for that reason that they were extracted in the first place.

The international race for the Marbles

While so much of the discussion about ownership of the Parthenon Marbles centered on Lord Elgin and his legal or illegal procurement of the sculptures, it is quite clear from the historical evidence that the ambition to own these precious objects transcended just the obsession, hubris, or greed of one man. In fact, it was the international competition for Parthenon treasures which, to a great degree, motivated and justified the British scramble for them. As Greenhalgh bluntly puts it, "For many in Britain, one of the arguments in favour of Elgin's coup was that it kept the works from the French."[45] The House of Commons Select Committee was quite explicit about this at its hearing in 1816,

> It may not be unworthy of remark, that the only other piece of Sculpture which was ever removed from its place for the purpose of export was taken by Mr. Choiseul Gouffier, when he was Ambassador from France to the Porte; but whether he did it by express permission, or in some less ostensible way, no means of ascertaining are with the reach of your Committee. It was undoubtedly at various times an object with the French Government to obtain permission of some of these valuable remains, and it is probable, according to the testimony of Lord Aberdeen and others, that at no great distance of time they might have been removed by that government from their original site, if they had not been taken away, and secured for this country by Lord Elgin.[46]

This was not just the competition between the British Museum and the Louvre, discussed earlier in the book. It was also the competition between Britain and other European states, first and foremost France. This competition and the likelihood of success in extracting antiquities from foreign lands

[44] Malcolm, "Elgin Marbles," p. 35.
[45] Greenhalgh, *Plundered Empire*, p. 405.
[46] Select Committee of the House of Commons, "Report," p. 7.

also directly reflected international relations at the time. The Ottomans were grateful to Great Britain for defeating Napoleon's France in Egypt and were more inclined to grant permission for extraction to British than to French representatives. The House of Commons Select Committee came to the same conclusion: the Ottomans were "beyond all precedent, propitious to what was desired on behalf of the English nation."[47]

Before Elgin ever went to Athens, French diplomat Auguste de Choiseul-Gouffier, who served as ambassador to Constantinople between 1784 and 1791, managed to obtain a type of *firman* from the Ottomans and removed two metopes and part of the Parthenon frieze, which he bequeathed upon his death to the Louvre.[48] The fragments are still there today. Choiseul-Gouffier was especially motivated to collect as many antiquities from Athens as possible and preempt Elgin from doing the same for Britain. In his instructions to his agent in Athens, the French painter and archaeologist Louis-François-Sébastien Fauvel (who would himself become the vice-consul of France in Athens in 1803), Choiseul-Gouffier writes, "Take everything you can, lose no opportunity to loot everything which is lootable in Athens and its surroundings . . . Spare neither the dead nor the living."[49]

The race for the Marbles, therefore, is intrinsically linked to the French–British rivalry and especially the status anxiety vis-à-vis the other.[50] France felt that its international status has slipped after its defeat in the Seven Years' War (1756–1763) and mobilized all its resources to restore superiority over Britain. French Foreign minister the duke of Choiseul agonized in 1767 over the French loss of status to Britain: "I am completely astounded that England . . . is dominant . . . One might reply that it is a fact. I must concur; but as it is impossible, I shall continue to hope that what is incomprehensible will not be eternal."[51] And when Napoleon declared "all my wars came from England," he was responding to British claims over superiority over the French. "English interest demands that France be reduced to the rank of secondary power," Napoleon complained.[52] Within this historical context, it is evident that Elgin was deeply anxious about being upstaged by the French, and much of his actions can be understood as an impatient response to the French interest in acquiring the same antiquities from the Acropolis. In May 1802, he warned Lusieri, his main agent on the ground, "I hear that French

[47] Select Committee of the House of Commons, "Report," p. 6.
[48] Beard, *Parthenon*.
[49] Quoted in Hoock, "British State," p. 55.
[50] On French/British imperial rivalry and different roles they assigned themselves in the international system, see Gildea, *Empires of the Mind*, ch. 1.
[51] Quoted in Onea, "Between Dominance and Decline," p. 140.
[52] Quoted in Onea, "Between Dominance and Decline," p. 142.

frigates will soon be coming into the archipelago. Every moment is therefore very precious in securing our acquisitions."[53]

The procurement of the Parthenon Marbles was discussed extensively and in the broader English society as an issue of international competition. For example, a written entry for the special section on the "Grecian Marbles" published in London's *Examiner* newspaper in 1811 says, "The fact is, the French are jealous of our good fortune in having secured those inspired productions by Lord Elgin's energy; *which puts us above them*, notwithstanding all their selections in Italy, Germany, and Spain, as to a School for Art."[54] "Which puts us above them" is as direct an allusion to international cultural status as there is. And in 1820, the magazine *Quarterly Review* noted that more tourists were visiting London than Athens because of the Marbles, which would now benefit England, as the country "will assert and win for herself as high a pre-eminence in art as she holds at this time in commerce, in science, in literature and in arms."[55]

The Marbles as status benchmarks

For both France and Britain, extracting and then displaying the Parthenon Marbles would be further evidence of the centrality of their cultural taste and sophistication but also financial, logistical, and transportation prowess—a combination of both nonmaterial and quite material status attributes. In his testimony to the House of Commons Select Committee in 1816, Elgin could not help but put in a small dig at the supposed poor state of the French navy: "My cases were at the harbour during the whole of the war; and if the French government had had any thing they could have put afloat, they would have taken them."[56] Elgin's main rival in the quest for the Parthenon treasures, Choiseul-Gouffier, wistfully acknowledged the French defeat in this pursuit,

> Lord Elgin gathered, throughout Greece, a rich harvest of precious monuments, which I had coveted long and vainly; it is difficult for me to see them in his possession without some degree of envy, but it should be a satisfaction for all those who cherish the arts to know these masterpieces have been saved from the barbarity of the Turks, and preserved by an enlightened amateur who will make them available for public enjoyment.[57]

[53] Quoted in Webb, "Appropriating the Stones," pp. 71–72.
[54] Quoted in Webb, "Appropriating the Stones," p. 72, emphasis mine.
[55] Quoted in Greenhalgh, *Plundered Empire*, p. 532.
[56] Select Committee of the House of Commons, "Report," p. 45.
[57] Quoted in Webb, "Appropriating the Stones," p. 54.

What Choiseul-Gouffier's statement indicates is that the Marbles themselves, as well as their ownership, represented symbols of civilization. In Choiseul-Gouffier's view, of course, France was at the pinnacle of civilization and should have been the rightful owner of the Marbles. Britain, however, could be a reluctant second, as it belonged to the same civilization. What was important was that the Marbles were saved from "the Turks," as they did not belong to the European sphere of civilization, and it is the Ottoman Turkey's outside position that made Elgin's looting morally justified.

The Parthenon Marbles, therefore, conferred on Great Britain high status as the guardian of Western civilization and a worthy descendant of Athens as it successfully rescued the Marbles from assured destruction under barbaric Turks and indifferent modern Greeks. As I describe later in the chapter, the standard of civilization, however, changed over time. While, at the time of the Marbles' extraction, the standard for which France and Britain competed was regarding who was the heir to classical civilization, the standard later became who was the custodian of global culture.

At the time, for Britain, the competition with France over the Marbles also involved top political and cultural leadership of the state. Even British Prime Minister Robert Banks Jenkinson, the Earl of Liverpool, chimed in on the Elgin Marbles affair. Recognizing that Elgin's actions were interpreted as theft by the rest of the world, Liverpool still thought the whole thing was worth it if it denied Paris the mantle of being the capital of the art world. In a letter to his foreign secretary in 1815, Liverpool wrote,

> The reasonable part of the world are for a general restoration to the original possessors; but they say, with truth, that we have a better title to them than the French, if legitimate war gives a title to such objects: and they blame the policy of leaving the trophies of the French victories at Paris, and making that capital in future the center of the arts.[58]

And again, the competition over art was seen through the lens of military competition. Liverpool ordered his foreign secretary to find a way to remove the art Napoleon collected from the Louvre, "It is most desirable . . . to remove them [the Napoleonic collections] if possible from France, as, whilst in that country, they must necessarily have the effect of keeping up the remembrance of their former conquests, and of cherishing the military spirit and vanity of the nation."[59]

[58] Quoted in Smith, "Lord Elgin," p. 331.
[59] Quoted in Wayne Sandholtz, *Prohibiting Plunder*, p. 63.

The British state was directly involved in this process of elevating British cultural status to dominate the French. This was not the private undertaking of entrepreneurial adventurers and amateur archaeologists. As Hoock demonstrates, "The foreign office and its diplomats organized the removal of antiquities to ports, the admiralty and royal navy provided transport, the treasury granted customs exemptions, the admiralty offered free storage at arsenals from Chatham to Woolwich, and detachments of gunners helped install massive sculptures in Bloomsbury."[60] In the case of the Parthenon Marbles, it is also clear that Elgin would have never been able to procure the sculptures had it not been for the role of the state—first in the diplomatic realm where the Ottomans were grateful to Britain for defeating the French in Egypt and, second, in the logistics realm where Elgin depended on British naval ships to transport his loot back to Britain. In fact, in his position as the British Ambassador to the Ottoman Porte, Elgin acted directly as an agent of the state, and on numerous occasions expected and was granted full state approval of his actions.[61]

The competition for the Parthenon Marbles went beyond Britain and France. In its description of the Parthenon sculptures in its possession, the British Museum noted in 1850, "The king of Bavaria, it is said, was on the watch to purchase them, should the British parliament have neglected the opportunity."[62] Elgin himself acknowledged this competition in displaying urgency that Britain, not other countries, be the beneficiary of his loot, by warning of the "importance they [other sovereigns] attach to the possession of objects of art."[63] And ultimately, it was the fear of international competition that played a critical role in persuading the British government to purchase the Marbles from Elgin in the first place. The transcript from the House of Commons Select Committee meeting of June 1816 acknowledges this quite directly, as upon questioning by a Member of Parliament whether any other state would purchase the Marbles if Britain did not, the Earl of Aberdeen argues in favor of the purchase with the following argument, "I think it extremely probable the King of Bavaria might, but I have no knowledge of that; and very possibly the Emperor of Russia, indeed the King of Prussia has bought a large collection of pictures; but this is mere conjecture."[64]

And indeed, in the mid-nineteenth century, Germany escalated its search for antiquities to populate its national museums, as its collections were

[60] Hoock, "British State," p. 55.

[61] Hoock, "British State," p. 61.

[62] Quoted in Greenhalgh, *Plundered Empire*, p. 514.

[63] Elgin's letter to William Richard Hamilton, undersecretary for foreign affairs at the British embassy in Paris, who was once Elgin's secretary, October 21, 1815, printed in Smith, "Lord Elgin," p. 332.

[64] Select Committee of the House of Commons, "Report," p. 121.

relatively poor compared to France and Britain. As early as 1812, King Ludwig I of Bavaria acquired the Greek Marbles of Aegina for his Glyptothek Museum in Munich.[65] King Ludwig also acquired a small fragment of the Parthenon (a horse hoof) that is still today in Munich. This need to possess prestigious objects of art only became more acute after German unification in 1871. It is in 1871 that German businessman Heinrich Schliemann began excavation of the remains of the city of Troy (in today's Turkey), one of the most significant archaeological remains of classical Greece. In a series of excavations between 1871 and 1890, Schliemann collected thousands of artifacts from the site, most famously the collection of gold jewelry known as Priam's Treasure. As part of the frenzy of enriching German museums with ancient Greek valuables, the Priam's Treasure collection was purchased in 1881 by the Royal Museums of Berlin, where it was displayed until World War II.[66]

It is also at the time of German unification that German archaeologist Carl Humann acquired the magnificent Pergamon sculptures from ancient Mysia (also in today's Turkey) and sent them back on German warships. Britain's ownership of the Parthenon Marbles was direct motivation for Germany's investment in the Pergamon expedition and complicated transport back to Berlin, where they are still displayed today. In a letter to the King of Prussia Wilhelm I in 1879, the Prussian Minister of Education implored,

> It is, however, of particular significance that the collection of the museums, which was until now very poor in Greek originals, consisting mostly of works from the Roman era, now possesses a Greek work of art of dimensions that are equal (or nearly) to the great rows of Attic and Asia Minor sculptures in the British Museum.[67]

The British Museum has become the status benchmark for European collecting of classical antiquities. But for Britain, the Marbles have also become indispensable for maintaining the British sense of self.

The Marbles in British imperial fantasies

For a few years after they arrived from Greece, the Parthenon Marbles were privately displayed in Elgin's house in London's Piccadilly before they were

[65] Leoussi, "Myths of Ancestry," p. 471.

[66] Greenfield, *Return of Cultural Treasures*. Priam's Treasure was displayed in Berlin first in the Ethnographic Museum, and then the Museum for Pre- and Early History until World War II. In 1945, during the battle for Berlin, the Soviet Art Committee took control of the collection and flew it to Moscow. The collection is still located in Moscow today, at the Pushkin Museum. Akinsha and Kozlov, *Beautiful Loot*.

[67] Quoted in Marchand, *Down from Olympus*, p. 95.

permanently housed in the British Museum in 1816.[68] It is at the British Museum that their new life began. They were no longer understood, interpreted, and narrated only as material objects that represented the greatness of an ancient civilization, but they now had a different purpose—to project the greatness, sophistication, and international cultural status of their new owner, the British Empire. This is why one of the stipulations of their sale, in trust, to the British Museum, was that they be known as the "Elgin Marbles."[69] These ancient artifacts were now "invested with new meaning and authority."[70]

The Marbles continued to play a diplomatic role for Britain, and to symbolize British cultural coup over its peers. They became a symbol of British victory over the French.[71] It was not just the original sculptures but also their copies that fulfilled this role. Elgin's team did make many models and casts of Parthenon sculptures before they actually began to remove them by force from the Acropolis. Even the casts themselves were internationally important. Parthenon casts made for excellent diplomatic gifts that Britain could exchange with its competitors. Furthermore, their ownership (which implied immediate access to the originals) claimed cultural superiority and a clear victory in the status war over antiquities. Once Elgin took them to Britain, the British sent the Parthenon casts to various diplomatic missions abroad.[72] In the acerbic words of Mary Beard, "It is reckoned that by the mid-nineteenth century there was hardly a sizeable town in Europe or North America that did not somewhere possess the cast of at least one of Elgin's Marbles."[73]

The Marbles were important for Britain internationally, as symbols of power and prestige, as messengers of status to both Britain's international rivals and its various and diverse imperial subjects.[74] The relationship between taking possession of the Marbles and claiming Britain's imperial greatness was explicit. For example, member of the British Parliament John Wilson Croker passionately argued in 1816 that keeping "these precious remains of ancient genius and taste would conduce not only to the perfection of the arts, but to the elevation of our national character, to our opulence, to our substantial greatness."[75] And here is contemporary writer Benjamin

[68] Greenfield, *Return of Cultural Treasures*, p. 56. For a brief time, they were also displayed at the Burlington House, also in Piccadilly.

[69] Gerstenblith, *Cultural Objects*, p. 73.

[70] Hamilakis, *Nation and Its Ruins*, p. 253.

[71] Gerstenblith, *Cultural Objects*, p. 70.

[72] Greenhalgh, *Plundered Empire*, p. 514.

[73] Beard, *Parthenon*, p. 18.

[74] Rose-Greenland, "Parthenon Marbles," p. 656.

[75] House of Commons Parliamentary Debate (June 7, 1816), vol. 34, col. 1034.

Robert Haydon also in 1816 expressing his hope for how the Marbles will be incorporated into the British national body:

> Thank God! The remains of Athens have fled for protection to England; the genius of Greece still hovers near them; may she, with her inspiring touch, give new vigour to British Art, and cause new beauties to spring from British exertions! May their essence mingle with our blood and circulate through our being.[76]

Just like Napoleonic France justified looting of Italian art by claiming that Paris was the new Rome, Georgian Britain justified looting of the Acropolis by claiming that London was the new Athens.

This idea that Britain, but especially *England*, was a cultural descendent of classical antiquity was not new. Already in the mid-eighteenth century, English nobles and art collectors expressed clear affinity for all things Greek and Roman. For example, Jonathan Richardson, a painter and an early art theorist, wrote in 1725 of England, "no nation under Heaven so nearly resembles the ancient Greeks and Romans as we. There is a haughty carriage, an elevation of thought, a greatness of taste, a love of liberty . . . which we inherit from our ancestors, and which belong to us as Englishmen."[77]

It is within this already established cultural context that Benjamin West, the president of the Royal Academy, wrote enthusiastically to Lord Elgin in 1808 to thank him for bringing the Marbles to London to its spiritual and cultural home: "Your Lordship, by bringing these treasures of the first and best age of sculpture and architecture into London, has founded a new Athens for the emulation and example of the British student."[78] The Marbles became ubiquitous in British popular culture of the time. They became frequently featured in political cartoons, postcards, and coloring books. And since the British Museum made many casts of the originals and sent them to regional museums, even non-Londoners could enjoy the Marbles or, at least, their replicas, and feel like they are participating in the cultural moment too.[79]

Britain's decisive victory over France at Waterloo in 1815 gave further impetus to this idea, and Waterloo and the Marbles became entangled. To celebrate Waterloo, a set of commemorative medals was designed which, on the front, displayed the head of Prince Regent George IV hovering above the Parthenon and, on the back, details of the Marbles Elgin brought to London.[80] With the visual help of the Marbles, the victory at Waterloo became

[76] Quoted in Webb, "Appropriating the Stones," p. 85.
[77] Richardson, "Essay on the Theory of Painting," quoted in MacGregor, "Aristocrats and Others," p. 74.
[78] Quoted in Rose-Greenland, "Parthenon Marbles," p. 662.
[79] Rose-Greenland, "Parthenon Marbles," p. 667.
[80] Webb, "Appropriating the Stones," p. 78.

for Britain what the victory at Marathon meant for classical Athens.[81] The Marbles cemented this connection between ancient Greece and modern Britain and their shared values.[82]

White Marbles

The Marbles, however, were used not only to showcase cultural affinity between the British and the ancient Greeks. They were also used to demonstrate their supposed physical and racial affinity, as contemporary British racial science held that Greeks were of "Scandinavian or Saxon origin" and, therefore, racially similar to and compatible with modern Britons.[83] This racialized logic, of course, was also what attracted later fascist aesthetic infatuation with classical Greek visual art, including and especially the Parthenon Marbles, and their aesthetic appropriation as the pinnacle of European cultural civilization by Nazi Germany.

The Marbles, in addition to many other symbolic purposes they served for the British imperial project, also became the material embodiment of British scientific racism of the nineteenth century. They were invoked to exemplify the supposed cognitive superiority of the white race. A newspaper article "Negro Faculties" published in 1811 in *The Examiner*, before the Marbles were purchased by the British government from Elgin, says, "The 'exquisite, unrivalled Greek form,' which is set forth as the epitome of the physiognomy of the 'white race,' is evident in the Elgin Marbles, 'which, when they are publicly studied by the academy, will enable England, in art as in arms to bid guidance to the world.'"[84]

The Marbles were racialized in nineteenth-century Europe (specifically England and France) through the process of "racial Hellenism," which was a consequence of the introduction of anthropological notions of race into the ideas of what constitutes national identity. The classical Greek body became the epitome of "biological perfection," and the Parthenon Marbles were the physical embodiment of biologically understood national identity.[85] More directly, as Leoussi documents, racial Hellenism contributed to the development of a new understanding of English national identity that constructed the modern English as being the direct racial descendants of ancient Greeks.

[81] Hamilakis, *Nation and Its Ruins*, p. 253.
[82] Lowenthal, "Classical Antiquities," p. 729.
[83] Hamilakis, *Nation and Its Ruins*, p. 253.
[84] Quoted in Rose-Greenland, "Parthenon Marbles," p. 666.
[85] Leoussi, "Nationalism and Racial Hellenism."

In the ungenerous but incisive words of Neal Ascherson, "England has had its turn and sucked its own bizarre identity-juice from these stones."[86]

Greek figurative sculpture—and its supreme expression in the Parthenon Marbles—then became a visual expression of the English self.[87] For Great Britain, which owned and displayed them, the Parthenon Marbles as aesthetic representations of whiteness were further used to project British superiority over its contemporary rivals. This superiority was also racialized—racial Hellenism was its own form of competition over, in this case, racial status, as "one European nation claimed to be more Greek than another."[88] The Marbles then contributed to the imperial "cult of whiteness" that found its fullest expression in fascist ideology of racial purity.[89]

This supposed "whiteness" of the Marbles became even more directly expressed during the notorious cleaning of the Marbles scandal in 1937, when Lord Joseph Duveen, who sponsored a gallery in the British Museum where the Marbles are still held today, financed the operation to whiten the Marbles in a misguided belief that they were originally carved in purely white stone. This unofficial and unsupervised process was carried away by scraping and chiseling away any discoloration, including original and still preserved authentic color, by brute force, using copper rods, wire brushes, and strong chemicals.[90] The cleaners removed the stones' patina, accumulated over centuries, and thus destroyed a veil of their authenticity.[91] When the officials of the British Museum discovered the damage, they thought it more prudent to cover up the incident instead of risking public embarrassment and accusations of incompetence. While a few articles did appear in the local press at the time, it was only with the publication of William St Clair's authoritative history of "Elgin's Marbles" in 1998 that the full extent of the scandal became apparent.[92] For St Clair, the whitening scandal confirmed the argument for restitution. He famously ended the book by declaring, "Now that the British Museum's stewardship of the Elgin Marbles turns out to have been a cynical sham for more than half a century, the British claim to a trusteeship has been forfeited."[93]

The process of making the Marbles white again permanently damaged them but served to demonstrate a particular, historically constituted,

[86] Ascherson, "End the Exile."
[87] Leoussi, "Myths of Ancestry," p. 467.
[88] Leoussi, "Nationalism and Racial Hellenism," p. 55.
[89] St Clair, "Imperial Appropriations," p. 86.
[90] Robertson, *Who Owns History?*, pp. 91–92.
[91] Yalouri, *The Acropolis*.
[92] Hamilakis, *Nation and Its Ruins*, p. 261. The opponents of Marbles' restitution, however, have consistently argued that the cleaning scandal was exaggerated. See, for example, the revamp of that claim in Malcolm, "Elgin Marbles."
[93] St Clair, *Lord Elgin*, p. 336, n. 11.

racialized cultural order. More broadly, over time the Marbles became so firmly incorporated into British cultural heritage that for many passionate advocates for their retention, they became *British*, and were no longer in any distant way, *Greek*. British appropriation of the Marbles was clear by their renaming "the Elgin Marbles" by the act of Parliament in 1816, which legally wiped out their Greek origins and turned them instead into an embodiment of British cultural superiority. But it was also further emphasized by the various (ultimately unrealized) attempts to physically reconstruct the Parthenon structure and erect its full-size replica in London, Cambridge, and Edinburgh in the 1810s and 1820s.[94] The obsession with and attachment to the Parthenon and its sculptures can be explained as a British desire to own and display a material symbol of its international status, and particularly its superiority over the French after the victory over Napoleon at Waterloo. The victorious Britain could bake in the sunny glow of the Parthenon and appropriate for itself the cultural symbol considered by most of its European contemporaries as the peak of human cultural achievement.

British imperial appropriation of the Parthenon was often quite direct and visually expressed. For example, the image of the Parthenon horsemen carved into the Marbles became a ubiquitous representation of British military might, especially during the height of British imperialism in the late nineteenth century. The Parthenon horsemen, now representing St. George slaying the dragon, were prominently featured on coins minted in the 1870s and, according to Leoussi, became associated with the British imperial race.[95] Fittingly, one version of the Parthenon-inspired horseman statue was sent to Rhodesia to be mounted on the tomb of Cecil Rhodes.[96] The Parthenon now served to visually represent Britain's imperial ambition.

The problem for Britain, however, was that the newly independent Greece wanted its treasures back.

State-building, heritage, and antiquity

After an eight-year-long war, Greece emerged as a modern state after winning its independence from the Ottoman Empire in 1829. The Greeks were helped by British, French, and Russian troops, including a high number of British volunteers, who out of romantic philhellenism joined the cause to preserve what in their view was the foundation of European civilization. For the

[94] Fehlmann, "As Greek as It Gets," pp. 357–58.
[95] Leoussi, "Myths of Ancestry," p. 477.
[96] Leoussi, "Myths of Ancestry," p. 477.

philhellenes, modern Greece was the obvious successor to its ancient predecessor, and independence from the "barbarian" Turks was the first step necessary for the revival of the Greek Golden Age in all its classical glory.[97] Lord Byron, the defender of Parthenon and the accuser of Elgin, was the most famous of those volunteers. He died in Greece in 1824 at the age of 36, after contracting a fever during the siege of Missolonghi.

The new Greece in 1829 was a much smaller state and hardly geographically mapped onto the ancient Greek world. Over time and through gradual acquisition of territory (much of it as late as the twentieth century), it came to be identified and, more important, to identify itself, with ancestral Greece.[98] Classical antiquities were a direct and tangible material reminder of this connection between modern and ancient Greece, a connection that was supposed to span millennia. Independent statehood, sovereignty, and national self-consciousness were all built on the political use of classical heritage of ancient Greece. This is why a Greek archaeologist exclaimed in 1838, "It is to these stones that we owe our political renaissance."[99] In other words, the new state's legitimacy was built on the foundation of antiquity.[100]

Like all modern states, Greece went through the process of inventing its tradition, and it tethered it permanently to classical Greece. Archaeology played a critical role here in providing the material foundation of the new nation. For Greece, classical archeology offered "the topological dream of the nation through the deployment of antiquities."[101] This construction of classical tradition and its connection to the present was not only made by modern Greece. In fact, as Lowenthal explains, it was "the awe in which the Western world has held the classical tradition [that] has shaped and reshaped Greek apprehension of their own past."[102] Modern Greek national identity, therefore, was at least in part constructed through the foreign gaze. This has also influenced external recognition of Greek international status, especially in the realm of cultural restitution. If modern Greece is understood as not locally but externally constructed in the nineteenth century, then this weakens Greek claims to ownership of classical antiquities which, instead, belong to the cultural heritage of the world. Britain, of course, promotes this position by also appointing itself the custodian of that world heritage.

[97] St Clair, *That Greece Might Still Be Free*.

[98] Lowenthal, "Classical Antiquities."

[99] Quoted in Lowenthal, "Classical Antiquities," p. 727.

[100] Marchand, "Dialectics of the Antiquities Rush," pp. 196–97.

[101] Hamilakis, *Nation and Its Ruins*, vii.

[102] Lowenthal, "Classical Antiquities," p. 733. On this point also see Marchand, "Dialectics of the Antiquities Rush," pp. 196–97 and, more broadly, Loukaki, *Living Ruins*.

The relationship between national heritage, campaigns for repatriation, and state-building is, of course, not a uniquely Greek phenomenon. This process is especially evident when it comes to archaeological sites located on the territory of a nation that is undergoing a process of state-building. These cultural sites came to serve as "legitimations of nationhood," and further as justifications for claims of statehood.[103] The struggles for repatriation of antiquities taken from the territories of what we today understand as modern Greece and Egypt (and similarly, modern Turkey and Italy, and as we'll see in the next chapter, modern Nigeria) then also crystalized a sense of unified national belonging. In other words, claims for repatriation of antiquities came *on behalf of a nation* (on behalf of "Egypt," "Greece," "Italy," and so on) even though these nations (and certainly these states) did not exist as such in the ancient era when these objects were produced. These objects, then, and the quest for their repatriation, served to construct their places of origin as something different and larger than the immediate location in which they were created.

The longing for the objects and the national campaigns for their restitution, then, also served as processes of national identity construction.[104] The objects' place of origin—and, significantly, national claims for their return to this place—was no longer Acropolis or Athens, but *Greece*. Not Rome, but *Italy*. This is why we can think of these cultural sites themselves as having political power, as "suturing" people to nations and nations to states.[105] They also serve as diplomats; they represent the country abroad.[106] Once a state declares cultural objects as its heritage, its patrimony, the objects are transformed into representations of the state and the nation. This is why these objects or cultural sites can focus national imagination and evoke strong, broadly shared national emotions.[107] They are no longer just material objects; they come to embody the state itself.

For contemporary Greek national imagination, the Parthenon, with its missing Marbles, has, then, since independence, represented a material trace that connected ancient Greece with contemporary Greece, and has served as a foundational block of contemporary Greek national identity. But the Parthenon now came to represent *all* of modern Greece, and not just Athens or Attica as in ancient times.[108] It became the most important "sacred site"

[103] Marchand, "Dialectics of the Antiquities Rush," p. 213.
[104] Barkan, "Amending Historical Injustices," p. 17.
[105] Greenland, *Ruling Culture*, p. 11.
[106] Greenland, *Ruling Culture*, p. 12.
[107] Barkan, "Amending Historical Injustices," p. 22.
[108] St Clair, *Who Saved the Parthenon?*, p. 503.

of the materialized Greek national dream.[109] Its symbolic role went beyond just the tight borders of modern Greece, but further into the Greek diaspora and the extended Greek cultural world. As St Clair evocatively writes, "as the visual embodiment of a grand unifying narrative that looked both back and forward in time, the Acropolis would create a new past, a new social memory, and therefore a new future."[110]

Parthenon's association with democracy and the apex of classical aesthetics then also portrayed contemporary Greece as a democracy and as the epitome of classical ideals, and further, as the birthplace of Western civilization. Parthenon (and the entire archaeological legacy of Greek antiquity of which Parthenon is just the most famous example), then, provided Greece with high international cultural status. Antiquities were no longer just cultural commodities, but they became Greece's status symbols, the country's principal symbolic capital.[111] Greece became not just the place where the Parthenon happened to be located today, but instead a direct descendant of ancient Greece and a direct heir of its culture and its political values. Ancient Greece became Greece.

But, further, it is not just the Parthenon and the Marbles that served to constitute Greek national identity; it is also the feeling of the Marbles *missing* (or being taken, or stolen, or disfigured, or mutilated, and so on) that provided further national cohesion and a sense of shared national cultural trauma, but also its shared national purpose. Greek Minister of Culture Antonis Samaras in 2009 referred to the separated Parthenon sculptures as a family portrait with "loved ones missing."[112] The Marbles embody the "nostalgia for the whole," for reunification, and for stability of the nation as it progresses through time. They are Greece's "imprisoned ancestors in exile," and modern Greeks should be their proper custodians.[113]

Perhaps the most distilled expression of this sentiment is included in the speech Melina Mercouri pointedly delivered in Britain, at Oxford University on June 12, 1986, in her capacity as then Greek Minister of Culture,

> You must understand what the Parthenon Marbles mean to us. They are our pride. They are our sacrifices. They are our noblest symbol of excellence. They are a tribute to the democratic philosophy. They are our aspirations and our name. They are the essence of Greekness.[114]

[109] Hamilakis, *Nation and Its Ruins*, p. 254.
[110] St Clair, *Who Saved the Parthenon?*, p. 504.
[111] Athanassopoulos, "'Ancient' Landscape."
[112] Kimmelman, "Elgin Marble Argument."
[113] Hamilakis, *Nation and Its Ruins*, p. 32, also ch. 7.
[114] Available at Melina Mercouri Foundation, https://melinamercourifoundation.com/en/the-parthenon-marbles/the-parhenon-marbles.

Melina Mercouri may have been the most passionate and internationally recognized Greek official demanding the return of the Parthenon Marbles, but she was hardly the first. While some of the continuing British resistance against repatriation relies on the claim that Greek demands for return are novel, in fact Greece has been asking for the Marbles for as long as the modern Greek state has been constituted.

"The missing soul" of Greece

Only four years after independence, in 1833, the Greek government began to request that the Parthenon Marbles be returned from the British Museum to Athens. The formal claim was issued by the King of Greece in 1836, who ordered the Greek ambassador to the UK to impart on the British that, "it would be sad for antiquity-lovers and not at all to the credit of the British people if this restoration remained incomplete owing to looting committed in the name of Britain by the late Earl of Elgin."[115] Greece offered to send to the UK copies of a few Parthenon reliefs, newly discovered. The UK rejected the request. Greece submitted a new request in 1844, this time directly to the British Museum. The museum again rebuffed the claim, but this time responded by sending a complete set of casts made of originals held in the Museum, generously adding, "free of all expense."[116] This gesture of course did not satisfy the King of Greece, but the casts were kept in Athens and are today displayed at the Acropolis Museum.[117] Another Greek proposal was put forward in 1890, this time a more modest one asking only for the return of architectural fragments. This, too, was declined.[118]

Successive Greek governments kept at it over the next hundred years, each appeal rebuffed or ignored. After the defeat of the Greek military junta in 1974, the new democratic government of Greece intensified their repatriation campaign, which gained new momentum after Greece joined the European Community, the precursor to the European Union, in 1981. UNESCO agreed with Greece that Elgin's removal "has disfigured a unique monument," and at its World Conference on Cultural Politics in Mexico City in 1982, issued a recommendation that "member states view the return of the Parthenon Marbles as an instance of the application of the principle that elements abstracted from national monuments should be returned to those monuments."[119] In

[115] Letter from the Secretary for Ecclesiastical Affairs and Public Education to the Secretariat of State for the King's Household and the Secretariat for Foreign Affairs (July 1836), quoted in Robertson, *Who Owns History?*, p. 103.

[116] Titi, *Parthenon Marbles*, pp. 126–28.

[117] Robertson, *Who Owns History?*, p. 37.

[118] Titi, *Parthenon Marbles*, p. 128.

[119] UNESCO, World Conference on Cultural Policies.

response to the UNESCO Resolution of 1982, a British lobby group, the British Committee for the Reunification of the Parthenon Marbles, was established in 1983, and has over time attracted high-profile supporters including the likes of Amal and George Clooney, Tom Hanks, and Stephen Fry.[120]

The Greek arguments for repatriation have changed over time to focus less on the illegality of Elgin's extraction (as was the case during Mercouri's time) to more recently emphasize the violation of the monument itself and the scientific and aesthetic necessity of monument reunification. The argument here is that the Marbles are not movable objects. Phidias did not sculpt them to travel and be displayed separately, but to be integrated into a very specific architectural structure. Elgin's crime, then, is not only theft; it is destruction of a cultural monument.[121]

This argument has gained some traction in the aftermath of highly visible destruction of major international cultural monuments, such as the Buddhas of Bamiyan by the Taliban in Afghanistan in 2001 or the destruction of Palmyra in Syria by the Islamic State in 2015. These highly publicized crimes also increased general awareness of the importance of preserving cultural heritage and may have helped consolidate the argument that cultural monuments that have been desecrated should be made whole.[122]

Greece has also gone to pains to assuage Britain that the claim on the Marbles is unique and that the end game is not the emptying of British museums of all things Greek. This emphasis on the uniqueness of the Marbles issue has, then, also led Greece to somewhat disassociate itself from other major international restitution claims, such as those by Nigeria regarding the Benin Bronzes. The 2002 French initiative to coordinate Greek and Nigerian restitution claims was rebuffed by Greece, which instead wanted to pursue its Parthenon claims alone.[123]

But the Greek insistence on the uniqueness of the Marbles has also, paradoxically, harmed the Parthenon restitution case as it detached it from the broader campaigns for repatriation and decolonization of museums. While other campaigns (such as the one for the return of the Benin Bronzes, discussed in the next chapter) gained momentum, the Marbles campaign has stalled. Elizabeth Marlowe has argued convincingly that the lack of solidarity with other restitution movements is the reason that, while the Bronzes are

[120] The British Committee for the Reunification of the Parthenon Marbles, https://www.parthenonuk.com/about-bcrpm/who-we-are. More recently, another international group, The Parthenon Project, led by the former British Conservative Culture Minister Lord Ed Vaizey, has been active in negotiating for a "win–win" solution for the dispute. The Parthenon Project, https://parthenonproject.co.uk.

[121] Chaniotis, "Divided Monument."

[122] Chaniotis, "Divided Monument."

[123] Hamilakis, *Nation and Its Ruins*, p. 265.

going home, the Marbles are still stuck in London.[124] But the main reason the Marbles are still in London has to do less with Greek diplomatic strategy and much more with what the Marbles continue to mean for the British sense of self.

Marbles after empire

The Parthenon Marbles went on to play a significant role in British national culture long after the British Empire came to an end. However, the persisting cultural and emotional significance of the Marbles for British national identity is, at least in part, related to Britain's enduring imperial nostalgia and longing. As Peter Mitchell notes, the empire is "the constant background noise" to British culture, as contemporary Britain lives in the ruins of its imperial past and the consequences of the violence (physical, material, cultural) its empire inflicted on its colonial subjects.[125] In this reading, Britain continues to suffer from its own imperial legacies by being unable to escape from its glorified national "undead past," its myths of former greatness, and fantasies that can never be fulfilled.[126]

Of specific interest for my purposes here is the resilient narrative in postimperial Britain of its exceptionalism and greatness. That "greatness" is central to British political identity—on both the political right and the left—has been well established.[127] This commitment to greatness, of course, is not unique to Britain (France will have much to say about that, as the previous chapter already described). In fact, it is often residual great powers, or states that had in the past enjoyed high status, that continue to be committed to greatness as an ongoing, constitutive part of their self-identity.[128] Put simply, they suffer from narcissism.[129] In the context of Britain, a clear example of a residual great power, the social narrative that Britain doesn't only *deserve* to be a global leader but that it, simply, *is*, is a long-established and broadly rooted story, an obsession with greatness that mostly goes unchallenged at the elite level.[130]

[124] Marlowe, "From Exceptionalism to Solidarity."

[125] Mitchell, *Imperial Nostalgia*. Also see Sanghera, *Empireland*.

[126] Beaumont, "Brexit"; Browning, "Brexit Populism"; Kenny and Pearce, *Shadows of Empire*; Lotem, *Memory of Colonialism*.

[127] Rogstad and Martill, "How to Be Great (Britain)?; Blagden, "Two Visions of Greatness"; Morris, "How Great Is Britain?"

[128] Webber, "Identity, Status and Role."

[129] Hagström, "Great Power Narcissism."

[130] Vucetic, *Greatness and Decline*.

An important manifestation of the British sense of greatness is its dedication to global leadership.[131] In fact, one of the most consistent ways in which the British understood what it meant to be *British* over at least the past century, has been as having a global role to play in the world.[132] For example, here is Tony Blair, at the time still an opposition leader, running for office in 1997,

> Century upon century it has been the destiny of Britain to lead other nations . . . That should not be a destiny that is part of our history. It should be part of our future. We are a leader of nations or nothing.[133]

While Blair's purpose in this speech was to criticize Conservative Prime Minister John Major's defense cuts and general isolationism, Blair still landed on the platform of British greatness—a different type of greatness to the Tory one for sure, but a greatness nonetheless, a pro-internationalist greatness that still recognizes international hierarchies and positions great powers such as Britain on the top and burdens it with responsibilities of caretaking and leadership.[134]

In this context, much of the British opposition to restitution claims was framed as an example of Britain's liberal fight against nationalism, terrorism (political as well as cultural), and religious fundamentalism. Here, again, Britain was portrayed as a global leader. Sir David Wilson, former director of the British Museum, stated in a 1986 BBC interview that the restitution campaign to return the Marbles to Greece was a form of "cultural fascism." "It is like burning books . . . that's what Hitler did."[135] Wilson's successor Neil MacGregor similarly argued in 2003 that the British Museum was "a resource against fundamentalism."[136] Directors of the British Museum, then, positioned their institution to be at the frontline of the British-led global struggle against the nationalist and tribal forces of darkness.

This pursuit (but also maintenance) of greatness then became a habit, a routinized form of political, and as I extend the argument, also *cultural* action. This self-understanding of Great Britain as, truly, *great*, as self-evidently a global leader, is important not only for its foreign policy narrowly understood, but also for its international cultural politics. This was apparent in the earlier discussion of the appropriation of the Parthenon Marbles as

[131] On the theoretical differentiation between identity, status, and role, see, for example, Webber, "Identity, Status and Role"; McCourt, *Britain and World Power*; Thies, "Role Theory."

[132] Vucetic, *Greatness and Decline*. On this point, also see McCourt, *Britain and World Power*; Gaskarth, *British Foreign Policy*.

[133] Boggan, "Election '97."

[134] Foley, "Race, Nation, Empire?"

[135] Quoted in Hitchens, "Elgin Marbles," p. 85.

[136] Gibbons, Kennedy, and Hencke, "Virtual Intervention."

British, as Britain understood itself to be the only nation with exceptional enough culture to be the proper heir and guardian of classical European treasures.

This position was elaborated frequently, as for example when Alan Howarth, former British Minister for the Arts, claimed at a House of Commons hearing in 2000, "I understand the emotional importance and the symbolic importance . . . to the Greek people of this case. I would also say with respect that we too in this country are heirs to the classical tradition."[137]

This British self-understanding of its greatness—political but also cultural—also explains how it has appointed itself a custodian of global culture, with a moral responsibility to preserve the world's most valuable art on behalf of humanity. This, fundamentally, is a question of status. Britain resists restitution of the Parthenon Marbles and many other artifacts it possesses because it resents the prospect of losing the status of an international cultural caretaker, status it conferred upon itself. It is also a position not dissimilar to its prior imperial notion of a civilizing mission, of an empire as a custodian of civilizations. It is a position laced with "latent imperial sensibilities."[138]

British politicians have been quite direct in tying the question of restitution to British cultural superiority. In his remarks at the House of Lords on May 19, 1997, Lord Wyatt of Weeford, sounding much like the Lords of mid-nineteenth century, asked, "My Lords, is the Minister aware that it would be dangerous to return the Marbles to Athens because they were under attack by Turkish and Greek fire in the Parthenon when they were rescued and the volatile Greeks might start hurling bombs around again?"[139] And in 2023, in response to the growing demands for restitution and a rekindled Greek reunification campaign, British Culture Secretary Michelle Donelan reiterated the same basic statement, "we shouldn't be sending them back, and actually they do belong here in the UK, where we've cared for them for a great deal of time, where we've allowed access to them."[140] Only Great Britain can be the proper caretaker. And only one institution—the British Museum—is deserving of this responsibility.

"A museum of the world, for the world"

While the debates about universal museums, described in the previous chapter, went on among international museum professionals and art experts,

[137] House of Commons Select Committee on Media, Culture and Sport.
[138] Ward and Rasch, "Introduction," p. 2.
[139] Quoted in Hitchens, *Elgin Marbles*, vii–viii.
[140] Razzall, "Parthenon Sculptures."

the British Museum as an institution fully embraced the universal vision and made it its most visible public-facing identity. But while the British Museum insisted on its universalism, it did so directly, and non-apologetically, from the vantage point of its Britishness.

What is of particular interest for my argument here is the extent to which the British Museum—as the premier state cultural institution of Great Britain—has conflated its role as a "world museum" with the role Great Britain, the state, conferred upon itself as the global leader. In other words, the British Museum came to view itself as leading and representing world culture just as the British state viewed itself as leading and representing the world. In this vision, the relationship of the museum to world politics is essential: the British Museum was founded, according to MacGregor, "to allow visitors to address through objects, both ancient and more recent, questions of contemporary politics and international relations."[141] But through its commitment to universalism, as Sylvester already noted, what the British Museum was doing was in fact describing *British* imperial history and *British* historical international relations and presenting them as the world's.[142] It is specifically the Marbles that have acted as "performers, trained as actors in a ceremony" about British imperial glory that "thought of itself as universal rather than merely national."[143]

Even deep into the postcolonial era, the British Museum continued to narrate the greatness of Great Britain through its location as the center of world culture. The Museum's former director and most prominent universalist Neil MacGregor argued this explicitly in relation to the Parthenon Marbles, "the Parthenon Marbles in the British Museum are in the best possible place for them, and they must remain here if the museum is to continue to achieve its aim, which is to show the world to the world."[144] Similarly, in his statement against restitution, British Culture Secretary Jeremy Wright said in 2019, "if you followed the logic of restitution to its logical conclusion there would be no single points where people can see multiple things."[145]

This role of the global cultural leader that the British Museum—as an institution of the British state—took upon itself became its defining mission, and it remains so until the present day. It is important for the British Museum to present itself as truly a world, global, encyclopedic museum, and not a *national* museum, even though it was established as such very clearly in the

[141] MacGregor, "Whole World."
[142] Sylvester, *Art/Museums*, p. 53.
[143] Ascherson, "End the Exile."
[144] BBC News, "Greek Minister."
[145] Quoted in Sanderson, "Minister Rules out Return."

eighteenth century. The British Museum, argued MacGregor, "was never a national collection," but instead a collection of the entire world.[146] And this position is implied in the British Museum's public position on the question of the Parthenon Marbles, which argues in its public statement on the matter, "The Trustees of the British Museum believe that there's a great public benefit to seeing the sculptures within the context of the world collection of the British Museum, in order to deepen our understanding of their significance within world cultural history."[147]

This universalist message is also displayed to visitors to the museum in captions next to the Marbles themselves. For example, one caption in the Duveen Gallery reads,

> At the British Museum, the sculptures form part of a wider global story. Here, the art of civilisations that preceded the Parthenon and those that came later can be seen together, as part of a world narrative.
>
> Since Elgin's time, all the remaining sculptures have been removed and will never be restored to the Parthenon. Once architectural ornaments displayed high above the ground, the sculptures have become objects of art to be appreciated at eye level.[148]

This idea that Marbles are no longer an integral part of the Parthenon structure and could be observed outside of its original context in a "world narrative" is a clear expression of museum universalism. But it still does not explain why the Marbles are to be appreciated at the eye level *in London* and not in Athens where a new museum was built just for this purpose.

In the context of Britain, its self-understanding as a global leader and its unresolved fantasies of greatness, it is the British Museum that has taken on itself the burdens and responsibilities of "showing the world to the world." In an essay titled "The Whole World in Our Hands," MacGregor asks, "Where else can the world see so clearly that it is one?"[149] Where else other than in London, where the world's objects, literally, are in the museum's hands. The British Museum also visually conveyed this position in its 2010 project, "History of the World in 100 Objects," which explicitly—and with astonishing arrogance—claimed that the entire history of the world can be explained by artifacts owned by the museum. This project paid no attention whatsoever to the provenance or restitution claims of any of these objects but treated

[146] Quoted in Levitt, *Artifacts and Allegiances*, p. 2.
[147] The British Museum, The Parthenon Sculptures.
[148] Author's visit to the British Museum, February 2024.
[149] MacGregor, "Whole World."

them, simply, as the property of the British Museum and, in the universalist language, "the world."[150] As the entrance to the British Museum simply states, "Welcome to the British Museum—a museum of the world, for the world."

In addition to the grandiosity of this project, a further obvious point is that the British Museum (and other universal museums) do not, of course, truly show the world to the world. These large museums only showcase a miniscule percentage of their vast holdings, and much of their collections, including innumerable objects with disputed provenance that are subjects of restitution claims, are never given the light of day.[151] The British Museum, for example, possesses more than 8 million artifacts, of which only 80,000 are actually on display.[152] This should not be surprising as the purpose of collecting has always been amassing vast quantities of precious objects in a cycle of cultural status competition with other grand state museums. The purpose of collecting is collecting; it is not showing the world to the world.

Marbles and British decline

The argument that the British Museum is the only institution capable enough and worthy enough of housing the treasures on behalf of all humanity cannot be separated from old, and persisting claims of Britain's cultural greatness, its unique position as the heir to classical civilizations, as a "nation fond of art." In fact, as the Head of Glasgow Museums Mark O'Neill quickly pointed out, the British Museum's justification for claiming its universal mission was made explicitly "on the specific qualities of British society during and since the eighteenth century."[153] The museum's insistence that no one else can be bestowed with such cultural responsibility then belies the universalist promise that it is not "tied to a particular notion of national identity, or . . . appropriated to a particular political end."[154]

For the purposes of my argument, however, what becomes quickly apparent is that, in promoting the universalism paradigm, the British Museum did so in yet another cycle of international status competition, and once again pitting Britain against France. In his manifesto outlining the universalist agenda of the British Museum, Neil MacGregor argues that the museum was founded in 1753 to be independent from the monarchy (unlike the Louvre

[150] The project description is available at https://www.bbc.co.uk/ahistoryoftheworld/about/british-museum-objects.

[151] Brusius and Singh, *Museum Storage*.

[152] Bridge, "British Museum's New Archives."

[153] O'Neill, "Enlightenment Museums," p. 192.

[154] MacGregor, "Whole World."

in France), that it was committed to Protestant ideas of liberty (as opposed to Catholic authoritarianism, as was the case in France), and to rationalism (unlike extremism, as in France). As to really drive the point to the readers, MacGregor writes, "the fact that we are the British Museum, and not a French one, is significant."[155] The importance of Britain winning the status competition over France in all things, including cultural things, is quite evident and has been consistent. But the question is, how many times can Britain win at Waterloo if Britain is, in fact, in decline?

While the widespread feeling of British decline was particularly internationally visible in the run-up to and in the aftermath of the Brexit referendum vote in 2016, it has been present in British self-narratives for much longer.[156] A straightforward way to understand decline, of course, is a perceived loss of status. It is "falling down the ranking of states."[157] But decline can also have a temporal dimension—it is loss of status over time not only vis-à-vis other states, but vis-à-vis the declining state's own prior, higher status.[158] Further, as much as rankings and status are socially constructed, so is decline. Whether a state is in decline reflects as much cultural and normative beliefs about the way things should be, as it does any objectively met set of benchmarks and indicators.[159] While decline is often understood narrowly to be an issue of military power and competitiveness or economic output, a broader understanding of decline defines it as an erosion of national status.[160] Building on this relationship between status and decline, I am interested in a broader sense of national decline, a feeling that not only a state's international military or economic status but also its international social, and especially cultural status, is not as it once was.[161] This nostalgia for the way things were, then, also produces a particular kind of cultural melancholia and mourning that is also, at its core, a mourning for lost status.[162]

The debates about repatriation of the Marbles to Greece are fraught with the same kind of anxiety and betrayal deeply embedded in the conservative cultural discourse that sees "things" (material artifacts such as the

[155] MacGregor, "Whole World" and response by O'Neill, "Enlightenment Museums."

[156] On Brexit and decline, see Browning, "Brexit Populism"; Franceca Melhuish, "Euroscepticism, Anti-Nostalgic Nostalgia"; Toomey and Shepherd, "Cultural Trauma." For a longer view of British declinism, see Vucetic, *Greatness and Decline*; Tomlinson, *Politics of Decline*; Gamble, *Britain in Decline*; Rubinstein, *Capitalism, Culture and Decline*.

[157] Ralston, "Make Us Great Again," p. 668.

[158] Freedman, "Status Insecurity."

[159] On the malleability of decline, understood as status loss, see Freedman, "Back of the Queue."

[160] Ward, "Decline and Disintegration."

[161] For an analysis of decline understood through competitive military capabilities, see MacDonald and Parent, *Twilight of the Titans*; Shifrinson, *Rising Titans*. For a cultural understanding of decline that aligns more closely with my argument, see Leheny, *Empire of Hope*.

[162] Gilroy, *After Empire*.

Parthenon sculptures, but also national statues, literary works, and other cultural products associated with the imperial past) slipping away and being replaced with a new kind of postimperial culture that is perceived as judgmental, accusatory, and painfully and unnecessarily introspective. This anxiety is, then, what explains the conservative backlash against attempts to decolonize museums by, at the very least, disclosing the problematic and often violent provenance of some of their most well-known artifacts.

The cultural backlash against decolonization of museums in Britain has been fierce. The tabloid *Daily Mail*, for example, attacked the art historian Alice Procter for leading shadow tours of British museums, which explained to interested visitors the problematic provenance of some of the objects on display. "Britain's museums have traditionally offered visitors the chance to appreciate our national treasures in all their glory. But sell-out tours of our biggest museums and galleries are now claiming that the artefacts represent 'the history of empire and genocide,'" bellowed the *Daily Mail*.[163] The reputation and journalistic quality of the *Daily Mail* aside, it is still striking that a popular newspaper so succinctly summarized not only the narrative of Britain's cultural greatness ("our national treasures in all their glory") but also expressed the indignation at the suggestion that these treasures tied back to British imperial history, including its history of violence.

It is here that I want to argue that the continuing appeals for restitution and repatriation of artifacts acquired by and held in British museums—and most visibly of all, the Parthenon Marbles—are perceived as challenges to British cultural greatness—or in my framework, its high international cultural status. From within this context, the claims for the Marbles' repatriation to Greece, then, came to be seen as taking away *British* property, as making Britain culturally smaller, less important, less great. As David Lowenthal so aptly observed, there has always been an "elision of the fate of the Elgin Marbles with that of the British imperial domain."[164] If the Marbles are "assets of our country," as the British Culture Minister Donelan claimed, then restitution is "asset-stripping of the British soul."[165] Giving back the Marbles, giving in to pressures for decolonization of museums and for global cultural justice, the fear of hallowing out of great British museums—"walls bare, sculpture courts deserted, store rooms despoiled"[166]—are then understood as manifestations

[163] Dilworth, "Art Historian." For the background and explanation of her shadow tours, see Procter, *Whole Picture*.

[164] Lowenthal, "Classical Antiquities," p. 729.

[165] Higgins, "Britain Treasures."

[166] Higgins, "Britain Treasures."

of Britain's political, as well as cultural, decline. Restitution comes to be seen as a death rattle and the Marbles the final relics of a former colonial empire.[167]

British Museum in the age of decolonization

Decolonization, however, is moving apace, the intransigence of the British Museum notwithstanding. There is dissent on the issue of repatriation even among the Museum trustees, including a public resignation over the fact that the museum, on the question of restitution, "hardly speaks."[168] Across other public museums in Great Britain, there are curators and art historians working actively to recontextualize, renarrate, and rehistoricize the displays at their museums.

Even among major "universal" museums there are subtle differences in approach. The Victoria & Albert Museum, for example, an institution established at the apex of British colonialism in mid-nineteenth century, has been more open about provenance of its artifacts and interested in engaging with questions of restitution. It has been negotiating with Ethiopia about the return of the Maqdala treasures and its leadership used language the British Museum has been reluctant to:

> There is no dispute about whether or not they were borrowed; they were looted and that's a story we have tried to tell very openly and very honestly at the V&A . . . Provenance is a big area for museums to invest in researching where these objects come from and how they came to be in these national collections. Being able to tell a much more rounded, holistic, accurate and honest story about those objects.[169]

In fact, the V&A hosted a first ever British exhibition into provenance of Nazi-era looted art. The museum was also explicit about its own holdings after provenance research disclosed that objects in its collection could be traced to Nazi-era looting.[170] It has also updated the objects' captions to now include information uncovered in the provenance search.[171]

[167] Chaniotis, "Divided Monument."

[168] Brown, "Trustee Resigns."

[169] Tim Reeve, the deputy director of the V&A Museum, interviewed in Campbell, "V&A in Talks." V&A, however, also claims that it is prohibited from reaccessioning its collection by the 1983 National Heritage Act.

[170] Victoria & Albert Museum, "Concealed Histories."

[171] Author's visit to the V&A Museum, January 2023.

Other museums have done more.[172] In 2020, the Pitt Rivers Museum in Oxford revamped its permanent exhibition and removed its well-known collection of human remains (the "shrunken heads") and explained its decision to the public. It also has a web portal outlining the procedure for restitution claims.[173] Also in 2020, Manchester Museum returned forty-three spiritual objects to the Australian Aboriginal heritage group.[174] The World Museum in Liverpool has redesigned its display and opened new exhibitions on colonial legacies and provenance, including provenance of its own collections.[175] These changes, of course, are not without controversy or without critics, those who deplore the "presentism" of the decolonization moment but also those who think decolonization has become tokenized and has not gone far enough.[176]

The argument that the Marbles are in the best care of Britain came to a crashing and possibly devastating blow with the British Museum great theft scandal of 2023, when it was disclosed that a museum curator stole upwards of 2,000 artifacts and sold many of them on eBay. The scandal has cost the British Museum director Hartwig Fischer his job but has also perhaps permanently damaged the reputation of the museum and especially its claim to being the ultimate caretaker of world culture. It is hard to argue that the British Museum is the best place to house the world's most precious objects when some of those objects are sold on eBay. Not wasting time in the wake of the theft scandal, Despina Koutsoumba, the director of the Association of Greek Archaeologists, said of the British Museum: "They have to return the Parthenon marbles because they're not safe."[177]

And so Greece continues to ask for the Marbles, and the UK continues to say no. But this issue is not going away, and every British Prime Minister keeps getting asked about their position on the Marbles. Boris Johnson, once a staunch (and somewhat surprising) supporter of repatriation during his student philhellenic days, has firmly refused repatriation during his tenure as PM in 2021.[178] And even Liz Truss, who served as the British PM for what seemed like no longer than a minute, had to declare her position (an unsurprising and firm "no") in October 2022.[179] Since 2022, however, there has

[172] For a survey of some of these developments, see the special issue of the *Journal of Museum Ethnography*, "Decolonizing the Museum in Practice," no. 32 (March 2019).

[173] Pitt Rivers Museum, https://www.prm.ox.ac.uk.

[174] Higgins, "Britain Treasures."

[175] World Museum Liverpool, https://www.liverpoolmuseums.org.uk/whatson/world-museum/exhibition/world-cultures-gallery.

[176] Dickson, "Ghosts of Colonialism."

[177] Weaver and Batty, "British Museum Director."

[178] Smith, "Boris Johnson's Zeal."

[179] Harris, "UK Prime Minister."

been a subtle change in public discourse about the Marbles in the British press. *The Times of London*, once a bastion of conservative opposition to all things restitution, published a surprising editorial in January 2022, arguing that the Greek demand for repatriation was "compelling."[180] The British public, for a while now open to restitution, has by 2022 indicated a majority approval of repatriation.[181] The Labour Party leadership has also indicated greater readiness to start the repatriation process.[182] These are indications that, for these groups, the Marbles are no longer seen as objects of status but increasingly objects of shame that threaten to erode Britain's status. It is the British conservative cultural establishment and the British Museum that have not caught on.

Greece has pressed on, hoping for a change of UK government and a more friendly negotiating partner. While all Greek governments have cared about the Parthenon issue, since Melina Mercouri's death in 1994, it was the center-right government of Kyriakos Mitsotakis that has perhaps most explicitly put this issue to the front of its diplomatic agenda. The Mitsotakis government pursued this strategy even though it has had a very fraught relationship with Greek archaeology institutions and had been accused of neglecting preservation and conservation of the Parthenon at home.[183] The Mitsotakis government has elevated the Parthenon issue out of its nationalist commitments, surely, but also possibly as a way to distract from myriad domestic problems plaguing contemporary Greek politics. Passionate pleas for the return of the Marbles and direct confrontation with the British prime minister could revitalize the government's popularity and enhance its domestic legitimacy.[184]

In late 2023, Mitsotakis reiterated the Greek claim that this was an issue of monument reunification, not ownership,

> This is not in my mind an ownership question, this is a reunification argument—where can you best appreciate what is essentially one monument? It's as if I told you that you would cut the Mona Lisa in half, and you will have half of it at the Louvre and half of it at the British Museum, do you think your viewers would appreciate the beauty of the painting in such a way? Well, this is exactly what happened with the Parthenon sculptures.[185]

[180] "The Times View on the Elgin Marbles."

[181] A November 2021 YouGov poll showed 59 percent of the British public approving of repatriation to Greece: https://yougov.co.uk/topics/travel/survey-results/daily/2021/11/23/9b053/2.

[182] Smith, "Keir Starmer Open to Return."

[183] Smith, "Acropolis Now."

[184] Prentoulis, "Is Rishi Sunak Using the Parthenon Marbles."

[185] Murray, "Greek PM Bemoans Lack of Progress."

But a few moments later, the ownership claim slips right back in, as Mitsotakis went on to say, "We feel that the sculptures belong to Greece and that they were essentially stolen . . . I think the answer is very clear. They do look better in the Acropolis Museum, a state-of-the-art museum that was built for that purpose."[186] Turkey's cultural officials seemed to affirm the Greek position that Britain's legal claim of ownership was bogus by stating at a UNESCO meeting, "We are not aware of any document legitimizing this purchase."[187] In apparent response to Mitsotakis's push, Britain's Prime Minister Rishi Sunak went on to cancel their scheduled meeting, causing a diplomatic scandal.[188]

And so the Marbles are still, and for now, displayed in the Duveen Gallery of the British Museum, its crown possession, its pride of place (Figure 3.2). They link today's Britain not only to the classical past and antiquity and Britain's self-understanding as a shepherd of that legacy, but also to Britain's own past and its now long-lost imperial glory. To give away the Marbles is not only to admit that Britain kept them illegally for more than two hundred years. It is also to admit that the empire is over, and that contemporary Britain is in decline. And this is why restitution is so passionately resisted.

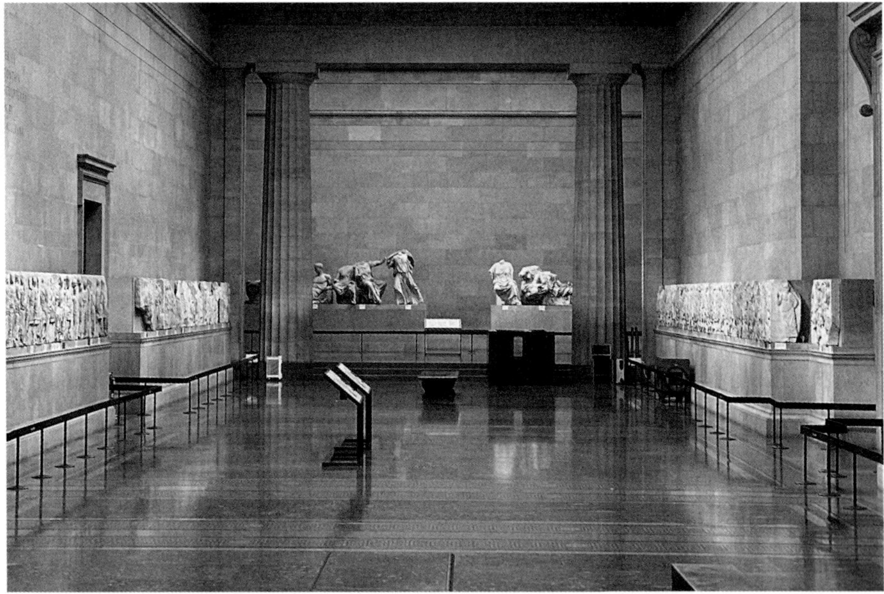

Figure 3.2 Parthenon Marbles on display at the Duveen Gallery, British Museum, London, during a special exhibition for members (reproduced from Wikimedia under Creative Commons Attribution-Share Alike 4.0 International license)

[186] Murray, "Greek PM Bemoans Lack of Progress."
[187] Zois, "Turkey Denies Firman."
[188] Marshall and Landler, "Amid Parthenon Dispute."

Whose Parthenon?

I have made the argument in this chapter that the British attachment to the Parthenon Marbles—at the time of collection, during centuries of display, and today in the global era of restitution—should be understood in the context of British competition for achieving and maintaining its international cultural status. States understand and seek status in different ways, and for Britain, keeping the world's most famous collection of sculptures is so intrinsically tied to its sense of self-worth as a global power but also as a former empire not quite ready to fold its wings, that restitution feels like a mortal blow.

But what about other national museums that hold fragments of the Parthenon in their own collections? Why would Denmark, Germany, or Austria still claim these pieces? What possible purpose does a small head found in the rubble of the Acropolis after the Venetian destruction in 1687 have for the National Museum of Denmark and for Danish cultural heritage (Figure 3.3)?

Apparently, these small fragments—two heads acquired in 1688 in Athens and a horse hoof acquired by the Danish consul general in Greece in 1835—mean quite a lot.[189] Responding to the 2023 request by the Acropolis Museum for the fragments to be returned to Athens, the National Museum of Denmark flatly refused, and it did so on the grounds of Danish international cultural status. In its public statement justifying the refusal to restitute the Parthenon pieces, the Museum stated that the fragments represent evidence of the great involvement of Danish artists, architects, and scholars in restoration, documentation, and exploration of ancient monuments. They symbolize Denmark's role in global culture. This gives the Parthenon fragments "a special role in Danish cultural history," in the words of the Museum director Rane Willerslev. Besides, the director added, as the vast majority of the Marbles are split between Athens and London, keeping the few small pieces in Copenhagen makes the objects "more important at the National Museum than if they were sent to Greece."[190] Keeping the fragments in Denmark was also important for domestic purposes: "it is important for Danes to know Denmark's place in European history," said Christian Sune Pedersen, head of research at the National Museum.[191] Possessing a fragment of perhaps the world's most famous monument elevates Denmark's rank in the international hierarchy of cultural status.

Outside of Great Britain, the relentless Greek pursuit of the scattered fragments of the Parthenon has already had some success. As a result of the Greek

[189] Author's visit to the National Museum of Denmark, Copenhagen, August 2022.
[190] National Museum of Denmark, "Greek Marble Heads."
[191] National Museum of Denmark.

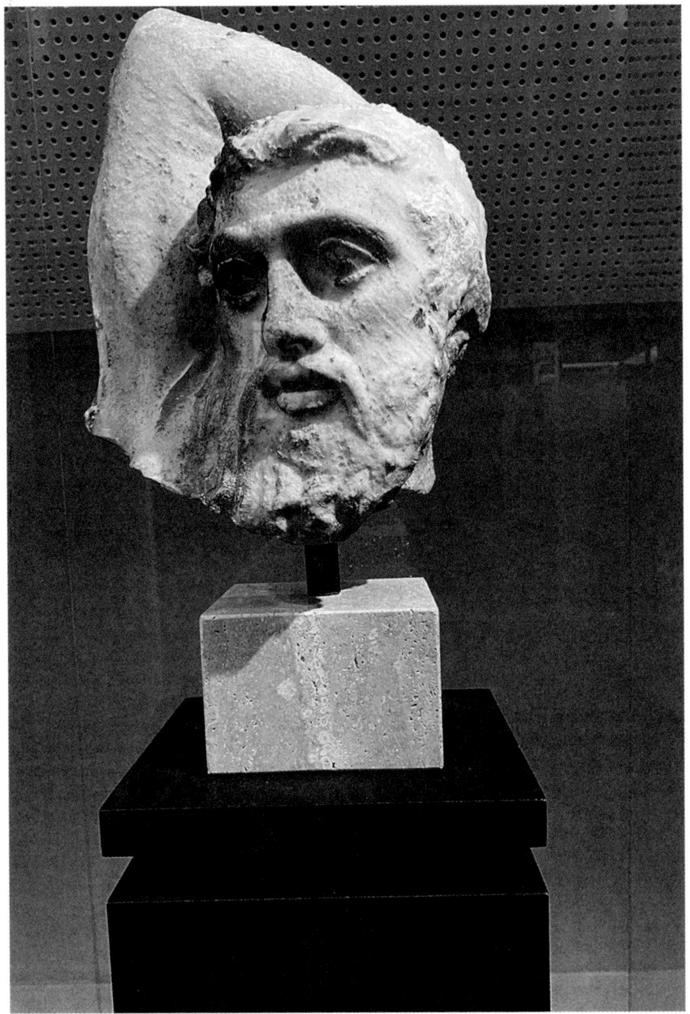

Figure 3.3 Centaur head fragment from the Parthenon, National Museum of Denmark, Copenhagen (photograph by author)

task force to locate all Parthenon fragments in various world museum collections, the first of the fragments was returned to Athens from the small collection at the University of Heidelberg, Germany, in 2006.[192] This was followed by returns from Palermo, Italy in 2022 and Vatican City in 2023, putting even more pressure on the British Museum to reconsider.[193]

[192] Bailey, "Germany's Heidelberg University."
[193] Smith, "Pope Francis Returns"; Harris, "Your Move, British Museum."

But there are still scattered pieces elsewhere. Two fragments are still located in the Bavarian State Collection of Antiques (Staatliche Antikensammlungen) in Munich. Acquired for the royal Bavarian collection by King Ludwig I, the fragments (hand of a rider and the left leg of centaur on one of the metopes) are in trust of the Wittelsbach dynasty, which refused to restitute them. In a response to an inquiry about restitution of fragments to Athens in 2007, the Compensation Fund that represents the dynasty wrote, "the collections of King Ludwig I represent in their extent and above all in their totality a high ideal value for the Wittelsbacher Ausgleichsfonds, for the House of Wittelsbach, and for the history of our country, which we are obliged to preserve."[194]

The problem with the Parthenon Marbles and competing claims on them is that they "symbolize a civilization at once specifically Greek and quintessentially European," as Lowenthal remarked.[195] The case of the destruction and dismemberment of the Parthenon is, then, a question not of desecration of cultural heritage of Greece, but of Europe and the world. Much ink has been spilled on the discussion of whether Elgin did, in fact, obtain the *firman* at all, whether the *firman* was legal, how much removal did it allow for and from where, how much bribery of Ottoman officials was involved (by Elgin's own admissions, quite a lot), how much did the Ottomans understand and care about the value of the Parthenon, was the Parthenon dilapidating under Ottoman neglect and Elgin "saved them" from ruin, were the Parthenon sculptures even the Ottomans' to give, how much was the removal Elgin's idea and how much was he influenced by his chaplain Hunt and his man on the ground Lusieri, and so on and so on.

These debates are endless and, in some ways, beside the point. What is indisputable is that Elgin's actions damaged the Parthenon structure, as well as the marble sculptures he took away, and that the inextricable part of the Parthenon temple and the entire Acropolis complex was forcibly removed and separated from its whole. The Parthenon was permanently desecrated because of one man's greed and his country's fantasies of international cultural status, all in the context of great power competition at the time. The history and the continuing debate about where the Parthenon Marbles belong is, therefore, a story of international politics. Reducing it to the attitudes and policies of a museum as if it were an institution completely independent from both the state in which it operates, and the broader international hierarchy and its status and power dynamics is a woefully incomplete account.

194 Quoted in Chaniotis, "Parthenon Sculptures."
195 Lowenthal, "Classical Antiquities," p. 727.

But more broadly, legal standards change over time, and moral and cultural values develop and grow.[196] Basing decisions for cultural politics in the twenty-first century on what was legal in colonial Europe in the eighteenth is not only impossible but also immoral. As we shall see in the next chapter, other states have decided that holding on to problematically obtained cultural objects is a drag on state status, not a force of its preservation, as Britain seems to have concluded. The international cultural status of the Parthenon Marbles as status symbols has changed, and the British narrative has been severely and fatally undermined by alternative status narratives. In that sense, perhaps as Neal Ascherson has argued, the Marbles have been in London too long for Britain's own good.[197]

[196] Chaniotis, "Divided Monument."
[197] Ascherson, "End the Exile."

4
The Bronzes

Often called the "forest kingdom" of the Edo people because of its location close to the lush and resource-rich rain forests, favorable geography, and proximity to the trans-Saharan trade routes, the Kingdom of Benin was, according to tradition, established in the twelfth century, and over time became a regional power.[1] At its peak in the sixteenth century, Benin dominated trade routes in pepper, cloth, and ivory along the Atlantic's Bight of Benin in the Gulf of Guinea.[2]

European traders and merchants arrived in the late fifteenth and early sixteenth centuries attracted by the tales of Benin riches. The first recorded European contact with Benin was in 1486 when the Portuguese navigator João Afonso de Aveiro arrived on its shores, sent on the exploratory expedition by the Portuguese King João II. Portuguese priests followed in 1515. Over the next few centuries, Benin developed a strong trade exchange with Portugal.[3] The English traders arrived in Benin in 1553, the Dutch in 1593.[4] Benin resources were traded for European guns and manillas (bronze and copper commodity currency, which were then used by Benin artists to cast bronze artifacts).[5]

Of course, also traded were enslaved people. The Portuguese traded goods for the enslaved with Benin, and then bartered them for other commodities, such as gold, with other African nations.[6] Even before the full establishment of the transatlantic slave trade, the rivers of the Niger Delta south of Benin were known in the sixteenth century as "the slave rivers."[7] Benin was unusual for refusing to sell male slaves to the Europeans for a long period.[8] However, by the eighteenth century, Benin reversed this position,

[1] For clarity, the contemporary state of Benin does not trace its origins to the precolonial Kingdom of Benin, but instead to the neighboring Kingdom of Dahomey. For a broader history of the region, see Green, *Fistful of Shells*.

[2] Northrup, "Growth of Trade." Also see Green, *Fistful of Shells*; Law, "Trade and Politics."

[3] Elbl, "Cross-Cultural Trade."

[4] For more on European encounters, see Ryder, *Benin and the Europeans*.

[5] Only recently did geologists determine that the Benin Bronzes were cast from German brass, traded in Benin by the Portuguese. See Skowronek, DeCorse, Denk, Birr, Kingsley, Cook, Dominguez, Clifford, Barker, and Otero, "German Brass for Benin Bronzes."

[6] Igbafe, "Slavery and Emancipation."

[7] Phillips, *Loot*, p. 18.

[8] Green, *Fistful of Shells*, p. 180, pp. 331–33. Instead of Benin men, enslaved people sold were female prisoners of war or those purchased from other places (the Igbo, Sobo, Ijaw and others). Bondarenko, "Benin," p. 57.

rejoined the international slave trade, and was selling 3,000 enslaved persons each year.[9]

Much of the written descriptions and drawings of precolonial Benin come to us through the European gaze, as European traders, missionaries, or great power emissaries arrived in West Africa as the region became more integrated into global economic and slave trade networks. It is the letters, drawings, paintings, and maps by European visitors that initially constructed the idea of "Africa" for European audiences at home.[10] With admiration, Lourenço Pinto, a Portuguese visitor to Benin in 1694, wrote,

> Great Benin, where the King resides, is larger than Lisbon, all the streets run straight and as far as the eyes can see. The houses are large, especially that of the king which is richly decorated and has Fine columns. The city is wealthy and industrious. It is so well governed that theft is unknown and the people live in such Security that they have no door to their houses.[11]

But the Europeans also noted the practice of human sacrifice, especially the ritualistic killing of the enslaved upon a noble's death. It is this practice, while likely often exaggerated by the fearful and suspicious Europeans, that was used as justification for the deposing of Benin's rulers and, ultimately, the destruction of the Kingdom at the end of the nineteenth century.

Much of the Benin political and cultural life centered on the Royal Palace. This massive complex in Benin City was built around atrium-style courtyards and galleries. The palace life was an intricate procession of many customs and rituals, in which the Oba (king), his chiefs, members of various guilds (drummers, butchers, priests, fertility cults, archers, marksmen, architects, sculptors, leather makers, iron workers, ceremonial executioners and so on), foreign merchants and dignitaries, and various support staff all took part.[12] Hundreds of rectangular brass plaques were affixed to wooden pillars supporting the roof of the palace. These plaques were decorative but also functional in the life of the Benin court. Their main purpose was to glorify the Oba and represent the history of his power and rule.[13]

[9] Bondarenko, "Benin," p. 57. For a relationship between slave trade and state-making in Africa, see Sharman, "Something New."

[10] European colonial descriptions of Benin (as well as other colonized territories, of course) should be relied on with caution, as they were written with a particular mercantile or mercenary purpose and most often with no understanding or particular interest in local cultural or social context. See Anagnost and Gueorguiev, "Edo Spaces" for this discussion. And yet, some of these sources provide the only written text we have to visualize what the landscape, architecture, and artifacts looked like, and so it makes sense to triangulate them with local oral history and other kinds of indigenous knowledge. This is the approach taken by the *Digital Benin* project, which combines written historiography with Edo oral history, www.digitalbenin.org.

[11] Quoted in Osarumwense, "Igue Festival," p. 2.

[12] Ezra, *Royal Art*.

[13] Gunsch, *Benin Plaques*.

These artifacts, commonly referred to as "bronzes," were made mostly out of leaded brass using the lost-wax casting technique. Other ones were made out of a range of other materials, such as coral, ceramic, ivory, and wood.[14] The art of Benin was also influenced by encounters with other cultures, including the Europeans. The Portuguese left a clear mark on Benin art, as Benin artists incorporated some of the Portuguese decorations into their own depictions and Portuguese-style details found their way into Benin's royal clothing and regalia.[15]

The surviving collection of several thousand ornaments, plaques, small sculptures, decorative figures, portrait heads, and jewelry created in the historic Kingdom of Benin is what we today refer to, collectively, as the "Benin Bronzes."[16] And much like the Parthenon sculptures on the Acropolis, various Benin sculptures, carvings, and artifacts were embedded into their architectural settings and their placement in space and relationship to their surrounding is what gave them ritualistic, religious, and artistic meaning.

This situating of the artifacts within their original setting is important as it makes it clear that their meaning was particular to the natural and built landscape that they were embedded in, and that their displacement from this locale and placement into museums continents away, often surrounded by other ethnographic curiosities from many different and often unrelated cultures, dramatically altered the meaning of these objects and stripped them of their original context. Further, what the Edo people may have considered to be one, singular collection of objects that provided them with meaning specifically because it was a one, united whole, has been deconstructed and disassembled into a series of separate objects and collections after the looting of 1897 and their dispersal throughout the world.

The punitive expedition of 1897

After a period of some decline, Benin's economy and trade blossomed in the nineteenth century as palm oil became a valuable commodity in Europe during the industrial revolution.[17] This made it increasingly attractive for Britain, which had set its goals on controlling the trade in West Africa and elevating its competitive economic status with other European powers. Benin, however, resisted British attempts to take over the trade routes and become a British protectorate. The Oba claimed monopoly over trade in the

[14] Ben-Amos, *Art, Innovation, and Politics*; Gunsch, *Benin Plaques*, Lundén, "Displaying Loot," p. 151.

[15] Phillips, *Loot*, pp. 20–21.

[16] For simplicity, I refer throughout the book to Benin "Bronzes" even though some of the objects were made of ivory or other materials.

[17] Northrup, "Compatibility"; Robins, *Oil Palm*.

kingdom and requested duties and customs for commerce. The relationship with the British soured, and the annoyed British emissaries began to describe Benin as a harrowing place of murder and human sacrifice. British consul Richard Burton, the first British government official to visit Benin City, wrote in 1863 that "nothing can be said in favour of Benin; the place has a fume of blood, it stinks of death."[18] Time and time again, Burton describes the "gratuitous barbarity" of the Benin people who, as other Africans in Burton's writing, are "less cruel because less intelligent than the European, the Asiatic and the American."[19] All this "degeneracy" of the Benin people led Burton to conclude, "It is a hopeless task to restore commerce to Benin. This people, who have long lost the trade, have declined in civilization."[20]

These kinds of descriptions were common in British writing at the time and created an image of Africa and Africans as savages in need of control that the audience back home readily accepted. This language then also served to sensitize the British public into the moral necessity of colonial occupation.[21] For example, an article in the *Illustrated London News* in 1897 described Benin as a "race of savages" who needed to be freed from their "superstition and ignorance."[22] In fact, in his dispatches as a consul, Burton stated this explicitly, "The civilisation of the coast, or rather its redemption from a worse state than the merest savagery, can be effected only by its passing into the hands of Europe."[23]

At the Berlin conference in 1884–85, the European powers divided control over African colonies and the Niger Districts were placed under the British sphere of influence. In 1885, Britain established its protectorate on the coast of Niger. In 1892, facing increasing British pressure, Benin's Oba Ovonramwen reluctantly agreed to a treaty with the British Vice-Consul Henry Gallwey. What the Oba consented to was "peace" as he was assured by Gallwey, but the British claimed that the Oba consented to full British control over Benin trade.[24] The British, however, were not satisfied with access to resources and accused Oba Ovonramwen of not respecting the treaty. A British delegation led by Acting Consul-General James Robert Phillips left the Niger Coast Protectorate for Benin in 1897. Phillips largely acted alone—he asked for, but was denied, explicit permission and military support for this mission. And yet, he ploughed ahead. He justified the expedition

[18] Burton, *Wanderings in West Africa*, p. 287.
[19] Burton, *Wanderings in West Africa*, p. 410.
[20] Burton, *Wanderings in West Africa*, p. 409.
[21] Coombes, *Reinventing Africa*; Osadolor and Otoide, "Benin Kingdom."
[22] *Illustrated London News*, January 23, 1897, quoted in Stahn, *Confronting Colonial Objects*, p. 168.
[23] Burton, *Wanderings in West Africa*, p. 220.
[24] Phillips, *Loot*, pp. 41–42.

in economic terms—commerce routes for the British will open and the expedition will pay for itself.[25]

While there is evidence that the Oba personally was not inclined to start a war with the British, his more bellicose chiefs, and especially Chief Ologbose, pushed for a more violent response.[26] The British delegation was attacked as they were nearing Benin City on January 4, 1897. Seven out of a group of nine British delegates were killed in the ambush, as were 124 of the 222 African porters and laborers who worked for the British expedition.[27] This became known in Britain as "the Benin massacre."

The British were outraged and felt additionally humiliated when their rivals, the Germans, reported in their own press that "the English were defeated in Benin."[28] The British press led the charge for retaliation, as "not only is English faith to be trusted and English friendship to be sought after, but . . . English justice, when outraged, is something to be feared."[29] The message was meant not only for the Oba of Benin, but for Britain's European rivals as well. Humiliated on the world stage, Britain was to gain its power status back through revenge. This is consistent with the research on status and territorial expansion, which demonstrates that states will seek opportunities to show their military and other coercive capabilities to other states when their international status has been challenged.[30]

Under the command of Rear-Admiral Sir Harry Rawson, an army of 1,200 British and native troops, supported by up to 2,100 native carriers descended on Benin on February 9, 1897.[31] The operation—named the Benin punitive expedition—lived up to its name. The British advanced through a narrow road and fired volleys into the forests on each side, killing scores of Edo soldiers who were hiding in the bushes. Parts of Benin city were set on fire. The Royal Palace and the surrounding areas also burned (Figure 4.1).

As they progressed, the British troops ransacked sacred altars used in rituals, and demolished compounds of the Queen Mother and other Benin chiefs. Writing in 1930, Henry Gallwey remembered the operation as a job well done:

[25] Quoted in Stahn, *Confronting Colonial Objects*, p. 166.

[26] Stahn, *Confronting Colonial Objects*.

[27] A British survivor's account of the ambush is available in Boisragon, *Benin Massacre*, Smithsonian Libraries (London: Methuen, 1897). British accounts rarely mentioned any non-British casualties. More details about casualties among the non-British working entourage are in Home, *City of Blood Revisited*. Also see Lundén, "Distorting History," p. 217.

[28] Phillips, *Loot*, p. 67.

[29] Phillips, *Loot*, p. 67.

[30] Barnhart, "Status Competition."

[31] Lundén, "Displaying Loot," p. 128.

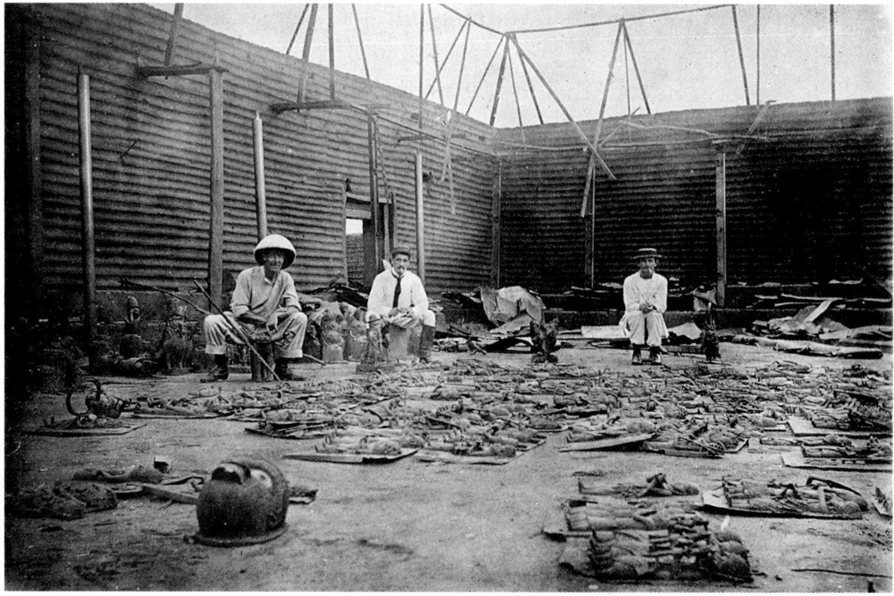

Figure 4.1 Interior of Oba's compound burnt during the British punitive expedition on Benin in 1897 (photograph by Reginald Granville, Wikimedia Commons)

> No time was lost in destroying the compounds of the Chiefs, who with the King were held responsible for the massacre of Mr. Phillips and his party. The execution pits were filled in and the crucifixion trees felled. In fact, to make the job a complete one, we blew up the roots of those hideous trees with dynamite, so that no trace whatever of them should remain. It is amusing to relate that before we had been a month in the city we had a nine-hole golf course. Our ninth hole was on the spot where the main crucifixion tree had stood. We thought it a great improvement![32]

After only nine days, Benin City fell. The Royal Palace burned to the ground on February 21.

British Consul-General Ralph Moor, who accompanied the expedition, provided the following justification for the violence:

> It is imperative that a most severe lesson be given the Kings, Chiefs, and Ju Ju men of all surrounding countries, that white men cannot be killed with impunity, and that human sacrifices, with the oppression of the weak and poor, must cease. All buildings on this site, saturated as it is with blood of human victims, will be levelled

[32] Galway, "Nigeria in the 'Nineties,'" pp. 241–42 [Galway changed the spelling of his last name].

> to the ground, and no building of any description will ever again be allowed to be erected thereon.[33]

The justification was thus framed as partly revenge, punishment, and deterrence, but also partly as a civilizing mission that would put an end to the practice of human sacrifice.[34]

Here, the comparison with the sacking of the Summer Palace outside Beijing is illustrative. The Summer Palace was thoroughly looted first in 1860 by the joint Anglo-French forces (as coincidence would have it, the British commander was one Lord Elgin, the son of the previous chapter's main protagonist), as a revenge for the killing of European hostages, and again during the Boxer Rebellion in 1900 by the broader alliance of European, American, and Japanese troops.[35] During both attacks, the anti-Chinese forces looted massive quantities of artifacts which then also globally dispersed and found their way into major museums and private collections around the world, such as, for example, the Château de Fontainebleau outside of Paris. As was the case in 1897 Benin, looting was part of a broader brutal attack which left scores of Chinese fighters and civilians murdered in particularly gruesome ways. And, both in China and in Benin, it was the Western looters that justified their action in the name of "civilizing" the barbarians.[36]

The looting of Benin

The British knew of norms against wartime looting—Admiral Rawson warned his troops, "all plundering and unnecessary destruction of property are to be strictly repressed."[37] Not only did no one seem to heed this request, but there is evidence the commanding officers allowed looting in part to motivate the troops and increase their morale.[38] The expedition troops plundered the Royal Palace and took with them more than 900 cast brass plaques which they discovered in palace storage. They also took ivory carvings and masks, including perhaps the most well known of Benin ivory artifacts—the mask of Queen Idia, the Queen Mother of Oba Esigie, the sixteenth-century

[33] Dispatch from Consul-General Moor to the Marquess of Salisbury, Benin City, February 24, 1897. Quoted in Stahn, *Confronting Colonial Objects*, p. 168.

[34] On separating fact and fiction regarding the Benin practice of human sacrifice, see Law, "Human Sacrifice."

[35] Hevia, "Looting and Its Discontents."

[36] For an extensive examination of this case, see Ringmar, *Liberal Barbarism*.

[37] Quoted in Phillips, *Loot*, p. 72.

[38] Lundén, "Displaying Loot," p. 147.

Oba, which they reportedly took from the Oba's bedroom.[39] They went through ceremonial buildings, religious sites, and houses of Benin nobles and commoners, and removed heads of former Obas decorated with carved ivory tusks from their ceremonial altars. Many of the brass plaques were permanently damaged as the soldiers removed them from the walls of the palace using their bayonets.[40]

The British troops also took jewelry, wooden boxes and stools, metal heads, statuettes, casts of animals, brass bells, gaming boards, hair pins, mirrors, clothing, needlepoint, ceremonial swords and axes, and whatever else looked like it would be valuable to sell, exotic to keep as a curiosity, or to showcase as a victory trophy. The looted items were piled together in the palace courtyard and the officers posed for photographs with their prize. Henry Gallwey was pleased and declared it "a regular harvest of loot!"[41]

Looting went on for quite some time. Even as late as March 12, four weeks after the fall of Benin, British officers were arriving to Benin to take away artifacts and valuables. One of the participating captains, Herbert Walker, observed another senior officer "wandering round with chisel & hammer, knocking off brass figures & collecting all sorts of rubbish as loot."[42] Walker himself took two Bronzes—a "bird of prophecy," known as an Oro bird, and a bell used to summon ancestors.[43]

Consul-General Moor was tasked with distribution of objects, but discipline was lax, and soldiers took many items for themselves. Moor also availed himself of some of the most valuable objects, such as ivory masks.[44] The objects the British assessed as most valuable—two tusks and two ivory leopards—were to be delivered to Queen Victoria.[45] Other senior officers were rewarded with valuable bronze plaques and decorated tusks. Some of the artifacts were sold to cover the costs of the expedition. About 1,000 material objects were claimed as official war booty. Around 300 were handed over to the British Museum. Many items, however, flooded the antiquities markets and were bought by various dealers and collectors and became dispersed throughout Europe and the United States. Today, a total of 5,426 individual Benin objects are to be found in more than 130 museums and art institutions

[39] Phillips, *Loot*.
[40] Penny, *Objects of Culture*, p. 72.
[41] Galway, "Nigeria in the 'Nineties,'" p. 241.
[42] Captain Herbert Walker's diary quoted in Otzen, "Man Who Returned," *BBC News*, February 26, 2015. In a remarkable example of restitution, Walker's grandson traveled to Benin City in 2014 to return his grandfather's two looted Bronzes to the current Oba.
[43] Otzen, "Man Who Returned."
[44] One of those is today in the British Museum. Another is at the Metropolitan Museum of Art in New York City, purchased and then donated by Nelson Rockefeller.
[45] The two ivory leopards are today also in the British Museum, on loan from the Crown.

around the world.[46] An unknown number of objects are dispersed across undisclosed collections or are in private hands.[47]

The Oba was captured and exiled to the city of Calabar. Six Benin chiefs were killed and hanged in the city square. The British appointed a Resident to oversee the protectorate. The 1897 expedition marked the beginning of the British occupation of Benin, which was initially incorporated into the British Niger Coast Protectorate, and eventually into what became the British colony of Nigeria. The British emancipated the enslaved people of Benin, but also instituted an elaborate system of forced labor, in line with their colonial practices elsewhere. That the purpose of the punitive expedition was mercantile was further substantiated by Ralph Moor himself, who wrote, "[a] rich country has thus been opened up to the influence of civilization and trade, containing extensive rubber forests, valuable gums, the usual products of palm-oil and kernels and possible many other valuable economic products."[48]

The expedition was hailed as a great success back in Britain—it was cheaper than anticipated, more efficient, and faster. In recognition, Admiral Rawson and Consul-General Moor were knighted. Newspapers reported on its great success: "Nothing could be more satisfactory than the work and results of the expedition. The blood of our countrymen had been avenged, and a system of barbarism rendered hideous by the most savage, horrible and bloodthirsty customs that even Africa can show has been effectually broken up . . . the cause of civilization has been advanced in this benighted district."[49] And, equally significant, the expedition's success demonstrated to the British rivals its military might, technological expertise, and triumph of values of "civilization" over those of native primitivism and barbarity.[50]

There were some, albeit lonely, dissenting voices in the British press. The socialist newspaper *The New Age* criticized British traders for using the pretext of stopping human sacrifice for lobbying for their own economic interests.[51] One of the authors argued that Britain, instead, should "have stopped our too numerous and abhorrent human sacrifices" back at home, such as the plight of British factory workers who are dying from miserable

[46] The most comprehensive online database of all known Benin artifacts (more than 5,000 discrete objects) is available on the *Digital Benin* portal, www.digitalbenin.org. It includes their detailed provenance, chain of ownership, and restitution claims and transfers. What makes the platform even more innovative is the inclusion of archival materials, eyewitness testimony to the 1897 expedition, as well as oral history sources that discuss the history, cultural significance, and provenance of the Bronzes.

[47] Hicks, *Brutish Museums*. For an attempt at calculating these numbers, see Lundén, "Distorting History," p. 218.

[48] Quoted in Obinyan, "Annexation of Benin."

[49] *Illustrated London News*, March 27, 1897.

[50] Lundén, "Displaying Loot," p. 131.

[51] For a similar argument, see Hobson, *Multicultural Origins*.

working conditions.[52] There were also numerous anti-colonial editorials in the West African newspaper *Lagos Weekly Record*, including one that pointed out Western hypocrisy on the issue of human rights, an argument that sounds much more contemporary than 1897: "What is the lynching of Negroes in the United States but human sacrifices?"[53]

After the British were finally done, the Kingdom of Benin, and its cultural riches, were no more.

The sacking of Benin and Britain's civilizing mission

The subjugation of Benin, the deposing of the Oba, and the clearing of the path for unchallenged British economic expansion was also a direct result of international status competition. Britain was desperate to fight off colonial expansion of France and Germany, and Benin stood in the way. A show of force through the punitive expedition was also a signal to these European rivals of British imperial domination.[54]

The attack on Benin came at the very peak of British imperialism. It was that same year, 1897, that Queen Victoria celebrated her Diamond Jubilee. Imperial Britain benefited enormously economically, of course, through access to vast natural resources of its colonies. But it also justified imperial expansion and control by claiming it was its Christian duty and obligation to "civilize" the colonized and rid them of their native prejudices, beliefs, and customs. Just as Britain claimed to have saved the Parthenon Marbles from their rot among the primitive Turks and Greeks, it now claimed that it was saving entire peoples and nations from themselves and fulfilling the great global mission of civilizing the world. "In the Empire we have found not merely the key to glory and wealth, but the call to duty, and the means of service to mankind," wrote the British foreign secretary and India's viceroy Lord George Curzon in 1908.[55]

By the end of the nineteenth century and the raid on Benin, British imperialism has also become rooted in strong racial ideology and an increasing stratification of the world based on racial science.[56] From this lens, British late nineteenth-century expeditions to Benin—and elsewhere in Africa—were narrated primarily as an opportunity for the civilized, Christian Britain,

[52] *The New Age*, February 6, 1896, quoted in Coombes, *Reinventing Africa*, p. 31.

[53] *Lagos Weekly Record*, November 6, 1897, quoted in Coombes, *Reinventing Africa*, p. 37.

[54] Hicks, *Brutish Museums*, p. 113. For a similar argument about the reasoning behind the punitive expedition, see Docherty, *Blood and Bronze*.

[55] Curzon, "True Imperialism," quoted in Cain, "Empire and the Languages of Character," p. 256.

[56] Rich, *Race and Empire*; Stepan, *Idea of Race*. For a broader overview of the late 19th century debates about Britain's role in the world, see Bell, *Idea of Greater Britain*.

the heir to classical Greece and Rome, to turn barbaric, savage, primitive Africans who feasted on human sacrifice into cultured societies. Central to this discourse was the British commitment to the abolition of slavery—an empire that once passionately participated and benefited from slavery by the late eighteenth century passionately embraced abolitionism.[57] By espousing abolitionism, Britain was also projecting a form of moral authority status, differentiating itself from its main European rivals, mostly France, the Low countries, Spain, and Portugal, who lagged in abolition legislation and practice.[58] By the logic of status competition, Britain was compelled to occupy slave-trading nations, such as the Kingdom of Benin, as occupation was the path to abolition and emancipation, and the pursuit of these goals positioned Britain at the top of the European moral hierarchy. It is from this abolitionist context that much of the narrative about colonization of Africa was justified—Britain was occupying African nations to free them from slavery. Of course, that resources could be extracted, money made, and territory conquered was just a bonus of the civilizational mission that Britain was conducting as a favor to the world.[59]

That Britain's civilizing project treated its colonized subjects barbarically goes without saying.[60] It is also important to note that the Benin punitive expedition was not an isolated or unusual deployment of troops. In its purpose, it was more akin to what we today would understand as a military invasion.[61] The word "expedition" is also a misnomer—these were punitive raids that Britain routinely engaged in—there were more than 200 British punitive expeditions between 1820 and 1900.[62] They were also extremely violent and often murderous.[63]

Here is Joseph Chamberlain, Secretary of the State for the Colonies, addressing the House of Commons in 1895, and explaining the importance of punitive expeditions for sustained British trade,

> No trade is possible as long as native disturbances are taking place, and when hon. Members, animated no doubt by philanthropic intentions, protest against expeditions, punitive or otherwise, which are now the only way we can establish peace between contending savage tribes in Africa, they are protesting against the only system of civilising and practically of developing the trade of Africa.[64]

[57] Olusoga, *Black and British*.
[58] Quirk and Richardson, "Anti-Slavery."
[59] These arguments did not disappear with the end of British colonialism. They live on in contemporary imperial apologia, such as Ferguson, *Empire*.
[60] Grant, *Civilised Savagery*.
[61] Brodie, "Problematizing the Encyclopedic Museum," p. 73.
[62] Ashcroft, "As Britain Returns."
[63] Ballard, "Swift Injustice."
[64] House of Commons Parliamentary Debate (August 22, 1895), Volume 36, Col. 641.

In fact, many punitive expeditions, such as the one on Benin, were driven by economic and trade interests, as corporations such as the Royal Niger Company sought and gained protection by the British state. The Royal Niger Company, however, also had an army of its own.[65] This extractive economic expansion backed by state and private organization of violence and terror was colonialism executed through corporate militarism.[66] And while many British narratives about its imperial past contain self-congratulatory stories about a uniquely British "soft touch" when dealing with indigenous groups—in comparison to the noted brutality of the German or Belgian genocidal colonial campaigns—historical evidence shows that the British punitive expeditions and other colonial practices also engaged in tremendous physical violence, making imperial Britain hardly the exception to colonial brutality.[67]

British officials explicitly understood their treatment of native populations in colonies to be based on a very different set of norms and rules than those they applied to nations they considered their peers. This also meant more direct economic and political management of the colonies. Again, Chamberlain is explicit,

> I regard many of our colonies as being in the condition of underdeveloped estates, and estates which can never be developed without Imperial assistance. It appears to me to be absurd to apply to savage countries the same rules which we apply to civilised portions of the United Kingdom.[68]

Similarly, even though by 1897 the international norms about cultural property and prohibition of looting were well established, and the looting of Benin occurred only two years before the 1899 Hague Convention on protection of cultural property discussed earlier in the book, the British (and other colonial powers) clearly did not think these norms applied to them. In fact, the *British War Office Manual of Military Law* from 1894, in force at the time of the Benin punitive expedition, explicitly states, "[t]he seizure of scientific objects, pictures, sculptures, and other works of art or science belonging to the public has derived some sanction from the repeated practice of civilized nations; but would seem incompatible with the admitted restriction of the rights of war to depriving the enemy of such things only as enable him to make resistance, and can only be justified as a measure of retaliation."[69] The British expedition, clearly, violated their own military manual, but they also

[65] For a broader history of the company, see Baker, *Trade Winds.*
[66] Hicks, *Brutish Museums.*
[67] Wagner, "Savage Warfare."
[68] House of Commons Parliamentary Debate (August 22, 1895), Volume 36, Cols. 641–42.
[69] Cited in Brodie, "Problematizing the Encyclopedic Museum," p. 72.

obviously did not understand the Edo of Benin to be a "civilized nation" and excluded them from any protection provided by international law.[70] They also did not understand the Benin Bronzes at the time to be "art," the way we understand it today, but only valuables to be sold as curiosities.

And this is how their new journey began once they were brought from Benin to London.

Bronzes in Covent Garden

Almost immediately upon the Bronzes' arrival, the British art connoisseurs realized that what the punitive expedition brought home were more than souvenirs or curios. The Bronzes quickly gained a reputation for their exceptional aesthetic value and historical importance.[71] The strong interest in the Bronzes—in Britain, but as we shall see, even more in Germany—followed the already developing curiosity and interest in the cultures and customs of non-European nations and the desire of ethnological museums to procure non-European objects for their collections.[72] Initially, there were some questions about how the people of Benin, truly, could have mastered the cast brass technique, or if indeed the technique originated with the Portuguese or even earlier, with ancient Egyptians.[73] There were fantastical tales of a "wandering tribe of alien craftsmen."[74] Eventually, the dilemmas of their origin subsided, and they became the most highly valued of all African art brought to Europe by that time.[75] The Bronzes were now recontextualized from war bounty into "artifacts" and their placement in European museums stripped them of the violence of their extraction.[76]

On May 25, 1897, the British government put up a selection of Benin objects not already handed over to the British Museum or kept as spoils of war by individual officers, for auction. This auction was followed by a number of smaller sales by various dealers. The auction houses initially showed more interest in selling carved ivory, which was to be sold by weight. But once the Bronzes were presented, they quickly became repriced as artworks, and their prices went up so quickly that a bidding war ensued.[77] It didn't hurt

[70] On the exclusion of non-Europeans from imperial Britain's understanding of international law and norms, see Vrdoljak, *International Law*, pp. 47–49.

[71] Coombes, *Reinventing Africa*, p. 43.

[72] Stahn, *Confronting Colonial Objects*, p. 172, building on Dark, *Introduction to Benin Art*.

[73] Coombes, *Reinventing Africa*, pp. 44–45.

[74] *Illustrated London News*, October 16, 1897, quoted in Phillips, *Loot*, p. 123.

[75] Barkan, "Aesthetics and Evolution," p. 36; Lundén, "Displaying Loot," p. 198.

[76] Brodie, "Problematizing the Encyclopedic Museum," p. 68.

[77] Penny, *Objects of Culture*, 76. According to the Digital Benin database, there are 931 Benin Bronze artifacts that were either bought or sold by Webster. They are today globally dispersed, with a large collection (164) in the Field Museum in Chicago.

sales that they were presented as evidence of Benin's gory practices of human sacrifice and other salacious rituals.[78]

General Lane Fox Pitt-Rivers purchased a huge number of artifacts for his private collection, which then became, in part, the Pitt Rivers Museum in Oxford, where more than a hundred Bronzes still remain.[79] Just one British auctioneer, Henry Stevens, sold hundreds of Benin Bronzes at his auction house in London's Convent Garden between 1898 and 1904. So did William Downing Webster, who purchased the Bronzes cheap from officers who took them during the 1897 expedition, and then resold them for much more. He sold them to individual collectors, but also to museums in Edinburgh, Dublin, Stockholm, Copenhagen, Basel, Leiden, Leipzig, Cologne, Dresden, Stuttgart, and Vienna, and thus became a major agent in the global diffusion of the Benin Bronze art.[80]

The first exhibition of Benin Bronzes at the British Museum was held between September 1897 and January 1898. The reception in the British press was, on balance, positive, but also quite confused as to what these objects actually *were*—art, weapons, crafts, ritualistic instruments, or something else even more difficult to comprehend.[81] But their connection to the ghastly rituals only made them more interesting to the public. After spending years depicting Benin as "the city of blood" engaged in routine human sacrifice, now here were the objects these same people produced, and they were . . . beautiful. Contemporary museum curators were amazed at the quality of craftsmanship and compared it favorably to the metal artwork produced in fifteenth- or sixteenth-century Europe.[82] Other museums in Britain quickly acquired small collections of the Bronzes of their own—in addition to the Pitt-Rivers collection, the Horniman Museum in London, the Bankfield Museum in Halifax, and the Museum of Liverpool obtained significant pieces.

That Britain now possessed these unusual treasures was also a clear expression of Britain's imperial domain and far reach. Ethnographic collections were representations of imperial power, and as more and more British expeditions went to far away corners of the empire, they brought back more and more objects. The greatly expanded ethnographic collections, then, were symbols of the greatly expanded British Empire. These collections were meant to illustrate to the British exhibition visitors the strange customs of the colonized lands and peoples—a typical description of an exhibition was "a series of artificial curiosities from the less civilised parts of the world."[83]

[78] Phillips, *Loot*, p. 138.
[79] Digital Benin database lists 148 objects as still property of the Pitt Rivers Museum in Oxford.
[80] Phillips, *Loot*, p. 139.
[81] Phillips, *Loot*, p. 122.
[82] Phillips, *Loot*, p. 123.
[83] Lundén, "Displaying Loot," p. 267.

These objects also rendered the colonial project and its value for everyday citizens much more tangible and enthralling than an abstraction on a map. The Bronzes and other artifacts brought back from the colonies made the empire more legible and also more legitimate in the eyes of the British public. But these colonial collections also signaled to Britain's rivals that the British Empire was in full swing. Since collecting material objects from occupied territories was one of the central practices of European colonialism, colonial powers measured their successes also through competitive collecting.[84]

African artifacts were almost always first displayed in natural history, ethnological, or anthropological museums, as curiosities of faraway exotic, primitive cultures. By the end of the nineteenth century, they began to be reclassified as educational materials.[85] In 1904, the British League of the Empire recommended that they be reclassified from curiosities into educational objects that would enlighten British students about the cultures and peoples of the British Empire.[86] But even further, these artifacts brought home to London, Paris, or Berlin further legitimized the imperial projects as they made the empire real for everyday citizens. While the distant, far-flung corners of European empires may have just been places to point on a map, material artifacts contemporaneously appearing in national museums made the imperial project much more tangible, concrete, and more easily presented as cultural and economic successes.

This move, also, came out of preconceived notions of social and racial hierarchies, and African art especially was used to narratively and visually explain these unfamiliar civilizations to European eyes.[87] This narrative was then replaced with the one about cultural guardianship—that the forces of modernity are ruining the African traditional way of life, which should now be preserved as artifacts in European ethnological or "world culture" museums.[88] Only over time did African art come to be interpreted as art that belonged in art museums. In other words, these objects over time became acsthcticized.[89]

Germany's collecting frenzy

Britain, however, did not compare favorably with its rivals on all counts. Germany, especially, was much more advanced in its ethnographic collections, and German interest in ethnology was much more directly state driven

[84] Gosden and Knowles, *Collecting Colonialism.*
[85] Coombes, *Reinventing Africa.*
[86] Coombes, "Museums."
[87] Schildkrout and Keim, *Scramble for Art.*
[88] Van Beurden, "Art of (Re)Possession."
[89] Van Beurden, "Value of Culture."

and financed.[90] The Ethnological Museum in Berlin also had, by the estimates of British ethnographers at the time, as much as ten times as many objects in its collections than did the British Museum.[91] These comparisons very much hurt the British sense of cultural supremacy and were expressed, with some chagrin, by the British anthropologist Northcote Thomas, who complained that "the greatest colonial empire the world has ever seen, lags far behind."[92]

As British ethnographers were stunned to find out, Germany had made ethnographic collecting a state priority. Between the 1870s and the onset of World War I, Germany's ethnological museums were considered the best in the world, with Berlin, Munich, Hamburg, and Leipzig leading the way, later followed by Stuttgart, Frankfurt, and Cologne.[93] Berlin's Ethnological Museum was generously funded by the government and a strong philanthropic network of individual donors and benefactors. Germany's acquisition of material objects was also a fully coordinated state effort. For example, in 1881, the director of German Royal Museums directed the Prussian Cultural Ministry to coordinate with ambassadors, envoys, consuls, and other diplomatic staff abroad and appraise them of the objects the Ethnological Museum in Berlin sought in order to facilitate their acquisition.[94] In 1896, the German Bundesrat—the Federal Council of the German Empire—decided that all material objects collected in the colonies should be displayed at the central location—the Ethnological Museum in Berlin. This provided a great incentive for colonial personnel and individual collectors to acquire massive quantities of objects, and this led to the exponential growth of the Ethnological Museum's collection, to the point of overcrowding.[95]

There are few reasons why Germany invested so heavily in ethnological museums, and they often seem, from today's perspective, to be contradictory. In part, there was genuine fascination with other cultures, a form of early cosmopolitanism, especially inspired by the legacy of the great German scientist Alexander Humboldt.[96] Adolf Bastian, the key figure in early German ethnology, and the founder of the Ethnological Museum in Berlin, subscribed to this vision and was critical of evolutionary Darwinism and its racist implications.[97]

But a critical element of Germany's curiosity in other cultures was also, of course, an imperialist drive, and some of it was certainly rooted in

[90] Penny, *In Humboldt's Shadow*.
[91] Penny, *Objects of Culture*.
[92] Quoted in Penny, *Objects of Culture*, p. 1.
[93] Gunsch, "Art and/or Ethnographica?," p. 25.
[94] Penny, *Objects of Culture*, p. 61.
[95] Stahn, *Confronting Colonial Objects*, p. 130. Also Penny, *Objects of Culture*.
[96] Penny, *In Humboldt's Shadow*.
[97] Stahn, *Confronting Colonial Objects*, p. 131.

race science.[98] As Susanne Zantop has demonstrated, Germany's relatively short-lived colonial rule masks a much longer period of colonial fantasies—a "colonialism without colonies" which was fundamental in the construction of German national identity. From "armchair conquistadors," German ethnographers became major collectors of other cultures' material objects, which explained the collecting mania that gripped Germany at the turn of the twentieth century.[99] This was the time of great German patriotic fervor and desire to demonstrate Germany's power on the world stage. German scholars measured their collections against those of other European museums and they yearned to lead the race.[100] But behind acquiring objects there was also clear intent to compete in the international marketplace of cultural artifacts, and to project Germany's international cultural status to its main rivals.

The most significant collector for the German state in this period was Felix von Luschan, Bastian's successor at the Ethnological Museum in Berlin. After the Hamburg Museum for Arts and Crafts purchased a Benin pedestal head in the summer of 1897, making Hamburg the first city in Germany to own a Benin Bronze, Luschan acted fast on behalf of his own museum in Berlin.[101] He traveled to London personally and immediately recognized Benin Bronzes for their artistic greatness, which he evaluated as "not second to contemporary European art."[102] By 1919, he systematically bought at auction and from various resellers a total of 580 objects for Germany's museums. This left the museums in London in the dust.[103] Luschan was also incredibly entrepreneurial and contacted the German Consul General in Lagos to purchase any Bronzes he found in Nigeria, again demonstrating the involvement of the state in procuring these artifacts.[104] A total of 263 additional Bronzes arrived in Germany directly from Nigeria. Luschan was so enthralled with the Bronzes that he announced he was ready to "buy up all available antiquities from Benin, regardless of price."[105]

As his passion for the Bronzes never wavered, Luschan became Europe's leading expert on Benin art.[106] He also went to some pains to persuade the skeptical German public that Africans, indeed, could produce exceptional art and that much of contemporary German race science was, in fact,

[98] Bach, "Brand of Brothers?" The 2023 German film, *Measures of Men* (dir. by Lars Kraume) takes this topic head-on.

[99] Zantop, *Colonial Fantasies*.

[100] Penny, *Objects of Culture*, p. 10.

[101] Plankensteiner, "Benin-Kings and Rituals," p. 86.

[102] Eisenhofer, "Felix Von Luschan," p. 63.

[103] Stahn, *Confronting Colonial Objects*, pp. 131–32.

[104] Eisenhofer, "Felix Von Luschan," p. 70.

[105] Quoted in Stahn, *Confronting Colonial Objects*, p. 172.

[106] Edo scholars, of course, described and wrote about Benin art themselves. Notable Edo writers in the 1930s were Chief A. Akpata and Jacob Egharevba. For more on Edo scholarship, see Nevadomsky, "Studies of Benin Art." My focus in this chapter, however, is on the way in which European powers used the Bronzes to elevate their international cultural status.

nonsense. He wrote in 1901, "Human beings which have brought casting to absolute perfection, human beings to whom with almost absolute certainty the discovery of iron-working may be attributed, human beings about whom we now know that they have stood in reciprocal contact with recognized cultured peoples may not be regarded as half-apes."[107]

Luschan also clearly understood his collecting of the Bronzes as being in the service of German colonialism and referred to the Berlin Ethnological Museum as "the greatest monument to our colonial troops."[108] He also was well aware, and apparently not particularly worried, that the Benin Bronzes had been looted. In a famous exchange, Richard Kandt, the German physician and explorer of Africa told Luschan, "Generally, it is difficult to acquire an object without employing at least some violence. I reckon that half the objects in your museum were stolen."[109]

Even beyond Luschan's entrepreneurial acquisitions, the fascination with collecting artifacts from Africa ran deep in Germany. Another major collector, Karl von Linden, acquired artifacts for the German public collection which eventually became the Linden Museum in Stuttgart. The collection was accumulated by individual acquisitions by German colonial staff, by employees in German corporations in the colonies, but also by missionaries, and diplomatic envoys.[110] In 1910, another German ethnologist Leo Frobenius conducted a special expedition to Africa which purpose was to collect African artifacts and populate German museums.[111]

German museums also began to serve as not only collection hubs but also distribution hubs for other museums and collections in Germany and abroad. Luschan's plan at the Berlin's Ethnological Museum seems to have been to purchase everything and control the international market of ethnographic artifacts. As one of the competitors complained, "[Berlin will] most likely purchase everything, in order to sell [the pieces they do not actually want] later."[112]

Acquiring and gifting the Bronzes was also a form of demonstrating individual cultural and social status. In the summer of 1898, the German consul in Lagos Eduard Schmidt obtained and then gifted to Kaiser Wilhelm two Benin brass leopards. In acknowledgment of this gesture, the Kaiser ordained Schmidt with the Order of the Red Eagle.[113] Just as collecting artifacts was one way of increasing Germany's international cultural status, so was trading

[107] Quoted in Lundén, "Displaying Loot," p. 329.
[108] Quoted in Zimmerman, *Anthropology and Antihumanism*, p. 154.
[109] Quoted in Hicks, *Brutish Museums*, p. 37.
[110] Stahn, *Confronting Colonial Objects*, p. 132.
[111] Marchand, "Leo Frobenius."
[112] Quoted in Penny, *Objects of Culture*, p. 67.
[113] Lundén, "Displaying Loot," p. 167. For more on this pay-to-play practice and bestowing of orders to significant individuals, see Zimmerman, *Anthropology and Antihumanism*.

them with other countries and thereby attaining international recognition. For example, the Museum of Ethnography in Leipzig managed to amass a considerable collection of objects by bestowing German decorative medals to international donors from Japan, Russia, El Salvador, Portugal, and Spain.[114] Populating German ethnological museums with objects was therefore an issue of high diplomacy and a priority of the newly established unified German state.

International status competition for the Bronzes

Much has been written about the global art implications of the arrival of Benin Bronzes, as well as other African art to Europe.[115] Many scholars believe that it was the Bronzes that introduced European publics to African art and began to change prevailing nineteenth-century beliefs that Africans were incapable of artistic expression.[116] Further, their technical sophistication was so high that it surpassed much of the European brass work of the same period, thus flipping the evolutionary racist theories on their head.[117] Their arrival in Europe may have significantly influenced European art and aesthetics. But their extraction from Africa and arrival to Europe also elevated the international cultural status of the states that came to possess them and fight to retain them.

The Germans were proud of what they had acquired, and they compared themselves favorably to the British. Hans Meyer, a patron of German ethnological acquisitions and collections, wrote in a letter to Luschan in 1898,

> It is actually a riddle to me, that the English let such things go. Either they have too many of them already or they have no idea what these things mean for ethnology, cultural history, and art history . . . whatever the case may be, the main thing remains, that *we* have these magnificent specimens.[118]

British collectors were outraged that so many Benin Bronzes slipped out of Britain and were purchased by Germany. Many in Britain considered the Bronzes to be rightfully British as, in the angry words of Henry Ling Roth (the British anthropologist whose brother Dr. Felix Roth was a surgeon who participated in the 1897 expedition and likely gave the items to Henry), the Bronzes cost the British government "thousands to obtain, as well as much

[114] Bedorf and Östberg, "African *Objets D'art*," pp. 30–31.
[115] For a broader look at the mass collection and extraction of art from Africa, see Schildkrout and Keim, *Scramble for Art*.
[116] Stahn, *Confronting Colonial Objects*, pp. 133–34; also Barkan, "Aesthetics and Evolution."
[117] Penny, *Objects of Culture*, p. 71.
[118] Letter dated March 26, 1898. Quoted in Penny, *Objects of Culture*, p. 75.

blood of our fellow countrymen."[119] Just as Britain had been competing with France over the Parthenon Marbles, it now competed with Germany over the Bronzes. Roth was especially incensed at the loss of such a precious collection:

> From what I can ascertain, the bulk of these bronzes has been secured by the Germans, and it is especially annoying to Englishmen to think that such articles, which for every reason should be retained in this country, have been allowed to go abroad. Not that I wish to, nor do I blame the Germans in the least for what they have done, but it is only one more example of their alertness, and of our apathy.[120]

But Roth also made a much broader point, and one that speaks directly to the question of international status. Britain, in his view, was far behind both Germany and a rising rival, the United States, in anthropological knowledge, and this was hurting British commerce, science, and politics. More specifically, it was hurting the British colonial project:

> For many years the Germans have foreseen that the study of native races and their development, a study known to us under the awkward name of Anthropology, is essential to every civilised community which trades with, or is called upon to govern native communities, and with their characteristic thoroughness they have become leaders in a branch of science in which the Americans alone have been able to equal them, and, as it now appears, are about to outstrip them . . . There remains the fact that with us the native races are not adequately studied, and we are consequently handicapped politically, scientifically, and commercially in competition with other nations.[121]

British ethnographers, especially those at the British Museum, responded by intensifying their procurement of Benin Bronzes. In May 1899, they acquired more plaques from the 1897 expedition commander Ralph Moor. In 1910, the British Museum purchased its most valued Benin artifact to date—the ivory mask of the Queen Mother (Figure 4.2). The museum ethnographers could now boast that Britain possessed "the finest thing that has come from Benin."[122] There were also fears in Britain that the new and large collection of African artifacts amassed by the German ethnologist Leo Frobenius would leave nothing of value in Africa for the British. Acting as an acquisition agent on behalf of the British Museum, the Hungarian-British

[119] Roth, *Great Benin*, xviii.
[120] Roth, *Great Benin*, Appendix IV, xix.
[121] Roth, *Great Benin*, Appendix IV, xix.
[122] Phillips, *Loot*, p. 134.

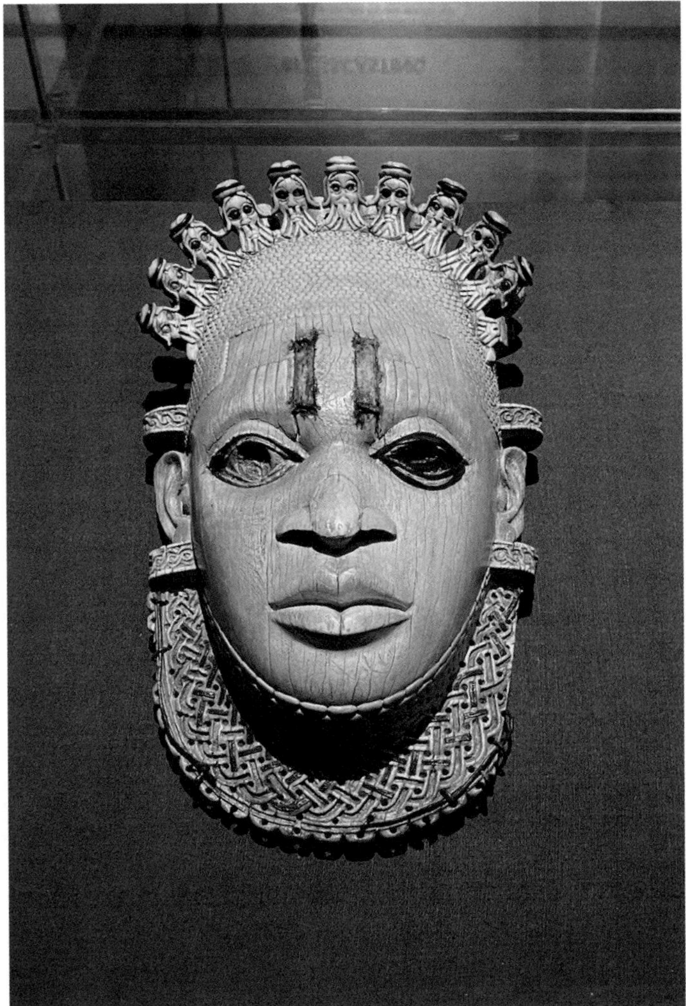

Figure 4.2 Queen Idia Mask, Benin, the British Museum (photograph by author)

anthropologist Emil Torday pledged to the museum that the Germans would not "undersell the old curiosity shop of Bloomsbury."[123]

The British were obsessed with Germany's advantage in ethnological collections in a similar manner to how they were obsessed with France regarding the Parthenon Marbles. Very early on, the British press began to refer to the Benin Bronzes as being part of British national heritage which was being pilfered by private sales to Germany. These appeals to heritage were part of

[123] Barkan, "Amending Historical Injustices," p. 21.

"a strategy calculated to inspire a sense of nationalist indignation."[124] British anthropologists played up this competition and British inferiority of collections to increase state support, but they framed it directly as an issue of status, within the context of "the perceived increasing threat posed by Germany to Britain's imperial supremacy."[125]

The international competition for the Bronzes as status symbols also revealed differences in the collector-states' understanding of them in the global context of art. In Britain, at the Pitt Rivers Museum in Oxford, which at the turn of the twentieth century had one of the largest collections of Benin art, the artifacts were displayed in an alleged evolutionary order of their creation. The purpose of this display was to present their evolutionary progress toward ever greater sophistication. This Darwinist approach, then, fit well with the great interest in evolutionary development that gripped Britain at the turn of the twentieth century. In Germany, on the other hand, under Luschan's guidance and influenced by Humboldt's theory of unified human history, the Benin objects were represented according to their geography. Instead of emphasizing their evolutionary development, Luschan focused on presenting these objects as evidence of global cultural diversity.[126]

In what was a stark difference from how British ethnologists thought of race at the time, Luschan wrote,

> The whole of human kind is composed of only one species: Homo sapiens. There are no "savage" people, there are only people with a culture that differs from ours. The distinguishing qualities of these so-called "races" essentially originated due to climatological, social, and other environmental factors.[127]

That the more progressive and cosmopolitan German approach was so thoroughly crushed and German ethnology used for the most perfidious of racist projects yet to come, is a tragedy in itself.[128]

Global circulation of the Bronzes

It was not just Britain and Germany that competed for the Bronzes to elevate their international cultural status. Austria's Imperial Royal Museum of

124 Coombes, "Ethnography, Popular Culture," p. 152.
125 Coombes, "Ethnography, Popular Culture," p. 152.
126 Gunsch, "Art and/or Ethnographica?," pp. 26–27; Lundén, "Displaying Loot," pp. 335—337.
127 Quoted in Gunsch, "Art and/or Ethnographica?," p. 27.
128 For a fascinating history of the takeover of German progressive ethnology by conservative and then fascist ideologies, see Penny, *In Humboldt's Shadow*; also Zimmerman, *Anthropology and Antihumanism*.

Natural History in Vienna was also seeking Bronzes. Already in 1897, the museum's chief ethnographer Franz Heger traveled to Berlin, where he purchased a Benin carved ivory tusk to enrich the Viennese collection. Heger also contacted individual travelers from Austria-Hungary and urged them to bring home artifacts from their journeys. Overall, Heger managed to purchase 181 Bronzes for Austria.[129] Art dealers and collectors played into these state competitions by creating a bidding war. In May 1898, the major British Bronzes dealer William Downing Webster manipulated Heger into paying top price for additional items, arguing that the Dresden Museum in Germany had already spent £1,000 for a major purchase.[130]

Other countries wanted in on the action, and the Bronzes were bought and sold frequently on the international art market. Museums in the Netherlands bought Bronzes, as did museums in Australia, New Zealand, Ireland, Russia, and Sweden.[131] Sweden, especially, followed the German model. Inspired by the donations-for-decorative-medals scheme that enriched the Museum of Ethnography in Leipzig, the Museum of Ethnography in Stockholm did the same. The Stockholm Museum was approached by a major German collector, Hans Meyer, who offered a donation of more than thirty Benin objects in exchange for a Swedish decorative medal. He received the Swedish Order of the Polar Star in 1907, but it came without the highest status of Grade of Commander 1st Class he initially requested. To Meyer, this was a grade one snub, and he angrily complained, in indignation, that he received more respect for similar services from Romania, Russia, and Portugal: "Surely, you understand how unpleasant it is for me to have to broach the matter in this fashion, but you no doubt also understand that I have no desire to be any less honored by Sweden than by other foreign powers, such as Russia and Rumania."[132] Meyer was upset, but what Sweden did with this scheme was populate its new museum with Benin Bronzes which were at the time already considered international objects of status. The new collection attracted visitors, established the Stockholm Museum of Ethnography as a world-class art institution, and, more important, helped put Sweden on the international cultural map.

The United States got in on the international market as well. From as early as 1898 on, the Field Museum in Chicago, the University of Pennsylvania Museum, and the Harvard University Museum began acquiring collections

[129] Plankensteiner, "African Art," pp. 16–17.

[130] Phillips, *Loot*, pp. 139–40.

[131] Lundén, "Displaying Loot," 168. France was a late entrant to the market in Benin Bronzes, but in the 1930s, Musée de l'Homme (descendant of the Musée d'Ethnographie du Trocadéro) purchased a few pieces. Today they are mostly in the Musée du quai Branly in Paris.

[132] Quoted in Bedorf and Östberg, "African *Objets D'art*," p. 32.

of Bronzes.[133] In the 1930s, US museums (such as the Smithsonian Institution in Washington, DC) and private collectors went on a buying spree and purchased many Benin pieces, initially from French dealers.[134] This also indicates a shift in the understanding and appreciation of Benin Bronzes—while initially they were acquired exclusively as ethnographic objects for ethnological museum collections, they now became desirable as objects of art and were purchased by American *art* museums, rather than ethnological ones.[135]

By 1901, state and private collections in Great Britain, Germany, and Austria possessed almost all available Benin art.[136] But the richness of these collections also fluctuated with world events. While initially the largest in the world, Germany's collection of Benin Bronzes dramatically shrunk during and in the immediate aftermath of World War II, while Britain's collection grew exponentially. During World War II, different collections of Bronzes in Britain also faired differently. Those already in the British Museum were evacuated with the rest of the museum collections and were safe from damage. Bronzes held at the Museum of Liverpool, however, were not evacuated and when the museum was bombed in 1941, some of the Bronzes were completely destroyed and some irreparably damaged in the fire that engulfed the museum.[137]

Some of the Bronzes at the Ethnological Museum in Berlin were also destroyed or lost in World War II. The museum was evacuated at the outset of the war, and various collections were dispersed throughout Germany. A large number of Bronzes (around 400) were evacuated to Silesia in Poland. This collection was taken by Soviet troops and transported to the Ethnographic Museum in Leningrad (now St. Petersburg) by the Soviet "Trophy Brigades." The Bronzes that remained in Berlin were initially taken by the Allied forces and then eventually returned in 1956 to the Ethnological Museum, which was then in West Berlin. The Bronzes continued to serve as tokens of international politics. The large cache taken to Leningrad was returned to Germany in 1977–78 but not to the Berlin museum from which they were taken but to the Ethnographic Museum in Leipzig, because Leipzig was in East Germany. This return was reported as a symbol of "friendship between communist nations."[138] With another major international event—Germany's

[133] Berzock, "African Art."
[134] The Metropolitan Museum in New York began to build its collection of the Bronzes in 1950.
[135] The first appearance of Benin art in a United States museum was in 1935 at the exhibition put up by the Museum of Modern Art (MOMA). The African Negro Art exhibition then toured across the US and was later put up for sale at an auction in New York. Gunsch, "Art and/or Ethnographica?"
[136] Gunsch, "Art and/or Ethnographica?," p. 23.
[137] Tythacott, "African Collection," p. 170.
[138] Ivanov, "African Art," p. 20.

reunification in 1990—the Berlin-Leningrad-Leipzig collection was returned to the Ethnological Museum in Berlin, but sixty-five of these Bronzes were and still are missing—destroyed, in private hands, or lost forever.[139]

The Bronzes are not only dispersed throughout the world but, just as was the case with the Parthenon Marbles, there are pieces of the same collection of objects that ended up on the opposite sides of the globe. A body of a Benin figure of a horseman is in a collection at the University of Zurich while its head is in the British Museum. Another sculpture has fragments divided between the National Museum in Benin City and the Penn Museum in Philadelphia.[140] And just like the Parthenon Marbles, a restitution case for these objects rests, in part, on a simple claim of artistic reunification.

Similarly to the case of the Parthenon Marbles, much of contemporary resistance to restitution of Benin Bronzes claims that the calls for restitution are novel and politically charged. However, some of the earliest calls for restitution came already in the 1940s, and from an unlikely source—the British colonial administrator in Nigeria. In 1942, Kenneth Murray, a British colonial official with a swanky title of Surveyor of Antiquities, published an article in the *Journal of the Royal African Society* in which he advocated for the establishment of a national museum in Nigeria which should be populated by returned Benin Bronzes and other removed artifacts.[141] Murray's argument today sounds strikingly modern. He argued that the artifacts taken to Europe have served only an "academic purpose," while if returned to Nigeria they would be in service of "the cultural life of the country itself."[142] He also demanded that any objects returned to Nigeria "must contain first-rate works, not those which remain after the cream has been taken by foreign museums."[143] Of course, Murray's demands should be considered within their own colonial subtext. After all, he was advocating the return of objects from other empires to a British colony, therefore elevating overall British stock of artifacts and reducing that of its competitors, primarily Germany.

Some of the Benin Bronzes taken to Britain have indeed made their way back to Nigeria, though not as restitution, but instead as sale. In the early 1950s, the British Museum sold some twenty Bronzes to the Colonial Government in Nigeria (in close coordination with Kenneth Murray) in preparation for the establishment of the National Museum in Lagos.[144] In 1950, the British Museum head of ethnography Hermann Braunholtz

139 Lundén, "Displaying Loot," pp. 170–71; Ivanov, "African Art."
140 Lundén, "Displaying Loot," p. 175.
141 Murray, "Art in Nigeria."
142 Murray, "Art in Nigeria," p. 247.
143 Murray, "Art in Nigeria," p. 247.
144 Lundén, "Displaying Loot," p. 169, also pp. 436—440.

informed the Museum Trustees that, out of his Benin collection, "about 30 are to all intents and purposes duplicate specimens, and therefore surplus to the Museum's requirements."[145] He recommended a sale to Nigeria as "there are hardly any in the country," but also because the sale proceeds could be used for the purchase of other desirable artifacts for the British Museum's collection. After offering a few Bronzes to a London dealer to test the price, the British Museum sold additional Bronzes to Nigeria in 1951 and 1953.[146] Nigeria, therefore, was made to pay back Britain for the artifacts Britain looted in 1897.

Further, it has become evident that the British Museum has been selling some of its Benin Bronzes to dealers and other museums as late as 1972, which would seem to be in clear violation of the 1963 British Museum Act that prohibits "deaccessioning" of its collection—the main official reason the museum refuses to restitute the Parthenon Marbles. That it was willing to get rid of "duplicates" (which today curators understand to be matching pairs, and so the British Museum in fact divided a unified artwork) of some art and not of others makes the invocation of the British Museum Act seem disingenuous. Even more damning is that the British Museum appears to have still been purchasing Benin Bronzes as late as 1986, well after there was hardly any question about their provenance and in clear violation of, by then, a firmly established international normative framework regarding acquisition and display of looted art.[147]

Restitution and status-seeking in the Cold War

But while Great Britain was holding onto these objects as symbols of its high international cultural status, for Nigeria, an independent state since 1960, the Bronzes were highly desired symbols of national identity and cultural heritage, the building blocks of statehood. Once again, the status value of the Bronzes had changed. Their value remained political, but they were now critically important for nation-building of a postcolonial state. Of course, restitution of cultural heritage was important to decolonizing states beyond just Nigeria. Reclaiming cultural heritage was a major element of decolonization, as the return of the artifacts would demonstrate the capabilities for "maintaining the cultural infrastructure necessary for sovereignty and the construction of a modern state."[148]

[145] Bailey, "British Museum."
[146] Bailey, "British Museum."
[147] Phillips, *Loot*, p. 239, n. 47.
[148] Bellisari, "Art of Decolonization," p. 642.

Art again played a major role in international status-seeking and state claims for recognition. It is in this specific political context that in 1966, Senegal hosted a major art exhibition, *The World Festival of Negro Arts* (*Art Nègre*), which was meant to present precolonial African art and culture to the world and demonstrate its international cultural significance and value.[149] The exhibition was first mounted in Dakar, Senegal, and then, with some controversy, traveled to Paris. Nigeria was a major participant in the project and here again, the Benin Bronzes played a big role in Nigeria's construction of its international cultural status. For the purposes of the *Art Nègre* exhibition, the Nigerian Federal Ministry of Information published a special issue of the magazine *Nigeria Today*, which was distributed in English and French. On its cover, the magazine carried the image of the Benin Queen Idia mask held at the British Museum. The headline, to make the message clear to all *Art Nègre* visitors, was "Our Cultural Heritage."[150]

It is within this international political context that Nigeria's efforts to repatriate Benin Bronzes should be understood. By the 1970s, various actors in Nigeria had already made repeated efforts to collect the dispersed Benin objects from various collections around the world. The government built a new museum in Benin City, and yet the museum had so few artifacts to display that, in 1972, Ekpo Eyo, a highly respected Nigerian scholar and director of the Nigerian Federal Department of Antiquities, sent an official request to the countries that possessed Benin Bronzes to repatriate some of their collections.[151]

The responses were predictable. From Austria came a message that the Benin Bronzes in possession of the Ethnological Museum in Vienna had been obtained legally and so there was no basis for restitution. Austrian officials also ruled out any loans to Nigerian museums, citing concerns regarding conservation. They did, however, suggest that Nigerian scholars might want to travel to Vienna to conduct research, but, of course, at their own expense.[152]

Eyo then met with the representatives of West Germany in Lagos and asked their assistance in facilitating a permanent loan of Benin Bronzes to Nigeria. His hope was that West Germany would see this as a relatively cheap way to signal cooperation with the Global South at the height of the Cold War. The prospect of restitution of Benin artifacts from Germany was greatly complicated by the realities of the Cold War and Germany's division into East and West. In fact, to a great extent, the governments in both East (GDR) and West (FRG) Germany used art restitution negotiations as an international status-claiming mechanism themselves. For example, East Germany

[149] On the broader significance of this exhibition, see Murphy, *First World Festival*.
[150] Savoy, *Africa's Struggle*, p. 9.
[151] Lundén, "Displaying Loot," p. 209.
[152] Savoy, *Africa's Struggle*, p. 19.

used its legacy collections of Benin Bronzes at the Museum of Ethnography in Leipzig to project its cultural status on the international stage. In 1971, the GDR postal authority issued a commemorative stamp displaying a "memorial head in the Udo style," which was a sketch of a Benin Bronze head in the collection of the Leipzig museum. The caption of the image read "German Democratic Republic. Ethnographic Museum Leipzig. African Bronze Head" (*Deutsche Demokratische Republik. Völkerkundemuseum Leipzig. Bronzekopf Afrika*), making sure that the holdings of such internationally valued artifacts are clearly marked as belonging to the GDR.[153]

On the West side, initially, the FRG government was in favor of restitution. In a letter to the president of the Prussian Heritage Foundation, the FRG Foreign Office noted, "Our embassy in Lagos supports the Nigerian request *for political reasons*, as they are convinced that Nigeria is surely unlikely to let the matter rest, considering its ever increasing awareness of its own tradition and culture, and that this might possibly develop into an unpleasant point of contention for us."[154] Indeed, the FRG Foreign Office was under considerable pressure to show interest in and good relations with Nigeria, as part of a Cold War status positioning vs. the East. Showing and, often, performing solidarity with the Global South was a routine feature of Cold War status-seeking politics.[155]

France, also, was using cultural politics to foster friendly relations with the Global South. In 1981, on an official visit to the People's Republic of Benin, French Minister of Culture Jack Lang compared, somewhat incoherently, the struggle of Africans against colonialism with the struggle of France to maintain its own culture, which was apparently under assault by US hegemony: "This is the same struggle, between us who want to defend our independence and you who also want to protect your culture and identities."[156] This performance of solidarity with the Global South was a clear strategy by the government of French socialist president François Mitterrand to build alliances across the world, preserve "special relationships" with its formal colonies, and bypass the increasing political domination of the "Anglo" (US/UK alliance), which the French perceived as, if not existentially threatening, then certainly extremely irritating.[157]

French interest in appearing to be a good ally of newly decolonized francophone Africa went beyond just speeches and led to concrete action. In 1982, the French Ministry of Foreign Affairs established an interdisciplinary working group that included scholars, government officials, and museum

[153] Savoy, *Africa's Struggle*, p. 17.
[154] Quoted in Savoy, *Africa's Struggle*, 16, emphasis added.
[155] Subotić and Vucetic, "Performing Solidarity."
[156] Lang, Cotonou speech.
[157] Schraeder, "Cold War to Cold Peace"; Kroslak, "France's Policy."

curators to discuss restitution of artifacts held in French museums.[158] The "Working Group of Africa" came up with a decidedly pro-restitution policy, much ahead of its other European peers:

> Based on the conviction that the return of cultural property is an act of solidarity and justice which, if it is properly understood and carried out well, will contribute not only to the restoration of and respect for the respective national cultural heritage, but will also demonstrate that this heritage, by remaining accessible to all, is part of the world heritage.[159]

While Western Europe was beginning to fracture in its hitherto unified front against restitution, East Germany was caught between a strong desire to keep its own Benin treasures in museums in Leipzig and Dresden but also to not appear as a traitor to the socialist cause. The GDR minister of culture elaborated this East German predicament in 1982:

> The GDR however also needed to take into account in its position vis-a-vis [*sic*] developing countries that the criterion of legality alone was often insufficient when faced with bourgeois-imperialist legal systems, especially from a foreign policy point of view, because this is tantamount to sanctioning bourgeois practices of looting. There is therefore . . . a danger of being seen by the developing countries as aligned with Imperialist states.[160]

Culture, therefore, was seen as an important vehicle for geopolitical influence at the delicate time of decolonization, and the FRG Foreign Office in 1972 implored the Prussian Heritage Foundation's leadership to seriously consider the importance of this political outreach: "There is no doubt that a positive gesture from us at this point would meet with great approval from many Africans in this phase of their cultural self-determination."[161] The leaders of the Foundation were unmoved by political concerns and instead argued that Nigeria's request and others that might soon follow would lead to the emptying of West German museums. The response speaks so directly to the question of international status that it is worth quoting at length:

> our main task [is] conserving our holdings, regaining losses, and raising Berlin to a cultural site of the highest rank, where excellent museum collections form a harmonious whole, with an exemplary presentation based on today's museum standards. Recurring wishes for donations and permanent loans which we continue to receive

[158] Savoy, *Africa's Struggle*, p. 122.
[159] Quoted in Savoy, *Africa's Struggle*, p. 122.
[160] Quoted in Savoy, *Africa's Struggle*, p. 123.
[161] Quoted in Savoy, *Africa's Struggle*, p. 20.

> from a variety of parties, make our work so much harder . . . Berlin's ethnological collections in Dahlem are on the point of receiving worldwide recognition. We keep hearing words of praise and gratitude from visitors from the countries where the collections originated, for preserving and maintaining with meticulous care a cultural heritage as a cohesive ensemble that has often been forgotten in the countries of origin. We are delighted that our collections form an excellent means of international understanding.[162]

What is remarkable about this position is that it makes it explicit that the value of these art objects for this national cultural institution, and by extension, for the FRG state, was in their location in Berlin. It is these objects that "raise Berlin to a cultural site of the highest rank" and give the city and the FRG its coveted international cultural status. Removal of the art from Berlin would diminish that status. As we shall see later in the chapter, in the 2020s, the value of these same objects for the German state was no longer in their location in Berlin, but its exact opposite—Germany elevated its international cultural status by returning them to Nigeria. But back in 1972, Nigeria's request was denied.

Museums vs. diplomacy

Nigeria's push for restitution continued, even in the face of continuous denials. In 1977, the Festival of International Black Art (FESTAC) was held in Lagos, as a follow-up to the 1966 Dakar World Festival of Negro Arts. The festival was to promote "black and African cultural values and civilization" and was a massive event organized and backed by the full apparatus of the Nigerian state. Artists from forty-eight countries, including international stars such as Stevie Wonder, performed.[163] FESTAC was to project postcolonial Nigeria's economic, political but also, critically, its cultural status. "We are no longer the Third World. We are the First World," boasted the festival's president Ochegomie Promise Fingesi.[164] To host the event, a new cultural center was constructed in Lagos. As a sign of global East–South relations, the building was designed and built by Bulgaria, as the small East European communist state was also using cultural capital to elevate its status abroad.[165]

The Benin Bronzes came to dominate this festival as well. Without consultation with their Senegalese partners, and to their significant annoyance, the Nigerian organizers selected the Benin Queen Idia mask as the

[162] Quoted in Savoy, *Africa's Struggle*, pp. 25–26.
[163] Phillips, *Loot*, p. 230, n. 2.
[164] Apter, *Pan-African Nation*, p. 21.
[165] Dragostinova, *Cold War*, p. 204.

festival's logo.[166] The logo was reproduced in all festival programs, marketing materials, and on banners and billboards throughout Lagos. This move then immediately positioned Nigerian, but also more broadly black and African art, as still a hostage of European colonialism, symbolized by the Benin Bronzes extracted from Africa and kept in Europe.

Diplomatic relations became even more heated after Nigeria asked the British Museum for a loan of the Queen Idia mask to display as the central art piece of the FESTAC. The museum declined the request, claiming the mask was "too fragile for transport."[167] Nigerian newspapers were extremely critical of the British Museum's rejection, with many articles accusing Britain of continuing its colonial policies. One author derided the museum's decision as an example of "poor, small Britain's history of international brigandry and thieving, in the tradition of Drake and Rhodes."[168] So incensed were Nigerians about this snub that the famous Nigerian writer the Nobel Laureate Wole Soyinka admitted in his 2005 autobiography that he advocated for stealing the Benin mask from London,

> The mask was stolen property and the aggrieved had a right to reclaim their property by any means. What I proposed instead was that a task force of specialists in such matters, including foreign mercenaries if necessary be set up to bring back the treasure—and as many others as possible—in one swift, once-for-all-time, coordinated operation.[169]

Just as in the case of West Germany discussed earlier, state and museum interests also collided in Britain. While the British Museum made the final decision, the British Foreign Office was in fact in favor of the loan for political reasons. The Foreign Office believed the loan to be a gesture of Britain's goodwill toward the Commonwealth and tried to persuade museum officials, ultimately unsuccessfully, to reconsider. From the objectives of British foreign policy, using the loan was a useful way to appease Nigeria, which was Britain's largest export market in the Global South at the time of Britain's financial crisis at home. More specifically, the Foreign Office feared that major deals with Nigeria, including arms deals, infrastructure contracts, and oil revenue would all be jeopardized over a simple ivory sculpture: "the affair is bound to damage our relations in almost every sphere,"

[166] Savoy, *Africa's Struggle*, p. 60. Also Malaquais and Vincent, "PANAFEST."
[167] Lundén, "Displaying Loot," p. 209. Also Coombes, "Ethnography, Popular Culture," p. 154.
[168] Phillips, *Loot*, p. 232, n. 13.
[169] Soyinka, *You Must Set Forth at Dawn*, p. 24. The fantasy of stealing back looted art from a fictionalized British Museum is, of course, the famous opening scene of the Marvel 2018 blockbuster film *Black Panther*. In the book's Conclusion, I come back to some of the contemporary performance art heists of looted art from European museums.

wrote British diplomats in a 1976 memo.[170] British Foreign Secretary David Owen was personally invested in the issue, arguing, "[the mask's] return would undoubtedly contribute more than any other gesture in improving Anglo-Nigerian relations."[171] But the British Museum was unmoved.

Back in West Germany, the government considered itself somewhat immune to the pressures to decolonize its museums that were beginning to build on Great Britain or France (and that the Netherlands and Belgium had by that point already begun to act upon). In preparation for the 1982 UNESCO meeting in Mexico City, the FRG Foreign Office prepared a brief for the German cultural delegates in which it described its state "as an efficient industrial nation without aspirations of domination or a colonial past."[172] German UNESCO Commission also continued to exert pressure on German museums to, if not fully restitute African art, then at least cooperate with African museums on joint projects: "These measures will greatly benefit the prestige of the Federal Republic in the long term, while the costs involved are relatively low."[173] The German Museum Association resented this approach and threatened to "use every means at its disposal to fight purely politically motivated tendencies to yield to restitution demands."[174]

This interesting split between the government and museums points to two things. First, art restitution was always considered an issue of political merit, and governments were aware that they could score important foreign policy points by being open to restitution requests. But second, these examples show that the frequent defense of retentionism by major world museums—"we would restitute if it wasn't for state pressure"—are often, in fact, quite the opposite. Sometimes, the state pressure was for restitution, but it was the museums that were intransigent. As we shall see, very similar objections emerged after the French president Emmanuel Macron in 2017 announced France's willingness to restitute, only to have French museums recoil.

After the end of the Cold War, Nigerian officials continued to demand restitution, even as most of their action resulted in failure. In 1991, Oba Erediauwa led a campaign that successfully collected one million signatures from various public figures all over the world demanding the return of the Bronzes. Realizing that the previous attempts by UNESCO to reignite the restitution issue have failed, the Pan African Movement of Nigeria, an international group dedicated to the maintenance and renewal of African culture,

[170] Quoted in Phillips, *Loot*, p. 232, n. 20.
[171] Quoted in Phillips, *Loot*, p. 234, n. 28.
[172] Quoted in Savoy, *Africa's Struggle*, p. 119.
[173] Quoted in Savoy, *Africa's Struggle*, p. 76.
[174] Quoted in Savoy, *Africa's Struggle*, p. 78.

coordinated the campaign with the Oba as the public-facing figure. The campaign made posters with pictures of some of the Bronzes under the banner "We Want Our Treasures Back" and distributed them in Nigeria and abroad.[175]

And then in the 2000s, some European museums that held the Bronzes slowly began to act on their own. In 2007, the Weltmuseum Museum in Vienna put up a major international exhibition, *Benin Kings and Rituals* and invited Oba Erediauwa to write the Preface to the exhibition catalog. In a passionate text, the Oba again appealed to "the people and the government of Austria [to] show humaneness and magnanimity and return to us some of the objects" still held in Austria.[176] The Vienna exhibition and the involvement of Nigerian representatives then led to the establishment of the Benin Dialogue Group, the first official multilateral international working group that included representatives from the Western museums (including major holders of the Bronzes, such as the British Museum, Berlin's Ethnology Museum, Vienna's Weltmuseum, and Oxford's Pitt Rivers Museum), as well as officials from the Nigerian government, the Royal Court of Benin, and the Nigerian National Commission for Museums and Monuments.

After a number of meetings, the Benin Dialogue Group agreed to organize a series of exhibition loans on a rotating basis that would bring the Bronzes from Western museums to the future Royal Museum in Benin City. Not authorized to speak on behalf of governments, the Group could not negotiate permanent restitution, only temporary loans, and this produced a degree of impatience and exasperation among Nigerian restitution activists: "Sometimes it looks like everyone is dancing around the main point," complained Victor Ehikhamenor, a Nigerian artist and a leading voice for restitution.[177]

And while the Benin Dialogue Group focused on loans and began to develop a protocol for how this cultural exchange would work, the new president of France decided to make art restitution a centerpiece of his foreign policy. The debate was no more about how to organize loans. Now, the focus was on permanent restitution.

Mr. Macron goes to Africa

In the contemporary debates about restitution, Emmanuel Macron's speech in Burkina Faso in November 2017 is often discussed as a watershed event.

[175] Shyllon, "Cultural Heritage Legislation," p. 251.
[176] The speech was printed in the exhibition catalog, Plankensteiner, *Benin Kings and Rituals.*
[177] Hickley, "Digital Benin."

Macron's wide-ranging speech attempted to reframe the role of France in Africa, by pledging new cooperation and solidarity, joint cultural and economic ventures, and relationships based on mutual respect instead of exploitation. The new French president was setting a new agenda for France, one in which relations with Africa were central—"Africa is carved into France's collective memory, in its culture, in its history, in its identity," Macron said.[178] The importance of Africa for France, of course, is not new, and has been a central feature of French foreign policy and its national identity since at least the nineteenth century. As Daniela Kroslak observed, "France needs Africa for its own image just as much as Africa needs France."[179] What Macron intended to do was initiate the most significant "reset" of French–African relations since decolonization in the 1960s.[180]

But while the speech itself was otherwise not particularly remarkable as it followed in a long tradition of French officials claiming solidarity and collaboration with their former African colonies (as was the case with Jack Lang discussed earlier), where Macron made the headlines was in his pivot to culture as a possible path to achieving these goals: "The first remedy is culture. In this area, I cannot accept that a large share of several African countries' cultural heritage be kept in France." Again suturing African culture onto the French, Macron declared, "your history, your heritage and, if you will allow me to say so, *our heritage*."[181] And then, the bombshell: "within five years I want the conditions to exist for temporary or permanent returns of African heritage to Africa."[182] Perhaps most unexpectedly, the French president then followed up by commissioning a report from two highly respected scholars—the Senegalese author and economist Felwine Sarr and the French art historian Bénédicte Savoy—and asked them to prepare a blueprint for how France could responsibly return African cultural objects back to their origin communities.

But there is what Macron did for global art restitution, and what he did for France. Macron made the engagement with the issues of colonialism and its memory in contemporary France a centerpiece of his presidential rhetoric. This shift, while still often limited, created a more discursive space for discussions of French colonial past.[183] This was important for France

[178] Emmanuel Macron's speech at the University of Ouagadougou, Burkina Faso, November 28, 2017, https://www.elysee.fr/en/emmanuel-macron/2017/11/28/emmanuel-macrons-speech-at-the-university-of-ouagadougou.

[179] Kroslak, "France's Policy," p. 66.

[180] Lebovics, "In the Diaspora," p. 109.

[181] Macron's speech.

[182] Macron's speech, emphasis added.

[183] Hassett, "Rupture and Reconciliation," p. 5.

as its relationship to its colonial past has been suspended in time and largely unprocessed.[184] France's new direction would then distinguish it from its European rivals, most obviously Great Britain, which lagged behind in acknowledging continuing legacies of colonialism. Art objects held in French museums now had a new kind of value—they were status symbols of France as an exemplary postimperial state, one that treated its former subjects with equality and dignity. Macron's commitment to art restitution in 2017, then, also symbolically rewarded the French state for acknowledging its implication in colonialism without, in fact, explicitly acknowledging its violent history and enduring legacies. Macron's memory project, then, can be understood as a strategy that "recognizes the past to exonerate the present."[185] More pragmatically, French bold action on restitution was also a clear attempt to re-establish France as a major actor in Africa that could stem the tide of increasing Chinese economic and political involvement. Re-engaging with African art, for France, was also a form of holding off other states' political influence through the domain of culture.

The Sarr–Savoy Report, published in November 2018, was initially mandated by Macron to deal specifically with the African collections at the Musée du quai Branly in Paris, as this museum alone held 67,000 African objects. The authors, however, provided a much broader assessment of French responsibility to restitute artifacts to African countries, and also introduced a far-reaching, revolutionary restitution agenda that would encompass not just French museums and Africa, but all of colonial heritage in world museums. Starting from a devastating assessment that 90 percent of all African cultural property is held in museums or private hands outside of Africa, the Sarr–Savoy Report concludes that full and immediate restitution should occur for all objects taken in punitive expeditions, such as the one on Benin, as well as all objects taken in "scientific expeditions" between the Berlin conference (1885) and the start of decolonization in the 1960s.[186]

The Report was much anticipated in both the Global South, where local scholars and museums were waiting to hear if they should begin preparations for a massive art transfer, but also in the museums in the West, which were bracing for a major earthquake. In France, reactions were mixed. Some scholars embraced the report and its ambitious agenda for creating a new "relational ethics" between Western museums and communities where the art originated. But there were also many, and vocal, critics of the report. The newspaper *Le Monde* accused the authors of taking an extremist position;

[184] Löytömäki, "Law and Collective Memory"; Lotem, *Memory of Colonialism.*
[185] Hassett, "Rupture and Reconciliation," p. 9.
[186] Sarr and Savoy, "Restitution of African Cultural Heritage," p. 57.

Le Figaro of attacking prestigious French institutions of cultural heritage. Former Minister of Culture Jean-Jacques Aillagon argued from a universalist position that French museums served a global function and were preserving African art for all the world to see.[187] The French Academy of Fine Arts took a similar universalist position, issuing a statement in support of circulation of artifacts, but not their full restitution.[188]

French museums, in general, have been quite opposed to revisiting the colonial provenance of their collections and have put forward a narrative that often portrays French colonialism's "positive aspects," such as, for example, Musée du quai Branly's statement that its collections benefited from "expeditions aimed at drawing up an inventory of the material cultures of the world."[189] On whose behalf and with whose support these expeditions went around the world, the museum did not say.

The conservative art press repeated the benevolent French colonialism narrative, as, for example, in this article published in the French art magazine *La Tribune de l'Art*,

> Let us be clear-headed, Africans should appreciate the fact that Europeans knew how to preserve a heritage condemned to disappear. Without the collectors, the 99% of objects [found] in Europe would have almost all disappeared, victims of ignorance, termites, and religious burnings of all kinds. African art, which has always been taken out of the ritual context, has left all Africans in total indifference, was it not the commercial value that it represents.[190]

Stéphane Martin, former president of the Musée du quai Branly, the main object of the report, dismissed its sweeping recommendations, disparaged its authors' scholarly credentials, and verbalized the worry of many in the traditional museum sector that "heritage will become the hostage of memory."[191] Directors of large museums outside of France were also critical. For example, the director of the Museum of Archaeology and Anthropology in Cambridge Nicholas Thomas wrote that Savoy and Sarr flattened the imperial cultural experience and ignored "accommodation, collaboration, innovation and interests on both sides in traffic in ideas and objects."[192] Some German museum directors used the report to do professional status politics of their own by claiming that German institutions had already been more advanced than France on issues of provenance research.[193]

[187] These examples are taken from Paquette, "France and the Restitution," p. 309.
[188] L'Académie des beaux-arts, "Restitution du patrimoine."
[189] Duhennois, "Restitution," pp. 126–27.
[190] Groux, "Restitutions," quoted in von Oswald, "Restitution Report."
[191] Rea, "French Museum Director."
[192] Hunt, Dorgerloh, and Thomas, "Restitution Report."
[193] von Oswald, "Restitution Report."

And then there was the issue of how the report was actually going to be implemented. Acting on the report, in July 2020 the Macron government submitted to the French Parliament the Draft law on the restitution of cultural goods to the Republic of Benin and to the Republic of Senegal. This cleared the path for the restitution of twenty-seven artifacts to the two West African countries.[194] Governments of Madagascar, Ivory Coast, Ethiopia, Mali, and Chad had also put in requests for restitution of their art from France.[195] Restitution was beneficial for the political elites of recipient countries as well. The return of the artifacts to Benin (in 2022) was a clear political success for the repressive regime of this country, while the return of the artifacts to Senegal (in 2019) was accompanied by a major arms deal and an additional financial loan from the French Development Agency.[196]

More broadly, the French approach to restitution also soon transformed into a form of development aid. Under the project "African Heritage: Realizing together our new cultural cooperation," French Culture Minister Franck Riester announced a series of subsidies by the French Development Agency toward museum and heritage initiatives in Benin and Ethiopia as an "innovative solution" to questions of restitution. Full and unconditional restitution as envisaged by the Sarr–Savoy Report was slowly beginning to look like a much more conditional development assistance.[197] Art extracted from outside of sub-Saharan Africa (the only focus of the Sarr–Savoy Report) remained outside of the French restitution debates and the momentum for their restitution was stalled through bureaucratic entanglements and never-ending cycles of expert commissions that recommended the creation of additional commissions.[198] In fact, the projects of actual implementation of the report followed the largely established French postcolonial project of *FranceAfrique*, a commitment by France to continue to exert influence in its former colonies.[199]

Bronzes after Sarr–Savoy

Sarr and Savoy wrote passionately about the importance of local communities experiencing and admiring their own ancestral art and the continuing injustice of being deprived of this experience as artifacts are under lock in Western museums:

194 Objects being restituted to Benin are not to be confused with the Benin Bronzes that, if restituted, would go to Nigeria. Rea, "France Has Approved."

195 Nayeri and Onishi, "Looted Treasures."

196 Hassett, "Rupture and Reconciliation," p. 15.

197 Paquette, "France and the Restitution," pp. 312–13.

198 Slyomovics, "Commissioning Memorial Reconciliation."

199 Lebovics, "In the Diaspora," p. 111.

> To fall under the spell of an object, to be touched by it, moved emotionally by a piece of art in a museum, brought to tears of joy, to admire its forms of ingenuity, to like the artwork's colours, to take a photo of it, to let oneself be transformed by it: all these experiences—which are also forms of access to knowledge—cannot simply be reserved to the inheritors of an asymmetrical history, to the benefactors of an excess of privilege and mobility.[200]

What the report did was, once again, transform the value of these status symbols. Their continuing ownership in Western museums has turned them into contemporary objects of shame, into international stigmata. The Sarr–Savoy Report fundamentally changed the debate about restitution, and directly influenced the destiny of the remaining Bronzes beyond France—particularly in Germany, Belgium, the Netherlands, Sweden, and also slowly, and begrudgingly, in Great Britain.[201]

Germany acted first. In anticipation of the Sarr–Savoy Report, in July 2018, the German Museums Association published the "Guidelines for the Care of Collections from Colonial Contexts," which mostly dealt with provenance research and less with restitution.[202] The message here was that Germany was changing its attitude toward objects of art acquired during colonial violence. "How can museums and collections justify having objects from colonial contexts in their collections, whose transfer to Germany contradicts our value system of today," asked German cultural officials.[203] To follow up, Germany expanded the mandate of the state Lost Art Foundation, which was set up in 2015 to investigate provenance of Nazi-looted art, to now also include colonial-looted art.[204] But this was not enough.

Local German debates were heating up regarding the planned opening of the Humboldt Forum, which was to house a large collection of artifacts extracted during the era of German colonialism, including the world's second largest collection of Benin Bronzes. Bénédicte Savoy resigned from the advisory board of the Humboldt Forum in protest at its continuing display of colonial-looted art, and famously asked, "how much blood is dripping from a work of art?"[205] Germany was also involved in long-standing bilateral

[200] Sarr and Savoy, "Restitution of African Cultural Heritage," p. 4.

[201] And it wasn't just the states. Nongovernmental organizations joined the global momentum for restitution as well. In 2019, the Open Society Foundation founded by George Soros announced its own plan to "strengthen efforts to restore cultural objects looted from the African continent" with a 15-million-dollar commitment to groups working on restitution of art to Africa. Open Society Foundation, "Open Society Pledges."

[202] German Museum Association, "Guidelines."

[203] Quoted in von Oswald, *Working through Colonial Collections*, p. 277.

[204] German Lost Art Foundation, "Confronting Colonial History."

[205] Bowley, "New Museum."

negotiations with Namibia regarding the return of human remains collected during Germany's genocide of the Herero and Nama people between 1904 and 1908.[206]

In the context of international pressures generated by the Sarr–Savoy Report and growing domestic calls for reckoning with colonial crimes, in 2019 Germany announced a much more ambitious set of guidelines for the return of artifacts taken from former German colonies. The agreement pledged, "All people should have the opportunity to meet their rich material cultural heritage in their countries and communities of origin, to interact with it and pass it on to future generations."[207] The guidelines asked museums to create detailed inventories of their collections and make them publicly available to allow for claims of restitution.

While these moves by Germany are the result of domestic activism and broader reassessment of Germany's past, they are also clearly indicative of Germany's desire to maintain its "global reputation as a normative model for democratic confrontations with difficult pasts."[208] This, again, is an issue of status—Germany's moral status as the leader in acknowledgment politics, an externally recognized status that has become a core of German self-identity.[209] Germany has worked hard to establish itself as the leader in Holocaust remembrance; it was now time for it to lead the way when it came to legacies of colonialism as well.[210] Restitution of Benin Bronzes was a good way to accomplish this goal.

In April 2021, Germany announced that it would return a "substantial" number (around 1,000) of the Bronzes from its collections, most held at the Humboldt Forum in Berlin, and the rest in museums in Berlin, Stuttgart, Cologne, Leipzig, and Hamburg, back to Nigeria. The agreement included permission for Germany to participate in archaeological excavation in Nigeria, provide training for local curators, take part in the construction of a new museum in Benin City, and most importantly, repatriate the Benin Bronzes.[211] Finally, Germany was leading the way—its announcement was the first by any state that also included a detailed timetable of when restitution would take place. Monika Grütters, Germany's minister of culture, expressed this clearly, "We are facing the historical and moral responsibility to bring Germany's colonial past to light and to come to terms with it . . . Dealing with

[206] Boehme, "Normative Expectations," p. 9.
[207] Schuetze, "Germany Sets Guidelines."
[208] Bach, "Colonial Pasts," p. 58.
[209] Bachleitner, "Ontological Security."
[210] On broader issues of Germany as a postcolonial state, see Schilling, "German Postcolonialism."
[211] Hickley, "And So It Begins."

the Benin Bronzes is a touchstone."[212] Hartmut Dorgerloh, the director of the Humboldt Forum, announced that the Forum was prepared to "exhibit only replicas or leave symbolic empty spaces" in preparation for the full return of Bronzes to Nigeria.[213]

All of this placed tremendous pressure on British museums to reconsider their opposition to restitution. While some smaller museums—the Horniman Museum in London or the Bristol Museum—expressed an interest in working within the framework offered by the Benin Dialogue Group, the British Museum, with its world's largest collection of Benin Bronzes, remained mum. That the British Museum owned more than 900 Bronzes, of which only a hundred are displayed and the rest hoarded in storage, made its silence that much more deafening (Figure 4.3).

In October 2021, the British Museum received the official request for the return of its collection of Benin Bronzes from Nigeria's Federal Ministry of Information and Culture. The museum acknowledged the request, put it on its webpage dedicated to "contested objects from the collection," but then responded vaguely to the request by reaffirming its commitment to working through the Benin Dialogue Group.[214] The museum did, however, significantly update the captions on one information panel describing Bronzes, which now referred to the collection as "Benin: Colonial Conquest and Military Looting."[215]

And while these narrative changes were responses to increasing social pressures to decolonize its collections, they also drew the ire of Britain's conservative government. British Culture Secretary Oliver Dowden went on the attack against museums revamping their permanent exhibitions, accusing them of pandering to the "noisy woke brigade who are trying to challenge all aspects of our history."[216] In a letter to museums, Dowden also expressed his opposition to the return and removal of contested objects and advised them not to get involved in activism or politics or else risk government funding.[217] And yet, some old opponents of restitution had a change of heart. In a surprise, the conservative newspaper *The Times* came out for the restitution of the Bronzes: "Where it can be shown—such as in the case of this Benin

[212] Marshall, "Germany Sets Out Plans."
[213] Oltermann, "Berlin's Plan."
[214] British Museum, "Contested Objects."
[215] Author's visits to the British Museum, May 2022 and February 2024. Also see Lundén, "The Benin Bronzes."
[216] James, "Culture Secretary."
[217] Letter from Culture Secretary on HM Government position on contested heritage, September 22, 2020, https://www.gov.uk/government/publications/letter-from-culture-secretary-on-hm-government-position-on-contested-heritage.

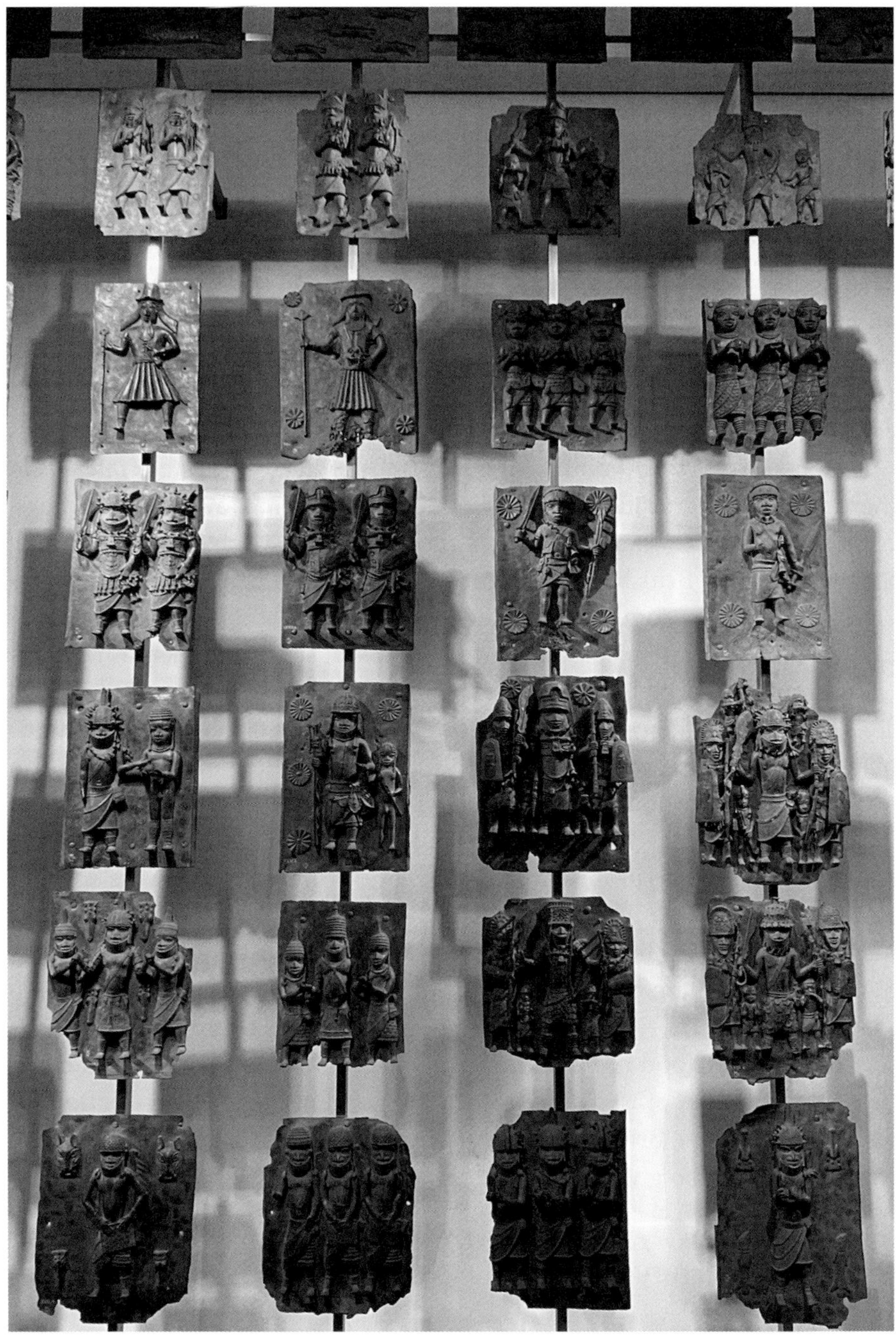

Figure 4.3 Display of Benin Bronzes, the British Museum (photograph by author)

bronze—that the removal of the piece was a criminal act, then repatriation should be the primary objective."[218]

Following similar national recommendations on restitution issued by Germany, the Netherlands, and other states, in 2023, the Arts Council England finally issued its own, overdue guidelines for museums. But the document "Restitution and Repatriation: A Practical Guide for Museums in England" was a much different kind of program.[219] It did not recommend restitution of looted colonial art held in English museums, but instead provided only a highly technical guide for museums to prepare for incoming restitution claims, and how to assess and process them. It was a statement of bureaucratic operating procedures, not a statement of a new set of standards and values. Great Britain was not ready.

It is also worthwhile noting how differently the British state reacted to the possibility of restituting the Benin Bronzes from how it reacted, and continues to react, when it comes to the Parthenon Marbles. In the case of the Marbles, the British government never seriously considered appeasing Greece, and any geopolitical goodwill gained by the gesture of repatriation was simply not discussed. And this is because the Parthenon Marbles were so fully absorbed into the idea of British cultural heritage that Britain considered them their own—and not something that Greece had any legitimate claims on. As I discussed at length in the previous chapter, this is also because, from the moment Elgin brought the Marbles to Britain, they were incorporated into the British national autobiography that claimed its roots in classical Greek civilization. The Marbles, in other words, were inalienable because they were already British. The Benin Bronzes, of course, were never integrated in the same way into the British self-understanding of its own heritage. Britain certainly did not trace its "civilizational roots" back to the Edo of Benin. British continuing possession of the Bronzes, therefore, should be understood more within the context of British self-professed status as the guardian of world heritage, manifested in the grand collections of world objects at the British Museum. This position, it seems, the British state was more willing to give up.

Bronzes' journey home

Looking at these developments through the lens of international status politics, France started the status competition, which motivated Germany to step up, which put pressure on other states to react so as not to have their

[218] "The Times View."

[219] Available at https://www.artscouncil.org.uk/supporting-arts-museums-and-libraries/supporting-collections-and-cultural-property/restitution-and-repatriation-practical-guide-museums-england.

own cultural status brought into question. And react they did. In 2020, the Netherlands published its own recommendations on the return of looted art to its former colonies.[220] Then came Belgium in 2022, with its bilateral agreement on restitution with its former colony, the Democratic Republic of Congo.[221] The United States did not produce a national plan for restitution, but some of its public museums, such as the Smithsonian Institution, published their own new guidelines and pledged repatriation. In a big ceremony in 2022, the Smithsonian returned twenty-nine Bronzes to Nigeria, and was joined by the National Gallery of Art in Washington, DC and the Rhode Island School of Design, which also handed over their Benin pieces.[222] The Metropolitan Museum of Art returned two of its own Bronzes in 2021.[223] The Penn Museum in Philadelphia has also agreed to repatriate its Benin Bronzes and has in the meantime revamped its display to clearly note the violent manner in which they were extracted.[224]

In Great Britain, the first Benin Bronze to be restituted to Nigeria did not come out of any government or major museum recommendation or report. It came from student activists at Jesus College at the University of Cambridge, who successfully lobbied the university to return a bronze cockerel.[225] Other smaller UK institutions decided to restitute Bronzes on their own, not waiting on the government to act. In October 2021, a day after the ceremony at the University of Cambridge, the University of Aberdeen in Scotland returned their own Benin Bronze to Nigerian representatives.[226] In April 2022, Glasgow City Council voted to return seventeen Benin Bronzes held in various city museums.[227] And in November 2022, the Horniman Museum in London became the first large UK public institution to return a significant part of its Benin Bronzes collection to Nigeria.[228]

And while many states increasingly realized that their Bronzes had to go back, saying goodbye proved hard. These artifacts were incorporated into their own cultural heritage through more than a hundred years of ownership but, more important, through active cultural appropriation and colonial and postcolonial cultural messaging. They *became* British, and German, and Austrian objects. These countries, now faced with strong winds of restitution,

[220] Summary of Report Advisory Committee on the National Policy Framework for Colonial Collections, https://www.raadvoorcultuur.nl/documenten/adviezen/2020/10/07/summary-of-report-advisory-committee-on-the-national-policy-framework-for-colonial-collections.
[221] Chow, "Inching Toward Restitution."
[222] Smithsonian Institution, "Smithsonian Returns."
[223] Ulaby, "Metropolitan Museum."
[224] Author's visit to Penn Museum, February 2024. Also see Brown and Davenport, "Museum Works to Repatriate."
[225] Khomami, "Cambridge College."
[226] Chow, "After Years of Debate."
[227] Greenberger, "Glasgow to Return."
[228] Sherwood, "London Museum Returns."

hosted farewell exhibitions, bidding them goodbye as they prepared to go back home. For many of these museums, these farewell exhibitions were also the first time their entire Benin Bronzes collections were taken from the storage depots to be displayed to the public. These farewell exhibitions now renarrated the Bronzes in a completely new way—as no longer trophies of war or decontextualized objects of African art, but now as symbols of resistance, longing, colonial violence, or looting.[229] They also clearly narrated the high international moral status of states that are sending the objects back.

In 2021, the Rautenstrauch-Joest Museum in Cologne (originally an ethnographic museum, now a museum of the "cultures of the world"), which holds the fourth largest collection of the Bronzes in Germany, presented its ninety-six Benin objects in the exhibition *RESIST! The Art of Resistance.*[230] The same Benin Bronzes were then presented in a different exhibition *I Miss You* in 2022, where they were narrated as objects of pain, loss, and grief.[231] The exhibition was meant to display the Bronzes as being missed by their creators and their descendants in today's Nigeria. Left unsaid in the exhibit, but implicit in its message, was also the grief Germany will experience once these precious objects are gone.

Hamburg's ethnological museum, the Museum am Rothenbaum (MARKK), organized its own farewell exhibition *Benin: Looted History*, in December 2021. The museum showed its entire collection of 179 Benin objects (bronzes, ivory artifacts, as well as jewelry) in its entirety for the first time in over a hundred years. This time, the Benin artifacts were displayed next to present-day objects and testimonies from citizens of Nigeria expressing their joy at seeing the Bronzes return. This exhibition was a particularly interesting and thoughtful model of recontextualizing both the Bronzes as artifacts but also the role of Germany in the colonial looting and trading. It was prepared by Barbara Plankensteiner, one of the world's leading experts on Benin Bronzes and a member of the Benin Dialogue Group. In explaining her vision behind this exhibition Plankensteiner said, "I want us to say goodbye to these works by once again honoring their quality and significance for a global history of art . . . while at the same time doing justice to their provenance as looted colonial property."[232]

For Germany, the restitution of Benin Bronzes to Nigeria was an issue of high diplomacy and an act that firmly positioned Germany as a leader in restitution implementation. The first group of Bronzes traveled from Germany

[229] Author's visit to Humboldt Forum, Berlin, March 2024.
[230] Available at https://rautenstrauch-joest-museum.de/RESIST-The-Art-of-Resistance.
[231] Available at https://www.rautenstrauch-joest-museum.de/I-MISS-YOU-EN.
[232] Abrams, "Send-Off Exhibition."

to Nigeria in December 2022, chaperoned by none other than Germany's foreign minister. Germany was fully committed to this project. France may have started the ball rolling, but it had yet to truly deliver on the promise of return. Germany did, and in the process managed to produce a subtle jab at France: "Macron took the very French route: a great speech by a great president, then it takes years for reality to match those words . . . We are operating in a German way. It isn't especially sexy, but it can be efficient," said Andreas Görgen, the secretary general of Germany's Federal Culture Ministry.[233]

Important for the purposes of my argument, Germany acted quite clearly out of concerns for its international status. In 2019, then German Chancellor Angela Merkel assembled a group of German historians to discuss the issue of restitution. Historians impressed on the Chancellor that some agreement with Nigeria had to be made prior to the opening of the much-criticized Humboldt Forum, or else "the spotlight of the entire world" would be on Germany and its problematic silence regarding its colonial past. To which Merkel apparently responded, "Then why don't we give them back?"[234]

Once measuring its international cultural status by collecting the Bronzes and competing with its rivals for ownership, Germany was now attaining status by competing with its rivals regarding the speed and completion of return. But Germany was claiming other, broader, changes with the restitution of Bronzes, changes that it also wished to express to the world as a favorable comparison to its international competitors. "This moment is also historic to us. We are facing up to our history of colonialism," said German foreign minister Annalena Baerbock at the restitution ceremony in Abuja.[235] The implication was that those states that refused restitution were not.

Where is home?

The demands for restitution to Nigeria, however, have been gravely damaged by persistent reports of thefts and damage and lack of care and resources in Nigerian museums. While some of these reports might be tendentious and recall the earlier Orientalist perceptions by Western museums and governments, a significant portion of them are accurate and have been well documented.[236] The problems were not reduced only to thefts and illegal trafficking of artifacts from museum collections, but also involved lack of

[233] Quoted in Marshall, Rogers, and Lassa, "How Germany Changed Its Mind."
[234] Marshall, Rogers, and Lassa, "How Germany Changed Its Mind."
[235] Marshall, Rogers, and Lassa, "How Germany Changed Its Mind."
[236] Lundén, "Displaying Loot," p. 173; Nwafor, "Culture, Corruption, Politics."

state funding of basic maintenance and museum infrastructure. By the 1990s, Nigerian museums were shells of what the 1977 FESTAC jubilee promised. The seeming lack of seriousness by the Nigerian government to deal with the suboptimal state of its museums has, then, further solidified the retentionist position of many museums that hold the Bronzes.

And then there is the problem of ownership within Nigeria. While Nigeria asked for the artifacts back, both directly from other states and museums, and also through international organizations such as UNESCO, a major complication regarding restitution of the Bronzes is that there are competing claims to ownership within Nigeria. One claimant is the state of Nigeria, which asserts that it is the international legal descendent of the former Kingdom of Benin after the intervening years of British colonial occupation. But even within Nigeria, there were competing claims made by the Nigerian federal government and the Edo state in which Benin City is located. Yet other claimants are the members of the Royal Edo House—even though the independent Kingdom of Benin de facto ceased to exist after the British punitive expedition in 1897, the royal lineage continued. In the view of the descendants of the royal family, the Bronzes should be returned to them, not to the state of Nigeria.

In 2000, Prince Edun Akenzua (Oba Erediauwa's brother) presented this view to the British Parliament in a memorandum requesting return of the Bronzes to the royal family. He argued, de facto, that the Bronzes were akin to a personal family archive and that this is where they belonged:

> Benin did not produce their works only for aesthetics or for galleries and museums. At the time Europeans were keeping their records in long-hand and in hieroglyphics, the people of Benin cast theirs in bronze, carved on ivory or wood. The Obas commissioned them when an important event took place which they wished to record. Some of them of course, were ornamental to adorn altars and places of worship. But many of them were actually reference points, the library or the archive.[237]

The contestation over who, within Nigeria, has the right to claim the Bronzes has already on numerous times interfered with the plans for restitution. In 2014, Mark Walker, whose grandfather Herbert Walker participated in the 1897 expedition and took many Benin objects, traveled to Nigeria to return these items to the Oba in Benin City. But the Nigerian government, through its representatives at the High Commission in London, requested

[237] Quoted in Stahn, *Confronting Colonial Objects*, p. 163.

that Walker instead hand over the Bronzes to the Nigerian minister of arts and culture in Abuja. Walker refused, and the Oba was incensed at the government's attempt to hijack the event and take the Bronzes.[238]

It is not just the Nigerian state and the royal Edo family that claimed ownership. It was also the descendants of slaves who argued that they should be the rightful owners of the objects their ancestors paid with their lives to make.[239] The New York–based Restitution Study Group (RSG) has filed a lawsuit against the Smithsonian Institution requesting a halt to the museum's restitution of twenty-nine Benin Bronzes to Nigeria. The RSG's argument was that restitution would deny the descendants of enslaved people in the United States from being able to view and enjoy the cultural artifacts their ancestors in the Kingdom of Benin helped create. The court, however, rejected this claim and allowed for the restitution to proceed.[240]

The complexity of ownership claims within Nigeria burst into the open in 2023, following the successful restitution of a large number of Bronzes from Germany. In a move that seemed to have caught Germany off guard, Nigeria's President Muhammadu Buhari issued a decree in March 2023, appointing Ewuare II, then Oba of Benin, the owner and administrator of the returned Bronzes. This decree was in apparent contradiction to the earlier government commitment to finance the construction of a new Benin Royal Museum that would house the treasures in Benin City. What, then, of the announced construction, privately funded, of the Edo Museum of West African Art, for which the world famous architect David Adjaye was commissioned as the chief designer? In indication of further German cultural involvement, it is Germany that was co-financing the new Edo Museum.[241] And then there was the issue of competing ethnic and national loyalties—the Oba insisted that the Bronzes be returned to Nigeria, but to an Edo museum, not a national Nigerian museum.[242]

The restitution of Benin Bronzes remains an issue of international politics. As some states have realized—Germany and the Netherlands through implementation and France through rhetoric—art restitution can be utilized quite effectively in pursuit of international status through the domain of culture. And other states, such as Great Britain, are experiencing status-seeking in a different way—by clinging to the material objects as embodiments of their former empire, as the last vestiges of a former imperial order in which

[238] Phillips, *Loot*, p. 222, n. 5.
[239] Okediji, "On Reparations Exodus."
[240] Aton, "Restitution Organization Sues."
[241] Sevillano, "Legitimate Concerns."
[242] Phillips, *Loot*, p. 288, no. 9.

they were on the top. In that sense they perpetuate "the ongoing colonialism of the object."[243] Refusal to return should, therefore, not be interpreted as a lack of action. Retentionism is also, on its own, a claim of status—of how the state perceives where it is in the international cultural hierarchy (high) and where it considers those that claim restitution to be (low).[244] Britain's steadfast refusal to create a restitution policy akin to those passed by Germany, the Netherlands, Sweden, or France, is a "fantasy of a continued British sovereignty" over its former imperial domain.[245]

And this brings us back to what the Benin Bronzes can tell us about states that possess them. The Bronzes were created as objects of status, they were acquired as objects of status, they were bought and sold as objects of status. They also elevated the cultural status of collectors, museums, and states that owned them. They became so highly valued, both in terms of their artistic and their commercial worth, that over time they were no longer just artifacts, but also "symbols of economic ability and power."[246] And with the changing norms about looted art ownership and display, the Bronzes' value changed yet again, to now represent objects of shame that needed to be returned to avoid their owners' status loss or decline. This change in the value ascribed to them is why contemporary debates about the Bronzes' restitution should be understood as expressions of state status and hierarchies in the international society.

[243] Donington, "Relics of Empire?," p. 126.
[244] For a similar point, see Lundén, "Displaying Loot," p. 113.
[245] Coombes, "Ethnography, Popular Culture," p. 155.
[246] Philip Dark, quoted in Felicity Bodenstein, "Notes for a Long-Term Approach," p. 286.

5
The Pictures

The history of Nazi-looted art is well known and is a source of much popular fascination. Many films, novels, and memoirs have told the story of stolen art, Holocaust survivors' difficult and often demoralizing pursuit to find and reclaim it, and the complex legal wrangling between families, governments, and museums.[1] Nazi looting of art was so extensive—estimates are in the several million unique pieces of art—that it defies imagination.[2] While massive art looting since Napoleon and throughout the era of European imperial expansion in the eighteenth and nineteenth centuries, as described in the previous chapters, populated European museums with innumerable works of art, the systematic looting of art by Nazi Germany during World War II was an effort on an altogether different scale. As the Nazis embarked on the full destruction of European Jewry, they also carried out the systematic extraction of all Jewish cultural property. But the Nazis did not steal only from the Jews; they also took whatever artifacts they wanted from museums in the countries they occupied—from France, Italy, the Netherlands, Belgium, and beyond.

Art looting for the Nazis was both a public and a private effort. Collecting art—through purchasing, looting, or gift exchanging—was an important practice of status-seeking for the Nazi elite, as it provided one of the key elements of the Nazi regime's legitimacy—claims of cultural superiority.[3] The greatest single beneficiary of Nazi art looting was Hermann Göring, who amassed 1,375 paintings, 250 sculptures, 108 tapestries, and 175 other art objects in his countryside home Carinhall, north of Berlin.[4] The speed with which Göring accumulated art was astonishing. Between 1940 and 1944,

[1] For example, films: *Woman in Gold* (2015, dir. Simon Curtis), *The Monuments Men* (2014, dir. George Clooney), *The Art Dealer* (*L'Antiquaire*, 2015, dir. François Margolin); novels: Waldman, *Love and Treasure*; Houghteling, *Pictures at an Exhibition*; memoirs: Goodman, *Orpheus Clock*; De Waal, *Hare with Amber Eyes*; de Perignon, *Vanished Collection*. Nazi-looted art was also the focus of the exhibition *Afterlives: Recovering the Lost Stories of Looted Art* at the Jewish Museum in New York City in 2021–22. Author's visit, December 2022.

[2] Nicholas, *Rape of Europa*.

[3] Petropoulos, "Not a Case of 'Art for Art's Sake,'" p. 108.

[4] Petropoulos, "Not a Case of 'Art for Art's Sake,'" p. 112.

he procured an estimated three paintings each week.[5] For Göring, these looted collections were meant to elevate his professional status and rank as the second most powerful man in Nazi Germany.[6] Göring was extremely proud of his collection until his very last days and bragged to his jailors at Nuremberg in 1945 that he owned the finest private collection of art in all of Europe.[7]

Much of this looting was carried out on direct Hitler's orders as part of his grand ambition to populate his personal Führermuseum, in his hometown of Linz, Austria with the world's best art, as judged by Hitler himself. Permanently obsessed with cultural status, Hitler also wanted to make sure that his collection was not only similar but vastly superior to other European collections of art. After visiting Mussolini in Rome and Florence in May 1938, Hitler realized that his art collection was woefully inadequate in comparison, and the plan to enrich his own museum with Europe's best art intensified.[8] By 1945, the collection for his Führermuseum grew to include 6,755 paintings, including major works by Vermeer, Rembrandt, and Leonardo da Vinci.[9]

The mass removal of art as an integral part of occupation, disenfranchisement and, ultimately, cultural genocide was obviously a central feature of the Nazi Holocaust. But the looting of European art was also in its rationale similar to Napoleon's "civilizing mission" of France, this time driven by Nazi Germany's racialized view of global hierarchy, according to which only Aryan Germany was civilized and culturally sophisticated enough to be the guardian of Europe's culture.[10] Similar to Napoleon, Hitler wanted to collect Europe's "best" art and showcase it in a museum named after himself. But Nazi looting of European art was also guided by the basic desire to show that the highest international cultural status is something that can be accomplished through military conquest, domination, and annihilation of any opposition.

Art and national socialism

Art and cultural policy were major aspects of the National Socialist political project from its inception, and the central theme of this policy was

[5] Wildman, "Revelations."

[6] Evans, "Art in the Time of War," p. 20.

[7] Petropoulos, "Not a Case of 'Art for Art's Sake,'" p. 112. Art collecting—in large part, through looting—was also a major project of Hans Frank, the ruler of occupied Poland, as well as of Joachim von Ribbentrop, the Nazi foreign minister, and Joseph Goebbels, the propaganda chief.

[8] Nicholas, *Rape of Europa*, p. 42.

[9] Petropoulos, "Not a Case of 'Art for Art's Sake,'" p. 110.

[10] Evans, "Art in the Time of War," p. 21.

the promotion of German culture and art. This was practiced through the glorification of art made by German artists, as well as excavation of "roots" of the great Germanic culture through investments in archaeology and art history. This interest in the origins of Germanic art also explains Nazi infatuation with the Old Masters, especially the painters of the Dutch and Flemish seventeenth-century "golden age," as the Nazis attributed the high aesthetic quality of these works to their "Germanic origin."

To recreate the glory of Germanic art in the Nazi worldview, art and culture had to be rebuilt based on racial and cultural purity. In the Nazi cultural vision, only classical art (ancient Greek or Roman) and German romantic or folkloric art were "unpolluted" by Jewish influence. Nazi-approved art was to be easily understood and accessible and it should celebrate life in the countryside, the traditional family, and Aryan beauty ideals.[11] Modern art, on the other hand, was narrated as "an act of aesthetic violence by the Jews against the German spirit."[12] Nazi propaganda chief Joseph Goebbels banned all art criticism in 1936 as it had been "perverted" by Jewish influence.[13] "The art critic will be replaced by the art editor . . . In the future only those art editors will be allowed to report on art who approach the task with an undefiled heart and National Socialist convictions," ordered Goebbels.[14] It was not just visual art—it was literature, music, performance art, theater, film, architecture—that was to be "synchronized" in line with Nazi goals.[15] The Nazi attempt to control all aspects of German arts and culture was, therefore, an effort to create a "total culture."[16]

So much of the priority was establishing the superiority of the German culture that on occasion Nazi projects would clash. For example, the SS had established in 1935 its own archeological unit, the *Ahnenerbe* led by Heinrich Himmler, which was searching for evidence of superiority and ancient origin of the German race.[17] But according to Albert Speer, Hitler's architect, Hitler was annoyed at the unintended consequences of this archeological research, which made Germany appear primitive in comparison to other European nations, and complained:

> Why do we call the whole world's attention to the fact that we have no past? It isn't enough that the Romans were erecting great buildings when our forefathers were still living in mud huts . . . All we prove by that is that we were still throwing stone

[11] Mosse, *Nazi Culture.*
[12] Grosshans, *Hitler and the Artists*, p. 86.
[13] Levi, *Modernist Form.*
[14] Quoted in Nicholas, *Rape of Europa*, p. 16.
[15] Hermand, *Culture in Dark Times.*
[16] Mosse, *Nazi Culture.*
[17] Arnold, "Past as Propaganda."

> hatchets and crouching around open fires when Greece and Rome had already reached the highest stage of culture. We really should do our best to keep quiet about this past.[18]

It is within this desire for internationally recognized cultural status that we should understand the relationship between Nazi ideology and its quest for a specific kind of art.

Already in the 1920s, the Nazi Party adopted the term "degenerate" art (*Entartete Kunst*) to describe modern art (particularly expressionism and abstract art) as something undesirable and alien to German culture, which needed to be eliminated. As soon as they came to power in 1933, the Nazis began to purge art institutions of "degenerate" art, banned modern artists from showing their work, and soon moved to confiscate vast quantities of art they deemed un-German.

In 1937, the Nazis organized a major exhibition of "degenerate" art in Munich, where 650 pieces of modern art, including many that today are considered masterpieces of modernism (paintings by Paul Klee, Wassily Kandinsky, Piet Mondrian, Marc Chagall, among others), were seized from German museums. In a speech on July 18, 1937, at the opening of the exhibition, Hitler declared, "We will, from now on, lead an unrelenting war of purification, an unrelenting war of extermination, against the last elements which have displaced our Art."[19] To the Nazis it did not matter much whether the banned modern artists were, in fact, Jewish or not. Instead, the Nazi policy on "degenerate" art demonstrates the fundamentally constructed nature of antisemitism, where any undesirable quality is considered Jewish and anything Jewish is considered undesirable, and so antisemitism served to reinforce policies in all other social realms. The purpose of the "Degenerate Art" exhibition, therefore, was to inflame the German public against modern art, but also to connect modernism with depravity and depravity with the Jews.

After the exhibition closed, some paintings were publicly auctioned off. Some were purchased by museums, some by private collectors, who were now able to acquire masterpieces for a fraction of what they were worth, even at the time. Göring also often availed himself of looted "degenerate" art, which he would then sell on the secondary art market and use the proceeds to buy his preferred style. Apparently, he was quite pleased with this deal and wrote in his diary that he was to "make some money from this

[18] Speer, *Inside the Third Reich*, pp. 94–95.
[19] Quoted in Nicholas, *Rape of Europa*, p. 20.

garbage."[20] In 1938, the German government formed a Commission for the Exploitation of Degenerate Art, which was to manage the marketplace for these artworks. A number of well-established German art dealers were put in charge of marketing and organizing the sale of this huge collection—almost 16,000 "degenerate" works of art were confiscated from German public collections alone.[21] One of those dealers was Hildebrand Gurlitt. His name will surface again in 2012, when a routine tax inquiry led German investigators into the Munich apartment of his son Cornelius, where a trove of "degenerate" art was discovered in one of the major Nazi-looted art findings in the 2000s.[22] But many of the modernist artworks were lost forever. Already practiced in large-scale book burnings, on March 20, 1939, the Nazis organized the burning of 1,004 paintings and sculptures and 3,825 watercolors, drawings, and prints deemed "degenerate." The destruction took place in the courtyard of the Berlin Fire Department.[23] Some artists and collectors tried to hide some of this art from ruin. Small caches of banned paintings were found in Berlin by the Soviet Army as they marched into the city in 1945, when they promptly seized the art themselves and took it to the Hermitage Museum in St. Petersburg. Much later, in 2010, another cache of banned art was discovered during the construction work on the Berlin underground subway.[24]

The looting of Jewish cultural property

The Nazis began looting Jewish property in 1933, as soon as they came to power in Germany. As the Nazi onslaught on Europe advanced, so did the dispossession and looting of the Jews. The complete Aryanization of cultural property of Austrian Jews, carried out as early as 1938, as well as the looting that followed Kristallnacht in November 1938 in Germany and Austria, provided troves of artworks for the Nazis to dispose of. Directors of German state collections were called in for a meeting in Munich in November 1938 "for a conference about the safekeeping of works of art belonging to Jews."[25] In Vienna, the most valuable was the Rothschild collection which was immediately confiscated. Then came the large collections of Jewish

[20] Nicholas, *Rape of Europa*, p. 23.
[21] Nicholas, *Rape of Europa*, p. 23.
[22] Hickley, *Munich Art Hoard*.
[23] Nicholas, *Rape of Europa*, p. 25.
[24] On Soviet seizures, see Akinsha and Kozlov, *Beautiful Loot*. On the 2010 discovery, see Hickley, "'Degenerate' Art Unearthed."
[25] Nicholas, *Rape of Europa*, p. 43.

families Gutmann, Bloch-Bauer, and many others. SS officers ransacked Jewish homes and took away art, silverware, furniture, and whatever else they could get their hands on.[26]

Many families fled and left their valuables behind, only to be collected by the SS or the neighbors or onlookers. Some Jews tried to ship their art abroad, but customs officials routinely ripped the crates and took the art themselves. Valuables deposited in bank vaults were no longer safe as the Nazi authorities simply ordered banks to open them and empty their contents.[27] Jews who could not escape were soon made to register all their possessions, which provided another easy stream of property for the Nazis to avail themselves of. But even within the Nazi regime there were early disputes as to where the looted art should go. Some Austrian Nazis argued that plundered art from Viennese Jews should remain in Vienna as the art—but not the Jews who owned it—were part of the city's cultural heritage.[28]

Then came the art taken from occupied Czechoslovakia and Poland in 1939. Within the first six months of the occupation of Poland, the Nazis extracted the most valuable art from Polish museums and private collections.[29] As was the case elsewhere, some of this art was sent to Germany to be considered for Hitler's Führermuseum, and some Nazi officials took for themselves. Hans Frank, the governor of occupied Poland, took many pieces for himself and also sent to Hitler 521 items he considered most valuable art.[30]

Frank didn't know much about art himself. His principal aesthetic appreciation of Leonardo da Vinci's *The Lady with an Ermine*, displayed in his private rooms at the Wawel Castle in Krakow after he took it from the Czartoryski Museum, was apparently the way the painting's subject Cecilia Gallerani parted her hair.[31] Instead, he relied on guidance from the Austrian art historian Kajetan Mühlmann. In Jonathan Petropoulos's estimation, Mühlmann was "arguably the single most prodigious art plunderer in the history of human civilization," as he directly guided the looting of art in Austria, and then in occupied Poland and the Netherlands.[32] In his position that carried the pompous title of the Special Delegate of the Reichsmarschall for the Securing of Artistic Treasures in the Former Polish Territories, it was Mühlmann who procured for Hans Frank Raphael's *Portrait of a Young Man*,

[26] O'Connor, *Lady in Gold*.
[27] Nicholas, *Rape of Europa*, p. 39, p. 124.
[28] Petropoulos, *Faustian Bargain*, p. 183.
[29] Radzilowski, "Thieves Stealing from Thieves."
[30] Petropoulos, *Faustian Bargain*, p. 191.
[31] In a particularly vivid description of the painting in Frank's possession, his son Niklas Frank recounts how his father commanded him, while pointing at Leonardo's masterpiece, "this is how you should comb your hair." Sands, *East West Street*, p. 248.
[32] Petropoulos, *Faustian Bargain*, p. 170.

also looted from the Czartoryski Museum in Krakow and never recovered. It is often considered the most valuable unrecovered painting looted by the Nazis.[33] As Nazi armed squads went to collect hundreds of thousands of valuable artworks from Polish museums, homes of Polish aristocracy, as well as churches and other religious sites, they gave their stealing (which they called "securing") a patina of academic inquiry: their work was called "coordinated scientific leadership."[34] Frank was more blunt. In his view of the job, "the Polish lands are to be changed into an intellectual desert."[35]

The complete dispossession of Polish Jews went in tandem with their complete removal from Poland. Everything of value was removed from Jewish homes. Synagogues were burned, Judaica objects, Torah scrolls, and other artifacts either vandalized or stored away for exchange. Frank's wife made regular visits to the Krakow ghetto to buy art and other material objects at bargain prices as the Krakow Jews sold and bartered all their possessions in exchange for food and basic survival supplies.[36] Art and objects the Nazis did not consider valuable were simply destroyed. Many of the artifacts were never returned and continue to be a cause of deep diplomatic rift between Poland and Germany.[37]

Mühlmann also led the art-looting project in the Netherlands. Under occupation, the Dutch Jews were required to take all their valuable possessions, mostly jewelry and art, to a central collection point in Amsterdam. The art was delivered to one of Mühlmann's agencies and was then assessed by his team of experts.[38] As always, Hitler and Göring were given first choice, and after their selection, the rest of the art was put up for sale. The proceeds from these auction sales were collected by the Finance Ministry and went into the war effort.[39]

But the Jews had their art taken in many other ways, in addition to extraction raids. Art dealers who had no qualms working with the Nazis purchased art from Jews under duress and often for a fraction of the artwork's value. Sometimes, Jews sold off their valuables in desperate attempts to leave Germany or other Nazi-occupied countries. Other times, Jewish-owned art was sold at *Judenauktionen*, organized public auctions of Jewish assets.[40] As in other morbid mechanisms of the Holocaust, it was Jewish property, including cultural assets, that were used to finance their own destruction. In fact, it is the looting of Jewish-owned art that in many ways signified a new phase in

[33] Radzilowski, "Thieves Stealing from Thieves."
[34] Petropoulos, *Faustian Bargain*, p. 188.
[35] Quoted in Petropoulos, *Faustian Bargain*, p. 189.
[36] Nicholas, *Rape of Europa*, p. 76.
[37] Manikowska, "Washington Principles."
[38] Petropoulos, *Faustian Bargain*, pp. 194–95.
[39] Petropoulos, "Not a Case of 'Art for Art's Sake,'" p. 114.
[40] Dean, *Robbing the Jews*.

the Holocaust, as the full takeover of Jewish property was a foreshadowing of the Final Solution.[41]

And then the Nazis got to France.

In Paris, the "center of Europe's art"

In 1940, the French museums knew what was coming and they organized a major operation to hide the most valuable art from the incoming Nazi onslaught. The most recognizable art, including the *Mona Lisa* and sculptures *Venus de Milo*, *Winged Victory*, and Michelangelo's *Slaves*, were moved to twelve separate castles outside of Paris, for safekeeping. As the Nazis were approaching, the *Mona Lisa* was moved again, to an old monastery further away from Paris, a safe haven for some 3,000 paintings, the last of which were moved on June 17, 1940, just a few days before France was occupied.[42] On June 30, Hitler ordered that all art objects in France be "safeguarded," which meant confiscated.[43] The French museum officials were also worried that Italy, Germany's ally, would now use the occupation to ask for its own art, looted by Napoleon, back. They were especially worried about the fate of Veronese's *Wedding Feast at Cana*, that had been at the Louvre since Napoleon's sacking of Rome, as I described in Chapter 2. In the end, nothing came of this, and the Louvre sighed a sigh of relief.[44]

Göring was especially interested in art from France as he—like many before—considered France the center of Europe's art, a country with the highest international cultural status. Göring wanted French art for Nazi Germany but also, of course, for himself, and Paris was the epicenter of the international art market. But France was also of particular interest to the Nazis because of the presence of many Jewish art dealerships and collections that dominated the Paris art world and provided an almost limitless reservoir of highly valued art for the Nazis to plunder.[45] Art was taken from individual Jewish homes, like everywhere else in occupied Europe, but also from large Jewish art collections and dealerships.[46] For the Nazis, it was especially unnerving that it was the Jews who were in possession of the best art in France. The Jews were not worthy of living, under Nazism, and they

[41] Hilberg, *Destruction of the European Jews*.

[42] Nicholas, *Rape of Europa*, p. 89. For a full account of the fate of the *Mona Lisa*, see Chanel, *Saving Mona Lisa*.

[43] Nicholas, *Rape of Europa*, p. 120.

[44] Nicholas, *Rape of Europa*, p. 122.

[45] For a particularly vivid and intricate view of Jewish art collecting in France, and its ultimate tragic end, see McAuley, *House of Fragile Things*.

[46] The Rothschild, Rosenberg, Seligmann, Schloss, David-Weill, Kann, Wildenstein, and Veil-Picard collections were some of the most prominent.

certainly were not worthy of disposing of Europe's artworks, these highly valued objects of status.[47]

In the first days and weeks of the occupation, Jewish art dealers scrambled to move or hide their collections. Initially, they had some help from French museum administrators, who agreed to stow away some of the paintings from the Wildenstein, Rothschild, David-Weill, and Kann collections. Other Jewish collectors had to fend for themselves. Peggy Guggenheim hid her paintings in a friend's barn. Paul Rosenberg stored his most valuable pieces in a bank vault near Bordeaux and others in a rented chateau. George Wildenstein deposited his paintings in a bank in Paris and in his house in the countryside. The Rothschild collection was vast and dispersed, and a portion of it was forever lost as one of the family members buried paintings in unmarked sand.[48]

A month into the occupation, the Vichy government passed a law stripping all those who fled France on the eve of the occupation of French citizenship, seizing their property and selling it for the benefit of the Vichy state. This made many Jewish dealers and collectors who fled immediately stateless and their collections the property of the state. But the decree also included immediate Aryanization of businesses and property of the Jews who had remained in France. Their art, also, became "heirless" and immediately confiscated.

In the end, many of the attempts to hide Jewish-owned art were in vain. The Nazis managed to take more than 5,000 art pieces from the Rothschild family collections alone (including such masterpieces as Vermeer's *The Astronomer* and Rembrandt's *The Standard Bearer*), more than 2,500 from the David-Weill collection, and more than 1,200 from the collection of Alphonse Kann.[49] Seizures were followed by Nazi mockery and humiliations. Upon seizing the gallery of Paul Rosenberg, the Nazis moved the "Institute for the Study of the Jewish Question" into its premises.[50] In total, it is estimated that the Nazis took more than 21,000 art pieces from the Jews of France.[51]

ERR and the methodology of plunder

The looting in France went on for the duration of the occupation and was carried out by the special unit, the ERR (*Einsatzstab Reichsleiter Rosenberg*), a Nazi outfit dedicated expressly for the extraction and appropriation of

[47] Feliciano, "Great Culture Robbery," p. 165.
[48] Nicholas, *Rape of Europa*, pp. 91–92.
[49] Feliciano, *Lost Museum*.
[50] Feliciano, "Great Culture Robbery," p. 167.
[51] Petropoulos, "Not a Case of 'Art for Art's Sake,'" p. 111.

cultural property. It was led by Alfred Rosenberg, the chief Nazi ideologue. The ERR was initially tasked with collecting cultural materials by the opponents of the Nazi regime (the Jews, communists, the Freemasons), which were then to be organized in a research institute dedicated to the study of Nazi's enemies.[52] Like many of the Nazis' megalomaniacal plans, this one never materialized, and the ERR was quickly reorganized into a simple plundering unit, with a special eye toward valuable artifacts in Jewish homes and institutions.[53]

The first train-full of the extremely valuable Rothschild collection took off from France to Germany in November 1941. The crates designated with an "H" were to be for Hitler's eyes first, those with a "G" for Göring.[54] If neither Göring nor Hitler were interested, the loot would then be offered to other Nazis down the chain.[55] Göring appointed the well-connected German art dealer Bruno Lohse as his liaison in Paris, and Lohse organized twenty exhibitions of this looted art for Göring's eyes only. Göring made individual trips to Paris on each occasion, to decide the fate of each artwork on display. The most valuable pieces—close to 600 artworks—Göring took for himself. Apparently, Göring's artistic taste was focused on the intersection of "German and nude."[56]

The ERR took the art from the Jews but also from French museums and other public and private collections. The plunder of France was organized as follows. Much of the art collected—now declared heirless—was initially held at the Louvre, but already by October 1941 there was so much of it that a new holding location was selected at a smaller Museum Jeu de Paume.[57] Then, this looted art organized by various categories was shipped to Germany in large transports. That the looting of art was a matter of great priority for the Nazi regime is also evident by the fact that the German foreign minister Joachim von Ribbentrop granted a special team of German art experts the title of "commercial attachés," whose sole job was to research, assess, and buy art in France.[58] In November 1941, the ERR issued a document justifying its confiscation of everything the French Jews owned. Written by Gerhard Utikal, head of ERR operations in Western Europe, this document argues that France, in

[52] Collins and Rothfeder, "Einsatzstab Reichsleiter Rosenberg."
[53] Petropoulos, *Art as Politics*.
[54] Feliciano, "Great Culture Robbery," pp. 167–68.
[55] Petropoulos, *Göring's Man in Paris*.
[56] Nicholas, *Rape of Europa*, p. 146.
[57] The online database "Cultural Plunder by the ERR" assembled by the Conference on Jewish Material Claims against Germany and the United States Holocaust Memorial Museum has an expansive searchable list of material objects looted from French and Belgian Jews that passed through Museum Jeu de Paume. This database includes more than 40,000 items, at https://www.errproject.org/jeudepaume.
[58] Feliciano, "Great Culture Robbery," p. 169.

fact, should be grateful to Germany for liberating it from its Jews. Germany was "safeguarding" Jewish-owned cultural property as "a small indemnity for the great sacrifices of the Reich made for the people of Europe in their fight against Jewry."[59]

If deemed to belong to the banned "degenerate art" category, pieces were held in a special room at the Jeu de Paume, which later came to be known as the "Room of Martyrs" (Figure 5.1). In July 1943, the Nazis staged another large bonfire in the gardens of the museum. A total of 500–600 paintings, including pieces by Pablo Picasso, Max Ernst, Paul Klee, and others were destroyed.[60] But the Nazi occupation authorities did not police French cultural practices to the extent they did in Germany, and they outsourced this to the Vichy regime. This meant that much of the "degenerate art" was freely exchanged on the French art market deep into the occupation, often by the same people who disparaged it, and often without any receipts or records of purchase.[61] This patchwork of policies, authorities, and a network

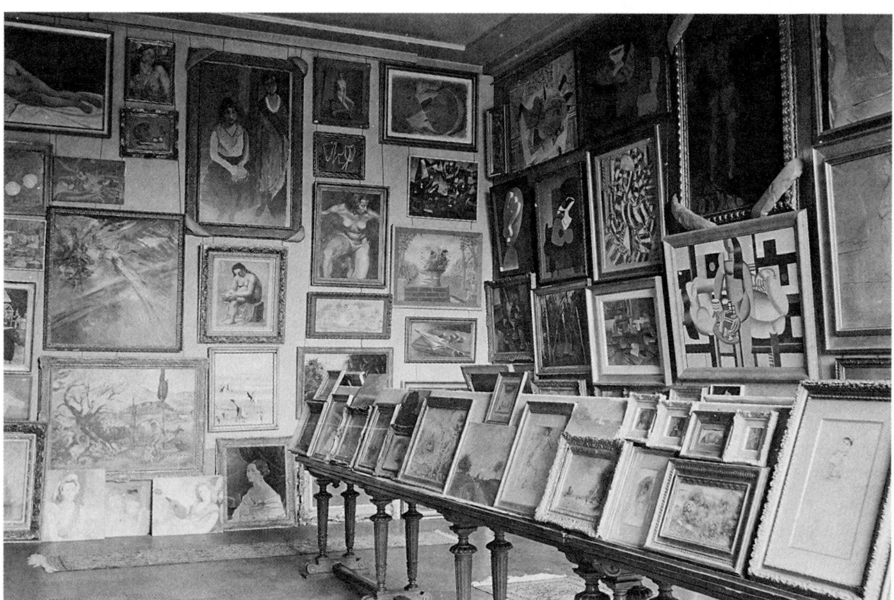

Figure 5.1 "Room of Martyrs" at the Jeu de Paume Museum, 1940 (Archives du ministère des Affaires étrangères, Quai d'Orsay, Paris, France, Catalogue Artcurial 2017, Wikimedia Commons)

[59] Quoted in Nicholas, *Rape of Europa*, p. 137.
[60] Dorléac, *Art of the Defeat*, p. 17.
[61] Petropoulos, *Faustian Bargain*; Nicholas, *Rape of Europa*.

of Nazi-affiliated French and German dealers and auction houses, then, also greatly hindered the postwar process of restitution of looted art to their original owners.

We know much of the details of the art-looting operations in Paris from a remarkable employee of Museum Jeu de Paume, Rose Valland. Working as an assistant curator at the museum, Valland realized quickly that she was witnessing the systematic plunder of art in France and a wholesale takeover of all Jewish cultural property. Unnoticed by the museum officials and Nazi occupying authorities, Valland meticulously documented each individual transport of artifacts that arrived to Jeu de Paume, compiled detailed inventory lists, and noted where the packages containing art were arriving from. Her wealth of knowledge of the Paris art scene also helped her immediately identify paintings from the major Paris art dealerships and collections. Working tirelessly, often overnight and on no sleep, Valland managed to document the provenance of some 20,000 works of art that passed through Jeu de Paume.[62] It is without question due to her heroic efforts that much of this art eventually found their way to their owners after the war.[63]

The volume of looted art from France alone is staggering. The final ERR report from July 1944 shows twenty-nine shipments of art to Germany from Paris that included 120 railway cars, which carried 4,170 crates of art.[64] In total, at least 100,000 pieces of art were taken from France to Germany. This means that one third of all art held in private French collections had been confiscated by the ERR, or as many as during all of the Napoleonic wars.[65]

Nazi art looting as international status politics

Not everyone in the German establishment approved of the looting. There was some opposition within the higher ranks of the Wehrmacht, as some

[62] On Valland's efforts, see, for example, Cœuré, "Cultural Looting"; Dorléac, *Art of the Defeat*. A comprehensive documentary film focusing on Valland is *Rose Valland, The Art Spy* (2015, dir. Brigitte Chevet). A fictionalized account of her activities at the Jeu de Paume is in Houghteling, *Pictures at an Exhibition*.

[63] In an interesting gendered aside, much has been made in subsequent research about her efforts of the fact that she was "unimposing," "unattractive," and basically invisible. She was also queer. Nobody noticed her around or figured out that she understood and read German and was engaged in an astonishing act of cultural protection and a dangerous act of resistance. It is, obviously, a testament to deep sexism that permeated her world that made her invisible to the Nazis. Unfortunately, sexism also permeated the early scholarship about this period and made Valland's role unappreciated for so long. Catrone, "A Feminine Legacy"; Campbell, "Monuments Women and Men."

[64] Special Staff for Pictorial Art Report of Work during the Period from October 1940 to July 1944. Prepared by Robert Scholz of the ERR. This document was entered into evidence at the International Military Tribunal at Nuremberg as PS-1015. It is available in the National Archives, file Office of United States Chief of Counsel: Trial Address "Plunder of Art Treasures" and Related Documents, NAID: 74,127,444.

[65] Feliciano, "Great Culture Robbery," p. 166.

officers in charge of "art protection" complained (truly grotesquely, considering the extent of Nazi mass atrocity) that the extensive looting was hurting Germany's international reputation.[66] Claims to reputation notwithstanding, German museums profited mightily from looting and dubious under-sales, and went on a spending spree. Many valuable artifacts could be bought for a good price, some directly in France, some in Switzerland, which became a major site of art exchange. Throughout the war, German museums would proudly announce in the newspapers their new acquisitions, which included antiquities, but also paintings, and even, on occasion, a painting by a modernist or a Jewish artist.[67]

The German museums' acquisitions were not completely random. In 1940, Goebbels sent the director of the Berlin museums Otto Kümmel and his team to France to make a list of all the art Germany claimed was historically looted by France from Rhineland, now part of the German Reich. The massive document, *Memorandum and Lists of Art Looted by the French in the Rhineland in 1794*, included a 300-page-long list of "works of art and valuable objects which since 1500 have been transferred to foreign ownership, either without our consent or by questionable legal transactions" from all German lands. The list included thousands of art pieces, including some that Hitler desperately wanted for his Linz Museum—Albrecht Dürer's *Self Portrait* and a number of Rembrandt paintings. Kümmel concluded his report with the statement that so overwhelming had the French looting been throughout history that, "it is questionable, if the entire French patrimony will suffice to replace these losses."[68]

These competing claims on cultural heritage have been especially vicious in the history of German–French relations. During World War I, France issued its own report of all the art France considered its own that was in possession of Germany (Dürer's paintings were on this list as well) and demanded its restitution as part of the Versailles Treaty negotiations on account of Germans' poor "artistic taste."[69] Twenty years later, it was the Germans claiming cultural superiority.

Nazi plundering of Jewish cultural property was, of course, not done by the ERR alone. The French police was instrumental in the destruction and dispossession of French Jewry. A specialized French–German unit was outfitted to raid Jewish art dealerships and private collections.[70] Jewish-owned art was,

[66] Nicholas, *Rape of Europa*, pp. 124–25.
[67] Feliciano, "Great Culture Robbery," p. 172.
[68] Nicholas, *Rape of Europa*, pp. 121–22.
[69] Nicholas, *Rape of Europa*, p 123.
[70] Jewish Digital Cultural Recovery Project, https://jdcrp.org.

therefore, looted by the Nazis but also by the French. Regardless of whether the art was officially deemed "degenerate," both the Germans and the French understood its value and wanted it for themselves. Art, again, was a claim of status. The French museums, also, wanted to keep looted Jewish property *in France* (while not returning it back to the Jews), and there was significant conflict between French museums, French authorities and the German occupation force regarding ownership and control of these large quantities of looted artifacts.

The seizure of the Schloss collection from France is indicative of this status competition.[71] As the ERR was closing in on the large Schloss holdings, the Louvre got involved and tried to block the German plan by invoking the possibility of "preemptive acquisition"—pre-purchasing the art to prevent it from leaving France. The Vichy Commissariat-General for Jewish Affairs (CGJA) was also concerned that too much of the seized Jewish property was being taken by Germans when, in fact, it belonged to Vichy France. So was the newly formed French Committee of Sequestration and Liquidation, which tried to keep heirless cultural property in France.[72] The Vichy authorities, of course, did not have a problem with Jewish dispossession, only with the fact that it was the Germans, and not the French, who were profiting from it.[73]

This concern for French cultural heritage played a role in the seizure of the Schloss collection in August 1943. The physical confiscation of the large collection from a bank vault in the French countryside and its transfer to Paris was carried out mostly by the CGJA, with local French police assistance. Now that the Vichy authorities possessed the collection, they had to act fast to prevent Germany from taking it over and incorporating it into Hitler's Führermuseum in Linz. This is where the Louvre came in, asserting the Schloss collection to be "culturally significant" for France and an indelible part of French cultural heritage. The collection was also internationally important for French cultural status: "specialists around the entire world" valued it and so it "should not be 'sold or removed from France without the Louvre keeping some key pieces,'" passionately argued Louvre's wartime director of paintings René Huyghe.[74]

[71] This presentation of the Schloss case is based primarily on Nicholas, *Rape of Europa*, pp. 172–73; Campbell Karlsgodt, *Defending National Treasures*, pp. 218–27, and Masurovsky, "Fate of the Adolphe Schloss Collection."

[72] Nicholas, *Rape of Europa*, p. 136.

[73] The French were more successful at keeping stolen Jewish art in the "unoccupied zone" in the South. This is where parts of the Rothschild family collection were found in an abandoned truck and immediately requisitioned by French museums. Nicholas, *Rape of Europa*, p. 136.

[74] Campbell Karlsgodt, *Defending National Treasures*, p. 222.

How significant was maintaining this collection for France, even under occupation and as a firm ally of Nazi Germany, is evident by the personal involvement of the Vichy Prime Minister Pierre Laval in this affair, who appointed the Minister of National Education to negotiate the retention of some of the Schloss collection at the Louvre. But not all the Schloss paintings remained in France. A much larger number—262 paintings—still ended up on a shipment to Germany after all. Jean-François Lefranc, a shady French art dealer who was personally involved in Aryanization of French Jewish cultural property and profited massively from its liquidation, claimed credit, "I should also be congratulated since most of the paintings in this collection are going to the museums of a country with an old culture, our neighbor."[75] Germany, for French collaborators, was close enough to French cultural status, that it was worthy of its stolen art.

Art dispersal at war's end

In August 1944, as the Allies were closing in on Paris, the ERR organized a massive shipment of French artworks to Germany. A total of forty-eight crates carrying close to 1,000 looted paintings, including priceless works by Cézanne, Degas, Gauguin, Picasso, Toulouse-Lautrec, and other artists, many of whom the Nazis designated as "degenerate," were put on a train to the East. Rose Valland informed the French Resistance of the shipment and the contents of each wagon. The Resistance railroaded the tracks which stranded the train north of Paris. On August 27, the Free French forces sent a small unit to secure the train. By extraordinary coincidence, the commander of the unit was Alexandre Rosenberg, the son of the French art dealer Paul Rosenberg, a large part of whose collection was on the train.[76] Alexandre Rosenberg was thus able to secure his own family's looted art, as well as hundreds of other paintings and return them to Paris for safekeeping.[77]

The Schloss paintings taken by Germany in 1943 ended up in the Führerbau storage facility in Munich, which served as a halfway station for

[75] Quoted in Masurovsky, "Fate of the Adolphe Schloss Collection."

[76] Nicholas, *Rape of Europa*, p, 292. This story is depicted in the 1964 film *The Train* (dir. John Frankenheimer), starring Burt Lancaster and Jeanne Moreau. While imprecise in many historical details, the film was important, as it was the first representation of the problem of Nazi-looted art in popular culture after the war. This was the point made by Marianne Rosenberg, Alexandre Rosenberg's daughter, in a webinar on the legacy of Rose Valland organized by the Sousa Mendes Foundation I attended on February 20, 2022.

[77] Not all of the Rosenberg collection was saved, however. To this day, the Rosenberg heirs are searching for several paintings that have never been recovered. Hickley, "Family Recovered"; Cohen and Mashberg, "Family, 'not Willing to Forget.'" For a family memoir of the search for the missing Rosenberg collection, see Sinclair, *My Grandfather's Gallery*.

looted art on its final journey to the Führermuseum in Linz. But by April 1945, the Allied forces were approaching Munich and the Nazi guards in charge of the facility left the post. For a few days before the US Army secured the premises, the Führerbau was unguarded and local civilians came and went, looting whatever they could find inside. A total of 1,000 paintings stored at the Führerbau were looted.[78] Out of the 262 paintings from the looted Schloss collection, ninety-eight were discovered circulating in and out of Munich, in the hands of locals who held on to them in the hope of exchanging them for other kinds of valuables. Out of a total of 333 paintings taken from the Schloss family, only 162 were eventually restituted to the Schloss heirs, while seven further paintings are subjects to legal claims.[79] The fate of 164 paintings from the collection is unknown.

As the Allied bombing increased in 1944 and the Germans began to retreat, they abandoned some of the looted art and hid it in various salt mines, cellars, castles, monasteries, schools, and other hiding spots, including a master trove of looted art deposited in the salt mine Alt Aussee near Salzburg, Austria. When the US Third Army discovered Alt Aussee on May 8, 1945, they found more than 100,000 art pieces, including some of Europe's major artworks, such as Jan van Eyck's fifteenth-century Ghent Altarpiece, Michelangelo's *Madonna of Bruges*, and thousands of other paintings and sculptures, taken mostly from Vienna and Paris.

Meanwhile, as the Soviet troops advanced across Central and Eastern Europe, their special art recovery units, the Trophy Brigades, searched for abandoned looted art and then, simply, seized it.[80] More than 3 million artifacts and objects were thus captured and taken to the Soviet Union—four trainloads of art were shipped from Germany to the Hermitage Museum in St. Petersburg and almost 3,000 crates to the Pushkin Museum in Moscow.[81] Regardless of where it was taken, as I describe later in the chapter, a lot of World War II looted art ended up in Eastern Europe after the war. The massive geographic dispersion of this art across the continent and across many different collections, public and private, then, further complicated efforts at restitution. After the war, about a million and a half Soviet-looted artifacts were returned to East Germany.[82] The rest was dispersed across illicit art markets, but much remains in Russia today.[83] Some estimates put the number of artworks looted from Germany by the Soviet troops as high as 1 million.[84]

[78] Lauterbach, *Central Collecting Point.*
[79] Connolly, "Nazi-Looted Painting."
[80] Akinsha, "Stalin's Decrees."
[81] Akinsha and Kozlov, *Beautiful Loot*, p. 164.
[82] Evans, "Art in the Time of War," p. 22.
[83] Evans, "Art in the Time of War," p. 22.
[84] Loudis, "Haul of Shame."

The Monuments Men (and women) in Munich

The issue of catastrophic cultural destruction and looting was clear to the Allies already during the war. In 1943, the Roosevelt administration formed the American Commission for the Protection and Salvage of Artistic and Historic Monuments in Europe (often referred to as the Roberts Commission after its chairman, the Supreme Court Justice Owen Roberts). The commission was guided by "the concern felt by the United States Government and by artistic and learned circles in this country for the safety of artistic treasures in Europe, placed in jeopardy by the War."[85] The commission then recommended the formation of the Monuments, Fine Arts, and Archives program (MFA&A), recruited US cultural experts to the unit, and structured it as a branch of the US Army. The MFA&A's initial work was focused less on restitution and more on cataloging major European cultural sites and creating maps to distribute to Allied forces so that they could avoid targeting them.[86] Britain formed its own version of the commission soon thereafter and the two groups of experts began to work together. Also in 1943, the Allied forces put together a joint document, the *Inter-Allied Declaration Against Acts of Dispossession Committed in Territories Under Enemy Occupation or Control*, signed by seventeen governments pledging to prevent and monitor cultural looting.[87]

The issues of cultural status featured prominently in the discussions about the conduct of the war. Allied command was receiving an increasing number of reports of cultural destruction that its operations were causing in Europe. Especially worrisome was the destruction of sites in Italy from Allied bombing raids. Experts from the Roberts commission warned that "this damage to Italian heritage would surely tarnish the reputation of Allied armies," which led Dwight Eisenhower, who by then was Chief of Allied Command in Italy, to warn the troops that Italian cultural sites "had shaped 'the civilization which is ours,'" and so wanton destruction of Italian culture was destruction of the civilizational values over which the war was fought in the first place.[88] Even during the conduct of the war, therefore, some countries were clearly recognized as states with high international cultural status. In addition to Italy, this status was also conferred on France. One of the

[85] Press release, "The American Commission for the Protection and Salvage of Artistic and Historic Monuments in Europe," August 20, 1943, NARA RG 331. Quoted in Campbell, *Museum Worthy*, p. 49, n. 9.

[86] This program was popularized by the 2014 film *The Monuments Men*. For a number of historical inaccuracies in the film, see Campbell Karlsgodt, "What's Wrong with This Picture."

[87] Campbell, *Museum Worthy*, p. 49.

[88] Strategic conduct of the war, however, often was in contrast to these lofty goals, and the Allies on numerous occasions destroyed or severely damaged cultural sites in pursuit of military objectives. Campbell, *Museum Worthy*, pp. 52–53.

pamphlets distributed to the US troops on the eve of the June 1944 invasion of Normandy read, "France is a great country . . . justly proud of her past achievements and of her enormous contribution to the political, scientific and intellectual progress of humanity."[89]

In the immediate aftermath of the war, the small staff of the MFA&A pivoted to work on restitution. The unit's intense but short-lived work was to collect, catalog, and distribute Nazi-looted art discovered all over Europe back to its countries of origin.[90] Of course, it was not just the Allies who worked on restitution. The Jewish community led its own efforts through the Jewish Cultural Reconstruction (JCR), an organization headed for a while by Hannah Arendt, which mandate was to manage and distribute heirless Jewish cultural property.[91] In 1944, the US created another agency, the Art Looting Investigation unit, placed under the Office of Strategic Services. Working together with the MFA&A, this agency prepared records of art theft and included them in indictments for war crimes and crimes against humanity at the Nuremberg Trials in 1945–46.[92]

To organize and coordinate the cataloging and matching of looted art pieces with their states of origin, the Allies established the Central Collecting Point (CCP) in Munich in the building that formerly housed the Nazi Party headquarters. Truckloads of art being discovered daily were then driven to Munich (the massive Alt Aussee collection began to arrive in June 1945) and the tiny staff of the MFA&A carried out the incredibly difficult and painstaking work of figuring out what art was there, what was its condition and, more important, who did it belong to.[93] Rose Valland was also instrumental in this operation as the MFA&A staff worked off her inventory lists to recover art looted from France.

Not everyone agreed that all of the looted art should be returned. A small group within the US government advocated transfer of some of the art from Germany to the United States as a form of "restitution in kind." This idea

[89] Supreme Headquarters Allied Expeditionary Force (SHAEF), "France: A General Survey to Be Read in Conjunction with the Handbook for Civil Affairs (France)," March 1944, NARA RG 331. Sounding much like contemporary TripAdvisor warning to American tourists, the pamphlet also warned the French "may sometimes seem surly and ungrateful even to their friends because of what they have suffered." Quoted in Campbell, *Museum Worthy*, p. 55.

[90] Sandholtz, *Prohibiting Plunder*, p. 155.

[91] Schidorsky, "Hannah Arendt's Dedication." For more background on the debates about JCR activities and divisions within the Jewish community about what to do with it, see Gallas, "Locating the Jewish Future."

[92] Sandholtz, *Prohibiting Plunder*, p. 152.

[93] Nicholas, *Rape of Europa*, pp. 358–61, Sandholtz, *Prohibiting Plunder*, p. 154.

came from the United States Group Control Council for Germany (USGCC) and was approved by President Harry Truman in July 1945. But the MFA&A staff rebelled. John N. Brown, Advisor on Cultural Matters for the Office of Military Government for Germany, wrote back a searing memo which presented this issue in the context of US reputation and its own claims to cultural status:

> The taking of masterpieces of art . . . which have been part of GERMANY'S national cultural heritage for years past . . . seems to the writer, and to his associates in the MFA&A Branch not only immoral but hypocritical. . . . All through the operational phase of the MFA&A it was constantly said by our officers in the field that the US Army had established this service in order to preserve and protect works of art and not for the purpose of carrying them off to the USA, as was often accused by our Allies as well as by enemy propaganda. To have the German propaganda turn out to be true would indeed be humiliating.[94]

But Brown's complaint was ignored, and a collection of 202 paintings from Germany arrived in New York on December 6, 1945, and from there was placed into storage at the National Library in Washington, DC. This move was very controversial even within the military and caused consternation and vehement objection by art historians and much coverage in the press. The United States was beginning to look like a looter itself. In the end, a compromise was reached. The paintings would be returned to Germany, but before they left, they would be shown at exhibitions in cities across the US, for the American public to enjoy and the proceeds of tickets to go to a fund for German children. This exhibition then toured the US to great success and was seen by 10 million people in twelve US cities.[95] The paintings went back to Germany in 1949.

The MFA&A had to deal with a staggering volume of art objects. By October 1945, 13,000 items were cataloged at the CCP in Munich alone. The Munich operation was often chaotic, as experts from France, Netherlands, Belgium, and other countries that requested their art returned mingled with the MFA&A staff. Things slipped, and mistakes were made. One of those mistakes—the erroneous shipment of an heirless "restitution" package to Yugoslavia on false pretenses by a conman art dealer—is one of the central stories of this chapter.

[94] Quoted in Sandholtz, *Prohibiting Plunder*, p. 162.

[95] Sandholtz, *Prohibiting Plunder*, p. 162; Nicholas, *Rape of Europa*, p. 405.

A fraud in Munich

On December 30, 1948, a man claiming to be the restitution official sent by the government of Yugoslavia showed up at the CCP in Munich with a list of 166 art objects he claimed were looted by the Nazis from Yugoslavia.[96] None of this was true. While he had connections at the Yugoslav Military Mission in Berlin, where he lived, he was not a Yugoslav restitution agent. He was a Croatian conman art dealer Ante Topić (also known as Mimara) who had by that time already been on the other side of the law.[97] The objects were not looted in Yugoslavia but instead had originated from the Göring and Hitler collections after being looted from Jewish dealerships or bought through Nazi shady art exchange deals in France, Italy, Germany, and elsewhere. They were being stored at the Munich depot after arriving from Alt Aussee and two other smaller Nazi hiding spots. Topić, of course, could not have known which paintings were in Munich without the inside help of a German art historian Wiltrud Mersmann, who worked as a junior curator at the CCP and helped compile the list for Topić after his successful romantic approach (the two later married).[98] M. H. McCord, the US Chief Reparations and Restitution Officer on the ground, approved the Topić claims on April 20, 1949, and on June 2, 1949, most of the art objects on the list were loaded onto trucks arranged by Topić and departed for Belgrade in four separate shipments (Figure 5.2).[99]

That something was wrong with this restitution case became apparent very soon. Within a year, the French government filed a claim for fifty-four items that Topić stole, showing documentation that they had been looted from France and should be returned. In a letter to the Yugoslav Military Mission in Berlin on June 1, 1950, Frank J. Miller, Office of Military Government of the United States (OMGUS) Property Division Chief, raised the concern that a wrong shipment had been sent to Yugoslavia. Miller notified the Yugoslavs that of the 166 items shipped to Yugoslavia only three (later it turned out it was only two) were indisputably of Yugoslav origin, while the rest had been

[96] The list included 56 paintings, 50 rugs, 2 tapestries, 2 crosses, 38 items of silver, 12 items of metal, 3 glasses, 1 manuscript, 1 group of coins, and 1 silver bar. National Archives, Record Group 260: Records of U.S. Occupation Headquarters, World War II, Series: Restitution Claim Records, File Unit Yugoslavia: Erroneous Restitution General Information, NAID: 34,716,204.

[97] In 1928, Topić stole a medieval ivory diptych from the Zagreb Cathedral and sold it to the Cleveland Museum. After its origins were discovered, the Cleveland Museum returned it in 1936 to the Zagreb Cathedral, where it still resides. Akinsha, "Ante Topic Mimara."

[98] Alford, *Herman Göring*, pp. 169–70.

[99] Letter from M. H. McCord, Chief, Reparations & Restitution Liaison Officer, OMGUS to Otto Yanisch, Officer of Military Government for Bavaria, Restitution Branch, April 20, 1949, National Archives, Record Group 260, NAID: 34,716,204.

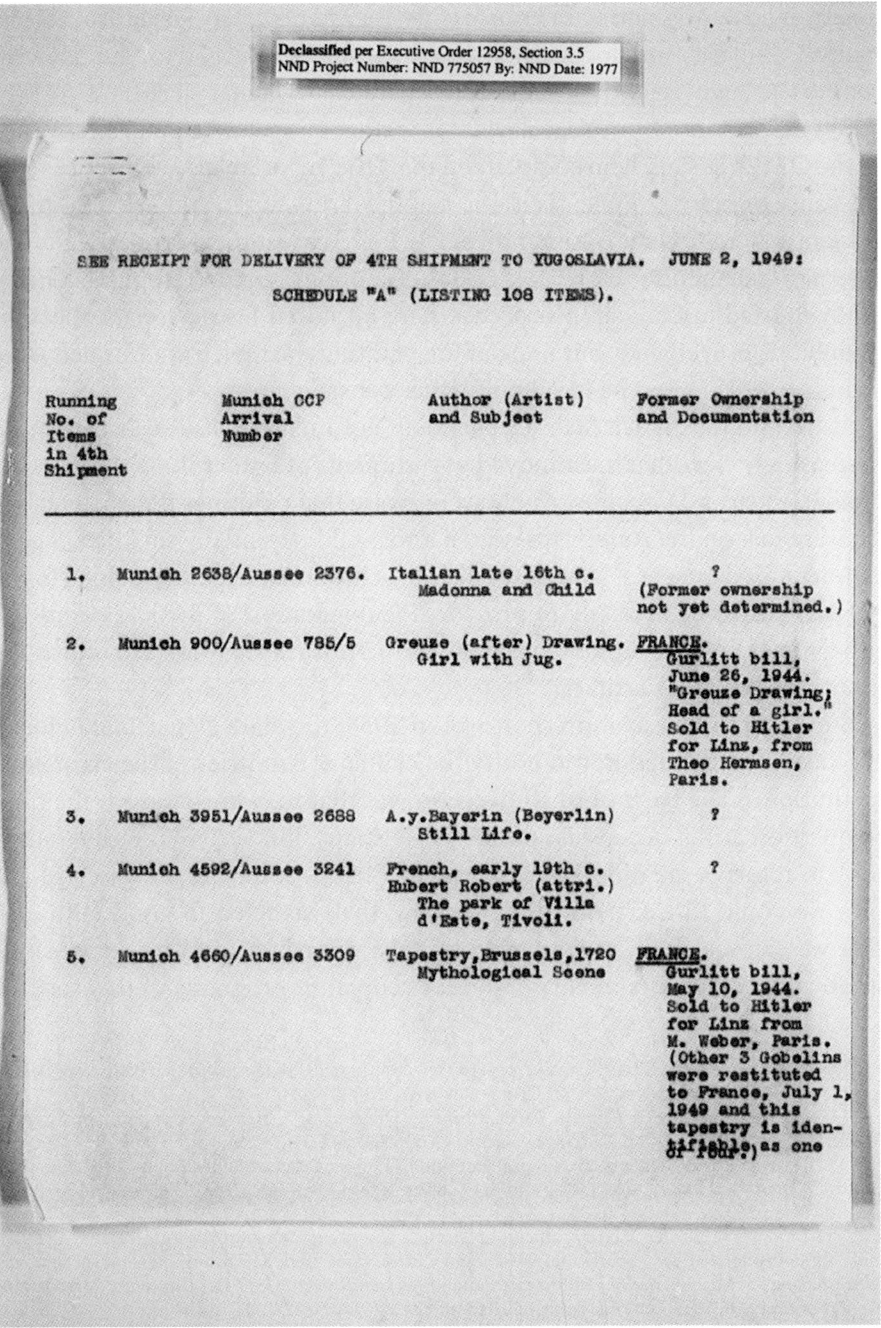

Declassified per Executive Order 12958, Section 3.5
NND Project Number: NND 775057 By: NND Date: 1977

SEE RECEIPT FOR DELIVERY OF 4TH SHIPMENT TO YUGOSLAVIA. JUNE 2, 1949:

SCHEDULE "A" (LISTING 108 ITEMS).

Running No. of Items in 4th Shipment	Munich CCP Arrival Number	Author (Artist) and Subject	Former Ownership and Documentation
1.	Munich 2638/Aussee 2376.	Italian late 16th c. Madonna and Child	? (Former ownership not yet determined.)
2.	Munich 900/Aussee 785/5	Greuze (after) Drawing. Girl with Jug.	<u>FRANCE</u>. Gurlitt bill, June 26, 1944. "Greuze Drawing; Head of a girl." Sold to Hitler for Linz, from Theo Hermsen, Paris.
3.	Munich 3951/Aussee 2688	A.y.Bayerin (Beyerlin) Still Life.	?
4.	Munich 4592/Aussee 3241	French, early 19th c. Hubert Robert (attri.) The park of Villa d'Este, Tivoli.	?
5.	Munich 4660/Aussee 3309	Tapestry,Brussels,1720 Mythological Scene	<u>FRANCE</u>. Gurlitt bill, May 10, 1944. Sold to Hitler for Linz from M. Weber, Paris. (Other 3 Gobelins were restituted to France, July 1, 1949 and this tapestry is identifiable as one of four.)

Figure 5.2 Partial list of the erroneous reparations shipment to Yugoslavia from the Central Collection Point in Munich, 1949 (National Archives and Records Administration, Record Group 260, NAID 34,715,878)

determined as originating in France (fifty-four items), Italy (seven), and Germany.[100] Full lists and documentation of items to be returned to Munich were sent to the Yugoslav Military Mission separately in January 1951.[101]

But no response from Yugoslavia was forthcoming, to the great annoyance of the OMGUS staff, who complained that "the Yugoslav case continues to be the cause of much trouble," as it was making it difficult to address "a number of claims from private German owners who have lost their property."[102] The international manhunt for Topić and the paintings began.[103] Topić was eventually located in Tangier, Morocco, where he stored his personal collection of dubious provenance, but none of the paintings he took from Munich were in his possession and he faced no further consequences.

At that point, the US State Department got involved, as it was becoming increasingly clear that the annoyed governments of France, Italy, Austria, the Netherlands, and Czechoslovakia were aware that paintings they had claims on were lost on the Americans' watch and could potentially sue the US government for damages.[104] Ardelia Hall, one of the major experts assigned to the MFA&A, worked tirelessly to provide documentation of the lost paintings' provenance and use diplomatic channels to pressure Yugoslavia to return the paintings and other artifacts.[105]

But Yugoslavia was nonresponsive. In 1956, the State Department closed the case, and decided not to notify the claimant countries of the erroneous restitution: "The basis of [this] decision was that we were acting at the time in question as the occupying power in Germany, that we voluntarily undertook to return a great deal of property to various countries, that we did the best we could to carry out this program, that we acted in good faith and that we cannot go on indefinitely trying to remedy or assume responsibility for possible errors in carrying out occupation programs of this sort."[106]

[100] Letter from Frank J. Miller, Chief, Property Division, to Chief, Yugoslav Military Mission, Berlin, June 1, 1950, National Archives, Record Group 260, NAID: 34,716,204.

[101] Letter from William G. Daniels, Chief, Property Division, to Chief, Yugoslav Military Mission, Berlin, January 8, 1951, National Archives, Record Group 260, NAID: 34,716,204.

[102] Letter from Edgar Breitenbach, Cultural Institutions Officer, Office of Public Affairs, to Theodore A. Heinrich, Henry E. Huntington Library and Art Gallery, California, March 14, 1952. National Archives, Record Group 260, NAID: 34,716,204.

[103] Testimonies of former MFA&A officers at Munich describing Topić for law enforcement agencies make for amusing reading: "a dark-complexed man with straight black hair, worn long and slicked back with pomade . . . His nails were well-manicured and his hands perfumed." Description of Mr. Mate A. Topic, February 16, 1956. National Archives, Record Group 260, NAID: 34,716,204.

[104] This is discussed in the Final Report of the Presidential Advisory Commission on Holocaust Assets in the United States, "Plunder and Restitution," December 2000.

[105] Ardelia Hall's contribution to the MFA&A project has been marginalized for years as the narrative congealed about the "Monuments Men." Her expertise, however, was outstanding and has been fully reevaluated. Reed, "Ardelia Hall."

[106] Donald A. Wehmeyer to Ardelia Hall, "Mistaken Restitution of Cultural Objects to Matutin (Mate) Topic," December 5, 1956, National Archives, Record Group 260, NAID: 34,716,128.

The problem was between Yugoslavia and the claimant countries, the State Department was saying, and the US was not willing to risk its international status as a competent occupying power on the case of an unfortunate clerical mix-up.[107]

That communist Yugoslavia was trying to fill its museums with heirless Nazi-looted art is clear from the letters Topić wrote personally to Yugoslav president Josip Broz Tito, updating him on his progress in Germany.[108] Justifying his lack of success so far, in a letter to Tito in January 1949, Topić wrote, "I need to use *other evidence*, and if I do so I am confident that I will do a very useful job for the country and with little expense complete our collections" [emphasis added]. Of course, always the conman, in the next sentence, he asks Tito to finance this endeavor.[109] But the purpose of the project was clear—the "very useful job for the country" was to fill up its museums and elevate its international cultural status.

Archival evidence indicates that the Yugoslav government realized that the restitution package from Munich was a fraud, but it had no intention of returning any of the art. In a lengthy legal memo in 1951, Milan Bartoš, a well-respected law professor and legal advisor to the Yugoslav Foreign Ministry admitted: "Yugoslav authorities know that the 'restituted' art objects did not belong to us" and advised the government to terminate its relationship with Topić.[110] The Yugoslav government, then, simply blamed the mishap on Topić and domestically interpreted the Munich shipments as legitimate war bounty, or reparations for damages incurred during the war.[111] As I detail below, this is the same justification that the Serbian government continues to use in rebuffing restitution claims today.

I will come back to the whereabouts of the erroneous shipment from Munich later in the chapter, but it is important to emphasize that postwar Yugoslavia was hardly unusual in readily accepting massive quantities of Nazi-looted art with not too many questions, or really any questions at all. Just as was the case with imperial and colonial-looted art, after World War

[107] The Topić shipment, however, was not the only mistake made during the restitution efforts in the immediate aftermath of the war. In 1946, Gustave Courbet's painting *View of Ornans*, looted from the Hungarian Jewish collector Mór Lipót Herzog by the Nazis, was erroneously restituted to Poland from the Nazi-looted art collection point in the Fischhorn Castle in Austria. Manikowska, "Washington Principles," p. 47. The painting has been in Poland until 2011, when it was restituted to the Herzog heirs with the help of the World Jewish Restitution Organization (WJRO)-affiliated Commission for Art Recovery. Esterow, "After 75 Years."

[108] Letters from Ante Topić Mimara to Josip Broz Tito, June 1 and June 17, Archive of Yugoslavia, fond 836 (KMJ), III-4/15.

[109] Letter from Ante Topić Mimara to Josip Broz Tito, Berlin, January 12, 1949, Archive of Yugoslavia, fond 836 (KMJ), III-4/15.

[110] Memo dated June 4, 1951.

[111] Ferenčak, "Umjetnine," p. 32.

II, Nazi-looted art was seamlessly incorporated into the cultural heritage of countries that got their hands on it and their violent provenance did not diminish their standing as objects of high status.

Heirless property and national heritage

Working hastily out of Munich until 1951, when the process of restitution was handed over to West Germany, the MFA&A distributed art to countries of origin, if that information could be determined. The understanding was that the postwar governments of formerly Nazi-occupied countries were then going to attempt to return the art to its rightful owners.[112] What many governments did, instead, was populate their national museums with vast quantities of this heirless art (2,000 art pieces in France, 4,000 in the Netherlands, and 600 in Belgium), often without even a cursory attempt to locate any survivors or family members who could claim it.[113] The burden of ownership proof that was placed on claimants was so onerous that many surviving family members could simply not provide the required documentation, many eventually giving up on the search. But more important—and directly relevant to the discussion regarding the status of the collections at the National Museum of Serbia—postwar governments of France, Netherlands, and Belgium simply considered heirless art as restitution in kind from Nazi Germany for wartime losses. As Elizabeth Campbell notes, the morbid irony here is that the restitution for war losses was, then, paid not by Nazi Germany, but by its victims, mostly Europe's Jews.[114]

This process of state appropriation of art objects for the purpose of constructing national heritage is what Campbell calls "patrimania," and was a central feature of European state museums' acquisition of Nazi-looted art after World War II.[115] These artifacts also served as agents of cultural nationalism for states competing for international status. Major European museums—the Louvre, the National Museum of Modern Art in Paris, the Rijksmuseum, and the Stedelijk Museum in Amsterdam—as well as many smaller, provincial museums across Western Europe that were "in need" of art, were distributed unclaimed heirless Nazi-looted art recovered from various German hideouts after the end of the war. The purpose of this massive cultural redistribution project was a sense of moral victory and justice of the

[112] Campbell Karlsgodt, "What's Wrong with This Picture,"; Nicholas, *Rape of Europa*; Sandholtz, *Prohibiting Plunder*.
[113] Campbell, *Museum Worthy*, p. 5.
[114] Campbell, *Museum Worthy*, p. 5.
[115] Campbell, "Claiming National Heritage," p. 797.

allied West against the Nazis. These beautiful and emotionally meaningful objects of art were to be displayed in public museums as a way of lifting the spirits of destroyed Europe.

But this frenzy of repopulating European museums with heirless Nazi-looted art also very specifically served the process of postwar national identity reconstruction out of the ashes of the war—these precious objects were meant "to restore a sense of national grandeur" to a broken-down continent.[116] Not much, if any, thought was given to the people who previously owned this art or to what happened to them to make the art heirless in the first place. This was not solely out of omission or neglect; it was out of a desire to put Europe back together after the catastrophe of World War II, and to build it back "without too much memory."[117] As one of the members of the Dutch postwar cultural property distribution committee said in 1946, "it is of utmost importance to make the great museums more glorious than they already are."[118] The national museums, in other words, were to be made great again—with paintings stripped off the walls of Europe's murdered Jews.

The objective to use this art to construct national heritage was explicit. Even when legally restituted, in practice many European states made it close to impossible for owners to take possession of their art. For example, postwar Austria instituted the "art tax," which levied a heavy tax on cultural property owners if they were to take their newly restituted art to their new countries of residence (United States, Israel, and so on). This tax was levied "in the name of preserving national heritage."[119] If not tax, then families were required to donate some of their artworks to Austria's museums, as a condition for taking the rest of their holdings outside of Austrian borders. This was apparently the deal the Viennese branch of the Rothschild family had to strike, and it enriched Austrian museums with 230 pieces of Rothschild-owned art.[120]

After MFA&A facilitated the return of some 60,000 pieces of looted art to France, 45,000 were restituted to their original owners. The unclaimed 13,000 were sold by the French state on the private markets, but some 2,000 heirless art pieces were declared extremely valuable and were labeled "MNR" (Musées Nationaux Récupération). They were held in de facto state trusteeship by various national museums (the Louvre, Musée d'Orsay, Pompidou Center, Rodin Museum, etc.), with, at least in the first few decades after the

[116] Campbell, "Claiming National Heritage," p. 820.

[117] Gaudenzi and Swenson, "Looted Art and Restitution," p. 511; also see Gaudenzi, "The 'Return of Beauty.'"

[118] Campbell, "Claiming National Heritage," p. 809.

[119] Czernin, "Austrian Evasion," p. 114, quoted in Sandholtz, *Prohibiting Plunder*, p. 224.

[120] Hochfield, "Wrestling with Restitution," p. 59.

war, minimal effort to try to locate their owners.[121] A separate commission was established in 1949 to select the best of the heirless art to enrich French museums, but also to decorate public buildings in need of freshening up after the war. This commission then coldly determined that if no claim was put forward by 1949, it was unlikely that the claimants survived, and the art could remain in the custody of the French state.[122] While France did not officially acquire heirless art but put the objects under museum custodianship instead, Belgium and the Netherlands simply placed unclaimed works under state ownership.[123]

European countries trying to reconstitute themselves after the catastrophe of the war, then, counted on their art collections to be their source of power and status in whatever postwar international order were to emerge. In so doing, they built on their previously constructed notions of cultural status. For example, it is this sense of cultural greatness that quickly mobilized Belgian officials to send the first state delegation to the Munich CCP and demand that the Ghent Altarpiece—a premier cultural status symbol of Belgium—be returned. They were remarkably successful, and the Altarpiece was the first piece of art to be restituted to its country of origin. It was sent from Munich to Brussels on August 21, 1945. Once safely back in Belgium, the Altarpiece was ceremoniously welcomed at the Royal Palace of Belgium, and an official signing ceremony took place, attended by Dwight Eisenhower and the Belgian Prime Minister. This object of art, then, also represented Belgium's re-entry into international society after years of Nazi occupation, and its new, firm alliance with the United States.[124] But this same sense of cultural greatness also guided Belgium's postwar non-restitution policy. Belgian state officials claimed that all heirless cultural property returned from Munich and elsewhere, including large quantities of Jewish-owned objects of art was, in fact, Belgium's state property, and the Belgian state was to use it to further enrich its great cultural heritage.[125]

In communist Central and Eastern Europe, heirless Jewish cultural property was simply nationalized. This of course was the case in the Soviet Union with the art looted by the Soviet Trophy Brigades, which became, seamlessly, property of the Soviet Union and displayed in Soviet, later Russian museums. In Poland, Jewish collections were just seized by the state after the war. Some of this art was placed in museums by Jews for safekeeping during the

[121] Between 1950 and 1993, only four MNRs were restituted to their owners. Lauter, "France's New Restitution Law."

[122] Campbell, "An Art Restitution Zeitgeist?"

[123] Campbell, *Museum Worthy*, p. 6.

[124] Graham, "Ghent Altarpiece," p. 347.

[125] Campbell, *Museum Worthy*, p. 185.

war, some was looted by the Nazis and stored there, as the Polish Jews were deported to ghettos and, later, to death camps. Large caches of art stolen from German Jews were also found after the liberation in the former German territories and major cities Wrocław (Breslau), Gdańsk (Danzig), or Szczecin (Stettin) that became part of Poland after 1945. After the war, all this art was nationalized, often moved from one museum to another, collections split and divided, and art objects entered into museum inventories with no mention of their prewar Jewish ownership.[126] In a chilling sign of the complete destruction of the largest prewar European Jewish community, Jewish property in Poland after the war was simply named "post-Jewish" (*mienie pożydowskie*).[127] The Jews and their property were, simply, erased from Polish history.

Holocaust memory and art restitution

The Jewish families' search for their stolen art after the war was almost always met with denial, resistance, redirection, and quite often overt antisemitism, as when some Dutch "Aryan guardians" (*bewariërs*), to whom their Jewish neighbors or friends entrusted valuables as they were being deported to camps, complained after the liberation, "Why did my Jew have to be the one to come back?"[128] But Holocaust victims and their families often pursued claims to get their art back persistently and doggedly, even in the face of obstruction, neglect, and even hostility. Family members often developed strong emotional attachment to a single piece of art they wanted returned. Sometimes, a single painting on the wall was all that a survivor remembered of their wartime apartment; it may have been the only thing that reminded them of their parents and grandparents who had perished. As Simon Goodman writes of his father's lifelong and ultimately unsuccessful search for his parents' vast art collection looted in the Holocaust,

> as the months passed and the terrible finality of his parents' deaths sank in, for my father those missing artworks took on an importance beyond their artistic or material worth. They were the last link to the happy days of his youth, the sole remaining connection to the life he had once known, and they were his murdered parents' last legacy.[129]

[126] Cieślińska-Lobkowicz, "Obligation of the State"; Manikowska, "Washington Principles."

[127] Manikowska, "Washington Principles," pp. 44–45.

[128] Goodman, *Orpheus Clock*, p. 167. On the role of "Aryan guardians" in occupied Netherlands, see also the 2024 Dutch documentary film *Bewariërs (Custaryans)* (dir. Sanne Kortooms and Timon Moll).

[129] Goodman, *Orpheus Clock*, p. 173.

But as the broader social and cultural understanding of the magnitude, importance, and legacy of the Holocaust became more socially salient over time, the attitudes about restitution of looted art also began to change. After a relative silence in the immediate aftermath of World War II, since the late 1970s, there has been a remarkable surge of interest in the Holocaust, spurred in part by the international fascination with trials of Nazi war criminals, but also by the increasing presence of the Holocaust in popular culture. The memory of the Holocaust that, until the 1990s, was mostly private memory within survivors' families, hidden from public view, transformed into a public memory that should concern everyone.[130]

As this surge of interest in the Holocaust continued, so did the interest in questions of stolen Jewish property. As various European governments began to open their war archives, more research could be carried out on the whereabouts of Nazi-looted art. A major step forward was the 1994 publication of Lynn Nicholas's *Rape of Europa*, a comprehensive archival study of Nazi looting, still considered one of the most authoritative reference books on this subject. Then came *The Lost Museum* (1995), a book of investigative reporting by Hector Feliciano, which documented the heirless MNR collection dispersed across French museums, and helped the heirs successfully locate some of the art they long considered forever lost. As the findings of the book gained much media attention, in 1997 then French Prime Minister Alain Juppé established a commission to investigate looted Jewish art during the Nazi occupation and the Vichy regime.[131]

Things were also beginning to move at the international level. As the cases of restitution of Jewish property looted in the Holocaust began to appear in front of US courts, the question of Jewish cultural property, especially the thousands of still unaccounted-for pieces of looted art, came to the front.[132] As already discussed in Chapter 2, a pivotal development regarding restitution of Nazi-looted art was the 1998 Washington Conference on Holocaust-era assets and a set of restitution guidelines it produced.[133]

A flurry of activities followed. In 1999, the Parliamentary Assembly of the Council of Europe adopted Resolution 1205 on Looted Jewish Cultural Property. This Resolution placed the question of restitution within the broader framework of historical and cultural justice. Its Article 8 states, "restitution of such looted cultural property to its original owners or their heirs (individuals,

[130] For more extensive discussion about the uptick in interest in the Holocaust in the 1990s, see Levy and Sznaider, "Memory Unbound"; Alexander, "On the Social Construction."

[131] Campbell, "Art Restitution Zeitgeist?"

[132] Bazyler, *Holocaust Justice*.

[133] US Department of State, "The Washington Principles."

institutions or communities) or countries is a significant way of enabling the reconstitution of the place of Jewish culture in Europe itself."[134] The Resolution then goes on to make a number of very specific and practical recommendations, including required legal changes across various European countries that would allow for restitution action to proceed. In France, the Study Mission on the Spoliation of Jews in France published a lengthy report in 2000 documenting Nazi looting operations in France.[135] A total of twenty-three works of art were returned to heirs because of this project.[136]

In 2003, the European Parliament adopted a very extensive Resolution and Report on a Legal Framework for Free Movement Within the Internal Market of Goods Whose Ownership is Likely to Be Contested, which also issued a very long list of specific changes needed to expedite the process of restitution of looted art, which the Resolution concluded was "ultimately a moral and ethical issue urgently calling for a moral and ethical solution."[137] In 2009, another conference was held in Terezin, the site of the Nazi concentration camp Theresienstadt outside Prague. It produced a further set of recommendations regarding Holocaust-era looted property, that went beyond just looted art.[138] Also in 2009, UNESCO adopted the Draft Declaration of Principles Relating to Cultural Objects Displaced in Connection with the Second World War which mostly reiterated similar recommendations.[139] More and more museums were put on notice to carefully re-evaluate the provenance of their art pieces and, instead of waiting to receive restitution claims by families, proactively seek rightful heirs of suspected Nazi-looted art in their collections. The surge in restitution cases also allowed scholars to reconstruct pre-Holocaust Jewish life and practices of collecting of the completely destroyed European Jewry.[140]

Since the adoption of the Washington Principles, there has been a massive increase in restitution claims by individual families filed against museums that hold Nazi-looted art. Some of these claims were successful, some were not, and the outcomes varied greatly. Some art pieces were fully restituted to families, some cases ended up in a financial settlement. In many cases, the

[134] Council of Europe, Resolution 1205.

[135] The commission, however, was silent on the practices of French cultural officials in securing Jewish-owned art for French museums (as was the case with the Schloss collection discussed earlier). A new commission was established in 2013, this time resulting in an additional eight restitutions. Campbell, "Art Restitution Zeitgeist?"

[136] Campbell, "Art Restitution Zeitgeist?," pp. 11–13.

[137] European Parliament, Committee on Legal Affairs.

[138] US Department of State, Terezin Declaration.

[139] UNESCO, Draft Declaration of Principles.

[140] Löffler, "'Living Room Art.'"

museums paid the families the estimated value of the art piece but got to keep it on display.

This was the case with the much-publicized case of Egon Schiele's *Portrait of Wally*, which was on loan at the Museum of Modern Art in New York but owned by the Leopold Museum in Vienna. Descendants of the Jewish collector Lea Bondi Jaray, who undersold *Wally* to a Nazi art dealer as she was desperate to flee Vienna in 1938, noticed the painting in New York in 1997 and filed a restitution claim. After a lengthy legal process, *Wally* was returned from New York to Vienna and the case was settled in 2010 when the Bondi Jaray descendants agreed to a financial payout that would leave the painting on display at the Leopold Museum.[141] And perhaps the most famous case of all, Gustav Klimt's *Woman in Gold*, was resolved when a descendent of the Viennese Jewish art collector family Bloch-Bauer, a California resident Maria Altmann, sued the Viennese gallery that owned the painting after it was looted by the Nazis. The case went all the way to the US Supreme Court. After Altmann eventually won the case in 2006, she sold the painting to the Neue Galerie in New York City, where it has since been displayed.[142]

In Germany, the Lost Art Foundation has maintained a publicly searchable database of looted art that could lead to new claims.[143] The French Ministry of Culture also has a searchable database of unclaimed heirless art, the MNRs.[144] In 2023, France also passed a sweeping new law that would facilitate the return of stolen cultural property to its rightful owners.[145] In the United States, a big move in this direction was the 2022 New York state law that required New York museums to have captions indicating if a displayed work of art had been looted by the Nazis, regardless of whether any restitution claims had been initiated. Major New York museums, such as the Guggenheim, MOMA, and the Whitney, have initiated new provenance research into their collections and have already disclosed art works that have likely "changed hands in continental Europe between 1932–1946" which makes their exact provenance a matter of heightened urgency.[146]

[141] Hickley and Schneeweiss, "Leopold Pays $19 Million."

[142] The case was made popular worldwide by the 2015 film *Woman in Gold* and the novel by Albanese, *Stolen Beauty*.

[143] Lauter, "France's New Restitution Law." German Lost Art database is available at https://www.lostart.de/en/start. A new searchable provenance database that came out of this project is Proveana, https://www.proveana.de, which includes provenance materials for Nazi-looted art as well as Soviet seizures and colonial-looted art.

[144] POP: La plateforme ouverte du patrimoine, https://www.pop.culture.gouv.fr/advanced-search/list/mnr.

[145] Lauter, "France's New Restitution Law."

[146] Cohen, "NY Museums Scramble."

The Museum of Jewish Heritage, also in New York, has for years held restitution ceremonies each time an art object looted by the Nazis has returned to their original owners or their families. But the issue of provenance search and display is also, fundamentally, an issue of historical memory. For Greg Schneider, executive vice president of the Conference on Jewish Material Claims Against Germany,

> Even if ultimately pieces are not returned to their rightful owners, this is still an important educational opportunity.... A lot of people go to museums who are not connected to the Holocaust, and certainly not heirs. For them to know that they are looking at a looted piece is important and opens up a new avenue for teaching about the Holocaust. The history is far greater than what you see hanging on the wall.[147]

All this bustle of activity indicates that holding onto Holocaust-looted art has become a form of international stigmata for states and their museums, who are incurring considerable financial and transaction costs in dealing with restitution claims in order to avoid international stigmatization. While collecting this art used to be a form of status-seeking, returning it to its rightful owners has now become a form of status management for states. As in the cases of the Parthenon Marbles and the Benin Bronzes discussed earlier, the status value of the same object of art has changed over time, and with that change has come a change in state decision-making over what to do with it.

The acceleration of restitution policies regarding Nazi-looted art has also paralleled the developments in restitution of colonial-looted art. For states that hold looted art in their public museums, pressures to restitute both groups of artifacts are coming thick and fast. For example, as the Netherlands was updating its laws regarding restitution of Nazi-looted art, it was also announcing repatriation of items looted during colonialism.[148] And in Belgium, a 2021 expert report urging the Belgian state to get serious about restitution of art and human remains taken from the Democratic Republic of Congo during its brutal colonial occupation, directly referenced the Washington Principles, as they "set up an important framework, also relevant for dealing with colonial loot, as they require a proactive role of possessors, call for understanding with regard to the problems with evidence, and put forward the importance of just and fair solutions to complicated

[147] Quoted in Cohen, "NY Museums Scramble."
[148] Oltermann and Boztas, "Netherlands to Return Treasures."

claims."[149] Restitution movements for imperial, colonial, and Nazi-looted art are, therefore, inextricably linked.

Restitution after communism

And while the normative expectations regarding restitution of Nazi-looted art have spread and become to a significant degree internationally institutionalized, some states, often in the former communist Central and Eastern Europe, have, however, rejected this normative framework and, instead, argued that this art belonged in their museums, regardless of how it had been initially obtained. The argument here is that retaining these collections equals "restitution in kind" (or "compensatory reparation") for the immense war damages these countries experienced in World War II. While presented in the language of international justice, this argument is, in fact, primarily about status. Whereas other major European imperial powers collected and looted "the best art" over centuries, these smaller, more peripheral states, often in Europe's East, had to be satisfied with cultural leftovers. For those states, possessing precious art—of questionable provenance or not—is still a ticket to high cultured status, and they will resist calls for restitution as long as they can.

Russia has been making this explicit argument for decades. Even though it nominally endorsed the Washington Principles, in 1998 the Russian Duma passed a Law on the Objects of Cultural Value Transferred to the USSR as a Result of the Second World War and Located on the Territory of the Russian Federation. The law, basically, legalized the Soviet capture of looted art. The law states that, since the Soviet Union did not start the war but lost 25 million people, more than any other nation, the "rescued" art may stay in Russia as "partial compensation for damage caused to the cultural heritage of the Russian Federation as a result of the looting and destruction of its cultural property by Germany and its military allies."[150] In a series of amendments since Vladimir Putin came to power, the Duma officially nationalized this art, which made its restitution legally impossible.[151]

But more than just an issue of a particularly self-serving understanding of wartime compensation, over time the looted art the Soviet Union captured from Nazi Germany became an integral part of the Soviet Union's cultural heritage, and later a cornerstone of Russia's own fantasies of its international

[149] Restitution Belgium, "Ethical Principles." Also see Campbell, *Museum Worthy*, p. 240.
[150] Quoted in Fisher and Weinberger, "Holocaust-Era Looted Cultural Property."
[151] Fisher and Weinberger, "Holocaust-Era Looted Cultural Property."

cultural status.[152] These new acquisitions build on already massive art holdings of European art in Russian museums, art collected over the centuries by Russian leaders, beginning with the reign of Catherine the Great. Again, the argument about material compensation is also a direct argument about status. The art looted from Germany by the Soviet Trophy Brigades has been referred to in Russia as "the last fruits of victory—the only ones the nation hasn't yet lost;" by refusing restitution, "Russia demonstrates that it is still a great power that can't be ordered around or humiliated by the West."[153]

Poland has also made legislative moves that de facto made it impossible for heirs of Nazi-looted art to claim restitution. The 2021 law has shut down claims older than thirty years, which of course would include all claims to Holocaust-looted art, but also claims for restitution of art that was seized by the communist regime, after it was taken from Holocaust victims.[154] And while the debate about restitution is very much alive in Poland, the Polish state has put all its efforts into recovering cultural property that was removed from Poland during the war, including mass quantities of Jewish cultural property, which it considers "Polish war losses" that should be restituted to the state of Poland, not to individual heirs.

Poland's actions also speak to its concerns about status—the refusal to restitute art looted from Polish Jews is presented as evidence that Poland was on the good side of history. In 2006, then director of the Polish Cultural Heritage Department summed this position clearly:

> We respect the provisions of the Washington Principles. But there is simply no such problem here. Poland was not Hitler's ally and Poland did not seize anything. We did not collaborate with the Nazis. It was in Poland that Jewish property was plundered, but it was not Poland that plundered.[155]

Polish concerns, instead, are about "the integrity of its national heritage," which gives Poland international cultural status.[156] This move, as Manikowska notes, then applies the Washington Principles designed to help restitute private property to heirs of Holocaust victims to Poland's public art stock instead.[157] The Polish Culture Ministry's Department for Cultural Heritage Abroad and Wartime Losses maintains an inventory of more than 63,000 "Objects Lost as a Result of World War II" from Poland, but does not

[152] Loudis, "Haul of Shame"; Campbell, *Museum Worthy*, p. 210.
[153] Akinsha and Kozlov, *Beautiful Loot*, p. 255.
[154] Fisher and Weinberger, "Holocaust-Era Looted Cultural Property," p. 80.
[155] Quoted in Manikowska, "Washington Principles," p. 56.
[156] Manikowska, "Washington Principles," p. 43.
[157] Manikowska, "Washington Principles," p. 44.

differentiate whether the objects were destroyed or in fact were looted from Polish Jews.[158]

Under this restitution scheme, return of an artifact from abroad to Poland has become a ritualized practice of status-claiming for the Polish state. Each return is accompanied by an official ceremony at the welcoming institution, all with restitution gadgets and souvenirs. The returned artifacts, however, remain in the Polish museums. Poland's restitution policy has no mechanism (because, of course, it has no interest) to establish who owned the artifact prior to its looting during World War II.[159] What makes an art object valuable for Poland is not its ownership provenance, but its *Polishness*.

Hungary, as well, has followed this pattern of non-restitution. Its three major museums, as well as a university in Budapest, still hold more than forty paintings (including three El Grecos, a Courbet, and a Corot) looted during the Holocaust in Hungary from the massive art collection owned by the Herzog family. As Nazi Germany occupied Hungary in 1944 and began rapid deportations of Hungarian Jews to death camps, Hungarian local collaborators pilfered Herzog collections that the family hid in salt mines or bomb shelters, and delivered them to Adolf Eichmann, who was personally overseeing the deportation of Hungarian Jews to Auschwitz. Eichmann designated a few pieces to be sent to Berlin, and the rest was stored at the Museum of Fine Arts in Budapest. After the war, Hungary simply took ownership of the works, distributed them to various museums, and continues to refuse cooperation on restitution to the heirs, despite many decades of legislation in European and US courts.[160]

And yet, other Central and Eastern European states have taken a dramatically different approach to restitution of Nazi-looted art. The Czech Republic, for example, has mandated all its public museums to conduct provenance research and, after the country adopted the Washington Principles, pay particular attention to Holocaust-looted art. This process identified 7,500 art objects likely looted from the victims of the Holocaust in the Protectorate of Bohemia and Moravia. In 2012, the Documentation Centre for Property Transfers of the Cultural Assets of WWII Victims (CDMP) was established, the purpose of which is provenance research into Holocaust-looted art. This

[158] Renewed efforts to return a number of paintings looted from Dutch Jews and currently on display at the National Museum in Gdańsk, including paintings looted from the major prewar Goudstikker art dealership in Amsterdam, remain unsuccessful. Nina Siegal, "Poland Urged"; Fisher and Weinberger, "Holocaust-Era Looted Cultural Property," p. 81. Also see Grimsted, "A Goudstikker Van Goyen."

[159] Manikowska, "Washington Principles," p. 54.

[160] Esterow, "After 75 Years"; Mashberg, "Martha Nierenberg." For detailed background on this case, see the presentation prepared by the law firm representing Herzog heirs: *Hungary on Trial: Herzog Family Sues for Return of Art Collection, the Last Hostage of the Holocaust*, https://hungarylootedart.com.

institution has documented close to 2,000 items that belonged in this category.[161] As part of this effort, in February 2023, the Czech Republic restituted fourteen art objects looted by the Gestapo during the war to the heirs of a Czech Jewish family. These objects were then displayed in Los Angeles as part of the exhibition *Reclaimed: A Family Painting*.[162]

More activities followed. CDMP published a report *Paintings from Jewish Collections at the National Gallery in Prague: Unidentified Owners*, followed by the brochure *Identifying Features*, which was a guide to the visual presentation (labels, tags, and so on) of art objects that belonged to Jewish collectors from the territories that are today the Czech Republic, and that would aid in identification and location of this art.[163] The Jewish Museum of Prague is an active actor in provenance research and restitution.[164] In fact, so much work has been done on provenance and restitution research in the Czech Republic that this country was one of only seven countries (and only one from the former communist Europe) that have been praised as having made major progress toward Nazi-looted art restitution in a 2024 worldwide report on Nazi-looted art prepared by the Claims Conference and the WJRO.[165]

Contrasting the Czech commitment with the refusal by Hungary and Poland is interesting. These differences are clearly not only dependent on change in government or the ruling party, as the particular and divergent paths regarding restitution taken by these states have been fairly consistent since the democratic transition after communism. Václav Havel, then still Czechoslovakia's first post-communist president, mentioned the issue of restitution of property, including Jewish property, in one of his very first speeches as president—in 1990.[166] Commitment to restitution of private property, then, was claimed by the Czech government from the very moment of democratic transition, and this was simply not the case in other post-communist countries.[167] This early commitment to restituting private property, then, provided the legal and political space for restitution of Jewish cultural property, space that has by that time not opened in Poland, Hungary, or Serbia.

Croatia, also, has stepped up its efforts regarding restitution of Nazi-looted art, after years of neglect. In preparation for taking the rotating presidency of

[161] Fisher and Weinberger, "Holocaust-Era Looted Cultural Property."

[162] CDMP, "RECLAIMED: a Family Painting," https://www.lootedart.cz/en/reclaimed-a-family-painting.

[163] CDMP, Publications, https://www.lootedart.cz/en/category/publications.

[164] Author's visit to the Jewish Museum of Prague, September 2018.

[165] The other six countries praised in the report were Austria, France, Germany, the Netherlands, United Kingdom, and the United States. Fisher and Weinberger, "Holocaust-Era Looted Cultural Property."

[166] Kraus, "Issue of Restitution."

[167] Author correspondence with Ewa Manikowska, May 12, 2024.

the International Holocaust Remembrance Alliance in 2024, Croatia began cooperation with the Claims Conference and the WJRO on cataloging all cultural property looted from Croatian Jews by the Croatian Ustasha, the homegrown fascist regime, as well as by the Nazis. Written by local researchers, a major report *Restitution of Movable Property in Croatia* was published in 2020, which lists names of original owners of art objects looted during World War II and then nationalized and placed in various Croatian cultural institutions, including its major museums.[168] This project then led to a series of additional extensive provenance searches of holdings in Croatia's museums and, finally, to a case of restitution to the heirs of Holocaust victims.[169] The Croatian Ministry of Culture made sure to emphasize to the international press that the Croatian government "shares the wish to provide Holocaust survivors and their heirs with a fair measure of justice."[170]

More broadly, these different approaches have to do with these states' own understanding of their status, and especially their different understanding of which international club they want to join and who they want to confer on them high cultural status. The Czech Republic, for example, aggressively pursued not only membership but leadership in various international organizations, including, importantly, UNESCO, as a way to elevate its international status.[171] Croatia did the same, targeting a different set of international institutions.[172] Croatia also acted out of its status as a European Union member state, often referring to its EU membership "as a framework in which it fulfilled its own responsibilities."[173] Choosing to aggressively pursue leadership in restitution politics was yet another strategy of international cultural status management.

Meanwhile, in Serbia, there was very little provenance research and no art restitution.

Looted art at the National Museum of Serbia

What happened to the paintings that Topić (Mimara) stole from Munich took many decades to unravel. The Munich shipments did arrive in Belgrade in 1949, and there are documents outlining the receipt of objects, as well as the

[168] Naida-Michal Brandl, "Restitution of Movable Property."
[169] Catherine Hickley, "Croatia Takes a Step."
[170] In 2023, the US heir of Dane and Frieda Reichsmann, Croatian Jewish collectors murdered in Auschwitz, was restituted paintings by Derain and de Vlaminck, as well as lithographs by Picasso and Cézanne. Catherine Hickley, "Croatian Museums Return Art."
[171] Hornát, Šlosarčík, Tomalová, and Váška, "International Organisations."
[172] Knezović and Lopes, "Croatia as a Small State."
[173] Šabić, "Impact of the Refugee Crisis," p. 59.

establishment of a committee to certify delivery of objects and their distribution.[174] The collection was then handed over to the Art Museum (today, the National Museum).[175] The Munich collection was a boon for the museum, as the Yugoslav elites invested heavily in this institution, which was a symbol of Yugoslavia's belonging in the sophisticated world of international art, as a "progressive member of European society with which it shares both historical traditions and value systems."[176]

Of the fifty-six paintings Topić stole from Munich, most are still in the possession of the National Museum.[177] Multisite archival research I conducted to partly reconstruct these paintings' origins also produced a veritable rolodex of Nazi dealers, fixers, and collectors.[178] For example, here is the partial provenance trace of a select few notable paintings still on display at the National Museum. *The Park on the Lake* by Hubert Robert and *Portrait of a Girl* by Aelbert Cuyp were confiscated by the ERR from the Rothschild collection in Paris on May 1, 1941.[179] They were first stored at the Jeu de Paume, and then selected by Göring for his personal collection at Carinhall. *A Landscape with*

[174] Ferenčak, "O provenijenciji," p. 244. Museum catalogs from 1952 also list some of the Munich shipment paintings as being in the inventory of the museum. For a list of catalogs with this information, see Ferenčak, "Umjetnine iz zbirke," p. 25. Archival records are in the Archive of Yugoslavia, Commission on Reparations, AJ-54-319-483.

[175] National Museum Record no. 501, July 2, 1949.

[176] Aleksandar Ignjatović and Olga Manojlović Pintar, "National Museums in Serbia," p. 795. The National Museum in Belgrade was founded in 1844. Its collection of European art dates from the early twentieth century. The museum's holdings were significantly expanded in the 1930s during the Kingdom of Yugoslavia, when the museum operated under the name the Museum of Prince Paul.

[177] The total number of stolen art objects was 166, of which fifty-six were paintings. Some investigations put the number of holdings at the National Museum today at forty-seven. Radio-Television Serbia, *Mimara*, (dir. Miodrag Ćertić), 2017.

[178] My reconstruction of the whereabouts of this collection is based on inventories and photographs contained in the archival documents at the National Archives in Washington, DC, Archives of Yugoslavia in Belgrade, the *Göring Catalogue*, online Database of Art Objects at the Jeu de Paume, online database of the Jewish Digital Cultural Recovery Project, multiple visits to the National Museum of Serbia in Belgrade, interviews with former employees of the National Museum, Serbian, Croatian, and Italian newspaper and TV coverage, in addition to cited secondary sources. I was not given access to the National Museum of Serbia's archives, nor to the paintings themselves and was unable to examine the artwork markings. The reconstruction of the collection I carried out here should, therefore, be taken as a first step in determining the provenance of these works, while the complete provenance would have to follow established methodologies of provenance research. For the fundamentals of provenance research, see Tompkins, *Provenance Research Today*.

[179] The Robert painting is described in the MFA&A provenance records as *Landscape with Lakes, Terrace and Figures*. Its Munich Collection Point (MCP) number is 7554. The *Göring Catalogue*, however, provides more information. It identifies the painting as *Paysage*, and reveals that it was taken by the ERR from the Rothschild collection in Paris on May 1, 1941. Dreyfus, *Catalogue Goering*, p. 404. This painting is also listed in the ERR Jeu de Paume database under inventory number R 373. This database also notes the following: "This item was repatriated erroneously to Yugoslavia. There is no information as to whether it was ever repatriated to France for restitution to the Rothschild family." Available at https://www.errproject.org/jeudepaume/card_view.php?CardId=18784. The Cuyp painting is listed in the *Göring Catalogue* as *Portrait d'une fillette*, with provenance in the same Rothschild collection seizure on May 1, 1941. Dreyfus, *Catalogue Goering*, p. 398. Its MCP number is 7556. National Archives, Record Group 260, NAID: 34,716,204. More information about this painting's provenance in the ERR Jeu de Paume database is available at https://www.errproject.org/jeudepaume/card_view.php?CardId=17253.

Cow by Camille Corot was acquired in France by Hans Lange, one of Hitler's personal art dealers, was then hidden at Alt Aussee, then stored in Munich, then arrived to the Belgrade museum as part of the Topić shipment. Another Robert painting, *Staircase of the Park of Palazzo Farnese at Caprarola*, has the same provenance.[180] In fact, so many valuable pieces in this collection had clear provenance in France, that Rose Valland herself got involved in the search for their return and pleaded to French officials in 1950, "I don't see any other way to get possession of these paintings than to claim them from Yugoslavia through diplomatic channels."[181]

Other extremely valuable works the National Museum in Belgrade acquired from Topić's Munich shipment can be traced to Italy, including *Portrait of Queen Christina of Denmark* (originally attributed to Titian) and *Madonna and Child with Donor* by Tintoretto. These paintings also came from Göring, who acquired them from Nazi-affiliated dealers in Italy.[182] Canaletto's *A View of the Grand Canal* and Guardi's *A View of San Marco* came to Munich from the collection of Martin Bormann, Hitler's private secretary. All of these paintings are still, to this day, and with no provenance acknowledgment, displayed at the National Museum of Serbia in Belgrade.[183]

Some of the artifacts from the Munich shipment were dispersed—some of the tapestries obtained by the notorious dealer Hildebrand Gurlitt in France and then sold to Hitler, and rugs traced to a French monastery that was the ERR collection point for seizures from Jews at the Belgian–Dutch border, found their way to the Museum of Applied Arts in Belgrade, Serbia. Others were used to decorate Yugoslav government buildings.[184] Two objects from this collection ended up in Zagreb, where they are currently displayed in the Mimara Museum—a seventeenth-century painted-glass Venetian wedding cup and a Syrian mosque lamp, initially part of the Göring collection.[185] And some of the artifacts have simply disappeared, never recovered, including a landscape by John Constable, confiscated by the Nazis from the Vienna Rothschild collection, as well as art pieces originally seized by Nazi dealers from the collection of Jacques Goudstikker in Amsterdam.[186]

[180] The painting's MCP number is 4592. Upon its arrival in Belgrade, it was recorded under the title *The Park of the Villa d'Este* in National Museum documents. See Brajović and Bošnjak, *Imaginarni vrtovi*.

[181] Letter from Rose Valland to Chief of Art and Cultural Restitution, Private Property and Interests Office, Paris, January 23, 1950. National Archives, Record Group 260, NAID: 34,715,878.

[182] Göring procured the Titian on December 2, 1941 and Tintoretto on February 8, 1942, from the Italian dealer Contini, via German dealer Hofer. Dreyfus, *Catalogue Goering*, p. 482, p. 516. While originally recorded as Titian, the painting's attribution by the National Museum has since been downgraded to a "Lombard painter."

[183] Author's multiple visits to the National Museum in Belgrade, December 2021 and December 2023.

[184] Akinsha, "Ante Topic Mimara."

[185] Ferenčak, "O provenijenciji," p. 244.

[186] Akinsha, "Ante Topic Mimara."

In 1967, Topić donated another large collection (close to 150 paintings and sculptures) to the Strossmayer Gallery in Zagreb.[187] In 1973, he donated further items to the government of the Republic of Croatia, then still part of the former Yugoslavia, in exchange for a generous lifetime annuity and a commitment to build a museum in his name to house the collection. He explained his donation as his "gift to the future, to the people," and predicted that "people from all over the world" would flock to Yugoslavia for the first time, to see this magnificent collection.[188] He, himself, was going to elevate Yugoslavia's international cultural status.

Yugoslav communist authorities believed this as well. Soon upon his death in 1987, a monumental museum was opened in his name in Zagreb, where his large collection (3,754 items) was to be housed. But it turned out that the magnificent paintings by Leonardo, Raphael, and Velásquez were, in fact, obvious forgeries. The entire collection of the Mimara Museum has been under suspicion ever since.[189] Art that was supposed to bring Croatia great international cultural status has only brought it ridicule and shame.

Back in Belgrade, the National Museum now had both the erroneous Munich shipment but also all the surviving paintings from the Erich Šlomović collection (discussed in the book's Preface), which has since been nationalized. These two collections—one seized from the victim of the Holocaust, the other fraudulently acquired from Europe's cache of Nazi-looted art—then formed the very heart of the National Museum's collection of international art. The state of Yugoslavia, and since its dissolution, the state of Serbia, built its cultural capital and its international cultural status through acquisition of looted art, just as did the Louvre or the British Museum two hundred years prior. The problem for the National Museum of Serbia, however, was that international norms had changed.

The Italian claim

In 2016, Italian prosecutors opened an investigation into the ownership of eight paintings, including paintings attributed to Titian, Tintoretto, and Carpaccio, displayed in the National Museum of Serbia as part of the 1949 restitution fraud (Figure 5.3).[190] Italian representatives traveled to Belgrade

[187] This donation does not appear to have included items stolen from Munich. However, more than a third of this collection Topić acquired on the Nazi art market, making this collection one of fundamentally tainted provenance. Ferenčak, "Umjetnine iz zbirke."

[188] *Mimara*, documentary.

[189] Andrew Decker, "Real and Fake."

[190] Two Italian investigative journalists published a book in 2024 arguing that it is seventeen, not eight Italian paintings as initially thought that are part of this collection. *ANSA*, "A Belgrado i quadri."

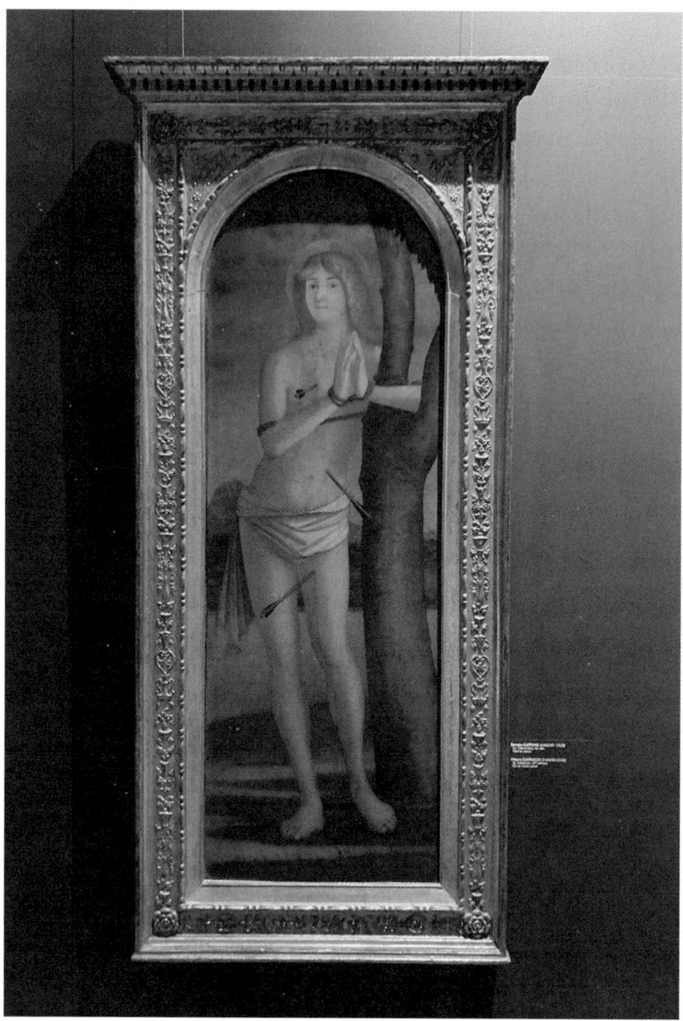

Figure 5.3 Vittore Carpaccio, *San Sebastian*, *c.*1495, part of the erroneous reparations shipment from the CCP Munich, 1949 (photograph by author)

and filed a claim directly with the Serbian Foreign Ministry, presenting evidence that the paintings by Italian masters were sold to Hermann Göring by Italian Nazi-affiliated dealers or were exchanged for pieces of art Göring previously looted from Jewish collections in France. They were then illegally taken from Italy to Germany, and this is the basis of the Italian claim of return.[191] Remarkably, these paintings have previously been displayed in

[191] Partial provenance of these paintings and the involvement of Italian dealers Alessandro Contini-Bonacossi and Eugenio Ventura can be reconstructed from archival materials available in National Archives, Record Group 260, NAID: 34,715,878. On the Italian art exchanges with Göring, see Pellegrini, "Göring in Italy."

Italy (in Bologna and Bari), as part of the 2004/05 traveling exhibition *From Carpaccio to Canaletto: Treasures of Italian Art from the National Museum of Belgrade* organized by the National Museum in cooperation with Italian curators, and did not raise any suspicion. The basis for the 2016 lawsuit, however, was a routine inquiry into missing Italian art one of the investigators was conducting in 2014. The Italian government now pursued these paintings with renewed vigor.[192] Never one to downplay the emotional appeal of Italian culture, Italian foreign minister Angelino Alfano announced, "We want to bring these eight prisoners of war home."[193]

The Italian claim caused consternation in the Serbian media, and was flatly rejected by the National Museum, which issued a statement that "all works of art in [our] collections are legally the property of the Republic of Serbia," and so the Italian claim had no merit.[194] But some of the arguments made in the press also demonstrated a fundamental disconnect between the Washington Principles and some Serbian cultural experts' understanding of provenance. Nikola Kusovac, a long-term head curator at the National Museum and member of its Executive Board, argued that the Italian ownership claim had no basis as "Göring bought paintings by Titian, Tintoretto and Carpaccio. I stress, he bought them with money and gold, and did not take them or loot them. At the end of World War II, these paintings fell into Allies' hands."[195] In a separate interview, Kusovac admitted that Göring was a war criminal, but "he was not a thief, but instead one of the most important interwar collectors," and besides, "dealing with the Göring collection was the only way to get even the crumbs from the vast artistic cache that was distributed by the victors after the war."[196] Bojana Borić Brešković, the National Museum director, also claimed, "these paintings were bought perfectly legally."[197]

This understanding of Göring's transactions as legal and normal flies in the face of the entire post–World War II understanding of the fundamentally tainted nature of all art dealing by the Nazi officials. The fact that some of these paintings were exchanged in Italy for paintings looted from the Jews

[192] In addition to requesting the paintings back, the prosecution also initially criminally charged three Italian curators involved in the 2004/05 Bologna/Bari exhibition. In 2019, the charges against them were dropped, as they could demonstrate lack of prior knowledge of the paintings' provenance. The Italian state restitution claim against the Serbian state for the return of the paintings, however, is ongoing. Santacatterina, "L'intricato caso."

[193] Musizza, "Si lavora per riportare."

[194] Mondo, "Italijani traže."

[195] Mondo, "Italijani traže."

[196] In the same interview, Kusovac also argued, with thinly veiled antisemitism, that the authors of a documentary film that exposed the Mimara fraud "were paid by the Rothschilds" to inflict damage on Serbia and its National Museum. Radio-Television Serbia, "Oko magazin."

[197] Radio Television Serbia, "Mira Adanja Polak." My request to interview the National Museum director has been unanswered.

of France should make their entire provenance records suspect, even before the complication of their fraudulent restitution from Munich to Belgrade. But in the understanding of the National Museum of Serbia, these paintings are, simply, *Serbian*, and claims to restitute them are claims to deny Serbian museums what is rightfully theirs.

The innocence of the museum's holdings and the offensiveness of Italy's claim were also presented as an issue of status recognition. Similar to the Polish position discussed earlier, what incensed Kusovac was "historical revisionism . . . forgetting of who was on the side of the Allies and who on the side of the Nazis."[198] It is Serbia's historical status as, always, on the right side of history that matters much more than the "technical" issue of provenance research. But then, almost admitting that the paintings could be illegally owned, Kusovac brought in the cultural status differential between Italy and Serbia, wondering why Italy fought to get these paintings back "when they are of lower quality than what [Italy] already possesses."[199] There was a disconnect, in other words, between Serbia's lower cultural status and its higher moral status.

The issue came back into public focus in February 2017 with the airing of a documentary on Serbian public television that outlined the broad contours of the fraudulent Topić shipment and the responsibility of the museum to conduct provenance research. In the documentary, Darko Tanasković, then Serbia's representative at UNESCO and president of the National Museum's Executive Board, argued that the issue at hand was one of international relations and, specifically, the injustice of the current international order which allowed looted art to remain in the British Museum and the Louvre but asked the National Museum of Serbia to send artifacts back. Like other Serbian state officials, Tanasković also argued that the paintings at the National Museum were the result of a fair reparations exchange: "When you destroy a National Library you have a moral obligation to give back something else—this is reparation in kind."[200] This position is shared by other Serbian cultural experts, who argue that the Munich collection is an ethically justified reparation for valuable art looted by the Nazis from Yugoslavia in World War II.[201] This was the case, for example, with Rembrandt's *Quintus Fabius Maximus*, which the Nazis looted from the Ostrog monastery in Montenegro, where the government of the Kingdom of Yugoslavia hid some of the art treasures before fleeing

[198] Nikoletić, "Revizija istorije."
[199] Nikoletić, "Revizija istorije."
[200] Radio-Television Serbia, *Mimara*.
[201] Author interviews on background with multiple cultural policy experts in Serbia.

the country from the Nazi onslaught in 1941. The painting was destroyed in the Allied bombing of Augsburg in 1944.[202]

Adding to the museum feeling under siege have been the contemporaneous legal claims on the much bigger Šlomović collection (Figure 5.4). This collection includes a number of masterpieces by Degas, Renoir, Gauguin, Derain, Utrillo, Picasso, and so on, and has been under a legal cloud for decades, as there are competing claims to ownership by Šlomović heirs in Israel, as well as descendants of the French dealer Ambroise Vollard, who had claimed that the paintings were, in fact, Vollard's, and not Šlomović's in the first place.[203] In the midst of all the conflicting claims to the collection, these very valuable paintings continue to be a source of embarrassment, unease, and status concerns for Serbia. For example, the National Museum needed to acquire special guarantees from the Netherlands that the Šlomović collection paintings would indeed be returned from a traveling exhibition in 2004 in The

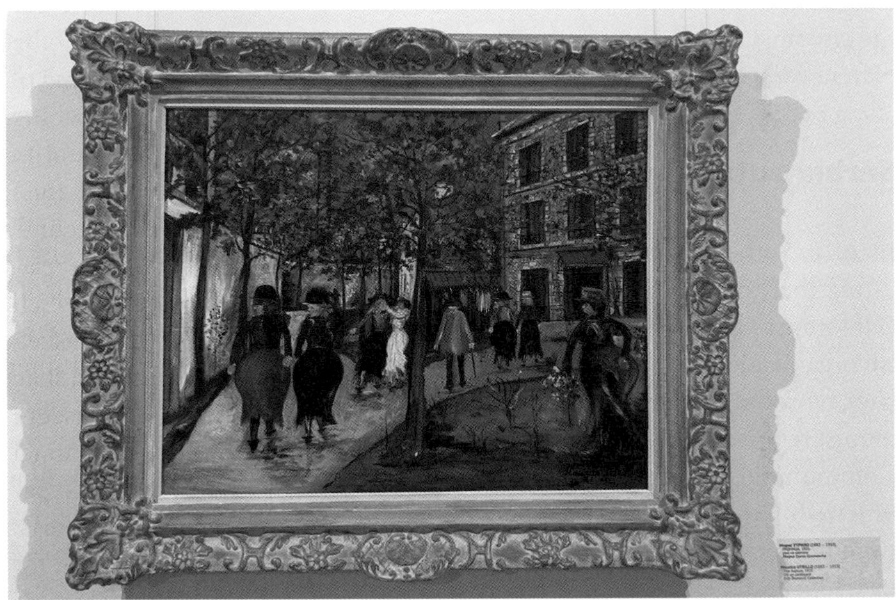

Figure 5.4 Maurice Utrillo, *The Asylum*, 1925, part of the Erih Šlomović collection at the National Museum of Serbia (photograph by author) (© 2024 Artists Rights Society (ARS), New York/ADAGP, Paris)

[202] For more background on the lost Rembrandt, see Jelena Todorović, "The Painting and Its Histories: The Curious Incident of Rembrandt's Painting *Quintus Fabius Maximus*," in *Regimes of Invisibility in Contemporary Art, Theory and Culture: Image, Racialization, History*, ed. Marina Gržinić, Aneta Stojnić, and Miško Šuvaković (Cham: Palgrave, 2017), pp. 159–68.

[203] D'Arcy, "The Mysterious Mr. Slomovic."

Hague. Switzerland, however, did not provide such guarantees, so a planned exhibition in Lausanne in 2004 had to be canceled out of fear of art seizure.[204] Art objects that gave Serbia great cultural status have now become objects of shame, as their international display exposed Serbia to accusations of looting and attempts at forced restitution.

After the National Museum reopened in 2018 after a fifteen-year-long renovation, the Šlomović collection was displayed again as a major part of the museum's modern European art holdings. Other than the words "Erich Šlomović collection" printed on individual painting captions, not a single caption anywhere in the permanent exhibition indicates that this vast and invaluable collection—the jewel of the National Museum's treasures—is art that belonged to the victim of the Holocaust and was handed over, under pressure, to the communist government after the war in exchange for "just compensation," a promise that was never fulfilled.[205] And while two National Museum curators announced in 2018 that the museum's remodeled exhibition would include a detailed biography of Erich Šlomović and the circumstances of his death as a model for "new museum education," this plan never came to be.[206]

Serbia outside of history

In 2016, Serbia passed the Law on Removing the Consequences of Confiscating the Property from Holocaust Victims with No Living Descendants (Holocaust Heirless Property Law).[207] The law, hailed by international Jewish organizations as quite generous by the standards of Holocaust restitution laws, returned property seized by the Nazis and later nationalized by the communist regime not to individual owners, but to Serbia's Association of Jewish Communities. It also obliged the government to compensate the Federation of Jewish Communities in Serbia with an annual donation of €950,000 for twenty-five years.[208] The 2016 law, however, is limited only to property looted *in Serbia* and it excludes Nazi-looted art that was brought into the country—such as the Topić collection erroneously sent to Belgrade from Munich in 1949. The law also requires that only the Jewish community in Serbia can

[204] Coblence and Laufer, "Memorandum."

[205] The National Museum website simply notes in the section on the history of the Museum, "Erich Šlomović collection was *received* in 1949" (my emphasis).

[206] Pejović and Grabež, "Nova muzejska edukacija." My inquiries with the museum curators about the status of the new display have been unanswered.

[207] The text of the law is available at http://www.parlament.gov.rs/upload/archive/files/lat/pdf/predlozi_zakona/234-16%20-lat.pdf.

[208] Subasic, "Serbia Returns Property." For broader context, see Subotić, *Yellow Star, Red Star*, ch. 2.

file claims for restitution.[209] As a result, it is extremely difficult for individuals, organizations, or governments outside of Serbia to make claims. Since the Federation of Jewish Communities of Serbia has not wanted to claim cultural property (on the grounds that doing so was too "political"), while immovable property has been processed under the 2016 law, movable cultural property has not.[210]

More broadly, however, the small and insecure Serbian Jewish community has been reluctant to open up the unpopular question of looted art and other cultural property, as these looted collections "have become part of the national corpus," and attempts to have them returned to private owners enjoy no general public support.[211] The history of communist Yugoslavia in which private cultural property was nationalized and turned into national cultural property exhibited in public museums contributes to the continuing unease museums express toward restitution of what they see as "public goods" into private ownership.[212] This is why attempts at restitution or even, more modestly, acknowledgment of provenance, have often been seen with suspicion by museum curators, and especially museum leadership.

Serbian museums have historically been state owned, and museum leadership has always been directly appointed by the state.[213] Museum directors—especially of major museums, like the National Museum of Serbia—therefore act primarily as agents of the state and are often active members of the ruling political party. Museum director Borić Brešković, in rebuffing restitution claims, simply claimed that all the art at the museum was the property of the Serbian state (which inherited it from the former Yugoslav state after its dissolution) and the museum was only its custodian.[214] It was the Serbian state, therefore, that had to make restitution decisions—a position shared by many national museums, including the British Museum, as already explored in Chapter 3.

More broadly, provenance research is in its infancy in Serbia and has not become a routine part of museums' practice, as objects of art are still valued mostly by their aesthetic qualities alone, and not by the broader social context of their creation and distribution.[215] They are also, however, explicitly valued

[209] Fisher and Weinberger, "Holocaust-Era Looted Cultural Property," p. 91.

[210] Author interview with Wesley Fisher, director of research, Claims Conference-WJRO, January 12, 2024.

[211] Author interview with Haris Dajč, Associate Professor of History, University of Belgrade, and former vice president of the Belgrade Jewish Community, December 20, 2023, Belgrade.

[212] Author interview with Višnja Kisić, UNESCO Chair in Cultural Policy and Management, University of the Arts, Belgrade, January 9, 2024.

[213] Ignjatović and Manojlović Pintar, "National Museums in Serbia."

[214] Radio Television Serbia, "Mira Adanja Polak."

[215] Kisić, interview.

as evidence of international cultural status. For example, the Hubert Robert painting, *The Staircase*, holds a pride of place in the National Museum, and was excitedly described in the Serbian press as evidence that "the National Museum can boast that it has one of the best Roberts in the world."[216] And while the provenance research on the two Robert paintings in the museum's collection has been conducted by the former museum curators and published in a monograph, the fact that they were part of the fraudulent Topić shipment was still being narrated as an issue of legitimate war reparations package and not as a problem of owning Nazi-looted art.[217]

Similarly, in 2024, the museum's foreign art curator discussed the large canvas *Adam and Eve in Paradise* by Marten de Vos in the context of Serbia's international cultural status: "[our foreign colleagues] are amazed at our collection . . . We are still for them a provincial museum, and they don't expect the wealth of foreign European art to be found in a provincial museum."[218] But the De Vos painting is at the National Museum in Serbia because it has been sent in error from Munich. According to the MFA&A records, it has been moved to the Nazi Alt Aussee salt mine hideout from the auction house Dorotheum in Vienna.[219] Under Nazi rule, Dorotheum served as a clearinghouse for the property seized from the Jews and then sold by the Gestapo office for the Disposal of the Property of Jewish Emigrants, known as Vugesta.[220]

These paintings, evidently, provide joy and pleasure and instill a sense of national pride among the Serbian public. What they do not do, however, is even begin to open up the decades-overdue discussion about whether these paintings should be in the National Museum at all. This question, however, was one that Serbia was eventually forced to confront.

In the absence of a coherent response from the National Museum, it is voices against restitution that have received the most attention in the Serbian press. But there are alternative voices among the Serbian cultural experts who have argued for more transparency, provenance research, cooperation with international institutions on issues of restitution policy and practice, and flipping the National Museum's script from one of defensiveness, disinterest, and silence, toward one of international professional expertise.[221]

[216] Dimitrijević, "Detektivska potraga."

[217] Brajović and Bošnjak, *Imaginarni vrtovi*.

[218] Bulatović, "Srpsko nacionalno blago."

[219] Lauterbach, *Central Collecting Point*, pp. 147–48. MCP id: 4844. It came to Dorotheum from France, where it was previously acquired in Paris in 1944 by the Nazi-affiliated dealer Theo Hermsen. National Archives, Record Group 260, NAID: 34,715,878. MFA&A initially attributed the painting to the artist Wtewael.

[220] Petropoulos, "Not a Case of 'Art for Art's Sake.'"

[221] Kisić, interview.

Some experts explained that the shock experienced by the museum today is the result of Serbia's international isolation during the 1990s, just at the time when international norms about provenance research were being developed, diffused, and institutionalized.[222] Serbia, in other words, has been outside of history.

Serbia's refusal to engage in debates about restitution and provenance of its major art collections have put it squarely outside of the coalescing international norms about dealing with looted art. This is particularly the case with Nazi-looted art, around which there has been emerging international consensus and a clear normative framework since the adoption of the 1998 Washington Principles. Serbia's attitude is, clearly, due in large part to the lack of expertise and practice in provenance research, as well as deep politicization of major cultural institutions that have almost no independence from the state. The National Museum as an institution is also increasingly isolated. Under the museum's politicized leadership, there is very little international cooperation and very few visiting exhibitions—the cornerstone of modern national museums.[223] But Serbia's behavior, also, reflects its own understanding of its international status, as well as anxiety about that status recognition internationally. Its problematic collections—the Topić collection of more than forty paintings, and the Šlomović collection of more than 350 paintings, drawings, prints, and art books, form the very core of the museum's collection of international art, and represent the most valuable collection of foreign art in Serbia.

The Serbian case is the case of a disconnect between the symbolic capital that art objects provide and the changing notions of what element of an art object provides status. In the case of the Benin Bronzes, the decision to return (in France, Germany, Belgium, Sweden, and so on) was guided by the desire for a different kind of status recognition (as a state that is exhibiting moral action and understands that art objects that have now become objects of shame need to be returned so that a state can *maintain* its cultural status). In Serbia, on the contrary, this dynamic simply does not exist. Serbia is a country anchored in its victimhood identity, and there is no narrative identity connection with violence or political crimes of the past in which Serbia acted on the wrong side of history.[224]

Serbia's major museums, and especially its flagship the National Museum, have been complicit in the refusal to discuss problematic events from Serbia's past. Serbia's museums have turned these violent episodes into events

[222] Radio Television Serbia, "Mira Adanja Polak."
[223] Author interviews with Serbian cultural policy experts.
[224] Damjanovic and Mason, "Suffering and Survivorship."

that cannot be heard.[225] If anything, restitution debates continued and perpetuated Serbia's sense of itself as a besieged victim. And this is because ownership of art objects, for Serbia, is what continues to lay the state's claim to international cultural status. While domestically they continue to be seen as status-granting, internationally, Serbia's continuing refusal to discuss their provenance makes these objects agents that lower Serbia's status. Objects of status have become objects of discomfort and international stigmatization.

[225] Ignjatović and Manojlović Pintar, "National Museums in Serbia," p. 786.

Conclusion

International Politics in the Age of Restitution

The year 2023 was to be "a year of decisive progress for restitutions," announced French culture minister Rima Abdul Malak, promising a sweeping change in French legislation regarding restitution for both Nazi-looted and colonial-looted art from France. The French policy on art restitution, Abdul Malak claimed, would be based on "nether denial nor repentance, but recognition."[1] While Abdul Malak referred to recognition of vague "tragedies of history," the French restitution posture also was a claim for status recognition. France was claiming to be the leader in international restitution efforts, a model for other states to follow. A country that has historically been conferred high international cultural status was now claiming high status recognition for its moral action regarding looted art return.

France was not going it alone. It formed a partnership with Germany to jointly fund provenance research into objects looted from their former colonies.[2] There was also renewed talk of North–South cooperation. In May 2023, museum directors from thirty-eight African and European countries signed a memorandum of cooperation at a conference in Senegal agreeing to collaborate on issues of restitution, digitization of collections, and joint exhibitions.[3]

Meanwhile, a number of countries carried out their own restitution projects. In July 2023 the Netherlands announced the return of 478 art objects to Indonesia, and six to Sri Lanka from two major Dutch museums—the National Museum of World Cultures and the Rijksmuseum. "This is a historic moment. It is the first time we are following recommendations of the [restitution] committee to give back objects that should never have been brought to the Netherlands," Dutch State Secretary for Culture and Media Gunay Uslu said.[4] In September 2024, 288 artifacts were returned to Indonesia in a ceremony at the Wereldmuseum in Amsterdam, where the objects had

[1] French Ministry of Culture, Transcription du discours de la ministre de la Culture.
[2] Villa, "France and Germany."
[3] Hickley, "African and European Museum Directors."
[4] Oltermann and Boztas, "Netherlands to Return Treasures."

been held.[5] The Fowler Museum at the University of California-Los Angeles returned seven artifacts looted by the British colonial forces from Ghana's Asante kingdom in 1874 and then purchased by the museum in the 1960s. Exactly 150 years later, at the restitution ceremony, director of the Fowler Museum Silvia Forni said, "We are globally shifting away from the idea of museums as unquestionable repositories of art, as collecting institutions entitled to own and interpret art based primarily on scholarly expertise, to the idea of museums as custodians with ethical responsibility."[6]

And other countries began the initial stages of the restitution process. In 2023, Belgium handed over a full digital inventory of 84,000 art pieces that its colonial occupation forces looted from the Congo and made plans to work with the Congolese partners on return of these items.[7] Austria proposed a new law that would require restitution of art objects acquired during the colonial era and held in Austrian museums.[8] After leading the process of Benin Bronzes return, Germany was laying the ground for restitution of some of the 40,000 art pieces its colonial administration extracted from Cameroon.[9] In preparation for future restitution, it was the scholar and activist Bénédicte Savoy again leading the charge, this time working with a team from Cameroon to catalog all objects of art from Cameroon currently in German museums. The information was published as an open access book in 2023 and formatted for mobile phone use so that when accessed from Cameroon, it could provide detailed information on the objects and geographical location from where they were taken.[10] The purpose of this joint project, then, was not just to provide the justice of return but also to help create a sense of shared cultural heritage in postcolonial Cameroon.[11] Restitution continued to serve nation-building purposes.

Also returned were human remains and artifacts taken from indigenous nations. The Royal British Columbia Museum in Canada returned a totem pole to the Nuxalk nation.[12] In August 2023, the National Museum of Scotland returned a totem pole to the Nisga'a Nation, which was notable as it was one of the first occasions a UK museum restituted objects to a North American indigenous nation.[13]

[5] Chutel, "Netherlands Returns."
[6] Africanews, "US Museum Returns."
[7] Chow, "Inching Toward Restitution."
[8] Solomon, "Amid Tightening."
[9] Solomon, "German Museums."
[10] Authors collective, Savoy, and Meyer, *Atlas of Absence*.
[11] Richard Tsogang Fossi, one of the coauthors of the Cameroon project, comments at the workshop "Objects from Afar," Humboldt Forum, Berlin, March 6–7, 2024.
[12] Elassar, "Nuxalk Nation's Totem Pole."
[13] CBC News, "Stolen Totem Pole."

The University of California-Berkeley repatriated nearly half of the 9,000 Native American remains it held in its Anthropology Museum.[14] Major museums in the United States—the American Museum of Natural History in New York City, the Field Museum in Chicago, the Peabody Museum of Archaeology and Ethnology at Harvard University—closed parts of their exhibitions that displayed Native American objects, responding to new federal regulations requiring museums to obtain consent from indigenous communities before displaying their cultural artifacts.[15]

There have also been major breakthroughs in returning looted antiquities. A high-profile return occurred in 2021, when the Museum of the Bible in Washington, DC, established by the Christian evangelical family that owns the Hobby Lobby superstore chain, restituted 12,000 artifacts, including thousands of clay tablets and seals—from ancient Mesopotamia back to Iraq, after a US federal investigation concluded these items were looted. On the plane to Baghdad were additional 7,000 Iraqi antiquities, also looted, and now returned by Cornell University. "This is not just about thousands of tablets coming back to Iraq again—it is about the Iraqi people. [Restitution] restores not just the tablets, but the confidence of the Iraqi people by enhancing and supporting the Iraqi identity in these difficult times," said Hassan Nadhem, the Iraqi minister of culture, tourism and antiquities.[16] Restitution, again, was understood as an integral part of nation-building.

There has been renewed energy in identifying and restituting Nazi-looted art as well. Germany, unsurprisingly, led the way. The city of Hagen restituted a painting by Auguste Renoir to the heirs of Jakob Goldschmidt, a Jewish collector whose art holdings the Nazis confiscated after he fled Germany in 1933. The city then repurchased the painting so it could stay on view in the Osthaus Museum in Hagen.[17] In January 2023, the Prussian Cultural Heritage Foundation restituted the sixteenth-century Statuette of Maria Lactans, also to the heirs of Jakob Goldschmidt.[18] The foundation also returned three paintings to the heirs of Ismar Littmann, a Jewish collector who died by suicide as the Nazis took power in 1933. Littmann's descendants agreed to donate one of the paintings by Carlo Mense back to the German state, and it went on display at the Neue Nationalgalerie in Berlin.[19] The city of Dusseldorf restituted a painting to the heirs of Max and Iris Stern, but a similar agreement with

[14] Hudetz, "UC Berkeley Takes Significant Step."
[15] Jacobs and Small, "Leading Museums."
[16] Arraf, "Iraq Reclaims."
[17] Aton, "Pierre-Auguste Renoir Painting."
[18] Axelrod, "Germany Returns."
[19] Prussian Cultural Heritage Foundation, "Restitution of Three Artworks."

the family resulted in the painting remaining on display at the Kunstpalast in the city.[20] In May 2023, the City of Frankfurt and Städelsches Kunstinstitut Museum also first restituted a painting to the heirs of Gustav Rüdenberg, the original owner, and then repurchased it in order to keep it on display. The museum also put up a memorial plaque to commemorate Rüdenberg's murder in the Riga Ghetto in 1941.[21]

There was also significant activity on Nazi-looted art beyond Germany. In February 2023, the National Gallery in Prague returned fourteen art pieces to the descendants of Jewish collector Johann Bloch, whose collection was seized after his death in 1940.[22] In April 2023, Abdul Malak, the French culture minister, returned three heirless "MNRs"—two paintings to the heirs of Agathe and Ernst Saulmann, and a painting that was at the Louvre to the heirs of another Holocaust victim, Harry Fuld.[23] In May 2024, two additional MNRs (paintings by Alfred Sisley and Auguste Renoir) were restituted to the descendants of the French Jewish collector Grégoire Schusterman.[24] In the United States, the Museum of Modern Art (MOMA) in New York City restituted a painting by Egon Schiele to the heirs of Fritz Grünbaum, murdered in Dachau in 1941, and a painting by Marc Chagall to the heirs of a German gallerist.[25]

This flood of restituted cases also comes on the heels of a strengthened set of Washington Principles. A new set of eleven guidelines adopted in March 2024, *Best Practices for the Washington Principles on Nazi-Confiscated Art*, clarified that the "just and fair solution" in cases of restitution "means just and fair solutions first and foremost for the victims of the Holocaust (Shoah) and other victims of Nazi persecution and for their heirs."[26] This strengthened language is important as it tips the scale of justice toward the victims of Nazi looting, and not the concerns for public art stock and wealth of collections of individual museums or states. Also clarified was the concept of "sale under duress," which under the updated guidelines now meant that any art sale "by a persecuted person during the Holocaust era between 1933–1945 can be considered equivalent to an involuntary transfer of property based on the circumstances of the sale."[27] Further, the updated principles will allow claimants to submit their requests for evaluation of provenance of a disputed artwork

20 Ghermezian, "German City of Dusseldorf."
21 Jewish News Syndicate, "Frankfurt Returns Painting."
22 Jewish News Syndicate, "Prague Museums Return."
23 French Ministry of Culture, "Three works stolen."
24 Solomon, "Renoir, Sisley Paintings."
25 Mashberg and Bowley, "Schiele Artworks Returned"; Villa, "MOMA Returned."
26 US Department of State, "Best Practices."
27 US Department of State, "Best Practices."

without the current holder (museum or even a private owner) needing to provide consent to this inquiry.

The revisiting of the Washington Principles also reaffirmed their groundbreaking role, a "ripple effect," in setting up norms for expanded provenance research and, ultimately, restitution of colonial-looted art. Stuart Eizenstat, the US Secretary of State Special Adviser on Holocaust Issues and a key architect of the 1998 Washington Principles, made this connection directly: "It's a great example of how voluntary international principles, if they're undergirded by strong moral and ethical principles, can have a dramatic impact . . . All of this is connected and just wouldn't have happened otherwise."[28]

Contemporary artists have also entered the restitution fray. At the 2024 Venice Art Biennale, the most prestigious international art show, the Brazilian pavilion exhibited an indigenously constructed feather mantle with a display caption that informed the audience that seven European museums continued to hold similar mantles in their collections. The Nigerian pavilion displayed clay copies of 150 Benin Bronzes. The Beninese pavilion exhibited glass sculptures of musical instruments taken from the Kingdom of Dahomey (today's Benin) and stored in the depots of the Musée du quai Branly in Paris.[29] Restitution was also a hot topic in film. The Golden Bear for the Best Film at the Berlin International Film Festival in 2024 was awarded to *Dahomey*, a film by the French-Senegalese director Mati Diop. The documentary followed the return of twenty-six art objects from France to Senegal, and the international negotiations surrounding the restitution. Diop herself presented the film as part of a broader agenda of restitution activism:

> It's quite clear that they were way too few compared with the 7,000 works that are still held captive in these museums. These 26 works are good but are not enough, and I certainly think that it is humiliating. I would say we need to think about more than just the way it was staged and all the governmental communication of this process . . . France has exploited this place for centuries. You need to do more. You need to go further. You need to breathe new life into this question, and that is what I was trying to do in this film. We need to think of restitution in a broad sense.[30]

Things were changing so fast and often in unexpected places, that for long-time restitution advocates such as Bénédicte Savoy, it seemed "as though the Berlin Wall has fallen."[31]

[28] Hickley, "Nations Agree."
[29] Marshall, "At Venice Biennale."
[30] Mouriquand, "Berlinale 2024."
[31] Quoted in Lauter, "Restitution, Repatriation Efforts."

A walk through a museum in the age of decolonization

And while some states are pressing forward with restitution and some are resisting, many museums have taken on this fight themselves as part of a much broader process of museum decolonization and renarration of their collections. Over the past few decades, there has been a marked shift in how museums around the world understand their role in the broader society and culture.[32] A major transformation has occurred, where many museums have moved away from pure art representation to, instead, function as agents of cultural and political action and innovation.[33] This transformation has been especially notable in some former imperial ethnological museums, which have abandoned their previous cataloging and exoticizing of "other people" to now narrate the history of European colonialism and begin to disclose the origins of their own collections.[34]

A short walk through some of the former ethnological museums give a sense of the new tone with which the museums are approaching their own histories and the histories of the states which established them. For example, in Copenhagen, the entry panel to the exhibition *Voices from the Colonies* at the Danish National Museum, says,

> Denmark was once a colonial power. Europe's seventh largest slave-trading nation. Driven by dreams of profit, power and exotic luxury goods. With consequences for countless people. These are the people you are about to meet. People whose lives were changed as a result of Danish colonialism.

Elsewhere in the exhibition, another caption reads,

> Ship after ship anchors off the west coast of Africa. Ship after ship packed to the rim with people. Suffocating overcrowded during the entire passage across the Atlantic. There is also fear, hardship, disease and hunger on board. The fate of the enslaved is still new and unknown. Approximately 110,000 Africans' lives are destroyed by the Danish slave ships.[35]

The Wereldmuseum (formerly Tropenmuseum) in Amsterdam includes perhaps the most explicit statement about the colonial roots of its collection. The entry caption reads,

[32] Wali and Collins, "Decolonizing Museums."
[33] Coombes and Phillips, *Museum Transformations.*
[34] Van Huis, "Contesting Cultural Heritage"; Macdonald, "New Constellations of Difference."
[35] Author's visit to the National Museum of Denmark, Copenhagen, August 2022.

> A large part of our collections was acquired during the colonial period. This was a period characterized by grossly unequal power relations and violence. As a consequence, some of the objects we care for, including objects in this exhibition, may have been obtained through looting or in other dubious and unjust situations. The museum is actively doing research to clarify the provenance of its collections.[36]

At the Museum of World Cultures in Gothenburg, Sweden, reflecting on the historical marginalization or "internal colonization" of the Swedish Sami people, the museum says,

> According to established methods of defining and assessing democracy, Sweden has been classified as a free state with full democracy since 1921. Yet during various times and circumstances, citizens have been disempowered and stripped of their rights.[37]

There were also changes in Britain. The Victoria & Albert Museum changed the representation of its Maqdala treasures looted from Ethiopia (see Figure C.1):

> The British troops [] ransacked Maqdala and the surrounding area, seizing a vast quantity of treasure that was mostly brought back to England. This crown and chalice, both important items from the Ethiopian Orthodox Church, are two of the most famous objects from Maqdala now in the V&A collection. Today there are many questions surrounding their history and ownership. The V&A has a responsibility to shine a light on the complex histories behind these objects, and to openly acknowledge the difficult questions relating to their provenance.[38]

At the Museum of Archaeology and Anthropology in Cambridge, the project *RePresent* contextualized the Benin Bronzes displayed at the museum in this way:

> Here lies an incredibly artistic object of a people once called barbaric, primitive and savage negroes adorning European Museums. Stolen by the British in 1897, after an unwarranted massacre and burning of a self-surviving kingdom. These blood Benin arts can be likened to the Sierra Leone blood diamonds.[39]

[36] Author's visit to the Wereldmuseum, Amsterdam, October 2023.
[37] Author's visit to the Museum of World Cultures, Gothenburg, October 2023.
[38] Author's visit to the Victoria & Albert Museum, London, January 2023.
[39] Author's visit to the Museum of Archaeology and Anthropology, Cambridge, May 2022.

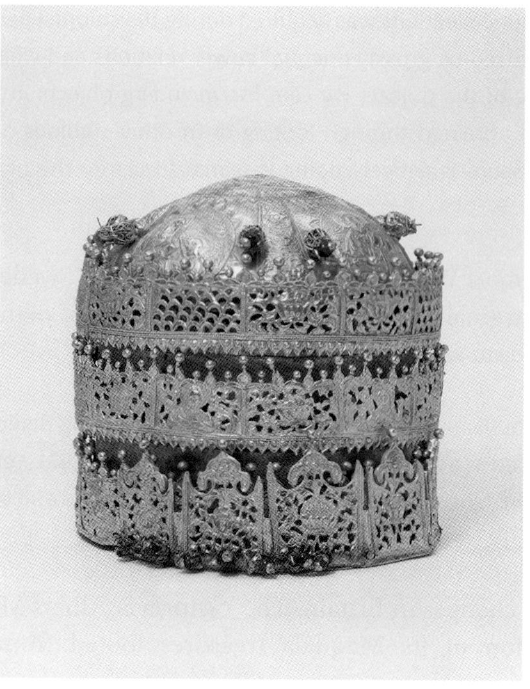

Figure C.1 Crown of Emperor Theodore of Abyssinia, Ethiopia, seventeenth–eighteenth century, Victoria & Albert Museum (© Victoria and Albert Museum, London)

The Penn Museum in Philadelphia narrates its very large collection of the Benin Bronzes under the title *Sacred Objects, Artistic Traditions, and the Colonization of an Empire*, and includes a "burned tusk" with the caption "The burnt tip of this carved tusk—taken from an ancestral altar—is possible evidence of the horrific destruction that ravaged the Kingdom."[40] There is also renewed attention to clearly displaying provenance and identifying the entire history of the object's ownership. The caption at one of the Benin Bronzes displayed at the Metropolitan Museum of Art in New York City lists its detailed provenance as: "Court of Benin, removed from the Royal Palace in 1897 during the British military occupation of Benin; Sotheby's, London, 1964; Paul Rose; Robert Owen Lehman, New York: Mr. and Mrs. Klaus G. Perls, New York, until 1990."[41]

[40] Author's visit to Penn Museum, Philadelphia, February 2024.
[41] Author's visit to the Metropolitan Museum of Art, New York City, August 2023.

And at the Humboldt Forum, after restitutions of art objects to Namibia and Nigeria, it is the process of restitution itself that has become the central object of the museum, no longer the artifacts alone. In the section that used to display art looted from Namibia, the caption reads:

> No objects are displayed here. Most of the objects discussed have been brought back to Namibia. This exhibition is a first step in understanding them: How can the objects reactivate historical and cultural knowledge? How can their return contribute to reconciliation? How can they help Germans and Namibians imagine the future?

Elsewhere in the museum, the captions put the new vision of this cultural institution in the context of its historical legacy and the burden of German political heritage,

> The critical appraisal of colonial crimes and power structures as well as the impact of racist ideology that continues to this day is one of the key tasks of the Humboldt Forum. In a building that contains reconstructed sections of the façade of the former Berlin Palace, presenting objects and their history in a way that is critical of racism is as difficult as it is important. As a symbol of the Prussian monarchy, the historical palace is associated with militarism, colonialism, and the repression of democratic movements.[42]

The British Museum may be open to change as well. Its *Reimagining the British Museum* project is a multiyear initiative in delivering curatorial briefs to new designers who will be working on redisplaying the collection over the coming years. The museum has also begun a number of new projects in collaboration with "source communities," such as The Endangered Material Knowledge Programme (EMKP), which calls attention to research and preserves the crafts, skills, practices, and knowledge of the material world that are in danger of disappearing. The museum "works very closely with external stakeholders, source communities/communities of origin and UK diaspora groups etc. to ensure that our temporary exhibition, public programming and curatorial research and stewardship work is done collaboratively and in consultation," the curator of the *Reimagining* project said.[43]

Many grand European national museums, which accumulated large collections of art to represent their states' imperial power and high international

[42] Author's visit to the Humboldt Forum, Berlin, March 2024.

[43] Author correspondence with Vikki Hawkins, project curator, *Reimagining the British Museum*, June 3, 2024.

cultural status, now compete in how to represent these collections to their publics, what language to use, what information to convey.[44] It is no longer the art object itself that is a symbol of status, it is the provenance history of that object and what it says about the state today that is a coveted symbol of status. One of the main points my book made was that both accumulation and restitution of looted art should be understood as fundamentally political acts that are related to how states understood their international status and how they chose to manage it—seeking higher status or preventing status loss. This fundamental point, then, also means that contemporary "restitution zeitgeist" is itself profoundly political and deeply entangled with the international political and cultural order.

The moral limits of art restitution

These projects of museum renarration have often, however, ignited strong cultural backlash, accusations of politicization, and then retrenchment.[45] They have also elicited scorn from decolonization activists with more maximalist demands, who scoffed at the cosmetic and sometimes tokenistic changes taking place in European museums.[46] For Bénédicte Savoy, for example, Germany's self-congratulatory posture after the internationally acclaimed restitutions to Namibia and Nigeria belied the complex web of contemporary neocolonialist policies, such as the difficulties in African researchers' getting German visas. For Savoy, therefore, restitution is more than just "moving things around"; restitution includes a much broader set of conversations around knowledge exchange and equal partnerships, including freedom of travel for African scholars researching their own cultural heritage held captive in European museums.[47] Even if we are living in a "restitution zeitgeist," what true and comprehensive restitution means continues to be a moving target.[48]

The surge in restitution cases and the increasing visibility of restitution as an international problem have also exposed the moral limits of restitution as a tool of global justice. In the case of return of cultural property to native and indigenous communities, restitution of material objects may ring hollow in

[44] For example, see Siegal, "Rijksmuseum Removing."
[45] Donington, "Relics of Empire?"; Onishi, "Turmoil Engulfs."
[46] Kassim, "Museum Will Not Be Decolonised"; Hassett, "Acknowledging or Occluding"; Shaw and Carrigan, "Reform or Reset?"
[47] Bénédicte Savoy, comments at the workshop "Objects from Afar," Humboldt Forum, Berlin, March 6–7, 2024.
[48] Campbell, "Art Restitution Zeitgeist?"

the absence of any meaningful discussion about return of the land to these communities.[49]

Historian Achille Mbembe worried that all the focus on art restitution would replace the broader political fight for accountability for colonial crimes.[50] An anonymous British Museum Trustee complained that "the museums were being asked to bear the entire moral weight of colonialism."[51] Other scholars objected that the blanket new restitution proposals (return everything taken before decolonization) would de facto delegitimize any African art prior to decolonization in the 1960s, and in the process remove agency from African artists themselves who worked and created art before that period.[52] There is also much diversity of opinion and vibrant debates within postcolonial countries themselves about what to do with looted art. These societies do not always speak with one voice and may have a variety of positions and solutions on restitution that go beyond bulk repatriation.[53] And then there is the moral concern about disproportionate effort being put toward the issue of restitution compared to other, much more pressing needs. Some Nigerians were already complaining about the vast amounts of money the Edo state had dedicated to building a new museum to host the Bronzes, while there was no money for schools and hospitals.[54]

There are deeper political critiques as well. For some scholars and activists, in both Global North and South, acts of restitution have been decried as cynical exchanges of art for economic resources, a continuation of neocolonial polices of extraction. Critics of these "rhetorical restitutions" noted that France reached an arms deal with Senegal, and Germany increased its economic imports from Namibia at the same time that restitution deals were being signed.[55] These economic side deals then make the restitution policies of former colonial states not progressive at all, but in fact should be understood as "neo-retentionist."[56] If colonial-looted artifacts were being returned without former colonial states looking critically at their own histories, argued Doris Duhennois regarding the case of France, restitution was nothing more than "a political gesture that helps conceal the reality of French colonial mentalities."[57]

[49] For an extensive discussion of this problem, see Esterling, *Indigenous Cultural Property.*
[50] von Oswald, "Restitution Report."
[51] Quoted in Phillips, *Loot*, p. 272, n. 38.
[52] Paquette, "France and the Restitution."
[53] Marlowe, "Review of Dan Hicks."
[54] Phillips, *Loot*, p. 286.
[55] Eyssette, "Restitution vs. Retention," p. 110.
[56] Eyssette, "Restitution vs. Retention," p. 111.
[57] Dris Duhennois, "Restitution of African Colonial Artefacts," p. 130. On this point see also Boehme, "Normative Expectations."

Similar critiques have also been levied at the so-called "digital" or "virtual restitutions" where what is transferred to source communities are digitized materials, not the artifacts themselves. In 2020, the AfricaMuseum in Tervuren, Belgium (formerly the Royal Museum for Central Africa) began a "digital restitution" project which promised to deliver to partner institutions in the Democratic Republic of Congo a "digital collection database."[58] In 2021, AfricaMuseum presented a set of digitized sound recordings of Rwandan musical traditions and digitized archives to the Rwanda Cultural Heritage Academy as a form of digital restitution to their former colony.[59] For the authors of these projects, digital restitution is important, as it fills the gaps in cultural memory and can provide a broader sense of shared culture than a decontextualized returned object alone.[60] For critics, digital restitutions are more akin to status virtue-signaling.[61]

And then there is the question of who is the rightful recipient of all this looted art. While restitution to families of original owners of Nazi-looted art is often difficult and time-consuming, especially in cases of "heirless" looted art, there are mostly clear legal guidelines for establishing claimant status and determining legal standing as a descendent of a victim of Nazi looting. While the process may involve a lot of detective work, there are legal signposts that can determine who, eventually, is recognized as a rightful owner.

But in the cases of colonial-looted art, art is restituted to states, not families, and claims of ownership can become much more heavily politically contested. For art that was looted before modern states were established, there are questions of which contemporary state should be the proper recipient of restituted art. The complexities of within-Nigeria competition for ownership of the Benin Bronzes were already discussed in Chapter 4, but what about the El Hadj Omer Tall sword restituted by France to Senegal, which could have perhaps also been restituted to Mali, as it was created in the precolonial empire of Toucouleur that would also include today's Mali?[62] And some of the artifacts procured by colonial administrators in the French Congo have likely been produced in what is today Gabon or the Central African Republic, before the Republic of Congo was established.[63] So which country should they be restituted to? All of these questions continue to revitalize

[58] AfricaMuseum, AFRISURGE.

[59] AfricaMuseum, "AfricaMuseum transfers."

[60] Van Bockhaven, "Les Congolais obtiendront."

[61] Eyssette, "Restitution Vs. Retention." For an engaging discussion about digital restitution by African digital heritage scholars Chao Tayiana and Molemo Moilo, see "Digital Restitution and Its Discontents."

[62] Arnoldi, Kéita, and Sidibé, "National Museum of Mali."

[63] Eyssette, "Restitution Vs. Retention," p. 113. For more details on this case, see Kaehr and Perrois, "Masterwork That Sheds Tears."

the much broader debate about whether restitution of individual artifacts is even a global public good, or a concession to nationalism and particularism, and whether cultural heritage should be national or universal, arguments I engaged with earlier in the book.[64]

To complicate the normative framework further, not all "source countries" seek restitution. International status and, more to the point, narratives about status, play into decisions regarding whether and how to approach restitution campaigns at all.[65] Seeking status is a claim that a state does not, in fact, already have high status and this can shape how states demand restitution. For example, Tibet's contested status has made it that much harder to successfully reclaim looted artworks—the concept of "nation" and its external recognition plays a critical role in restitution efforts.[66]

On the other hand, China has chosen not to pursue restitution openly in a manner Greece or Nigeria have, presumably because it does not want to signal weakness as a victim of looting. Looting of its artifacts, and especially the sacking of the Summer Palace in 1860, remains a matter of great national humiliation in China.[67] Instead, China has engaged in an intricate and sustained campaign of purchasing Chinese-looted art at international auctions privately or through diplomatic, often behind-the-scenes bilateral negotiations with states that are in possession of this art.[68] More spectacularly, there have been increasing reports of robberies of Chinese artifacts from Western museums as part of a coordinated Chinese state effort to get those artifacts back to China.[69] Other countries have opted to seek higher international cultural status not through restitution but its opposite—through supporting exhibitions and displays of their art in major international museums abroad. The objective here is to expose Western audiences to Japanese, Saudi, Egyptian, Chinese, or Turkish art and culture and through this exposure and aesthetic appreciation elevate their state status.[70]

And then there is the question of unwanted heritage and unwanted restitution. For example, the US Army still holds a collection of 327 objects of Nazi propaganda and military art, including four watercolors painted by Hitler himself. These objects of little artistic value or interest other than to historians

[64] For recent entrants to this debate, see Kuper, *Museum of Other People*; Frum, "Who Benefits"; Mattez, "Restitution of Cultural Property." For the critique of the Humboldt Forum along those lines, see Dätsch, "Common, shared, contradictory."

[65] On the importance of paying attention to narratives about status in status research, see Beaumont, *Grammar of Status Competition*.

[66] Singh, "Repatriation Without Patria."

[67] Wang, *Never Forget*.

[68] Herman, *Restitution*; Azimi and Kerviel, "Complex Issue."

[69] Palmer, "Great Chinese Art Heist."

[70] McClellan, *Art Museum*, p. 258.

(or the apparently sizeable number of Nazi aficionados on the Internet), were discovered in 1945 in Germany by a special "reversed-Monuments Men" team of the US Army and taken to the United States. Germany never asked for these objects back and they remain at a US Army warehouse in Fort Belvoir, Virginia. For guardians of this unwanted art, such as Sarah Forgey, the US Army's chief art curator, there is a political reason to keep them locked up:

> The rationale in 1945 was that we take possession of these works to keep them out of dangerous hands . . . The fear was that there would be a revival of Nazism. Look at the world today. That rationale seems more valid in 2020 than it's been in a long time.[71]

Beyond European museums

More broadly, a serious critique levied at the maximalist arguments for restitution is that they continue to perpetuate Eurocentrism, in that the entire debate is about the West and what the European states and museums do. Once again, it is the Western states that are the heroes of their own story.[72] This critique can be levied against this book as well, as the main focus of my inquiry was the role looted art played in European states status-seeking and status-management strategies. To that end, this book paid much more attention to the narratives of European states and their museums than to those in the "source countries" where the art originated or to individual stories of families who were looking for the art stolen from them in World War II. This imbalance in the book in favor of European museums that hold this art is not an omission of negligence, but a choice of focus. Art looted from "source countries" plays a huge political and cultural role in those countries, as the discussion about restitution campaigns launched by Nigeria and Greece already demonstrated earlier in the book. Art looted by the Nazis also weighs heavily in narratives and identities of individual families, many of whom have made this search for restitution the central feature of their intergenerational memory, often to much personal loss and sacrifice.

The analytical focus of this book, however, was on a particular piece of the much larger story about looted art—my interest was in the changing value of looted art for states that own it. Zooming out to other pieces of the broader restitution landscape would necessitate a very different set of

[71] Quoted in Filkins, "Inside the U.S. Army's Warehouse."
[72] For some of these arguments, see von Oswald, "Restitution Report."

questions and empirical investigations. It would also necessitate widening the scope of inquiry and the universe of restitution cases to tease out other possible dynamics at work, in addition to concerns with status. Questions of national identity and nation-building or moral justice and reparations for past wrongs are also questions that would require a much richer set of examples than the limited number of cases I explored in the book. Part of the problem here is that the possible pool of cases is limitless. The global diffusion of looted art and the geographic dislocation of these objects makes each object a possible case of its own, as does each family that has lost it, each state that owns it, each museum that houses it, each state that demands its return, and so on.

A broader lens at the changing global art landscape would also note that, in parallel to the restitution campaigns, there has also been a slew of new major museums openings in the Global South as part of the broader international "museum boom." Perhaps the glitziest and most highly anticipated of these museums is the Museum of West African Art (MOWAA) in Benin City, Nigeria, which is to house, in part, the restituted Benin Bronzes. But new museums are springing up everywhere. The Grand Egyptian Museum is set to open next to the Giza pyramids and should house 100,000 Egyptian antiquities—presumably some restituted from European museums. In Cameroon, there is a newly renovated National Museum that may display art restituted from Germany or France. There is a new National Museum in Accra, Ghana, and the Manhyia Palace Museum in Kumasi, the capital of the former Asante Empire, that could house Asante art Ghana has been requesting from British museums. The new Itumbaha Museum in Nepal is showcasing artifacts restituted from Europe and elsewhere.[73] This museum renaissance in the Global South has led some scholars to declare that the encyclopedic or universal museum as a cultural project, is dead. "The encyclopedic museum had an idea that it could serve as an opportunity to learn more about the world and in turn about ourselves, but this opportunity has never been democratic," Aindrea Emelife, curator at the MOWAA in Benin City said. New museums in the Global South were trying to "deconstruct the museum model itself," connecting art to the society that created it and recontextualizing art as part of living experience.[74]

International politics and the questions of international status feature prominently in the Global South "museum boom" as well. For example,

[73] For further detail on these new museums, see Iwu, "Nigeria's New Museum."
[74] Quoted in Iwu, "Nigeria's New Museum."

China has steadily invested in various African states' infrastructure and economic projects, but also increasingly in African cultural projects, including projects that deal directly with art and restitution. Most notably, China financed the major Museum of Black Civilizations in Dakar, Senegal, with the investment of 35 million dollars.[75] The museum opened in 2018 and set the standard for similar new museums to be built in other African countries.[76] It was not just China that used this channel of influence. South Korea has financed a major new museum in Kinshasa, in the Democratic Republic of Congo.[77] North Korea has also had a long-term relationship with Namibia and its architectural firms have carried out a series of projects there, including the country's flagship Namibian Independence Memorial Museum in Windhoek.[78]

The story of the remarkable change in restitution practices, however, needs to be further recentered from European museums to acknowledge the strength, persistence, and success of many activist campaigns that originated in the "source countries" themselves. Beyond the brief discussion of campaigns in Nigeria and Greece in the context of the Benin Bronzes and the Parthenon Marbles, there have been strong and sustained campaigns in many other countries—Namibia, Ghana, Mexico, Nepal, Cambodia, Ethiopia, Ivory Coast, Mali, Senegal, Benin, Indonesia, Sri Lanka, Democratic Republic of Congo, Cameroon, and many others.[79]

It is not just states but also individual activists who have taken on the case of restitution. The idea that stolen art should, simply, be taken back from European museums has been vocalized at least since the 1970s, as already discussed in Chapter 4. But there are renewed efforts at the so-called "guerilla restitution." In September 2020, Mwazulu Diyabanza, a Congolese restitution activist, walked into the Africa Museum in Berg en Dal in the Netherlands and took an African funereal post from its podium and walked out, while loudly chanting the crimes of European colonialism ("We came to recuperate what is rightfully ours . . . They have pillaged, humiliated, stolen") and recording his act on Facebook Live.[80] Diyabanza has also attempted what he named "active diplomacy" from the Louvre, from where he took an eighteenth-century guardian spirit figure from the island of Florès in Eastern Indonesia, before a guard stopped him. He did the same at the Museum of

[75] Lebovics, "In the Diaspora."
[76] Bocoum and Ndiaye, "Le Musée Des Civilisations Noires."
[77] Mukundayi and Van Beurden, "Korea and the New National Museum."
[78] Kirkwood, "Postindependence Architecture."
[79] For a recent quick overview of a few of the ongoing campaigns, see Garcia, "Mexico's Splashy Campaign"; Villa, "Met Returns"; Mashberg and Bowley, "Cambodia Says"; Hickley, "How 4 Countries."
[80] Brown, "Mwazulu Diyabanza."

African, Oceanic, and Amerindian Arts in Marseille. After he repeated the stunt at the Musée du quai Branly in Paris, when the police came in, Diyabanza greeted them with a memorable and since much repeated line, "Ah the police are here. Officer, I want to report a theft."[81]

Diyabanza has since created a wider network—the Multicultural Front against Pillaging (Front Multiculturel Anti Spoliation (FMAS))—which is aimed at global restitution of colonial-looted art as well as artifacts taken from indigenous nations:

> We have to give a voice to these people and push them to join our action so we can pressure western governments to return everything. This restitution must be immediate and unconditional and carried out with dignity and respect—and it must happen everywhere in Europe. The museums and institutions of these countries must understand that we are determined.[82]

Another restitution activism group, Looty, has digitally recaptured looted art objects on display in European museums and then showed their replicas on the Internet, for the publics in the "source countries" to enjoy. In August 2023, the group "digitally repatriated" the Rosetta Stone from the British Museum, by producing a QR code which people in Egypt standing at the location where the Rosetta Stone is thought to have been discovered would be able to point at and watch the Stone appear in an augmented-reality art installation. The group has done a similar installation with a digital copy of the Benin Bronzes and displayed it at the Venice Architecture Biennale in 2023. For these activists, the mission is to protect the object's narrative from the colonial museum's appropriation. "The physical still has power . . . Let's at least get the power of digital in our own hands, for us to be able to tell that story, rather than leave it up to museums to then start representing things digitally, and then own that narrative," said one of Looty's founders, Chidirim Nwaubani.[83]

The Chicago-based Iraqi artist Michael Rakowitz proposed in 2020 to donate his art piece, *The Invisible Enemy Should Not Exist (Lamassu)* to Tate Modern in London, which would then share its ownership with an institution in Iraq. Rakowitz's installation replicated a Mesopotamian antique sculpture dated to 700 BCE and demolished by the Islamic State in 2015. In exchange for donating his work, Rakowitz demanded that the British Museum return one of its two Assyrian lamassu sculptures, that were discovered in the city

[81] Lebovics, "In the Diaspora," p. 120.
[82] Willsher, "We Want Our Riches Back."
[83] Nayeri, "A 'Digital Heist.'"

of Nineveh by the British archaeologist Sir Austen Henry Layard in 1847. In a letter to the British Museum, Rakowitz wrote, "Given all that has been destroyed in Iraq, and the intersection of that destruction with the west's insatiable appetite for the objects of the east while not always, if ever, extending that concern to its people, this return of an original would be more than just restitutive. It would be restorative."[84] Tate Modern was happy to receive the gift, but the British Museum, so far, had no plans to restitute the lamassu to Iraq.[85]

Restitution activists have credited these campaigns with raising the visibility of the restitution issue and putting pressure on governments in France, the Netherlands, and Germany to begin serious restitution projects. They also build on the broad appeal of "restitution bandits" in popular culture, such as Killmonger from *The Black Panther* or the Mu'tafikah gang in Ishmael Reed's novel *Mumbo Jumbo*, who liberate artifacts from Western museums in order to create "renewed enthusiasms for the Ikons of the aesthetically victimized civilizations."[86] It is fitting in the context of my book that in Reed's novel, these museums are called the "Centers of Art Detention."

Art and international status—a research agenda

The main goal of this book was to demonstrate the political importance of art objects for states and the enduring power they have for state strategies of status-seeking and status management. In doing so, I hoped to create a space for a new research agenda in International Relations that explores the relationship between art and international status. This agenda builds on a number of theoretical and political implications of my book.

The first theoretical implication is that the markers of international status are not static. They change over time with the global cultural and normative shifts that take place across international society. In the context of art, art objects themselves have been read and interpreted differently at the time of original collection than they are interpreted today. The very purpose of collecting these artifacts has also changed over time. Napoleon's looting of Italy, Elgin's capture of the Parthenon sculptures, and the nineteenth-century antiquities rush were all rooted in contemporary, narrow conceptions of the Greco-Roman classical civilization and its foundational role for European culture, as well as the fascination with exotic disappeared civilizations like

[84] Weaver, "Artist Asks British Museum."
[85] Harris, "Tate May Acquire."
[86] Quoted in Lucas, "Forgotten Movement."

ancient Egypt or Assyria. The collection and possession of these artifacts was then evidence of high culture—both the artifacts themselves and the countries that now owned them conveyed high cultural status.

The extraction of material objects from European imperial pursuits across Africa, Asia, or Latin America, however, was evidence of something else. These objects were often collected in punitive expeditions where the theft of locally valuable objects was an integral part of colonial politics of humiliation and cultural erasure. The purpose of artifacts' removal was the symbolic expression of defeat and demonstration of colonial control, but also acquisition of specific objects that were not for sale. These stolen objects were then displayed in European colonial museums as parts of exhibitions that manifested scientific-racist arguments about civilizational development and progress, with objects from colonized territories there to represent civilizational primitive beginnings, and European objects the civilizational pinnacle. The artifacts and states that owned them also reflected status, but of a different kind—the "low" status of primitive civilizations and the "high" status of the Europeans who extracted the objects through "civilizing missions" abroad.

Nazi looting had a different purpose yet. It was part of a broader Nazi attempt at creating a total culture, based on racialized ideology of German and Aryan supremacy. Removing "degenerate art" from public display was part of this cultural totalitarianism. But looting served other purposes as well. It was a means for individual Nazi officers to gain personal cultural status by creating collections of stolen art, but also for Hitler's grand ambition of amassing all of Europe's "best art" in Germany and making Germany the cultural center of the world. Art looting for the Nazis, obviously, was also a form of cultural genocide. Dispossession of European Jews was a crucial step toward their complete physical annihilation.

The second theoretical implication that the problem of looted art demonstrated was the changing meaning of material objects for states. The same artifact meant different things to different actors at different point in time—as a symbol of empire, a symbol of national identity, a symbol of power, a symbol of civilization, a stigmata of shame. Over time, and through global cultural entanglements, new meanings got ascribed to the artifacts themselves, not just to the norms of who should own them. This is because material objects, such as artifacts, have social lives of their own; they have biographies, they have geographies, and their meaning changes within the changing context in which they are displayed.[87]

[87] Appadurai, *Social Life of Things* and especially Kopytoff, "Cultural Biography of Things."

Art objects, of course, do not become status symbols by themselves; they do not intrinsically have value and meaning. Affixing ownership and provenance of an art object to a state also affixes national identity to the object while elevating state status. By becoming nationalized, part of national cultural heritage, these objects become important in both nation-building (as we saw in the case of the Parthenon and post-independence Greece), as well as in legitimating state actions internationally, including violent imperial, colonial, and racist projects of cultural domination (as we saw in the role the Parthenon Marbles, Benin Bronzes, and looted art played in the domination projects of imperial France and Britain and, later, Nazi Germany). This link between art objects and national identity, then, also explains why states (Great Britain in the case of the Marbles, Serbia in the case of Nazi-looted art) have such a hard time letting these objects go. They would have much to gain, status-wise, with restitution, but their profound narratives of the self, and the way in which these art objects became significant for their national identity, make restitution ontologically difficult, if not impossible.

The third theoretical implication concerns the historical contingency and the changing notion of what is considered a "standard of civilization." As I demonstrate in the context of looted art, these standards were products of different conceptions of status, morality, and "civilization" in the different historical periods under study. If during the late eighteenth century, the standard of civilization was manifested in attachment to Greco-Roman antiquity, in the late nineteenth century in the colonial boundary-making between Europeans and non-Europeans, during World War II in the Nazi construction of an "Aryan civilization," after 1945 the standard moved toward individual rights, and in the twenty-first century toward global social justice, which necessitated giving looted art back. This focus on the historical contingency of the art object's status value introduces an important dynamic aspect to status research. Opposite actions (looting and restitution) were used for status-seeking and status management at different historical periods, which demonstrates that the standards for status recognition also change over time.

A further theoretical implication is the dialectic of alternative and competing normative orders. The new normative framework of the "restitution zeitgeist" has created an international normative order of restitution which, like other normative orders, stigmatizes deviance from the norm, and stigmatization in an international society leads to status loss.[88] What Serbia, for

[88] Adler-Nissen, "Stigma Management."

example, has chosen is a form of counter-stigmatization—by claiming that the countries demanding restitution, such as Italy, were fascists on the wrong side of history, so their moral claim is invalid. This strategy of stigma management, however, also includes joining an alternative international normative order, such as the one led by Russia. This alternative order presents international restitution norms as deviant and justifies nonrestitution with its own set of morally righteous actions, such as retaining looted art as a just compensation for wartime losses.

And while Russia's aggressive and deviant international behavior, including blatant art looting throughout Ukraine, has clearly diminished its international cultural status, paradoxically, this same behavior could be interpreted as actually elevating its great power status. Russia's behavior, at least since 2014, has been stigmatized by large segments of the international community, but Russia is, again, recognized as a great power to be feared and reckoned with. It is the flaunting of international norms that has, in fact, elevated Russia's international status, at least status understood in the realm of power politics. This, then, implies that, instead of thinking of a single international order, it may be more productive to conceptualize the world in terms of status orders that coexist but contradict one another.[89] The case of art restitution demonstrates that there is an alternative status order (of restitution) that is in the process of becoming more salient or dominant than the previous status order (of art accumulation through looting), and some states are stuck in between, hedging their bets.

And yet, with all the excitement about the progress in global restitution, looting on a grand scale continues in Ukraine, Syria, Egypt, Peru, Iraq, Romania, and elsewhere. The final theoretical implication from this book, therefore, concerns a broader question of how international norms ebb and flow and don't diffuse in any linear or teleological fashion. There were attempts to formalize prohibition of looting already in the nineteenth century, which were then disregarded, then institutionalized again, and then continuously ignored by some states and respected by others. The same nonlinear process has followed attempts to mobilize restitution campaigns—they began early, then disappeared, then re-emerged in a different form at a different historical juncture. This path of normative change and retrenchment then also demonstrates the often circuitous evolution of well-established international political and cultural practices.

[89] Røren, "Belligerent Bear."

Restitution as repair

The big final question is, do we truly live in the age of restitution? Will the international cultural landscape look quite different in a decade from now, with cultural hubs beginning to decenter from the small Western core into the East or the Global South? Will the repatriation of major artworks from European museums allow Dakar, Lagos, Benin City, Phnom Penh, or Chennai to compete for cultural hub status with London, Paris, or New York? Or will restitution movements fail because of a nationalist backlash against acknowledging state crimes from the past? Will major international museums roar back and reassert their claims on universal cultural heritage of all humankind, heritage they appointed themselves global guardians of? When the UK refuses Nigeria's requests for repatriation of the Benin Bronzes from the British Museum, the argument is often that these valuable objects will become less internationally visible, as many more visitors come to London than to Benin City.[90] But of course, an argument could be made that if the Benin Bronzes were to be displayed in Benin City, this would elevate Nigeria as a cultural destination, raising its international cultural status. State decisions on art restitution, then, should be understood as not only responses to moral arguments, but also exercises in international power and control.

But the concept of restitution itself includes many different practices and possibilities. Restitution is often understood as the restoration of something lost or stolen to its proper owner. This can be done through the return of the stolen object or through financial or other material compensation for loss. But, more broadly, restitution is about making whole what was once broken. It is about re-establishing order.[91] And this includes nonmaterial responses, such as acknowledgment of past injustice, proper disclosure of provenance, the history of ownership of an object, and attempts at repair. In the world of art restitution, practices I described in the book range from repatriation of objects to their countries of origin, return of artwork to individuals who originally owned them, financial compensation by museums to original owners in exchange for retaining the artwork, agreements between original and current owners on loaning the artwork for temporary exhibitions, public acknowledgment of artwork provenance, changing the captions and panel displays at museums, and so on. Restitution, in other words, does not always end in artwork return, and there are many additional possibilities of redress.

[90] For example, this is one of the main arguments in Jenkins, *Keeping Their Marbles*.
[91] Herman, *Restitution*.

To get at a complete picture of this broad field of restitution, one of the goals of this book was to provide the comprehensive history of art restitution since World War II and firmly connect the efforts to restitute art looted in the Holocaust with efforts to reclaim colonial-looted art. These restitution campaigns are often thought of as separate and distinct, historically removed from one another. Yet, as my book demonstrates, we cannot fully understand the contemporary restitution movements without understanding what came before, and how today's efforts build on the heroic efforts to find and save hundreds of thousands of artifacts stolen by the Nazis and their collaborators. What the search for Nazi-looted art developed was not only the legal language for restitution but also an understanding of provenance as an inseparable element of an artifact's value. This was a revolution in art appraisal and practice, and it has informed how we view the value of artifacts stolen during colonial occupations and displayed in the world's most famous museums.

The last goal of the book was to connect the much more well-known cases of the Parthenon Marbles and Benin Bronzes with the much less-known cases of looted art in smaller museums away from the central nodes of international cultural hierarchy. Global attention has for decades been paid to the world's major museums—the British Museum, the Louvre, the Musée du quai Branly, the Humboldt Forum—and to their responses to restitution claims. But looting of art and the continuing injustice of denied restitution is an international problem, and smaller museums out of the global spotlight have managed to avoid reckoning with looted art objects in their possession for too long. One of my hopes for this book is that it will bring these cases to international attention and help start the slow process of acknowledgment and repair.

References

Abrams, Amah-Rose. "A Send-Off Exhibition of 179 Looted Objects in Hamburg Marks 'the Beginning of the Return' of Germany's Benin Bronzes to Nigeria." *Artnet Magazine*, December 17, 2021.

Abungu, George. "The Declaration on Universal Museums: A Contested Issue." *ICOM News* 57, no. 1 (2004): pp. 3–5.

Adler-Nissen, Rebecca. "Stigma Management in International Relations: Transgressive Identities, Norms, and Order in International Society." *International Organization* 68, no. 1 (2014): pp. 143–76.

Advisory Committee on the Assessment of Restitution Applications for Items of Cultural Value and the Second World War in The Hague (the Restitution Committee), "Binding Opinion Regarding the Dispute about Restitution of *Painting with Houses* by Wassily Kandinsky, currently in the possession of Amsterdam City Council." Report number: RC 3.141, October 22, 2018, https://www.restitutiecommissie.nl/en/recommendation/bild-mit-hausern-by-wassily-kandinsky.

AfricaMuseum. "AfricaMuseum transfers over 4000 sound recordings to Rwanda." October 28, 2021, https://www.africamuseum.be/en/research/news/africamuseum_transfers_over_4000_sound_recordings_to_rwanda.

AfricaMuseum. AFRISURGE: Transformative Heritage: politics, peacebuilding and digital restitution of cultural heritage in contemporary Northeast DR Congo, 2020, https://www.africamuseum.be/en/research/discover/projects/prj_detail?prjid=717.

Africanews. "US Museum Returns Ghana's Looted Artifacts After 150 Years." February 9, 2024, https://www.africanews.com/2024/02/09/us-museum-returns-ghanas-looted-artifacts-after-150-years.

Ajana, Btihaj. "Branding, Legitimation and the Power of Museums: The Case of the Louvre Abu Dhabi." *Museum and Society* 13, no. 3 (2015): pp. 322–41.

Akinsha, Konstantin. "Ante Topic Mimara, 'the Master Swindler of Yugoslavia.'" *ARTnews* 100, no. 8 (September 2001): pp. 155–58.

Akinsha, Konstantin. "Stalin's Decrees and Soviet Trophy Brigades: Compensation, Restitution in Kind, or 'Trophies' of War?". *International Journal of Cultural Property* 17, no. 2 (2010): pp. 195–216.

Akinsha, Konstantin, and Grigoriĭ Fedotovich Kozlov. *Beautiful Loot: The Soviet Plunder of Europe's Art Treasures*. New York: Random House, 1995.

Albanese, Laurie Lico. *Stolen Beauty*. New York: Atria Books, 2017.

Alexander, Jeffrey. "On the Social Construction of Moral Universals: The Holocaust from War Crime to Trauma Drama." *European Journal of Social Theory* 5, no. 1 (2002): pp. 5–85.

Alford, Kenneth. *Herman Göring and the Nazi Art Collection: The Looting of Europe's Art Treasures and Their Dispersal After World War II*. Jefferson, NC: McFarland, 2012.

Anagnost, Adrian, and Manol Gueorguiev. "Edo Spaces, European Images: Iterations of Art and Architecture of Benin." In *Perspectives on In/stability*, edited by Delinda Collier and Robyn Farrell Chicago: Art Institute of Chicago, 2022. https://www.artic.edu/digital-publications/36/perspectives-on-instability/14/edo-spaces-european-images-iterations-of-art-and-architecture-of-benin.

Anderson, Benedict. *Imagined Communities: Reflections on the Origin and Spread of Nationalism*. London: Verso, 1991.

ANSA. "A Belgrado i quadri dei nazisti, l'Italia li rivuole." *ANSA*, March 20, 2024.

Appadurai, Arjun. *The Social Life of Things: Commodities in Cultural Perspective.* Cambridge: Cambridge University Press, 1986.

Appiah, Kwame Anthony. "Whose Culture Is It?" *The New York Review of Books*, February 9, 2006, 38–53.

Apter, Andrew. *The Pan-African Nation: Oil and the Spectacle of Culture in Nigeria.* Chicago: University of Chicago Press, 2008.

Arnold, Bettina. "The Past as Propaganda: Totalitarian Archaeology in Nazi Germany." In *Histories of Archaeology: A Reader in the History of Archaeology*, edited by Tim Murray and Christopher Evans, pp. 120–44. Oxford: Oxford University Press, 2008.

Arnoldi, Mary Jo, Daouda Kéita, and Samuel Sidibé. "The National Museum of Mali, 1960–Present: Protecting and Promoting the National Cultural Heritage." In *National Museums in Africa*, edited by Debora L Silverman, George Abungu, and Peter Probst, pp. 139–58. London: Routledge, 2021.

Arraf, Jane. "Iraq Reclaims 17,000 Looted Artifacts, Its Biggest-Ever Repatriation." *The New York Times*, August 3, 2021.

Arvanitis, Kostas, and Louise Tythacott. *Museums and Restitution: New Practices, New Approaches.* Farnham: Ashgate, 2014.

Ascherson, Neal. "End the Exile." *The Guardian*, June 20, 2004.

Ashcroft, AC. "As Britain Returns to an Expeditionary Strategy, Do We Have Anything to Learn from the Victorians?" *Defence Studies* 1, no. 1 (2001): pp. 75–98.

Askew, Marc. "The Magic List of Global Status: UNESCO, World Heritage and the Agendas of States." In *Heritage and Globalisation*, edited by Sophia Labadi and Colin Long, pp. 33–58. London: Routledge, 2010.

Athanassopoulos, Effie-Fotini. "An 'Ancient' Landscape: European Ideals, Archaeology, and Nation Building in Early Modern Greece." *Journal of Modern Greek Studies* 20, no. 2 (2002): pp. 273–305.

Aton, Francesca. "Pierre-Auguste Renoir Painting Restituted to the Heirs of a Jewish Banker Fleeing Nazi Persecution and Repurchased by a German City." *ARTnews*, June 7, 2023.

Aton, Francesca. "Restitution Organization Sues to Keep Smithsonian's Benin Bronzes from Returning to Nigeria." *Artnet Magazine*, December 6, 2022.

Auslander, Leora, and Tara Zahra. "The Things They Carried: War, Mobility, and Material Culture." In *Objects of War: The Material Culture of Conflict and Displacement*, edited by Leora Auslander and Tara Zahra, pp. 1–22. Ithaca: Cornell University Press, 2018.

Authors collective, Bénédicte Savoy, and Andrea Meyer. *Atlas of Absence: Cameroon's Cultural Heritage in Germany.* Heidelberg: Heidelberg University Library, 2023.

Axelrod, Toby. "Germany Returns 16th-Century Statuette Sold Off by Nazis to Jewish Banker's Heirs." *The Times of Israel*, January 31, 2023.

Azimi, Roxana, and Sylvie Kerviel. "The Complex Issue of Looted Chinese Art Restitution." *Le Monde*, May 5, 2024.

Bach, Jonathan. "Brand of Brothers?: The Humboldt Forum and the Myths of Innocence." *German Politics and Society* 39, no. 1 (2021): pp. 100–11.

Bach, Jonathan. "Colonial Pasts in Germany's Present." *German Politics and Society* 37, no. 4 (2019): pp. 58–73.

Bachleitner, Kathrin. "Ontological Security as Temporal Security? The Role of 'Significant Historical Others' in World Politics." *International Relations* 37, no. 1 (2023): pp. 25–47.

Bailey, Martin. "British Museum Sold Benin Bronzes." *The Art Newspaper* 13, no. 124 (2002): pp. 1–5.

Bailey, Martin. "Germany's Heidelberg University Returns Parthenon Fragment to Greece." *The Art Newspaper*, January 31, 2006.

Bailey, Martin. "We Serve All Cultures, Say the Big, Global Museums: World's Leading Institutions Release a Declaration on Restitution." *The Art Newspaper*, December 31, 2002.

Baker, Geoffrey L. *Trade Winds on the Niger: Saga of the Royal Niger Company, 1830-1971*. London: Radcliffe Press, 1996.

Ballard, Chris. "Swift Injustice: The Expedition of Imperial Punishment." *Journal of Colonialism and Colonial History* 18, no. 1 (2017). https://dx.doi.org/10.1353/cch.2017.0020.

Bandelj, Nina, and Frederick F Wherry. "Introduction: An Inquiry into the Cultural Wealth of Nations." In *The Cultural Wealth of Nations*, edited by Nina Bandelj and Frederick F. Wherry, pp. 1–22. Stanford: Stanford University Press, 2011.

Barkan, Elazar. "Aesthetics and Evolution: Benin Art in Europe." *African Arts* 30, no. 3 (1997): pp. 36–41.

Barkan, Elazar. "Amending Historical Injustices: The Restitution of Cultural Property—an Overview." In *Claiming the Stones, Naming the Bones: Cultural Property and the Negotiation of National and Ethnic Identity*, edited by Elazar Barkan and Ronald Bush, pp. 16–46. Los Angeles: Getty Research Institute, 2002.

Barnhart, Joslyn. "Status Competition and Territorial Aggression: Evidence from the Scramble for Africa." *Security Studies* 25, no. 3 (2016): pp. 385–419.

Bazyler, Michael J. *Holocaust Justice: The Battle for Restitution in America's Courts*. New York: NYU Press, 2005.

BBC. "Cambridge University College Hands Back Looted Cockerel to Nigeria." October 27, 2021.

BBC. "Greek Minister on Marbles Mission." November 11, 2002, http://news.bbc.co.uk/2/hi/entertainment/2440211.stm.

Beard, Mary. "The Latest Scheme for the Parthenon." *The New York Review of Books*, March 6, 2013.

Beard, Mary. *The Parthenon*. Cambridge: Harvard University Press, 2010.

Beaumont, Paul, and Pål Røren. "Status Symbols in World Politics." *Cooperation and Conflict* 60, no. 1 (2025): pp. 3—26.

Beaumont, Paul, Lucas de Oliveira Paes, and Cristiana Maglia. "Prestige and Punishment: Status Symbols and the Danger of White Elephants." *Cooperation and Conflict* 60, no. 1 (2025): pp. 166—92.

Beaumont, Paul. "Brexit, Retrotopia and the Perils of Post-Colonial Delusions." *Global Affairs* 3, no. 4–5 (2017): pp. 379–90.

Beaumont, Paul. *The Grammar of Status Competition: International Hierarchies and Domestic Politics*. Oxford: Oxford University Press, 2024.

Bedorf, Franziska, and Wilhelm Östberg. "African *Objets D'art* as Currency in a Bid for the Polar Star—and for Recognition on the European Scene." In *Whose Objects? Art Treasures from the Kingdom of Benin in the Collection of the Museum of Ethnography, Stockholm*, edited by Wilhelm Östberg, pp. 30–43. Stockholm: Museum of Ethnography, 2010.

Bekenova, Kristina. "African Museums and Their Participation in the Debates on the ICOM New Museum Definition." *Museum History Journal* 16, no. 2 (2023): pp. 141–61.

Bell, Duncan. *The Idea of Greater Britain: Empire and the Future of World Order, 1860–1900*. Princeton: Princeton University Press, 2007.

Bellisari, Andrew. "The Art of Decolonization: The Battle for Algeria's French Art, 1962–70." *Journal of Contemporary History* 52, no. 3 (2017): pp. 625–45.

Ben-Amos, Paula G. *Art, Innovation, and Politics in Eighteenth-Century Benin*. Indianapolis: Indiana University Press, 1999.

Bennett, Tony. *The Birth of the Museum: History, Theory, Politics*. London: Routledge, 2013.

Bergvelt, Ellinoor, Debora J Meijers, Lieske Tibbe, and Elsa van Wezel, eds. *Napoleon's Legacy: The Rise of National Museums in Europe, 1794–1830*. Berlin: G+ H Verlag, 2009.

Berzock, Kathleen Bickford. "African Art at the Art Institute of Chicago." *African Arts* 32, no. 4 (1999): pp. 19–93.

Blagden, David. "Two Visions of Greatness: Roleplay and Realpolitik in UK Strategic Posture." *Foreign Policy Analysis* 15, no. 4 (2019): pp. 470–91.

Bocoum, Hamady, and El Hadji Malick Ndiaye. "Le Musée Des Civilisations Noires: A Continuous Creation of Humanity." In *National Museums in Africa: Identity, History and Politics*, edited by Raymond Silverman, George Abungu, and Peter Probst, pp. 127–38. Abingdon: Routledge, 2021.

Bodenstein, Felicity. "Notes for a Long-Term Approach to the Price History of Brass and Ivory Objects Taken from the Kingdom of Benin in 1897." In *Acquiring Cultures: Histories of World Art on Western Markets*, edited by Bénédicte Savoy, Charlotte Guichard, and Christine Howald, pp. 267–88. Berlin: De Gruyter, 2018.

Boehme, Franziska. "Normative Expectations and the Colonial Past: Apologies and Art Restitution to Former Colonies in France and Germany." *Global Studies Quarterly* 2, no. 4 (2022): pp. 1–12.

Boffey, Daniel. "Dutch Art Panel's Ruling Against Jewish Family Criticised as 'Step Back.'" *The Guardian*, December 5, 2018.

Boggan, Steve. "Election '97: Patriotic Blair Sets out Global Vision." *The Independent*, April 21, 1997.

Boisragon, Alan Maxwell. *The Benin Massacre*. London: Methuen, 1897.

Bondarenko, Dmitri M. "Benin." In *Encyclopedia of the Middle Passage*, edited by Toyin Falola and Amanda Warnock, pp. 56–58. Westport, CT: Greenwood Press, 2007.

Bourdieu, Pierre. *Distinction: A Social Critique of the Judgement of Taste*. Cambridge, MA: Harvard University Press, 1984.

Bowden, Brett. "In the Name of Progress and Peace: The 'Standard of Civilization' and the Universalizing Project." *Alternatives* 29, no. 1 (2004): pp. 43–68.

Bowley, Graham. "A New Museum Opens Old Wounds in Germany." *The New York Times*, October 12, 2018.

Boztas, Senay. "Jewish Descendants Welcome Report Encouraging Return of Looted Art." DutchNews.nl, December 8, 2020. https://www.dutchnews.nl/news/2020/12/jewish-descendants-welcome-report-encouraging-return-of-looted-art.

Brajović, Saša, and Tatjana Bošnjak. *Imaginarni vrtovi Ibera Robera*. Belgrade: Narodni muzej, 2012.

Brandl, Naida-Michal. "Restitution of Movable Property in Croatia." Zagreb: Claims Conference and World Jewish Restitution Organization, 2020.

Bridge, Mark. "British Museum's New Archives in Shinfield for Hidden Treasures." *The Times*, August 20, 2019.

British Museum. "Contested Objects from the Collection," https://www.britishmuseum.org/about-us/british-museum-story/contested-objects-collection/benin-bronzes.

British Museum. "The Parthenon Sculptures: The Trustees' statement," 2015. https://www.britishmuseum.org/about-us/british-museum-story/contested-objects-collection/parthenon-sculptures/parthenon.

Brodie, Neil. "Problematizing the Encyclopedic Museum: The Benin Bronzes and Ivories in Historical Context." In *Unmasking Ideology in Imperial and Colonial Archaeology: Vocabulary, Symbols, and Legacy*, edited by Bonnie Effros and Guolong Lai, pp. 61–82. Los Angeles: Cotsen Institute of Archaeology Press, 2018.

Brown, Jeffrey, and Anne Azzi Davenport. "Museum Works to Repatriate Artifacts Looted from West Africa." In *PBS News Hour*, 2022.

Brown, Kate. "Mwazulu Diyabanza, the Robin Hood of Restitution Activism, Has Been Fined for Removing a Congolese Funerary Statue from a Dutch Museum." *Artnet Magazine*,

January 12, 2021. https://news.artnet.com/art-world/mwazulu-diyabanza-netherlands-1936340.

Brown, Mark. "New Museum in Nigeria Raises Hopes of Resolution to Benin Bronzes Dispute." *The Guardian*, November 14, 2020.

Brown, Mark. "Trustee Resigns from British Museum over BP Sponsorship and Artefacts Repatriation." *The Guardian*, July 16, 2019.

Browning, Christopher R. *Fateful Months: Essays on the Emergence of the Final Solution*. New York: Holmes & Meier, 1985.

Browning, Christopher S. "Brexit Populism and Fantasies of Fulfilment." *Cambridge Review of International Affairs* 32, no. 3 (2019): pp. 222–44.

Brusius, Mirjam, and Kavita Singh, eds. *Museum Storage and Meaning: Tales from the Crypt*. Abingdon: Routledge, 2017.

Brusius, Mirjam, and Kavita Singh, eds. "Introduction." In *Museum Storage and Meaning: Tales from the Crypt*, edited by Mirjam Brusius and Kavita Singh, pp. 1–33. London: Routledge, 2018.

Bulatović, Valentina. "Srpsko nacionalno blago koje zasenjuje strance—od turista do svetskih pop zvezda." *Sputnik Srbija*, May 18, 2024. https://lat.sputnikportal.rs/20240518/srpsko-nacionalno-blago-koje-zasenjuje-strance-od-turista-do-svetskih-pop-zvezda-1172258620.html.

Burton, Richard F. *Wanderings in West Africa from Liverpool to Fernando Po*. London: Tinsley Brothers, 1863.

Cain, Peter J. "Empire and the Languages of Character and Virtue in Later Victorian and Edwardian Britain." *Modern Intellectual History* 4, no. 2 (2007): pp. 249–73.

Campbell, Elizabeth. "An Art Restitution Zeitgeist? Museum Ethics and the Law in the Early Twenty-First Century." *The Journal of the Western Society for French History* 49, no. 2 (2024): pp. 3–18.

Campbell, Elizabeth. "Claiming National Heritage: State Appropriation of Nazi Art Plunder in Postwar Western Europe." *Journal of Contemporary History* 55, no. 4 (2020): pp. 793–822.

Campbell, Elizabeth. "Monuments Women and Men: Rethinking Popular Narratives Via British Major Anne Olivier Popham." *International Journal of Cultural Property* 28, no. 3 (2021): pp. 409–24.

Campbell, Elizabeth. *Museum Worthy: Nazi Art Plunder in Postwar Western Europe*. New York: Oxford University Press, 2024.

Campbell, Elizabeth. "What's Wrong with This Picture: Casual Disregard for History in George Clooney's the Monuments Men (2014)." *Historical Journal of Film, Radio and Television* 36, no. 3 (2016): pp. 392–414.

Campbell Karlsgodt, Elizabeth. *Defending National Treasures: French Art and Heritage under Vichy*. Stanford: Stanford University Press, 2011.

Campbell, Lucy. "V&A in Talks over Returning Looted Ethiopian Treasures in 'Decolonisation' Purge." *The Guardian*, October 7, 2020.

Carrier, David. *Museum Skepticism*. Durham, NC: Duke University Press, 2006.

Cascone, Sarah. "The Dutch Government Just Promised to Return Any Stolen Colonial-Era Objects in Its Collections Back to Their Countries of Origin." *Artnet Magazine*, February 4, 2021, https://news.artnet.com/art-world/netherlands-restitution-guidelines-1941734.

Catrone, Aubrey. "A Feminine Legacy: Contemporary Views of Rose Valland's Sacrifice in Occupied France." *Journal of Art Crime* 15 (2016): pp. 59–62.

CBC News. "Stolen Totem Pole Formally Welcomed Home to Nisga'a Territory After Nearly a Century in Scottish Museum." (2023). September 28. https://www.cbc.ca/news/canada/british-columbia/memorial-totem-pole-returned-1.6981891.

Chambers, Iain, Alessandra De Angelis, Celeste Ianniciello, and Mariangela Orabona, eds. *The Postcolonial Museum: The Arts of Memory and the Pressures of History*. Abingdon: Routledge, 2016.

Chan, Tak Wing. *Social Status and Cultural Consumption*. Cambridge: Cambridge University Press, 2010.

Chanel, Gerri. *Saving Mona Lisa: The Battle to Protect the Louvre and Its Treasures from the Nazis*. London: Icon Books, 2018.

Chaney, Edward. *The Evolution of the Grand Tour: Anglo-Italian Cultural Relations since the Renaissance*. London: Routledge, 2014.

Chaniotis, Angelos. "Divided Monument, Dividing Monument: The Controversy over the Parthenon Sculptures," Virtual Lecture Series. Athens: College Year in Athens, November 29, 2023.

Chaniotis, Angelos. "The Parthenon Sculptures—Now That the British Museum Has Lost Its Charm." *E-kathimerini*, September 22, 2023.

Chow, Vivienne. "After Years of Debate, Two Universities Have Become the First U.K. Institutions to Restitute Benin Bronzes." *Artnet Magazine*, October 29, 2021.

Chow, Vivienne. "Inching Toward Restitution, Belgium Has Handed over an Inventory of 84,000 Artifacts to the Democratic Republic of Congo." *Artnet Magazine*, February 22, 2022.

Chutel, Lynsey. "The Netherlands Returns Hundreds of Cultural Artifacts to Indonesia." *The New York Times*, September 20, 2024.

Cieślińska-Lobkowicz, Nawojka. "The Obligation of the State or a Hobby of the Few: The Implementation of the Washington Principles in Poland." In *Holocaust Era Assets: Conference Proceedings*, edited by Jakub Klepal, Irena Kalhousová, and Jiří Schneider, pp. 979–92. Prague: Forum 2000 Foundation, 2009.

Clunan, Anne L. "Why Status Matters in World Politics." In *Status in World Politics*, edited by T.V. Paul, Deborah Welch Larson, and William C. Wohlforth, pp. 273–96. Cambridge: Cambridge University Press, 2014.

CNN. "Cambridge University to Return Benin Bronze to Nigeria in Historic Moment." October 16, 2021, https://www.cnn.com/style/article/benin-bronze-return-intl-gbr-scli/index.html.

Coblence, Alain, and David Laufer. "Memorandum on the Collection of Erich Šlomović in the National Museum of Belgrade Presented to H.E. Boris Tadić, President of the Republic of Serbia." New York: Commission for Art Recovery, 2005.

Codrea-Rado, Anna. "Emmanuel Macron Says Return of African Artifacts Is a Top Priority." *The New York Times*, November 29, 2017.

Cœuré, Sophie. "Cultural Looting and Restitution at the Dawn of the Cold War: The French Recovery Missions in Eastern Europe." *Journal of Contemporary History* 52, no. 3 (2017): pp. 588–606.

Cohen, Haley. "NY Museums Scramble to Acknowledge Nazi-Looted Art." *The Jerusalem Post*, August 26, 2022.

Cohen, Patricia, and Tom Mashberg. "Family, 'not Willing to Forget,' Pursues Art It Lost to Nazis." *The New York Times*, April 26, 2013.

Collins, Donald E, and Herbert P Rothfeder. "The Einsatzstab Reichsleiter Rosenberg and the Looting of Jewish and Masonic Libraries During World War II." *The Journal of Library History* 18, no. 1 (1983): pp. 21–36.

Connelly, Joan Breton. *The Parthenon Enigma: A Journey into Legend*. London: Bloomsbury, 2014.

Connolly, Kate. "Nazi-Looted Painting to Be Auctioned as Owners' Heirs Fail to Halt Sale." *The Guardian*, April 23, 2017.

Coombes, Annie E., and Ruth B. Phillips. *Museum Transformations: Decolonization and Democratization*. London: John Wiley & Sons, 2020.

Coombes, Annie E. "Ethnography, Popular Culture and Institutional Power: Narratives of Benin Culture in the British Museum, 1897–1992." *Studies in the History of Art* 47, Symposium Papers XXVII: The Formation of National Collections of Art and Archaeology (1996): pp. 142–57.

Coombes, Annie E. "Museums and the Formation of National and Cultural Identities." In *Grasping the World: The Idea of the Museum*, edited by Donald Preziosi and Claire Farago, pp. 278–97. Abingdon: Routledge, 2019.

Coombes, Annie E. *Reinventing Africa: Museums, Material Culture, and Popular Imagination in Late Victorian and Edwardian England*. New Haven, CT: Yale University Press, 1994.

Corder, Mike. "Dutch Museums Will Return Art and Artifacts That Were Looted from Sri Lanka and Indonesia." *AP News*, July 6, 2023. https://apnews.com/article/art-restitution-indonesia-sri-lanka-netherlands-a5a151374c06b292cf0a34114d371726.

Council of Europe, Parliamentary Assembly, Resolution 1205, Looted Jewish Cultural Property, November 4, 1999, https://assembly.coe.int/nw/xml/XRef/Xref-XML2HTML-en.asp?fileid=16726&lang=en.

Cuno, James. "View from the Universal Museum." In *Imperialism, Art and Restitution*, edited by John Henry Merryman, pp. 15–33. New York: Cambridge University Press, 2006.

Cuno, James. *Who Owns Antiquity? Museums and the Battle over Our Ancient Heritage*. Princeton, NJ: Princeton University Press, 2010.

Curtis, NG. "Universal Museums, Museum Objects and Repatriation." In *Museum Studies: An Anthology of Contexts*, edited by Bettina Messias Carbonell, pp. 73–81. Chichester: Wiley and Sons, 2012.

Curzon, George Nathaniel. "The True Imperialism." *The Nineteenth Century and After* 63, no. 371 (1908): pp. 151–65.

Czernin, Hubertus. "The Austrian Evasion." *ARTnews* 97, no. 6 (1998): pp. 112–19.

D'Arcy, David. "The Mysterious Mr. Slomovic." *Artnet Magazine*, January 10, 2007, http://www.artnet.com/magazineus/features/darcy/darcy1-10-07.asp.

Damjanovic, Rebecca, and Robert Mason. "Suffering and Survivorship: Mythologies and Contested Narratives of War in Serbian Museums." *Museum and Society* 21, no. 1 (2023): pp. 74–86.

Dark, Philip J.C. *An Introduction to Benin Art and Technology*. Oxford: Clarendon Press, 1973.

de Perignon, Pauline Baer. *The Vanished Collection*. New York: New Vessel Press, 2022.

De Waal, Edmund. *The Hare with Amber Eyes: A Family's Century of Art and Loss*. New York: Macmillan, 2010.

Dean, Martin. *Robbing the Jews: The Confiscation of Jewish Property in the Holocaust 1933–1945*. New York: Cambridge University Press, 2008.

Decker, Andrew. "Real and Fake in the 'Zagreb Louvre.'" *ARTnews*, Summer, 1987.

DeGroff, Daniel. "Ethnographic Display and Political Narrative: The Salle De France of the Musée D'ethnographie Du Trocadéro." In *Folklore and Nationalism in Europe During the Long Nineteenth Century*, edited by Timothy Baycroft and David Hopkin, pp. 113–35. Leiden: Brill, 2012.

Dickson, Andrew. "The Ghosts of Colonialism at the Pitt Rivers Museum." *Prospect Magazine*, October 6, 2022.

Dilworth, Miles. "Art Historian, 23, and Museum Guide Is Using Sell-Out Tours to Label Lord Nelson a 'White Supremacist' and Brand Queen Victoria a 'Thief.'" *The Daily Mail*, April 22, 2018.

DiMaggio, Paul, and Walter W. Powell. "The Iron Cage Revisited: Institutional Isomorphism and Collective Rationality in Organizational Fields." *American Sociological Review* 48, no. 2 (1983): pp. 147–60.

DiMaggio, Paul. "Classification in Art." *American Sociological Review* 52, no. 4 (1987): pp. 440–55.

Dimitrijević, Milica. "Detektivska potraga za sudbinom slika." *Politika*, August 4, 2012.

Docherty, Paddy. *Blood and Bronze: The British Empire and the Sack of Benin.* New York: Oxford University Press, 2022.

Donington, Katie. "Relics of Empire? Colonialism and the Culture Wars." In *Embers of Empire in Brexit Britain*, edited by Stuart Ward and Astrid Rasch, pp. 121–32. London: Bloomsbury, 2019.

Dorléac, Laurence Bertrand. *Art of the Defeat: France 1940–1944.* Los Angeles: Getty Publications, 2008.

Dragostinova, Theodora K. *The Cold War from the Margins: A Small Socialist State on the Global Cultural Scene.* Ithaca: Cornell University Press, 2022.

Dreyfus, Jean-Marc. *Le Catalogue Goering.* Paris: Flammarion, 2015.

Duhennois, Doris. "Restitution of African Colonial Artefacts: A Reassessment of France's Post-Colonial Identity." *International Journal of Francophone Studies* 23, no. 1–2 (2020): pp. 119–42.

Duncan, Carol, and Alan Wallach. "The Universal Survey Museum." In *Museum Studies: An Anthology of Contexts*, edited by Bettina Messias Carbonell, pp. 46–61. Chichester: Wiley & Sons, 2012.

Dunn, Kevin C. *Imagining the Congo: The International Relations of Identity.* New York: Springer, 2003.

Duque, Marina G. "Recognizing International Status: A Relational Approach." *International Studies Quarterly* 62, no. 3 (2018): pp. 577–92.

Duque, Marina G. "The Concept of Status in International Politics." Working Paper. 2024.

DutchNewsl.nl. "Interest of Museums Irrelevant in Assessing Nazi Looted Art Claims: Report." December 7, 2020, https://www.dutchnews.nl/news/2020/12/interest-of-museums-irrelevant-in-assessing-nazi-looted-art-claims-report.

DutchNewsl.nl. "Jewish Family Complains About Committee That Rules on Nazi Looted Art." March 19, 2020. https://www.dutchnews.nl/news/2020/03/jewish-family-complains-about-committee-that-rules-on-nazi-looted-art.

Dyson, Stephen L. *In Pursuit of Ancient Pasts: A History of Classical Archaeology in the Nineteenth and Twentieth Centuries.* New Haven: Yale University Press, 2008.

Effros, Bonnie. "Berber Genealogy and the Politics of Prehistoric Archaeology and Craniology in French Algeria (1860s–1880s)." *The British Journal for the History of Science* 50, no. 1 (2017): pp. 61–81.

Eggeling, Kristin A. "Cultural Diplomacy in Qatar: Between 'Virtual Enlargement,' National Identity Construction and Elite Legitimation." In *Cultural Diplomacy and International Cultural Relations: Volume I*, edited by Oliver Bennett, pp. 59–73. London: Routledge, 2020.

Eisenhofer, Stefan. "Felix Von Luschan and Early German-Language Benin Studies." *African Arts* 30, no. 3 (1997): pp. 62–67.

Elassar, Alaa. "The Nuxalk Nation's Totem Pole Was Stolen and Sold to a Museum. After Waiting 110 Years, They Finally Have It Back." *CNN*, February 19, 2023. https://www.cnn.com/2023/02/19/americas/nuxalk-nation-totem-pole-royal-bc-museum-reaj/index.html.

Elbl, Ivana. "Cross-Cultural Trade and Diplomacy: Portuguese Relations with West Africa, 1441–1521." *Journal of World History* 3, no. 2 (1992): pp. 165–204.

Esterling, Shea Elizabeth. *Indigenous Cultural Property and International Law: Restitution, Rights and Wrongs*. Abingdon: Routledge, 2024.

Esterow, Milton. "After 75 Years and 15 Claims, a Bid to Regain Lost Art Inches Forward." *The New York Times*, October 16, 2020.

European Parliament. Cross-border restitution claims of works of art and cultural goods looted in armed conflicts and wars, January 17, 2019, https://eur-lex.europa.eu/legal-content/EN/TXT/?uri=CELEX%3A52019IP0037#ntr9-C_2020411EN.01012501-E0009.

European Parliament. Resolution and Report of Committee on Legal Affairs and the Internal Market, November 26, 2003, https://www.europarl.europa.eu/doceo/document/A-5-2003-0408_EN.html.

Evans, Richard J. "Art in the Time of War." *The National Interest*, no. 113 (2011): pp. 16–26.

Eyssette, Jérémie. "Restitution vs. Retention: Reassessing Discourses on the African Cultural Heritage." *African Studies Review* 66, no. 1 (2023): pp. 101–26.

Ezra, Kate. *Royal Art of Benin: The Perls Collection in the Metropolitan Museum of Art*. New York: Metropolitan Museum of Art, 1992.

Fehlmann, Marc. "As Greek as It Gets: British Attempts to Recreate the Parthenon." *Rethinking History* 11, no. 3 (2007): pp. 353–77.

Feigenbaum, Gail, and Inges Reist, eds. *Provenance: An Alternate History of Art*. Los Angeles: Getty Publications, 2012.

Feliciano, Hector. *The Lost Museum: The Nazi Conspiracy to Steal the World's Greatest Works of Art*. New York: Basic Books, 1997.

Feliciano, Hector. "The Great Culture Robbery: The Plunder of Jewish-Owned Art." In *The Plunder of Jewish Property During the Holocaust: Confronting European History*, edited by Avi Beker, pp. 164–76. Cham: Springer, 2001.

Ferenčak, Ivan. "O provenijenciji nekoliko umjetnina iz Muzeja Mimara u Zagrebu." *Radovi Instituta za povijest umjetnosti*, no. 45 (2021): pp. 237–48.

Ferenčak, Ivan. "Umjetnine iz zbirke Ante Topića Mimare u Strossmayerovoj galeriji." Ph.D. thesis, University of Zadar, 2021.

Ferguson, Niall. *Empire: How Britain Made the Modern World*. London: Penguin UK, 2012.

Filkins, Dexter. "Inside the U.S. Army's Warehouse Full of Nazi Art." *The New Yorker*, January 4, 2021.

Fisher, Wesley A., and Ruth J. Weinberger. "Holocaust-Era Looted Cultural Property: A Current Worldwide Overview." *Claims Conference and World Jewish Restitution Organization*, March 5, 2024. https://art.claimscon.org/wp-content/uploads/2024/03/11-March-2024-Holocaust-Era-Looted-Cultural-Property-A-Current-Worldwide-Overview.pdf.

Fiskesjö, Magnus. "Commentary: The Global Repatriation Debate and the New 'Universal Museums.'" In *Handbook of Postcolonial Archaeology*, edited by Jane Lydon and Uzma Z. Rizvi, pp. 303–10. Abingdon: Routledge, 2016.

Foley, James. "Race, Nation, Empire? Historicising Outward and Inward-Facing British Nationalism." *International Relations* (2023), https://doi.org/10.1177/00471178231196073.

Folk, Zachary. "British Museum Lends Ghana Looted Gold Artifacts—Here's Why It Won't Fully Return Them." *Forbes*, January 25, 2024.

Fradier, George. "Editorial." *Museum* 31, no. 1 (1979): pp. 2–3.

Freedman, Joshua. "Back of the Queue: Brexit, Status Loss, and the Politics of Backlash." *The British Journal of Politics and International Relations* 22, no. 4 (2020): pp. 631–43.

French Ministry of Culture. "Three works stolen during the Nazi period," April 24, 2023, https://www.culture.gouv.fr/en/news/Three-works-stolen-during-the-Nazi-period.

French Ministry of Culture. Transcription du discours de la ministre de la Culture, Rima Abdul Malak, de présentation des vœux aux acteurs culturels - le 16 janvier 2023, à la Grande Halle de La Villette, January 17, 2023, https://www.culture.gouv.fr/presse/discours/Transcription-du-discours-de-la-ministre-de-la-Culture-Rima-Abdul-Malak-de-presentation-des-vaeux-aux-acteurs-culturels-le-16-janvier-2023-a-la.

Frum, David. "Who Benefits When Western Museums Return Looted Art?" *The Atlantic*, September 14, 2022.

Gallas, Elisabeth. "Locating the Jewish Future: The Restoration of Looted Cultural Property in Early Postwar Europe." *Naharaim* 9, no. 1–2 (2015): pp. 25–47.

Galway, Henry L. "Nigeria in the 'Nineties.'" *Journal of the Royal African Society* 29, no. 115 (1930): pp. 221–47.

Gamble, Andrew. *Britain in Decline: Economic Policy, Political Strategy and the British State*. London: Bloomsbury, 1994.

Garcia, Juan. "Mexico's Splashy 'My Heritage Is Not for Sale' Campaign Hides a More Troubling Reality for Conservationists." *ARTnews*, February 23, 2024.

Gaskarth, Jamie. *British Foreign Policy: Crises, Conflicts and Future Challenges*. Cambridge: Polity, 2013.

Gaudenzi, Bianca, and Astrid Swenson. "Looted Art and Restitution in the Twentieth Century—Towards a Global Perspective." *Journal of Contemporary History* 52, no. 3 (2017): pp. 491–518.

Gaudenzi, Bianca. "The 'Return of Beauty'? The Politics of Restitution of Nazi-Looted Art in Italy, the Federal Republic of Germany and Austria, 1945–1998." *European Review of History* 28, no. 2 (2021): pp. 323–46.

Geczy, Adam. "Curating Curiosity: Imperialism, Materialism, Humanism, and the Wunderkammer." In *A Companion to Curation*, edited by Brad Buckley and John Conomos, pp. 23–42. New York: Wiley, 2019.

Genocchio, Benjamin. "Seized, Reclaimed and Now on View." *The New York Times*, April 27, 2008.

German Federal Government. "Framework Principles for dealing with collections in colonial contexts," March 13, 2019, available at https://www.auswaertiges-amt.de/blob/2210152/b2731f8b59210c77c68177cdcd3d03de/190412-stm-m-sammlungsgut-kolonial-kontext-en-data.pdf.

German Lost Art Foundation. "Confronting Colonial History: The German Lost Art Foundation Launches a New Funding Programme." February 4, 2019, https://kulturgutverluste.de/en/press/confronting-colonial-history-german-lost-art-foundation-launches-new-funding-programme.

German Museum Association. "Guidelines for the Care of Collections from Colonial Contexts." Berlin: German Museum Association, July 2018. Updated version from 2021, https://www.museumsbund.de/wp-content/uploads/2021/03/mb-leitfaden-en-web.pdf.

Gerstenblith, Patty. *Cultural Objects and Reparative Justice: A Legal and Historical Analysis*. Oxford: Oxford University Press, 2023.

Ghermezian, Shiryn. "German City of Dusseldorf Restitutes to Heirs of Jewish Gallery Owner Portrait from Mayor's Office." *The Algemeiner*, April 25, 2023.

Gibbons, Fiachra, Maev Kennedy, and David Hencke. "Virtual Intervention in Battle over Parthenon Marbles." *The Guardian*, October 7, 2003.

Gilady, Lilach. *The Price of Prestige: Conspicuous Consumption in International Relations*. Chicago: University of Chicago Press, 2018.

Gildea, Robert. "Myth, Memory and Policy in France since 1945." In *Memory and Power in Post-War Europe: Studies in the Presence of the Past*, edited by Jan-Werner Muller, pp. 59–75. Cambridge: Cambridge University Press, 2002.

Gildea, Robert. *Empires of the Mind: The Colonial Past and the Politics of the Present*. Cambridge: Cambridge University Press, 2019.

Gilks, David. "Attitudes to the Displacement of Cultural Property in the Wars of the French Revolution and Napoleon." *The Historical Journal* 56, no. 1 (2013): pp. 113–43.

Gilroy, Paul. *After Empire*. London: Routledge, 2004.

Goffman, Erving. "Symbols of Class Status." *The British Journal of Sociology* 2, no. 4 (1951): pp. 294–304.

Gong, Gerrit W. *The Standard of "Civilization" in International Society*. Oxford: Clarendon Press, 1984.

Goodman, Simon. *The Orpheus Clock: The Search for My Family's Art Treasures Stolen by the Nazis*. New York: Simon and Schuster, 2015.

Gosden, Chris, and Chantal Knowles. *Collecting Colonialism: Material Culture and Colonial Change*. Abingdon: Routledge, 2020.

Graham, Jenny. "The Ghent Altarpiece After World War II: Restitution, Restoration, and Redemption." *International Journal of Cultural Property* 28, no. 3 (2021): pp. 343–67.

Grant, Kevin. *A Civilised Savagery: Britain and the New Slaveries in Africa, 1884–1926*. Abingdon: Routledge, 2014.

Gray, Clive. *The Politics of Museums*. Houndmills: Palgrave, 2015.

Greek City Times, "Sicily returns a fragment of the Parthenon to Greece," January 6, 2022, https://greekcitytimes.com/2022/01/06/sicily-returns-a-fragment-of-the-parthenon-to-greece.

Green, Hilary. "Shifting Landscapes and the Monument Removal Craze, 2015–20." *Patterns of Prejudice* 54, no. 5 (2020): pp. 485–91.

Green, Toby. *A Fistful of Shells: West Africa from the Rise of the Slave Trade to the Age of Revolution*. London: Penguin UK, 2019.

Greenberger, Alex. "Glasgow to Return Its Benin Bronzes as Part of the Largest Repatriation in Scotland's History." *Artnet Magazine*, April 14, 2022.

Greenfield, Jeanette. "The Return of Cultural Property." *Antiquity* 60, no. 228 (1986): pp. 29–35.

Greenfield, Jeanette. *The Return of Cultural Treasures*. Cambridge: Cambridge University Press, 1996.

Greenhalgh, Michael. *Plundered Empire: Acquiring Antiquities from Ottoman Lands*. Leiden: Brill, 2019.

Greenland, Fiona. *Ruling Culture: Art Police, Tomb Robbers, and the Rise of Cultural Power in Italy*. Chicago: University of Chicago Press, 2021.

Grimsted, Patricia Kennedy. "A Goudstikker Van Goyen in Gdańsk: A Case Study of Nazi-Looted Art in Poland." *International Journal of Cultural Property* 27, no. 1 (2020): pp. 53–96.

Grosshans, Henry. *Hitler and the Artists*. New York: Holmes & Meier, 1983.

Groux, Réginald. "Restitutions: et si on faisait un peu d'histoire . . ." *La Tribune de l'Art*, December 4, 2018.

Gunsch, Kathryn Wysocki. "Art and/or Ethnographica?: The Reception of Benin Works from 1897–1935." *African Arts* 46, no. 4 (2013): pp. 22–31.

Gunsch, Kathryn Wysocki. *The Benin Plaques: A 16th Century Imperial Monument*. Abingdon: Routledge, 2017.

Haas, Ernst B. *When Knowledge Is Power: Three Models of Change in International Organizations*. Berkeley: University of California Press, 1990.

Hagström, Linus. "Great Power Narcissism and Ontological (in) Security: The Narrative Mediation of Greatness and Weakness in International Politics." *International Studies Quarterly* 65, no. 2 (2021): pp. 331–42.

Hamilakis, Yannis. *The Nation and Its Ruins: Antiquity, Archaeology, and National Imagination in Greece*. Oxford: Oxford University Press, 2007.

Hansen, Lene, and Johan Spanner. "National and Post-National Performances at the Venice Biennale: Site-Specific Seeing Through the Photo Essay." *Millennium* 49, no. 2 (2021): pp. 305–36.

Harris, Gareth. "Tate May Acquire Michael Rakowitz's Lamassu Sculpture—Will It Convince the British Museum to Return the Original to Iraq?" *The Art Newspaper*, January 24, 2023.

Harris, Gareth. "UK Prime Minister Liz Truss Rules Out Deal with Greece over Parthenon Marbles." *The Art Newspaper*, October 5, 2022.

Harris, Gareth. "Your Move, British Museum: Sicily Sends Back Parthenon Fragment to Athens." *The Art Newspaper*, January 6, 2022.

Hassett, Dónal. "Acknowledging or Occluding 'the System of Violence'?: The Representation of Colonial Pasts and Presents in Belgium's Africamuseum." *Journal of Genocide Research* 22, no. 1 (2020): pp. 26–45.

Hassett, Dónal. "Rupture and Reconciliation: The Neoliberal Logics of Emmanuel Macron's Colonial Memory Policies." *Modern & Contemporary France* 32, no. 1 (2024): pp. 31—53.

Herman, Alexander. "Restitution—What's Really Going On?" *The Art Newspaper*, September 28, 2021.

Herman, Alexander. *Restitution: The Return of Cultural Artefacts*. London: Lund Humphries, 2021.

Herman, Joost. "The Dutch Drive for Humanitarianism: Inner Origins and Development of the Gidsland Tradition and Its External Effects." *International Journal* 61, no. 4 (2006): pp. 859–74.

Hermand, Jost. *Culture in Dark Times: Nazi Fascism, Inner Emigration, and Exile*. New York: Berghahn Books, 2013.

Hevia, James L. "Looting and Its Discontents: Moral Discourse and the Plunder of Beijing, 1900–1901." In *The Boxers, China, and the World*, edited by Robert Bickers and RG Tiedemann, pp. 93–113. Lanham: Rowman & Littlefield, 2007.

Hickley, Catherine. "A Family Recovered Most of What the Nazis Stole. But Not This." *New York Times*, November 6, 2018.

Hickley, Catherine. "African and European Museum Directors Pledge to Cooperate at Dakar Conference." *The Art Newspaper*, May 2, 2023.

Hickley, Catherine. "And So It Begins: Germany and Nigeria Sign Pre-Accord on Restitution of Benin Bronzes." *The Art Newspaper*, October 15, 2021.

Hickley, Catherine. "Croatia Takes a Step Toward Returning Art Looted During the Holocaust." *The New York Times*, November 3, 2022.

Hickley, Catherine. "Croatian Museums Return Art Looted During Holocaust to Jewish Heir." *The New York Times*, September 22, 2023.

Hickley, Catherine. "'Degenerate' Art Unearthed from Berlin Bomb Rubble." *Bloomberg*, November 8, 2010.

Hickley, Catherine. "Digital Benin: A Milestone on the Long, Slow Journey to Restitution." *The Art Newspaper*, June 8, 2020.

Hickley, Catherine. "How 4 Countries Are Preparing to Bring Stolen Treasures Home." *The New York Times*, August 9, 2023.

Hickley, Catherine. "How Recent Anti-Racism Protests Have Pushed a Longstanding Debate About Colonial Looting in Europe." *The Art Newspaper*, August 14, 2020.

Hickley, Catherine. "Nations Agree to Refine Pact That Guides the Return of Nazi-Looted Art." *The New York Times*, March 5, 2024.

Hickley, Catherine. *The Munich Art Hoard: Hitler's Dealer and His Secret Legacy*. London: Thames and Hudson, 2015.

Hickley, Catherine, and Zoe Schneeweiss. "Leopold Pays $19 Million to Keep Schiele's 'Wally.'" *Bloomberg*, July 21, 2010.

Hicks, Dan. *The Brutish Museums: The Benin Bronzes, Colonial Violence and Cultural Restitution.* London: Pluto Press, 2020.

Higgins, Charlotte. "Britain Treasures the Parthenon Marbles, but Consider This: Returned to Greece, Could They Be More Valuable?" *The Guardian*, January 24, 2023.

Hilberg, Raul. *The Destruction of the European Jews.* New Haven: Yale University Press, 2003.

Hitchens, Christopher, ed. *The Elgin Marbles: Should They Be Returned to Greece?* London: Verso, 1997.

Hitchens, Christopher, ed. "The Elgin Marbles." In *The Elgin Marbles: Should They Be Returned to Greece?*, edited by Christopher Hitchens, pp. 16–92. London: Verso, 1997.

Hitchens, Christopher, ed. *The Parthenon Marbles: The Case for Reunification.* London: Verso Books, 2016.

Hobhouse, John Cam. "A Note on Lord Elgin's Pursuits in Greece." In *A Journey Through Albania and Other Provinces of Turkey in Europe and Asia to Constantinople, During the Years 1809 and 1810*, edited by John Cam Hobhouse, pp. 345–49. London, 1813.

Hobson, John M. *Multicultural Origins of the Global Economy: Beyond the Western-Centric Frontier.* Cambridge: Cambridge University Press, 2020.

Hochfield, Sylvia. "Wrestling with Restitution." *ARTnews* 97, no. 7 (1998): pp. 59.

Home, Robert. *City of Blood Revisited: A New Look at the Benin Expedition of 1897.* London: Rex Collings, 1982.

Hoock, Holger. "The British State and the Anglo-French Wars over Antiquities, 1798–1858." *The Historical Journal* 50, no. 1 (2007): pp. 49–72.

Hoock, Holger. *Empires of the Imagination: Politics, War, and the Arts in the British World, 1750–1850.* London: Profile Books, 2010.

Hornát, Jan, Ivo Šlosarčík, Eliška Tomalová, and Jan Váška. "International Organisations as Status Enhancers: The Case of the Czech Republic." *Europe-Asia Studies* 75, no. 10 (2023): pp. 1626–50.

Houghteling, Sara. *Pictures at an Exhibition.* New York: Knopf, 2010.

House of Commons Select Committee on Media, Culture and Sport, Examination of Witnesses, June 8, 2000, https://publications.parliament.uk/pa/cm199900/cmselect/cmcumeds/uc371/uc371804.htm.

Hudetz, Mary. "UC Berkeley Takes Significant Step to Repatriate 4,400 Native American Human Remains." (2023). November 2. https://nagpra.berkeley.edu/news/uc-berkeley-takes-significant-step-repatriate-4400-native-american-human-remains.

Hunt, Tristram, Hartmut Dorgerloh, and Nicholas Thomas. "Restitution Report: Museum Directors Respond." *The Art Newspaper*, November 27, 2018.

ICOM, *Study on the Principles, Conditions and Means for the Restitution or Return of Cultural Property in View of Reconstituting Dispersed Heritages*, special issue of *Museum* 31, no. 1 (1979): pp. 62–66.

Igbafe, Philip A. "Slavery and Emancipation in Benin, 1897–1945." *The Journal of African History* 16, no. 3 (1975): pp. 409–29.

Ignjatović, Aleksandar, and Olga Manojlović Pintar. "National Museums in Serbia: A Story of Intertwined Identities." In *Building National Museums in Europe 1750–2010*, edited by Peter Aronsson and Gabriella Elgenius, pp. 779–815. Linköping: Linköping University Press, 2011.

Impey, Oliver R., and Arthur MacGregor. *The Origins of Museums: The Cabinet of Curiosities in Sixteenth and Seventeenth-Century Europe.* Oxford: Clarendon Press, 1985.

Ivanov, Paola. "African Art in the Ethnologisches Museum in Berlin." *African Arts* 33, no. 3 (2000): pp. 18–39.

Iwu, Chidinma. "Nigeria's New Museum of West African Art Calls into Question the Future of Encyclopedic Museums." *ARTnews*, February 22, 2024.

Jacobs, Julia, and Zachary Small. "Leading Museums Remove Native Displays Amid New Federal Rules." *The New York Times*, January 26, 2024.

James, Liam. "Culture Secretary Accuses Churchill Charity of 'Pandering to Noisy Woke Brigade.'" *The Independent*, September 10, 2021.

Jenkins, Ian Dennis. *The Parthenon Sculptures*. Cambridge: Harvard University Press, 2007.

Jenkins, Tiffany. *Keeping Their Marbles: How the Treasures of the Past Ended Up in Museums… And Why They Should Stay There*. Oxford: Oxford University Press, 2018.

Jewish News Syndicate. "Frankfurt Returns Painting to Heirs of Jewish Collector Murdered in the Holocaust." May 4, 2023. https://www.jns.org/frankfurt-returns-painting-to-heirs-of-jewish-collector-murdered-in-the-holocaust.

Jewish News Syndicate. "Prague Museums Return 14 Artworks to Heirs of Jewish Collector." February 14, 2023. https://www.jns.org/prague-museums-return-14-artworks-to-heirs-of-jewish-collector.

Joy, Charlotte. *Heritage Justice*. Cambridge: Cambridge University Press, 2020.

Jules-Rosette, Bennetta, and JR Osborn. *African Art Reframed: Reflections and Dialogues on Museum Culture*. Urbana-Champaign: University of Illinois Press, 2020.

Kaehr, Roland, and Louis Perrois. "A Masterwork That Sheds Tears . . . And Light: A Complementary Study of a Fang Ancestral Head." *African Arts* 40, no. 4 (2007): pp. 44–57.

Kalaycioglu, Elif. *The Politics of World Heritage: Visions, Custodians and Futures of Humanity*. Oxford: Oxford University Press, 2025.

Kassim, Sumaya. "The Museum Will Not Be Decolonised." *Media Diversified* 15 (2017): pp. 109–22.

Kenny, Michael, and Nick Pearce. *Shadows of Empire: The Anglosphere in British Politics*. Cambridge: Polity, 2018.

Khomami, Nadia. "Cambridge College to Be First in UK to Return Looted Benin Bronze." *The Guardian*, October 15, 2021.

Kimmelman, Michael. "Elgin Marble Argument in a New Light." *The New York Times*, June 23, 2009.

Kirkwood, Meghan L.E. "Postindependence Architecture Through North Korean Modes: Namibian Commissions of the Mansudae Overseas Project." In *A Companion to Modern African Art*, edited by Gitti Salami and Monica Blackmun Visonà, pp. 548–71. Chichester: Wiley Blackwell, 2013.

Knezović, Sandro, and Marco Esteves Lopes. "Croatia as a Small State in Contemporary International Relations." Zagreb: Hanns-Seidel-Stiftung, 2018.

Kopytoff, Igor. "The Cultural Biography of Things: Commoditization as Process." In *The Social Life of Things: Commodities in Cultural Perspective*, edited by Arjun Appadurai, pp. 64–91. Cambridge: Cambridge University Press, 1986.

Kraus, Tomáš. "The Issue of Restitution in the Czech Republic." *The CEU Jewish Studies Yearbook* 3 (2002/2003): pp. 87–98.

Kroslak, Daniela. "France's Policy Towards Africa: Continuity or Change?". In *Africa in International Politics: External Involvement on the Continent*, edited by Ian Taylor and Paul Williams, pp. 73–94. Abingdon: Routledge, 2004.

Kuo, Christopher. "Setback for Heirs in Long-Running Nazi Art Restitution Case." *The New York Times*, January 10, 2024.

Kuper, Adam. *The Museum of Other People: From Colonial Acquisitions to Cosmopolitan Exhibitions*. London: Profile Books, 2023.

L'Académie des beaux-arts, "Restitution du patrimoine culturel africain: l'Académie des beaux-arts défend l'inaliénabilité et la circulation des collections," November 28, 2018, https://www.academiedesbeauxarts.fr/sites/default/files/inline-files/cp%20restitution%20des%20biens%20culturels.pdf.

La Follette, Laetitia. "Looted Antiquities, Art Museums and Restitution in the United States since 1970." *Journal of Contemporary History* 52, no. 3 (2017): pp. 669–87.

Lang, Jack. Speech in Cotonou, Benin, September 17, 1981, https://www.vie-publique.fr/discours/251904-jack-lang-17091981-relations-nord-sud-politique-culturelle.

Larson, Deborah Welch. "Social Identity Theory: Status and Identity in International Relations." In *Oxford Research Encyclopedia of Politics*. Oxford: Oxford University Press, 2017, https://doi.org/10.1093/acrefore/9780190228637.013.290.

Larson, Deborah Welch, and Alexei Shevchenko. *Quest for Status: Chinese and Russian Foreign Policy*. New Haven, CT: Yale University Press, 2019.

Lauter, Devorah. "France's New Restitution Law for Nazi-Looted Art Reveals the Country's Inconsistent Efforts in Dealing with Its Complicated Past." *ARTnews*, October 9, 2023.

Lauter, Devorah. "Restitution, Repatriation Efforts See Halting Progress Across Europe and the US, Amid Shifts in Public Opinion." *ARTnews*, February 19, 2024.

Lauterbach, Iris. *The Central Collecting Point in Munich: A New Beginning for the Restitution and Protection of Art*. Los Angeles: Getty Publications, 2019.

Law, Robin. "Human Sacrifice in Pre-Colonial West Africa." *African Affairs* 84, no. 334 (1985): pp. 53–87.

Law, Robin. "Trade and Politics Behind the Slave Coast: The Lagoon Traffic and the Rise of Lagos, 1500–1800." In *European and Non-European Societies, 1450–1800*, edited by Robert Forster, pp. 275–302. Abingdon: Routledge, 2019.

Lebovics, Herman. "In the Diaspora, Not Dead: Africa's Heritages in French Museums." *French Cultural Studies* 32, no. 2 (2021): pp. 108–31.

Leheny, David. *Empire of Hope: The Sentimental Politics of Japanese Decline*. Ithaca: Cornell University Press, 2018.

Leira, Halvard, and Benjamin De Carvalho. "The Importance of Being Civilized: Opera Houses as Status Symbols in International Relations." *Conflict and Cooperation* 60, no. 1 (2025): pp. 27—53.

Lemaire, André. "Tribute or Looting in Samaria and Jerusalem: Shoshenq in Jerusalem?". In *Homeland and Exile*, edited by Gershon Galil, Markham (Mark) Geller, and Alan Millard, pp. 167–77. Leiden: Brill, 2009.

Leoussi, Athena S. "Myths of Ancestry." *Nations and Nationalism* 7, no. 4 (2001): pp. 467–86.

Leoussi, Athena S. "Nationalism and Racial Hellenism in Nineteenth Century England and France." *Ethnic and Racial Studies* 20, no. 1 (1997): pp. 42–68.

Levi, Neil. *Modernist Form and the Myth of Jewification*. New York: Fordham University Press, 2013.

Levitt, Peggy. *Artifacts and Allegiances: How Museums Put the Nation and the World on Display*. Berkeley: University of California Press, 2015.

Levy, Daniel, and Natan Sznaider. "Memory Unbound: The Holocaust and the Formation of Cosmopolitan Memory." *European Journal of Social Theory* 5, no. 1 (2002): pp. 87–106.

Lidz, Franz. "The Robot Guerrilla Campaign to Recreate the Elgin Marbles." *The New York Times*, July 8, 2022.

Lin, Alex Yu-Ting, and Saori N. Katada. "Striving for Greatness: Status Aspirations, Rhetorical Entrapment, and Domestic Reforms." *Review of International Political Economy* 29, no. 1 (2022): pp. 175–201.

Lindsay, Ivan. *The History of Loot and Stolen Art: From Antiquity until the Present Day*. London: Unicorn Press, 2014.

Liphshiz, Cnaan. "A Jewish Family Sold This Kandinsky Painting to Survive the Nazis. Amsterdam Is Keeping It Anyway." *Jewish Telegraphic Agency*. July 18, 2019. https://www.jta.org/2019/07/18/global/a-jewish-family-sold-this-painting-to-survive-the-nazis-amsterdam-is-keeping-it-anyway.

Liphshiz, Cnaan. "Reversing Earlier Stance, Netherlands to Return Looted Kandinsky to Jewish Family." *The Times of Israel*. September 29, 2022. https://www.timesofisrael.com/netherlands-returns-looted-kandinsky-painting-to-jewish-family.

Löffler, Emily. "'Living Room Art' and the Material Culture of Provenance: Retracing Bourgeois Everyday Life and Art Collecting Practices Through Restitution Files." *International Journal of Cultural Property* 28, no. 3 (2021): pp. 369–88.

Longair, Sarah, and John McAleer, eds. *Curating Empire: Museums and the British Imperial Experience*. Manchester: Manchester University Press, 2017.

Lotem, Itay. *The Memory of Colonialism in Britain and France: The Sins of Silence*. Cham: Springer Nature, 2021.

Loudis, Jessica. "Haul of Shame—the 'Trophy Art' Taken from Germany by the Red Army." *Apollo*. January 6, 2020. https://www.apollo-magazine.com/red-army-trophy-art-germany.

Loukaki, Argyro. *Living Ruins, Value Conflicts*. Abingdon: Routledge, 2016.

Lowenthal, David. "Classical Antiquities as National and Global Heritage." *Antiquity* 62, no. 237 (1988): pp. 726–35.

Lowenthal, David. *The Heritage Crusade and the Spoils of History*. Cambridge: Cambridge University Press, 1998.

Löytömäki, Stiina. "The Law and Collective Memory of Colonialism: France and the Case of 'Belated' Transitional Justice." *International Journal of Transitional Justice* 7, no. 2 (2013): pp. 205–23.

Lucas, Julian. "The Forgotten Movement to Reclaim Africa's Stolen Art." *The New Yorker*, April 14, 2022.

Lundén, Staffan. "Displaying Loot: The Benin Objects and the British Museum." Gothenburg University, 2016.

Lundén, Staffan. "Distorting history in the restitution debate. Dan Hicks's *The Brutish Museums* and fact and fiction in Benin historiography." *International Journal of Cultural Property* 31, no. 2 (2024): pp. 202–225.

Lundén, Staffan. "The Benin Bronzes: Whose Stories Get Told, Silenced or Neutralized?" In *The Politics of Cultural Restitution in Global Perspective*, edited by Bianca Gaudenzi. Göttingen: Vanderhoeck & Ruprecht Unipress, forthcoming.

M'Bow, Amadou-Mahtar. "A Plea for the Return of an Irreplaceable Cultural Heritage to Those Who Created It." *Museum* 31, no. 1 (1979): pp. 58.

MacDonald, Paul K., and Joseph M. Parent. *Twilight of the Titans: Great Power Decline and Retrenchment*. Ithaca: Cornell University Press, 2018.

MacDonald, Paul K., and Joseph M. Parent. "The Status of Status in World Politics." *World Politics* 73, no. 2 (2021): pp. 358–91.

Macdonald, Sharon. "Collecting Practices." In *A Companion to Museum Studies*, edited by Sharon Macdonald, pp. 81–97. Oxford: Blackwell Publishing, 2006.

Macdonald, Sharon. "Museums, National, Postnational and Transcultural Identities." In *Museum Studies: An Anthology of Contexts*, edited by Bettina Messias Carbonell, pp. 273–86. Chichester: Wiley & Sons, 2012.

Macdonald, Sharon. "New Constellations of Difference in Europe's 21st Century Museumscape." *Museum Anthropology* 39, no. 1 (2016): pp. 4–19.

MacGregor, Arthur. "Aristocrats and Others: Collectors of Influence in Eighteenth-Century England." In *British Models of Art Collecting and the American Response*, edited by Inge Reist, pp. 73–85. Farnham: Ashgate, 2014.

MacGregor, Neil. "Britain Is at the Centre of a Conversation with the World." *The Guardian*, April 18, 2007.

MacGregor, Neil. "The Whole World in Our Hands." *The Guardian*, July 23, 2004.

MacKay, Joseph. "Art World Fields and Global Hegemonies." *International Studies Quarterly* 66, no. 3 (2022): sqac029.

Malaquais, Dominique, and Cédric Vincent. "PANAFEST: A Festival Complex Revisited." In *The First World Festival of Negro Arts, Dakar 1966: Contexts and Legacies*, edited by David Murphy, pp. 194–202. Liverpool: Liverpool University Press, 2016.

Malcolm, Noel. "The Elgin Marbles: Keep, Lend or Return? An Analysis." London: Policy Exchange, 2023.

Manikowska, Ewa. "The Washington Principles *à Rebours*: Explaining Poland's Current Restitution Policy." *International Journal of Cultural Property* 30, no. 1 (2023): pp. 42–61.

Manoschek, Walter. "The Extermination of the Jews in Serbia." In *National Socialist Extermination Policies: Contemporary German Perspectives and Controversies*, edited by Ulrich Herbert, pp. 163–85. New York: Berghahn Books, 2000.

Marchand, Suzanne. "The Dialectics of the Antiquities Rush." In *Pour une histoire de l'archéologie XVIIIe siècle–1945: Hommage de ses collègues et amis à Eve Gran-Aymerich*, edited by Annick Fenet and Natacha Lubtchansky, pp. 191–206. Bordeaux: Ausonius, 2015.

Marchand, Suzanne. *Down from Olympus: Archaeology and Philhellenism in Germany, 1750–1970*. Princeton: Princeton University Press, 2003.

Marchand, Suzanne. "Leo Frobenius and the Revolt Against the West." *Journal of Contemporary History* 32, no. 2 (1997): pp. 153–70.

Marlowe, Elizabeth. "From Exceptionalism to Solidarity: The Rhetoric of the Case for the Parthenon Sculptures' Return." *Cardozo Arts & Entertainment Law Journal* 41 (2022): pp. 125–50.

Marlowe, Elizabeth. "Review of Dan Hicks, *The Brutish Museums: The Benin Bronzes, Colonial Violence and Cultural Restitution*." *International Journal of Cultural Property* 28, no. 4 (2021): pp. 575–86.

Marshall, Alex. "As Europe Returns Artifacts, Britain Stays Silent." *The New York Times*, December 20, 2021.

Marshall, Alex. "At Venice Biennale, Artists Make a Case for Returning Looted Artifacts." *The New York Times*, May 3, 2024.

Marshall, Alex. "Germany Sets Out Plans to Return Benin Bronzes." *The New York Times*, April 30, 2021.

Marshall, Alex, and Mark Landler. "Amid Parthenon Dispute, Sunak Cancels Meeting with Mitsotakis." *The New York Times*, November 27, 2023.

Marshall, Alex, Thomas Rogers, and Rahila Lassa. "How Germany Changed Its Mind, and Gave the Benin Bronzes Back." *The New York Times*, December 20, 2022.

Mashberg, Tom. "Martha Nierenberg, Entrepreneur Who Sought Art's Return, Dies at 96." *The New York Times*, July 30, 2020.

Mashberg, Tom, and Graham Bowley. "Cambodia Says It's Found Its Lost Artifacts: In Gallery 249 at the Met." *The New York Times*, August 18, 2022.

Mashberg, Tom, and Graham Bowley. "Schiele Artworks Returned to Heirs of Owner Killed by Nazis." *The New York Times*, September 20, 2023.

Masurovsky, Marc. "The Fate of the Adolphe Schloss Collection." *Jewish Digital Cultural Recovery Project* (2021). https://pilot-demo.jdcrp.org/essays/fate-of-the-schloss-collection.

Mattez, Anaïs. "Restitution of Cultural Property: The Rise and Fall of a Cosmopolitan Ideal." *International Journal of Heritage Studies* 30, no. 2 (2024): pp. 165–80.

McAuley, James. *The House of Fragile Things: Jewish Art Collectors and the Fall of France*. New Haven: Yale University Press, 2021.

McAuliffe, Padraig. "Complicity or Decolonization? Restitution of Heritage from 'Global' Ethnographic Museums." *International Journal of Transitional Justice* 15, no. 3 (2021): pp. 678–89.

McClellan, Andrew. *Art and Its Publics: Museum Studies at the Millennium.* New York: John Wiley & Sons, 2008.

McClellan, Andrew. *Inventing the Louvre: Art, Politics, and the Origins of the Modern Museum in Eighteenth-Century Paris.* Berkeley: University of California Press, 1999.

McClellan, Andrew. *The Art Museum from Boullée to Bilbao.* Berkeley: University of California Press, 2008.

McCourt, David M. *Britain and World Power since 1945: Constructing a Nation's Role in International Politics.* Ann Arbor: University of Michigan Press, 2014.

Melhuish, Francesca. "Euroscepticism, Anti Nostalgic Nostalgia and the Past Perfect Post Brexit Future." *JCMS: Journal of Common Market Studies* 60, no. 6 (2022): pp. 1758–76.

Merryman, John Henry. "A Licit International Trade in Cultural Objects." *International Journal of Cultural Property* 4, no. 1 (1995): pp. 13–60.

Meyer, John W., John Boli, George M. Thomas, and Francisco O. Ramirez. "World Society and the Nation State." *American Journal of Sociology* 103, no. 1 (July 1997): pp. 144–81.

Miles, Margaret Melanie. *Art as Plunder: The Ancient Origins of Debate About Cultural Property.* Cambridge: Cambridge University Press, 2008.

Mitchell, Peter. *Imperial Nostalgia: How the British Conquered Themselves.* Manchester: Manchester University Press, 2021.

Mitchell, Timothy. "The Limits of the State: Beyond Statist Approaches and Their Critics." *American Political Science Review* 85, no. 1 (March 1991): pp. 77–96.

Mohdin, Aamna, and Rhi Storer. "Tributes to Slave Traders and Colonialists Removed Across UK." *The Guardian*, January 29, 2021.

Mondo. "Italijani traže da Narodni Muzej vrati slike?" November 30, 2016, https://mondo.rs/Zabava/Kultura/a960747/Narodni-muzej-slike-iz-Italije-istraga.html.

Morris, Justin. "How Great Is Britain? Power, Responsibility and Britain's Future Global Role." *The British Journal of Politics and International Relations* 13, no. 3 (2011): pp. 326–47.

Mosse, George Lachmann. *Nazi Culture: Intellectual, Cultural and Social Life in the Third Reich.* Madison: University of Wisconsin Press, 2003.

Mouriquand, David. "Berlinale 2024: Golden Bear Goes to Mati Diop's Restitution Documentary 'Dahomey.'" *Euronews.* February 24, 2024. https://www.euronews.com/culture/2024/02/24/berlinale-2024-golden-bear-goes-to-mati-diops-restitution-documentary-dahomey.

Mukundayi, Augustin Bikale, and Sarah Van Beurden. "Korea and the New National Museum in the Democratic Republic of the Congo: Building a Museum, Building Relations?" In *National Museums in Africa: Identity, History and Politics*, edited by Raymond Silverman, George Abungu, and Peter Probst, pp. 110–26. Abingdon: Routledge, 2021.

Murphy, David, ed. *The First World Festival of Negro Arts, Dakar 1966: Contexts and Legacies.* Liverpool: Liverpool University Press, 2016.

Murray, Jessica. "Greek PM Bemoans Lack of Progress on Return of Parthenon Marbles." *The Guardian*, November 26, 2023.

Murray, Kenneth C. "Art in Nigeria: The Need for a Museum." *Journal of the Royal African Society* 41, no. 165 (1942): pp. 241–49.

Musgrave, Paul, and Daniel H. Nexon. "Defending Hierarchy from the Moon to the Indian Ocean: Symbolic Capital and Political Dominance in Early Modern China and the Cold War." *International Organization* 72, no. 3 (2018): pp. 591–626.

Musizza, Walter. "Si lavora per riportare in Italia un'opera trafugata del Tiziano." *Corriere delle Alpi*, March 20, 2018.

National Museum of Denmark, "Greek marble heads stay in Denmark," November 22, 2023, https://natmus.dk/nyhed/graeske-marmorhoveder-bliver-i-danmark.

Nayeri, Farah. "A 'Digital Heist' Recaptures the Rosetta Stone." *The New York Times*, August 11, 2023.

Nayeri, Farah, and Norimitsu Onishi. "Looted Treasures Begin a Long Journey Home from France." *The New York Times*, October 28, 2021.

Neils, Jenifer. "'With Noblest Images on All Sides': The Ionic Frieze of the Parthenon." In *The Parthenon: From Antiquity to the Present*, edited by Jenifer Neils, pp. 199–224. New York: Cambridge University Press, 2005.

Nevadomsky, Joseph. "Studies of Benin Art and Material Culture, 1897–1997." *African Arts* 30, no. 3 (1997): pp. 18–27.

Nicholas, Lynn H. *The Rape of Europa: The Fate of Europe's Treasures in the Third Reich and the Second World War*. New York: Vintage, 1994.

Nikoletić, Dragana. "Revizija istorije u 24 slike." *NIN*, December 6, 2016.

Northrup, David. "The Compatibility of the Slave and Palm Oil Trades in the Bight of Biafra." *The Journal of African History* 17, no. 3 (1976): pp. 353–64.

Northrup, David. "The Growth of Trade Among the Igbo Before 1880." *The Journal of African History* 13, no. 2 (1972): pp. 217–36.

Nwafor, Okechukwu. "Culture, Corruption, Politics: National Museum of Unity Enugu and the Struggle for the Survival of Cultural Institutions in Nigeria." *Critical Interventions* 4, no. 2 (2010): pp. 118–31.

O'Connor, Anne-Marie. *The Lady in Gold: The Extraordinary Tale of Gustav Klimt's Masterpiece, Portrait of Adele Bloch-Bauer*. New York: Vintage, 2015.

O'Neill, Mark. "Enlightenment Museums: Universal or Merely Global?". *Museum and Society* 2, no. 3 (2004): pp. 190–202.

Obinyan, Thomas Uwadiale. "The Annexation of Benin." *Journal of Black Studies* 19, no. 1 (1988): pp. 29–40.

Okediji, Moyo. "On Reparations Exodus and Embodiment." *African Arts* 31, no. 2 (1998): pp. 8–10.

Oltermann, Philip, and Senay Boztas. "Netherlands to Return Treasures Looted from Indonesia and Sri Lanka in Colonial Era." *The Guardian*, July 6, 2023.

Oltermann, Philip. "Berlin's Plan to Return Benin Bronzes Piles Pressure on UK Museums." *The Guardian*, March 23, 2021.

Olusoga, David. *Black and British: A Forgotten History*. London: Pan Macmillan, 2016.

Onea, Tudor A. "Between Dominance and Decline: Status Anxiety and Great Power Rivalry." *Review of International Studies* 40, no. 1 (2014): pp. 125–52.

Onishi, Norimitsu. "Turmoil Engulfs Canadian Art Museums Seeking to Shed Colonial Past." *The New York Times*, October 9, 2023.

Oost, Tabitha I. "From 'Leader to Pariah'? On the Dutch Restitutions Committee and the Inclusion of the Public Interest in Assessing Nazi-Spoliated Art Claims." *International Journal of Cultural Property* 28, no. 1 (2021): pp. 55–85.

Open Society Foundation. "Open Society Pledges Support for African Cultural Heritage Restitution," November 12, 2019. https://www.opensocietyfoundations.org/newsroom/open-society-pledges-support-for-african-cultural-heritage-restitution.

Osadolor, Osarhieme Benson, and Leo Enahoro Otoide. "The Benin Kingdom in British Imperial Historiography." *History in Africa* 35 (2008): pp. 401–18.

Osarumwense, Charles O. "Igue Festival and the British Invasion of Benin 1897: The Violation of a People's Culture and Sovereignty." *African Journal of History and Culture* 6, no. 2 (2014): pp. 1–5.

Ostrower, Francie. "The Arts as Cultural Capital Among Elites: Bourdieu's Theory Reconsidered." *Poetics* 26, no. 1 (1998): pp. 43–53.

Otzen, Ellen. "The Man Who Returned His Grandfather's Looted Art." *BBC News*, February 26, 2015.

Palmer, Alex B. "The Great Chinese Art Heist." *GQ*, August 16, 2018. https://www.gq.com/story/the-great-chinese-art-heist.

Paquette, Jonathan. "France and the Restitution of Cultural Goods: The Sarr-Savoy Report and Its Reception." *Cultural Trends* 29, no. 4 (2020): pp. 302–16.

Pejović, Marina, and Gordana Grabež. "Nova muzejska edukacija: Jevrejsko kulturno nasleđe u nacionalnom kontekstu." In *Graničnici sećanja: Jevrejsko nasleđe i Holokaust*, edited by Nevena Daković and Vera Mevorah, pp. 237–50. Beograd: Jevrejski istorijski muzej, 2018.

Pellegrini, Emanuele. "Göring in Italy: The Ventura Case." In *Transfer of Cultural Objects in the Alpe Adria Region in the 20th Century*, edited by Christian Fuhrmeister and Barbara Murovec, pp. 145–62. Cologne: Böhlau, 2022.

Penny, H. Glenn. *In Humboldt's Shadow: A Tragic History of German Ethnology*. Princeton: Princeton University Press, 2021.

Penny, H. Glenn. *Objects of Culture: Ethnology and Ethnographic Museums in Imperial Germany*. Chapel Hill: University of North Carolina Press, 2002.

Perry, Victor. *Stolen Art*. Hewlett, NY: Gefen Publishing, 2000.

Petropoulos, Jonathan. "Not a Case of 'Art for Art's Sake': The Collecting Practices of the Nazi Elite." *German Politics & Society* 32 (Summer 1994): pp. 107–24.

Petropoulos, Jonathan. *Art as Politics in the Third Reich*. Chapel Hill: University of North Carolina Press, 1999.

Petropoulos, Jonathan. *The Faustian Bargain: The Art World in Nazi Germany*. New York: Oxford University Press, 2000.

Petropoulos, Jonathan. *Göring's Man in Paris: The Story of a Nazi Art Plunderer and His World*. New Haven: Yale University Press, 2021.

Phillips, Barnaby. *Loot: Britain and the Benin Bronzes*. New York: Simon and Schuster, 2021.

Plankensteiner, Barbara. "African Art at the Museum Für Völkerkunde in Vienna." *African Arts* 38, no. 2 (2005): pp. 12–37.

Plankensteiner, Barbara, ed. *Benin Kings and Rituals: Court Arts from Nigeria*. Ghent: Snoeck, 2007.

Plankensteiner, Barbara. "Benin-Kings and Rituals: Court Arts from Nigeria." *African Arts* 40, no. 4 (2007): pp. 74–87.

Pogrebin, Robin, and Graham Bowley. "After Seizures, the Met Sets a Plan to Scour Collections for Looted Art." *The New York Times*, May 9, 2023.

Povoledo, Elisabetta. "In Rome, a New Museum for Recovered Treasures Before They Return Home." *The New York Times*, July 17, 2022.

Prentoulis, Marina. "Is Rishi Sunak Using the Parthenon Marbles as a Distraction? Perhaps—But So Are the Greeks." *The Guardian*, December 1, 2023.

Procter, Alice. *The Whole Picture: The Colonial Story of the Art in Our Museums & Why We Need to Talk About It*. London: Cassell, 2020.

Prussian Cultural Heritage Foundation, "Restitution of Three Artworks from the Littmann Collection and Gifting of Carlo Mense's 'Doppelbildnis (Rabbi S. und Tochter)' to the Neue Nationalgalerie," press release, February 15, 2023, https://www.smb.museum/en/whats-new/detail/restitution-of-three-artworks-from-the-littmann-collection-and-gifting-of-carlo-menses-doppelbildnis-rabbi-s-und-tochter-to-the-neue-nationalgalerie.

Quirk, Joel, and David Richardson. "Anti-Slavery, European Identity and International Society: A Macro-Historical Perspective." *Journal of Modern European History* 7, no. 1 (2009): pp. 68–92.

Quynn, Dorothy Mackay. "The Art Confiscations of the Napoleonic Wars." *The American Historical Review* 50, no. 3 (1945): pp. 437–60.

Rabinow, Rebecca A., Douglas W. Druick, Ann Dumas, Gloria Groom, Anne Roquebert, and Gary Tinterow, eds. *Cezanne to Picasso: Ambroise Vollard, Patron of the Avant-Garde*. New York: Metropolitan Museum of Art, 2006.

Radio-Television Serbia. *Mimara*, February 14 (Part I), February 15 (Part II), and February 22, 2017 (Part III), https://www.youtube.com/watch?v=JnUvWX_fwAk.

Radio-Television Serbia. "Mira Adanja Polak: Ekskluzivno—istinu zna samo Mimara," March 18, 2018, https://www.youtube.com/watch?v=zJ5c_CIU0kU&t=2s.

Radio-Television Serbia. "Oko magazin: Misterija Mimara," March 10, 2017, https://www.youtube.com/watch?v=WQlcTKs0Pj8.

Radzilowski, John. "Thieves Stealing from Thieves, Victims from Victims: The Culture, Morality, and Politics of Stolen Art in Twentieth Century Poland." *The Polish Review* 61, no. 4 (2016): pp. 3–17.

Ralston, Robert. "Make Us Great Again: The Causes of Declinism in Major Powers." *Security Studies* 31, no. 4 (2022): pp. 667–702.

Razzall, Katie. "Parthenon Sculptures Belong in UK, Says Culture Secretary Michelle Donelan." *BBC News*, January 11, 2023.

Rea, Naomi. "A French Museum Director Pushes Back Against a Radical Report Calling on Macron to Return Looted African Art." *Artnet Magazine*, November 28, 2018.

Rea, Naomi. "France Has Approved the Return of 27 Artworks to Benin and Senegal, Signaling What May Be a New Era for Restitution." *Artnet Magazine*, November 5, 2020.

Reed, Victoria. "Ardelia Hall: From Museum of Fine Arts to Monuments Woman." *International Journal of Cultural Property* 21, no. 1 (2014): pp. 79–93.

Renshon, Jonathan. *Fighting for Status: Hierarchy and Conflict in World Politics*. Princeton, NJ: Princeton University Press, 2017.

Renshon, Jonathan. "Status Deficits and War." *International Organization* 70, no. 3 (2016): pp. 513–50.

Restitution Belgium. "Ethical Principles for the Management and Restitution of Colonial Collections in Belgium," June 2021, https://restitutionbelgium.be/en/report.

Reuters. "Austria Says Talks Underway on Returning Parthenon Marbles to Greece." May 2, 2023, https://www.reuters.com/world/europe/austria-says-talks-underway-returning-parthenon-marbles-greece-2023-05-02.

Rich, Paul B. *Race and Empire in British Politics*. Cambridge: Cambridge University Press, 1990.

Ringmar, Erik. *Liberal Barbarism: The European Destruction of the Palace of the Emperor of China*. New York: Palgrave, 2013.

Robertson, Geoffrey. *Who Owns History?: Elgin's Loot and the Case for Returning Plundered Treasure*. London: Biteback Publishing, 2019.

Robins, Jonathan E. *Oil Palm: A Global History*. Chapel Hill: The University of North Carolina Press, 2021.

Rogstad, Adrian, and Benjamin Martill. "How to Be Great (Britain)? Discourses of Greatness in the United Kingdom's Referendums on Europe." *European Review of International Studies* 9, no. 2 (2022): pp. 210–39.

Røren, Pål. "The Belligerent Bear: Russia, Status Orders, and War." *International Security* 47, no. 4 (2023): pp. 7–49.

Røren, Pål. "Status Seeking in the Friendly Nordic Neighborhood." *Cooperation and Conflict* 54, no. 4 (2019): pp. 562–79.

Rose Greenland, Fiona. "The Parthenon Marbles as Icons of Nationalism in Nineteenth Century Britain." *Nations and Nationalism* 19, no. 4 (2013): pp. 654–73.

Roth, Henry Ling. *Great Benin: Its Customs, Art and Horrors.* Halifax: F. King, 1903.

Rubinstein, William D. *Capitalism, Culture and Decline in Britain: 1750–1990.* London: Routledge, 2002.

Rudenstine, David. "Trophies for the Empire: The Epic Dispute Between Greece and England over the Parthenon Sculptures in the British Museum." *Cardozo Arts & Entertainment Law Journal* 39 (2021): pp. 377–505.

Rydell, Robert W. *All the World's a Fair: Visions of Empire at American International Expositions, 1876–1916.* Chicago: University of Chicago Press, 2013.

Ryder, Alan Frederick Charles. *Benin and the Europeans, 1485–1897.* New York: Humanities Press, 1970.

Šabić, Senada Šelo. "The Impact of the Refugee Crisis in the Balkans: A Drift Towards Security." *Journal of Regional Security* 12, no. 1 (2017): pp. 51–74.

Saltzman, Cynthia. *Plunder: Napoleon's Theft of Veronese's Feast.* New York: Farrar, Straus and Giroux, 2021.

Sanderson, David. "Minister Rules out Return of Treasures." *The Times*, April 22, 2019.

Sandholtz, Wayne. "Plunder, Restitution, and International Law." *International Journal of Cultural Property* 17, no. 2 (2010): pp. 147–76.

Sandholtz, Wayne. *Prohibiting Plunder: How Norms Change.* Oxford: Oxford University Press, 2007.

Sands, Philippe. *East West Street: On the Origins of "Genocide" and "Crimes Against Humanity."* New York: Alfred A. Knopf, 2016.

Sanghera, Sathnam. *Empireland: How Imperialism Has Shaped Modern Britain.* New York: Pantheon, 2023.

Santacatterina, Marta. "L'intricato caso dei dipinti italiani 'deportati' a Belgrado e mai restituiti." *Finestre sull' arte*, May 15, 2024.

Sarr, Felwine, and Bénédicte Savoy. "The Restitution of African Cultural Heritage: Toward a New Relational Ethics." Paris: French Ministry of Culture, 2018.

Savoy, Bénédicte. *Africa's Struggle for Its Art: History of a Postcolonial Defeat.* Princeton, NJ: Princeton University Press, 2022.

Schidorsky, Dov. "Hannah Arendt's Dedication to Salvaging Jewish Culture." *The Leo Baeck Institute Yearbook* 59, no. 1 (2014): pp. 181–95.

Schildkrout, Enid, and Curtis A. Keim. *The Scramble for Art in Central Africa.* Cambridge: Cambridge University Press, 1998.

Schilling, Britta. "German Postcolonialism in Four Dimensions: A Historical Perspective." *Postcolonial Studies* 18, no. 4 (2015): pp. 427–39.

Schraeder, Peter J. "Cold War to Cold Peace: Explaining US-French Competition in Francophone Africa." *Political Science Quarterly* 115, no. 3 (2000): pp. 395–419.

Schuetze, Christopher F. "Germany Sets Guidelines for Repatriating Colonial-Era Artifacts." *The New York Times*, March 15, 2019.

Scott, Cynthia. *Cultural Diplomacy and the Heritage of Empire: Negotiating Post-Colonial Returns.* London: Routledge, 2019.

Select Committee of the House of Commons, "Report from the Select Committee of the House of Commons on the Earl of Elgin's Collection of the Sculptured Marbles." London: John Murray, 1816.

Sevillano, Elena G. "Legitimate Concerns, or Neocolonialism? Germany Expresses Worry About the Fate of the Benin Bronzes, Following Their Restitution to Nigeria." *El Pais*, May 19, 2023.

Sharman, J.C. "Something New out of Africa: States Made Slaves, Slaves Made States." *International Organization* 77, no. 3 (2023): pp. 497–526.

Shaw, Anny, and Margaret Carrigan. "Reform or Reset? How Cultural Institutions Are Facing a Reckoning over Racism." *The Art Newspaper*, July 3, 2020.

Sherwood, Harriet. "London Museum Returns Looted Benin City Artefacts to Nigeria." *The Guardian*, November 28, 2022.

Shifrinson, Joshua R. Itzkowitz. *Rising Titans, Falling Giants: How Great Powers Exploit Power Shifts*. Ithaca: Cornell University Press, 2018.

Shyllon, Folarin. "Cultural Heritage Legislation and Management in Nigeria." *International Journal of Cultural Property* 5, no. 2 (1996): pp. 235–68.

Siegal, Nina. "Poland Urged to Look for Nazi-Looted Art Still Held in Its Museums." *The New York Times*, January 12, 2022.

Siegal, Nina. "Rijksmuseum Removing Racially Charged Terms from Artworks' Titles and Descriptions." *The New York Times*, December 10, 2015.

Silverman, Debora L. "Diasporas of Art: History, the Tervuren Royal Museum for Central Africa, and the Politics of Memory in Belgium, 1885–2014." *The Journal of Modern History* 87, no. 3 (2015): pp. 615–67.

Sinclair, Anne. *My Grandfather's Gallery: A Family Memoir of Art and War*. New York: Farrar, Straus and Giroux, 2014.

Singh, Kavita. "Repatriation Without Patria: Repatriating for Tibet." *Journal of Material Culture* 15, no. 2 (2010): pp. 131–55.

Singh, Kavita. "The Museum Is National." In *No Touching, No Spitting, No Praying: The Museum in South Asia*, edited by Saloni Mathur and Kavita Singh, pp. 107–31. Abingdon: Routledge, 2015.

Skowronek, Tobias B., Christopher R. DeCorse, Rolf Denk, Stefan D. Birr, Sean Kingsley, Gregory D. Cook, Ana María Benito Dominguez, et al. "German Brass for Benin Bronzes: Geochemical Analysis Insights into the Early Atlantic Trade." *PLOS One* 18, no. 4 (2023): pp. e0283415.

Slyomovics, Susan. "Commissioning Memorial Reconciliation: The Stora Report and Algeria's Ottoman Cannon in France." *Modern & Contemporary France* 31, no. 1 (2023): pp. 17–32.

Smith, Arthur Hamilton. "Lord Elgin and His Collection." *The Journal of Hellenic Studies* 36 (1916): pp. 163–372.

Smith, Helena. "Acropolis Now: Greeks Outraged at Concreting of Ancient Site." *The Guardian*, June 10, 2021.

Smith, Helena. "Boris Johnson's Zeal to Return Parthenon Marbles Revealed in 1986 Article." *The Guardian*, December 18, 2021.

Smith, Helena. "Keir Starmer Open to Return of Parthenon Marbles, Reports Say." *The Guardian*, November 25, 2023.

Smith, Helena. "Pope Francis Returns Three Fragments of Parthenon to Greece." *The Guardian*, March 25, 2023.

Smithsonian Institution, "Smithsonian Returns 29 Benin Bronzes to the National Commission for Museums and Monuments in Nigeria," October 11, 2022, https://www.si.edu/newsdesk/releases/smithsonian-returns-29-benin-bronzes-national-commission-museums-and-monuments.

Solomon, Tessa. "Amid Tightening of Cultural Protections Worldwide, Austria Proposes New Restitution Laws." *ARTnews*, June 20, 2023.

Solomon, Tessa. "German Museums Hold 40,000 Artifacts Looted from Cameroon, New Study Finds." *ARTnews*, June 5, 2023.

Solomon, Tessa. "Renoir, Sisley Paintings Sold under Duress During Nazi Occupation of France Returned." *ARTnews*, May 22, 2024.

Soyinka, Wole. *You Must Set Forth at Dawn—A Memoir*. New York: Random House, 2007.

Speer, Albert. *Inside the Third Reich*. New York: Simon and Schuster, 1997.

St Clair, William. "Imperial Appropriations of the Parthenon." In *Imperialism, Art and Restitution*, edited by John Henry Merryman, pp. 65–97. New York: Cambridge University Press, 2006.

St Clair, William. "Looking at the Acropolis of Athens from Modern Times to Antiquity." In *Cultural Heritage Ethics: Between Theory and Practice*, edited by Constantine Sandis, pp. 57–102. Cambridge: Open Book Publishers, 2014.

St Clair, William. *Lord Elgin and the Marbles*. Oxford: Oxford University Press, 1998.

St Clair, William. *That Greece Might Still Be Free: The Philhellenes in the War of Independence*. Cambridge: Open Book Publishers, 2008.

St Clair, William. *Who Saved the Parthenon?: A New History of the Acropolis Before, During and After the Greek Revolution*. Cambridge: Open Book Publishers, 2022.

Stahn, Carsten. "Confronting Colonial Amnesia: Towards New Relational Engagement with Colonial Injustice and Cultural Colonial Objects." *Journal of International Criminal Justice* 18, no. 4 (2020): pp. 793–824.

Stahn, Carsten. *Confronting Colonial Objects: Histories, Legalities, and Access to Culture*. Oxford: Oxford University Press, 2023.

Stepan, Nancy. *Idea of Race in Science: Great Britain, 1800–1960*. Basingstoke: Springer, 1982.

Stevens, Matt. "In a Nod to Changing Norms, Smithsonian Adopts Policy on Ethical Returns." *The New York Times*, May 3, 2022.

Stevens, Matt. "Smithsonian Moves Toward Returning Benin Bronzes." *The New York Times*, November 5, 2021.

Stockings, Craig, and Eleanor Hancock. *Swastika over the Acropolis: Re-Interpreting the Nazi Invasion of Greece in World War II*. Leiden: Brill, 2013.

Stray, Christopher A. "Culture and Discipline: Classics and Society in Victorian England." *International Journal of the Classical Tradition* 3 (1996): pp. 77–85.

Subasic, Katarina. "Serbia Returns Property Taken in Holocaust to Tiny Jewish Community." *Times of Israel*, March 30, 2016.

Subotić, Jelena. *Yellow Star, Red Star: Holocaust Remembrance After Communism*. Ithaca: Cornell University Press, 2019.

Subotić, Jelena, and Srdjan Vucetic. "Performing Solidarity: Whiteness and Status-Seeking in the Non-Aligned World." *Journal of international Relations and Development* 22 (2019): pp. 722–43.

Sylvester, Christine. *Art/Museums: International Relations Where We Least Expect It*. Abingdon: Routledge, 2015.

Tayiana, Chao, and Molemo Moilo. "Digital Restitution and Its Discontents," December 21, 2021, https://www.delfinafoundation.com/whats-on/digital-restitution-and-its-discontents The Times. "The Times View on Returning Benin Bronzes: Home Territory." *The Times*, March 25, 2021.

The Times. "Ian Jenkins Obituary." *The Times*, December 15, 2020.

The Times. "The Times View on the Elgin Marbles: Uniting Greece's Heritage." *The Times*, January 11, 2022.

Thies, Cameron. "Role Theory and Foreign Policy." *Oxford Research Encyclopedia of International Studies*. Oxford: Oxford University Press (2010), https://doi.org/10.1093/acrefore/9780190846626.013.291.

Thomas, Hugh. *Conquest: Montezuma, Cortés, and the Fall of Old Mexico*. New York: Simon & Schuster, 1993.

Thompson, Erin L. *Possession: The Curious History of Private Collectors from Antiquity to the Present*. New Haven, CT: Yale University Press, 2016.

Titi, Catharine. *The Parthenon Marbles and International Law*. Cham: Springer, 2023.

Todorović, Jelena. "The Painting and Its Histories: The Curious Incident of Rembrandt's Painting *Quintus Fabius Maximus*." In *Regimes of Invisibility in Contemporary Art, Theory and Culture: Image, Racialization, History*, edited by Marina Gržinić, Aneta Stojnić, and Miško Šuvaković, pp. 159–68. Cham: Palgrave, 2017.

Tomlinson, Jim. *The Politics of Decline: Understanding Postwar Britain*. London: Routledge, 2014.

Tompkins, Arthur, ed. *Provenance Research Today: Principles, Practice, Problems*. London: Lund Humphries, 2020.

Toomey, Michael, and Alistair J.K. Shepherd. "Cultural Trauma, Populist Grand Narratives, and Brexit." *Global Studies Quarterly* 3, no. 4 (2023): pp. 1–12.

Towns, Ann E. *Women and States: Norms and Hierarchies in International Society*. Cambridge: Cambridge University Press, 2010.

Tythacott, Louise. "The African Collection at Liverpool Museum." *African Arts* 31, no. 3 (1998): pp. 18–94.

Ulaby, Neda. "Metropolitan Museum of Art Sends Three Benin Bronzes Home to Nigeria." *NPR*, June 9, 2021.

UNESCO. Draft Declaration of Principles Relating to Cultural Objects Displaced in Connection with the Second World War, 2009, https://unesdoc.unesco.org/ark:/48223/pf0000183433.

UNESCO. Report of the Committee of Experts, Doc. SHC-76/CONF.615/3 (1976), at https://unesdoc.unesco.org/ark:/48223/pf0000023694.

UNESCO. World Conference on Cultural Policies: Final Report, Mexico City, July 26-August 6, 1982, https://unesdoc.unesco.org/ark:/48223/pf0000052505.

United Nations General Assembly. Address by General Mobutu Sese Seko, President of the Republic of Zaire, 28th session, October 4, 1973, available at https://documents-dds-ny.un.org/doc/UNDOC/GEN/NL8/304/33/PDF/NL830433.pdf.

United Nations General Assembly. Resolution 3187 on the Restitution of Works of Art to Countries Victims of Expropriation, December 1973, available at https://digitallibrary.un.org/record/190996.

United Nations General Assembly. Resolution on the Return or restitution of cultural property to the countries of origin (2021), available at https://documents-dds-ny.un.org/doc/UNDOC/GEN/N21/375/04/PDF/N2137504.pdf?OpenElement.

US Department of State. "Best Practices for the Washington Conference Principles on Nazi-Confiscated Art." edited by Office of the Special Envoy for Holocaust Issues. Washington, D.C., 2024.

US Department of State. "Terezin Declaration on Holocaust Era Assets and Related Issues." June 2009, https://www.state.gov/prague-holocaust-era-assets-conference-terezin-declaration.

US Department of State. *Treaties and Other International Agreements of the United States of America, 1776–1949*. Volume 2: Multilateral (1918–1930). Washington, D.C.: Department of State.

Van Beurden, Jos. *Inconvenient Heritage: Colonial Collections and Restitution in the Netherlands and Belgium*. Amsterdam: Amsterdam University Press, 2022.

Van Beurden, Sarah. *Authentically African: Arts and the Transnational Politics of Congolese Culture*. Athens: Ohio University Press, 2015.

Van Beurden, Sarah. "Loot: Colonial Collections and African Restitution Debates." *Origins: Current Events in Historical Perspective*. March 2002. https://origins.osu.edu/read/loot-colonial-collections-and-african-restitution-debates.

Van Beurden, Sarah. "The Art of (Re)Possession: Heritage and the Cultural Politics of Congo's Decolonization." *The Journal of African History* 56, no. 1 (2015): pp. 143–64.

Van Beurden, Sarah. “The Value of Culture: Congolese Art and the Promotion of Belgian Colonialism (1945–1959).” *History and Anthropology* 24, no. 4 (2013): pp. 472–92.

Van Bockhaven, Vicky. “Les Congolais obtiendront-ils la restitution qu’ils demandent?: Suggestions du nord-est de la RDC par rapport à la politique de restitution Belge prévue.” *Afrika Focus* 35, no. 1 (2022): pp. 190–98.

Van Huis, Iris. “Contesting Cultural Heritage: Decolonizing the Tropenmuseum as an Intervention in the Dutch/European Memory Complex.” In *Dissonant Heritages and Memories in Contemporary Europe*, edited by Tuuli Lähdesmäki, Luisa Passerini, Sigrid Kaasik-Krogerus, and Iris van Huis, pp. 215–48. Cham: Springer, 2019.

Van Laar, Timothy, and Leonard Diepeveen. *Artworld Prestige: Arguing Cultural Value.* Oxford: Oxford University Press, 2013.

Vardas, George. “From the Depths of Despair: Lord Elgin and the Parthenon Sculptures.” *Greek City Times*, May 13, 2022.

Veblen, Thorstein. *The Theory of the Leisure Class.* Abingdon: Routledge, 2017 [1899].

Victoria & Albert Museum, “Concealed Histories: Uncovering the Story of Nazi Looting,” https://www.vam.ac.uk/articles/about-the-concealed-histories-display#slideshow=6872&slide=0.

Villa, Angelica. “Amsterdam to Restitute Kandinsky Painting to Heirs After Years-Long Dispute.” *ARTnews*, August 30, 2021.

Villa, Angelica. “France and Germany Forge Joint Fund for Colonial-Era Research.” *ARTnews*, October 11, 2023.

Villa, Angelica. “Met Returns Two Artifacts to Nepal and Promises an ‘Open Dialogue.’” *ARTnews*, August 17, 2022.

Villa, Angelica. “MOMA Returned Valuable Chagall Painting with Disputed Provenance in 2021.” *ARTnews*, February 12, 2024.

von Oswald, Margareta. “The ‘Restitution Report’ First Reactions in Academia, Museums, and Politics.” *How to Move On with Humbolt’s Legacy? Rethinking Ethnographic Collections* (2018). https://web.archive.org/web/20221129014325/https://blog.uni-koeln.de/gssc-humboldt/the-restitution-report.

von Oswald, Margareta. *Working Through Colonial Collections: An Ethnography of the Ethnological Museum in Berlin.* Leuven: Leuven University Press, 2022.

Vrdoljak, Ana Filipa. *International Law, Museums and the Return of Cultural Objects.* Cambridge: Cambridge University Press, 2006.

Vucetic, Srdjan. *Greatness and Decline: National Identity and British Foreign Policy.* Montreal: McGill-Queen’s Press, 2021.

Wagner, Kim A. “Savage Warfare: Violence and the Rule of Colonial Difference in Early British Counterinsurgency.” *History Workshop Journal* 85 (2018): pp. 217–37.

Waldman, Ayelet. *Love and Treasure.* New York: Anchor, 2014.

Wali, Alaka, and Robert Keith Collins. “Decolonizing Museums: Toward a Paradigm Shift.” *Annual Review of Anthropology* 52 (2023): pp. 329–45.

Wang, Zheng. *Never Forget National Humiliation: Historical Memory in Chinese Politics and Foreign Relations.* New York: Columbia University Press, 2014.

Ward, Steven. “Decline and Disintegration: National Status Loss and Domestic Conflict in Post-Disaster Spain.” *International Security* 46, no. 4 (2022): pp. 91–129.

Ward, Steven. *Status and the Challenge of Rising Powers.* Cambridge: Cambridge University Press, 2017.

Ward, Stuart, and Astrid Rasch. “Introduction.” In *Embers of Empire in Brexit Britain*, edited by Stuart Ward and Astrid Rasch, pp. 1–14. London: Bloomsbury, 2019.

Weaver, Matthew. “Artist Asks British Museum to Return Assyrian Treasure to Iraq in Swap.” *The Guardian*, January 20, 2023.

Weaver, Matthew, and David Batty. "British Museum Director Hartwig Fischer Resigns After Suspected Thefts." *The Guardian*, August 25, 2023.

Webb, E.T. "Appropriating the Stones: The 'Elgin Marbles' and English National Taste." In *Claiming the Stones/Naming the Bones: Cultural Property and the Negotiation of National and Ethnic Identity*, edited by Elazar Barkan and Ronald Bush, pp. 51–96. Los Angeles: Getty Research Institute, 2002.

Webber, Mark. "Identity, Status and Role in UK Foreign Policy: Brexit and Beyond." *International Politics* (2023): pp. 1–12, https://doi.org/10.1057/s41311-023-00482-4.

Wildman, Sarah. "The Revelations of a Nazi Art Catalogue." *The New Yorker*, February 12, 2016.

Williams, Dyfri. "Lord Elgin's Firman." *Journal of the History of Collections* 21, no. 1 (2009): pp. 49–76.

Willsher, Kim. "'We Want Our Riches Back'—the African Activist Taking Treasures from Europe's Museums." *The Guardian*, February 7, 2021.

Winfield, Nicole. "Pope Returns Greece's Parthenon Sculptures in Ecumenical Nod." *Associated Press*, December 16, 2022, https://ictnews.org/outside/pope-returns-greeces-parthenon-sculptures-in-ecumenical-nod.

Winter, Tim. "Heritage Diplomacy." *International Journal of Heritage Studies* 21, no. 10 (2015): pp. 997–1015.

Wohlforth, William, Benjamin De Carvalho, Halvard Leira, and Iver Neumann. "Moral Authority and Status in International Relations: Good States and the Social Dimension of Status Seeking." *Review of International Studies* 44, no. 3 (2018): pp. 526–46.

Yalouri, Eleana. *The Acropolis: Global Fame, Local Claim*. Abingdon: Routledge, 2020.

Yanık, Lerna K., and Jelena Subotić. "Cultural Heritage as Status Seeking: The International Politics of Turkey's Restoration Wave." *Cooperation and Conflict* 56, no. 3 (2021): pp. 245–63.

Zantop, Susanne. *Colonial Fantasies: Conquest, Family, and Nation in Precolonial Germany, 1770–1870*. Durham: Duke University Press, 1997.

Zimmerman, A. *Anthropology and Antihumanism in Imperial Germany*. Chicago: University of Chicago Press, 2010.

Zois, Nikolas. "Turkey Denies Firman Giving Lord Elgin Rights to Sell Parthenon Sculptures." *E-kathimerini*, June 4, 2024.

Index

For the benefit of digital users, indexed terms that span two pages (e.g., 52–53) may, on occasion, appear on only one of those pages.